Zechariah Chafee, Jr.

Defender of Liberty and Law

Gardner Cox's oil portrait of Chafee (1952),
which hangs in the Harvard Law School Library.

Zechariah Chafee, Jr.

Defender of Liberty and Law

Donald L. Smith

Harvard University Press
Cambridge, Massachusetts
London, England   1986

This book is printed on acid-free paper, and
its binding materials have been chosen
for strength and durability.

Library of Congress Cataloging in Publication Data

Smith, Donald L., 1928–
   Zechariah Chafee, Jr., Defender of Liberty and Law

   Bibliography: p.
   Includes index.
   1. Chafee, Zechariah, 1885–1957.   2. Law teachers—
United States—Biography.   3. Freedom of speech—
United States.   4. Civil rights—United States.
I. Title.
KF373.C388S6   1986   340′.07′1173 [B]   85-27213
ISBN 0-674-96685-6 (alk. paper)

For Clarence and Margaret Mitchell
and in memory of
Marlin Carr and John Trebilcock

Acknowledgments

Because this is a biography of a professor, I wish to acknowledge the encouragement I derived from the publication, not long after I started my research, of Ray Allen Billington's *Frederick Jackson Turner*. Especially heartening was an anecdote in the preface recounting how a colleague had encouraged Professor Billington to write "a realistic life of a classroom teacher." Of course, Turner and Chafee, who knew each other during the former's years on the Harvard history faculty, made substantial contributions to intellectual life besides teaching. Had they not, it is doubtful that books about them would have been written.

Further encouragement, together with constructive criticism, was provided by persons who read all or portions of the manuscript. My colleague Daniel W. Pfaff read each chapter as it was completed and was always available to discuss my progress. Or lack of it. The following persons, who read at least portions of the manuscript, helped clarify both my thought and my prose at various points and saved me from some embarrassing factual errors: Irving Dilliard, Erwin N. Griswold, Gerald Gunther, Dean Mills, and Edward D. Re. They are, of course, blameless for any surviving errors and wrongheaded interpretations.

Professor Chafee's son, Zechariah Chafee III, answered numerous questions by mail in addition to allowing me to interview him in his home in St. Davids, Pennsylvania. He also lent me various items from his collection of family papers and memorabilia. And he permitted me to do research in his father's papers in the Harvard Law

School Library, the Harvard University Archives, and the Brown University Archives.

Professor Chafee's longtime friend and college roommate, Claude R. Branch, invited me to be his house guest during a week spent working in the Brown University Archives. He also arranged for me to have a temporary membership in Providence's venerable Hope Club, where we dined nightly after he returned from a day spent practicing law in Boston. He obviously enjoyed reminiscing about Chafee even more than he enjoyed playing tennis, which he continued to do at the age of 88.

One of the most delightful aspects of doing research at Harvard was getting to know Erika Chadbourn, who is equally adept at keeping a scorecard in Fenway Park and at organizing collections in the Harvard Law School Library, where she served as curator of manuscripts before retiring in 1985. For their cheery manner and all types of assistance, including promptly fulfilling requests by mail, I am indebted to the staff of the Harvard University Archives; its curator, Harley P. Holden, allowed me to do research in the Chafee Papers there. My week at Brown was pleasant as well as productive thanks to Martha L. Mitchell, the university's archivist, and her staff, who even shared coffee and cake with me as they observed a staff member's birthday.

Kathy Good, a charming and versatile undergraduate, performed numerous library and typing chores during the summer of 1983. Others who helped lighten the load in various ways are: David S. Allen, William N. Allen, Donald J. DeMaio, Rita Kugelman Dettmar, Donald E. Dusing, Jean Dusing, LaDawn H. Dutrow, Jill Challender Shelley, Christine L. Templeton, Dee J. Vonada, and Shelba J. Winfree. Toni Benner, truly a good neighbor, and Patricia E. Kidder expertly processed drafts of the manuscript the old-fashioned way—on a typewriter.

I come now to that portion of the acknowledgments in which the role of the author's family is traditionally noted. My wife, Mary, and daughters, Kaia and Gretchen, made no direct contributions to the research or writing. But if they do not know what the book says, they know better than anyone what went into it; and without their love, support, and innumerable sacrifices, it would not have been possible. Moreover, my wife was always willing to drop whatever else she might be doing to perform such tasks as double-checking the renumbering of footnotes—the kind of tedium, in other words, that falls under the "for worse" clause of the marriage contract.

Two sabbaticals facilitated work on the book. Several grants from the College of Liberal Arts Research Office at the Pennsylvania State University assisted with travel expenses; for this aid, my thanks go to Deans Thomas F. Magner and Joseph W. Michels.

Gerald Gunther gave me permission to quote from letters by Chafee, Learned Hand, and Oliver Wendell Holmes, Jr., printed as an appendix to his article, "Learned Hand and the Origins of Modern First Amendment Doctrine: Some Fragments of History," *Stanford Law Review*, 26 (1975), 719–773.

Chief Judge Edward D. Re and Oceana Publications, Inc., granted me permission to quote from Re's *Freedom's Prophet*.

The Harvard Law Review Association granted me permission to quote from Chafee's article "Freedom of Speech in War Time," *Harvard Law Review*, 32 (1919), 932–973. Copyright © 1919 by the Harvard Law Review Association.

Morris L. Cohen, librarian of the Harvard Law School at the time I started my research, granted me access to the Chafee Papers there. His successor, Harry S. Martin III, gave me permission to publish the contents of manuscripts or excerpts therefrom in the following manuscript collections in the Harvard Law School Library: American Bar Association Bill of Rights Committee Papers, Louis D. Brandeis Papers, Lawrence G. Brooks Papers, Zechariah Chafee, Jr., Papers, Felix Frankfurter Papers, Learned Hand Papers, Thomas Reed Powell Papers, and Austin W. Scott Papers. And Paul A. Freund, Professor of Law Emeritus and Carl M. Loeb University Professor Emeritus at Harvard, granted additional permission for use of materials from the Brandeis and Frankfurter Papers.

The following persons permitted me to use materials from various other unpublished sources: Mary Chafee Andrews (interview), Shirlyn G. Brien (two manuscripts by Anne C. Brien), John G. Brooks (interview with Lawrence G. Brooks), Patience M. Canham (letter to me from Erwin D. Canham), Francis H. Chafee (interview), John H. Chafee (interview with John S. Chafee), William G. Chafee (letter to Zechariah Chafee III), Zechariah Chafee III (interview; letter to me), Sheila G. Cook (interview with Elisabeth Chafee Gamble), Copenhaver Cumpston (interview with John M. Maguire), Mary E. Derieg (letter to me from Fredrick S. Siebert), Erwin N. Griswold (two letters to me), Luis Kutner and Myres S. McDougal (letter to me from Harold D. Lasswell), Margaret T. McManus (interview), Theodore Peterson (manuscript), Alexander E. Racolin (letter to me), Robert H. Reno (letter to Irving Dilliard from Grenville Clark), Richard S. Schwartz (interview), Gordon K. Scott (interview with Austin W. Scott), and Cecily von Gemmingen (interview with Claude R. Branch).

The staff of the Harvard University Press were, quite simply, splendid to work with. In particular, I wish to express my gratitude to Aida Donald, who encouraged me virtually from the moment she read my original query letter, and to Elizabeth Hurwit, whose delightful disposition and deftness with green pencil and blue tag make her an ideal manuscript editor.

It is fitting that these last words for the book are being written on the one-hundredth anniversary of Professor Chafee's birth.

7 December 1985

Contents

ILLUSTRATIONS

The Reluctant
Civil Libertarian

O n 1 June 1968 a letter printed in the *Providence Journal* complained: "Although there have been recurring references of late to Mr. John S. Chafee as 'the father of the governor,' I have been waiting for someone to mention the fact that he also had a brother named Zechariah Chafee, Jr. Are Professor Chafee and his works so soon forgotten, even by the spokesmen for liberty? If so, perhaps they will accept a citation from Mr. Justice Felix Frankfurter, whom they may remember. Of Professor Chafee, he wrote: 'The extent to which . . . he influenced the thought and temper of public opinion and action in that pervasive aspect of national life known as civil rights has no match in the legal professoriate.' "

Chafee's leading work is *Freedom of Speech;* its publication in 1920, four years after he joined the Harvard Law School faculty, earned him a permanent place in the pantheon of civil libertarians. That his work in this field was never forgotten is demonstrated by the fact that the items used most by scholars doing research in the library of the Harvard Law School—where repose the papers of Oliver Wendell Holmes, Jr., Louis Brandeis, Learned Hand, Felix Frankfurter, and Roscoe Pound—are the boxes about civil liberties in the Chafee collection. The fruits of that scholarly research include journal articles that have revised the traditional view of the development of First Amendment doctrine and of Chafee's contribution to it.[2]

Much more neglected, if not wholly forgotten, are Chafee's numerous contributions outside the field of freedom of speech. "Evidence, commercial paper, associations, copyright, trademark, unfair competition, . . . various branches of equity and equitable remedies—these are among the topics to which Mr Chafee made distinctive and important contributions," a law school colleague wrote after his death on 8 February 1957.[3] Equity was his specialty, and for more than a quarter-century Harvard law students knew him best as a teacher of that subject.

The fact that he was interested in so many things other than free expression helps explain why he was both an unlikely civil libertarian and a somewhat reluctant one: an unlikely one partly because, as he often expressed it, his people "had money." Both sides of his family were well-off industrialists in Providence, and he himself served for years as chairman of an iron foundry operated by several generations of Chafees. He usually pointed to his business background in countering charges of radicalism in much the same way he noted that his industrial experience made trade unions philosophically unacceptable to him. When Harvard hired him, it was not to teach Constitutional Law but rather to teach Bills and Notes and Insurance in addition to Equity.

Such a background was not calculated to endow him with a fundamental interest in civil liberties. Like most Americans, he explained, he had had "no enthusiasm or even interest in the importance of free speech," adding that he suspected that such an interest is "an acquired taste like olives." That explanation seems too simple. For he had a temperament that he said forbade his "floating down the stream" and that made him uneasy about the special privileges he enjoyed. "I see no reason why I should be out mountain climbing and enjoying life," he said in an early 1920s reference to jailed members of the Industrial Workers of the World, "while some other chap who started life with less money and gets a little angrier and a little more extreme should be shut up in a prison for five or ten years . . . When I am loafing around on my boat, or taking an inordinately large number of strokes on the golf course, I occasionally think of these poor devils who won't be out for five or ten years and [I] want to do a bit to make the weight of society less heavy on them."[4] In addition, as a Rhode Islander he was steeped in the tradition of Roger Williams. And his devotion to Greek and the culture of ancient Greece—his undergraduate major was classics—helped sensitize him to the importance of free expression in a democracy.

It is true that he backed into the First Amendment field through his teaching of Equity. But having done so, he quickly sought to resolve the free speech problem—in one early article he confidently proclaimed it solved—so that he could get back to legal issues that interested him more. It was not to be. He had written *the* book on this intractable subject, and he was stuck with it. Finding himself saddled with such a persistent problem, he responded in two principal ways: by reiterating throughout his forty-year career that the best way to decide free speech questions consisted of balancing social and individual interests; and by ignoring First Amendment developments for long periods. More than one civil liberties lawyer asking his advice must have been shocked to receive a reply similar to the one sent to John Beardsley, who in the early 1930s was preparing to argue before the U.S. Supreme Court in behalf of Yetta Stromberg, a victim of California's "red flag" statute. There was little he could do to help, Chafee said, because he had "not given much close attention to free speech problems for a long time."[5]

If he was inattentive to free speech concerns for considerable periods, he was also very much a man of his time in the insensitivity he sometimes revealed on racial matters. For instance, the draft of a talk he gave commemorating the sesquicentennial of the Bill of Rights uses a racial anecdote—perhaps deleted prior to delivery—to make the point that free speech should not be shelved during emergencies.[6]

When *Free Speech in the United States* was published at about the same time, it was criticized by some reviewers for its inadequate discussion of the U.S. Supreme Court's decision upsetting the conviction of Angelo Herndon, a black Communist organizer from New York, under a Georgia anti-insurrection statute.[7] Seeking to justify his treatment of the case—his judgment was that of "all the chief sedition defendants discussed in this book," Herndon was the only one who actually "did create a 'clear and present danger' of unlawful acts"—Chafee said he was dissatisfied not with the court's decision but rather with the situation in the South: "Another way of expressing it is to say that free speech is much harder to operate in an undemocratic environment. Discussion gets much closer to violence where the usual methods of political expression are seriously impeded . . . The single party system seems to be fastened on the South so firmly that it is likely to last there much longer than in Fascist Italy."[8]

Chafee's moderate approach to the racial issue was influenced to some extent by the fact that he had several cousins—one of them also a lawyer—in and around Aiken, South Carolina, where he visited on several occasions. He alluded to this southern connection in a letter to a black law student who had criticized both his published account of the *Herndon* case and an out-of-class comment suggesting that southern Negroes were not "ready" to vote. Emphasizing his belief that there was "no solution of the problem which can be reached on paper, even if that paper be the United States Constitution," he said: "The right solution must be worked out in the lives of Southern men and women of all types." And he counseled patience: "It is quite natural that Negroes should feel resentful when they see how much is still denied them, but may it not be wise to look in the other direction occasionally and feel happy to think how much has been attained."[9]

A decade and a half later, however, he conceded that there had been no real progress in the field of racial equality. In his last major public address, delivered at Morgan State College in Baltimore less than two months before he died, he discussed the question of whether or not the federal government should be able to take action against wrongdoers when state justice breaks down and seriously damages the interests of all Americans.[10] He told the predominantly black audience that he had "a good deal of sympathy" for the states' rights school of thought (which he rechristened "the states' responsibilities school") because "My grandfather's first cousin went to Charleston about 1840 . . . and I have intimate associations with my Southern cousins in the third generation." But he went on to say that his experiences while serving on United Nations bodies on press freedom had led him to abandon "complete gradualism" because "it is now nearly ninety-two years since Appomattox and that is being patient a long time . . . Unless the states make a determined effort to end outrageous denials of human rights by their own laws during the next few years, the national government will have to possess the residual power [I have] described if we are to preserve leadership in the free world."

The speech was silent on school segregation, a subject that he felt had been abundantly discussed by others. But a week before his death, the *Harvard Law School Record* published his views under the headline "Chafee Scores Failure to Plan Desegregation." Criticizing the U.S. Supreme Court for failing to provide school authorities with a blueprint for implementing its desegregation decisions and instead turning "all the dirty work" over to federal district courts, he said he did not think the problem could be solved by fragmentary litigation. Instead, he called upon the president to "do something to better the situation."[11]

Chafee's doubts about the propriety of lower federal courts correcting racial imbalance in the schools were consistent with the negative or noninterventionist view of government held by classical liberals. He consistently reflected their dread of big government and always described himself as a Cleveland Democrat. He was fundamentally conservative, and his great defense of free speech was, in a significant sense, a reflection of his conservatism.

"Our wisest conservatives," Arthur M. Schlesinger, Sr., has written, have always understood the safety-valve function of free speech. "Liberty of expression may not at first seem a moderating influence, since it is an open invitation to all malcontents to agitate their grievances. But that is just the point. For orderly progress it is better that crackpots rant in public than plot in private, and the very act, moreover, subjects their beliefs to comparison with the more constructive ideas of others. Only in this way can the critics be criticized, their proposals cut down to size, and an appropriate course be arrived at democratically."[12] In *Free Speech in the United States* Chafee expressed the safety-valve justification for expression this way: "Nothing adds more to men's hatred for government than its refusal to let them talk, especially if they are the type of person anarchists are, to whom talking a little wildly is the greatest joy of life. Besides, suppression of their mere words shows a fear of them, which only encourages them to greater activity in secret."[13]

That interpretation of free speech reflects the pragmatic side of Chafee; but there was a Platonic side as well. Indeed, he considered himself a Platonist: he was interested in concepts and theories, and he enjoyed thinking a legal problem through to a solution. This was essentially the method he used in drafting the federal Interpleader Act of 1936, a highly specialized measure for solving multiple claims for the same debt against insurance companies, banks, and similar businesses. Although he was a Platonist in important respects, he formulated no general philosophy of law. There is, however, a thread that unites his disparate writings on the law. It is the idea of balance and the belief that most legal problems should be solved by balancing interests. His fondness for the balancing metaphor is clearly linked to both his personal life and the age in which he lived.

He had been affected by the ideas of Roger Williams, who emphasized both individual liberty and collective welfare. He grew up at a time when individualism was giving way to collectivism, and intellectuals were searching for balance between the individual and the community or the social organization. He longed to be a writer but filial duty originally propelled him into the iron business. He felt a debt to blacks because a black woman had helped rear him, but he also sympathized with white southern attitudes because of his relatives in the South. His family were well-to-do industrialists, but he married a woman of modest background whose mother was a social worker, a Socialist, and an admirer of the Soviet Union. He believed in making money, but his social status pricked his conscience. He attended Harvard Law School whose general pedagogical attitude was one of "realizing that there is often much to be said on both sides of a question and endeavoring to hear both sides and judge between them." And his mentor was Roscoe Pound, who, borrowing from a German legal philosopher named Rudolf von Jhering, stressed the need to balance interests in deciding legal disputes. Balance, it may be said without exaggeration, was the leitmotiv of his life and work.

Instead of developing a general philosophy of law, Chafee attacked legal problems in a systematic way chiefly through the preparation of journal articles. In a sense, he was a "pamphleteer"—a term used to describe him by his Harvard law colleague John M. Maguire. Not one of his seven books intended for a general readership was a book as such; all were derived from articles, lectures, memoranda, reviews, and so on, and his books at times suffered from the redundancies and lack of coherence peculiar to this genre. As for the dozen or so casebooks bearing his name, sometimes as coauthor or coeditor, he slyly noted that they were largely written by judges. Even the classic *Freedom of Speech* was criticized by his friend Harold J. Laski—in a letter to Justice Holmes, not Chafee—for being a nonbook: "It is good and solid; but it suffers from the almost complete absence of literary virtues and from a tendency to repetition which makes it at times a little boring. This, I suppose, because it is reprinted articles; but if one is going to write a book, one is going to write a book. On the other hand, I read F. J. Turner's *Frontier in American History* which I insist you get—quite obviously the biggest contribution to the interpretation of America in my time—the book of a real master with a great thesis to maintain."[14]

If Chafee never quite evolved into a "real master" with a "great thesis," it may have been partly because of the times in which he wrote. Coincidentally, in a tribute to Laski written after his friend's death on 24 March 1950, Chafee looked back to the year 1916, when Laski arrived at Harvard from Cambridge, England, as a time when "forward-looking men and women were still engaged in rethinking our traditional political, economic and social conceptions and considering how they could be best altered to meet the new needs of an industrial and highly developed country. All possibilities were open to examination, under the guiding principle, 'Prove all things; hold fast that which is good.' Men's minds moved with a freedom which is now incomprehensible, for thinking had not yet been hardened into queer shapes by the emotions aroused by war and conflicting reactions to the Russian Revolution."[15]

It was also in 1916 that Chafee left Providence, where he had practiced law for three years, to join the Harvard faculty, a position that he enthusiastically accepted with the hope that it would make him a participant in the vital task of reforming American law. The dampening effect of post–1916 events on his reformer's zeal may be conveniently gauged by the difference in tone between two essays on the law he prepared for collections about American society edited by the liberal expatriate Harold Stearns. In the earlier essay, printed in 1922, he cited the need to "make over the common law system of an agricultural population a century ago to meet the needs of the city-dwelling America of today," and then described both necessary reforms and ways of achieving them.[16] In the later essay, published in 1938, he noted that the legal improvements he had called for in the earlier volume were "mostly unaccomplished" but he did so with resignation.[17]

Although he became more reconciled as he grew older to the difficulty of accomplishing significant legal reforms, through his "pamphleteering" he continued to peck away at effecting improvements in areas of particular interest to him, notably commercial law and equity. His most tangible achievement was the federal Interpleader Act, which he considered "the accomplished task to which I look back most gladly" because it was a "means of speedily and satisfactorily settling hundreds of disputes between citizens of different states."[18] In fact, he once suggested—wryly, to be sure—that his epitaph should be (in imitation of Jefferson's, which omits mention of his presidency): drafter of the Interpleader Act and translator of "Pervigilium Veneris." The latter refers to the translation he wrote as a Brown undergraduate of the well known Latin spring poem beginning "Love, oh love upon the morrow . . . ," a rendition printed several times in the *Boston Herald* and in at least one anthology.

Because he was more interested in concepts than in the natural-science methodology increasingly being imported into the law, he favored improving the law through sharpening its language rather than through collecting data. (He was not unmindful, however, of the important distinction, stressed by Roscoe Pound at Harvard and legal realists at Columbia and Yale, between "law in books" and "law in action.") In a 1941 essay entitled "The Disorderly Conduct of Words," for example, he described what the legal profession could learn from semanticists, and vice versa: "Because we believe reason to be our best guide, we must exert ourselves in legal expression to make our thoughts fit things and our words fit our thoughts, to keep down the emotional element, and above all to pick and choose among possible emotions. The evocation of a sense of fairness may be within the emotive function as truly as the stimulation of hatred and greed, but it is a much more legitimate aim."[19]

Part of the essay—which was amusing as well as acute—represented a "long reply to the [realists'] superficially tempting plan of dropping general concepts out of the administration of justice," a reply that did "not take the position that all such concepts are now satisfactory or that they are all wisely handled" but insisted that "judges and law teachers should be constantly engaged in the task of making these phrases fit present conditions better. We need a big spring cleaning to see which terms embody useful principles like 'good faith,' and which are enough worn out to throw away like 'malice' and 'conclusive presumption.' " It "is one thing to say that abstractions must be used cautiously, and quite another to urge that, unless they can be verified by the methods of the natural sciences, they must not be used at all," just as "the fact that the houses in which we live happen to be ugly or inconvenient is no reason for tearing them down and sleeping in the woods."[20]

Although interested in reform, Chafee was no activist. In general, he believed he could accomplish more by limiting himself to the role of the detached scholar and commentator on legal issues. Consistent with this view—no doubt partly shaped by the fact that various activities and writings early in his career had almost cost him his teaching post—was his refusal to become an active member of the National Advisory Committee of the American Civil Liberties Union (ACLU). He aided the ACLU with both scholarly and financial contributions, but he feared that by becoming a committee member in a public capacity his credibility would suffer. Similarly, he seldom appeared in court after having taken part in a controversial deportation case in 1920, although he advised practicing lawyers and, as a member of the American Bar Association's Bill of Rights Committee during the years 1938–1947, he helped prepare briefs for several leading cases in the U.S. Supreme Court—the closest he came to realizing his ambition of sitting on that tribunal.

Just as he questioned the advisability of becoming an activist, so he had serious doubts about his leadership ability. He was convinced that he was "no chairman," a point he regularly made in declining administrative or leadership responsibilities. On several occasions, though, he did agree to serve on or even head bodies concerned with important social and political issues. Because these activities are not discussed in the body of this biography, I will summarize them here.

In May 1923 he became chairman of the Committee of Inquiry on Coal and Civil Liberties, financed by the ACLU and the League for Industrial Democracy and created in response to an invitation from the U.S. Coal Commission. Because his committee's report contained criticisms of mine operators, the private police they employed, and the company towns they ran, some influential Harvard law alumni questioned, for the second time in three years, his fitness to remain on the faculty.[21]

For five years starting in 1928, he served as president of the Massachusetts Council for the Abolition of the Death Penalty. Because the campaign against capital punishment gained impetus from the electrocutions of Sacco and Vanzetti in 1927, it seemed a favorable time to lead the opposition even though accepting such a post went against his better judgment. An idealist with a Jeffersonian faith in the power of education, he assumed the council would be able to enlighten the public, whose elected representatives would then abolish the law. But capital punishment was still on the books in 1944 when he donated his council correspondence to the Harvard University Archives and sent along this wistful note: "Possibly these [materials] will be of interest someday to a student of unsuccessful reforms in this vicinity."[22]

From 1929 to 1931 he assisted in the work of the National Commission on Law Enforcement and Observance (the Wickersham Commission), whose most diligent member was Chafee's dean, Roscoe Pound. Created by President Hoover in response to the widespread crime associated with prohibition, the commission had one of its key subcommittees study lawless enforcement of the law including police use of the third degree. Serving with Chafee on this body were Carl S. Stern and Walter H. Pollak, both civil libertarians and then law partners in New York. As an ACLU counsel, Pollak had in 1925 persuaded the U.S. Supreme Court that the First Amendment's speech and press guarantees protect against infringements by state governments as well as by the federal government.[23] Two of the three reports produced by the subcommittee were officially printed: one on unfairness in prosecutions, the other on the third degree.[24] Years later, referring to the United Nations Universal Declaration on Human Rights, Chafee noted that his Wickersham experience in studying the third degree had left him pessimistic about investigations of human rights violations: "We spent $40,000 and two years on the job. Yet our report was greeted by the police with two answers which they regarded as conclusive: first, there wasn't any third degree; and second, they couldn't do their work without it."[25]

Thus, in varying degrees, his service for the coal commission, the anti-death penalty group, and the Wickersham Commission all brought frustration or downright disappointment. A fourth foray into public service—this one primarily unofficial in nature—proved much more satisfying. This was his work on behalf of congressional reapportionment and mainly took the form of journal articles and correspondence in which he sought to explain in laymen's terms mathematical methods for allocating among the states the seats in the U.S. House of Representatives. But his interest and expertise in this area also resulted in his serving in 1950 on a committee of the American Political Science Association that made recommendations for reapportionment based on the census of that year.

Questions of reapportionment gave Chafee, an accomplished amateur mathematician, a chance to combine his interest in numbers theory with his mastery of the law and his concern for justice. "No group of persons is more vitally concerned with the problem of Congressional reapportionment than the bar," he stated at the outset of his first article on the problem, published in 1929. "Laws are inevitably affected by the composition of the law making body. Loyal obedience to statutes depends largely upon the widespread conviction that they were justly enacted, and this conviction is seriously weakened by an unfair allotment of representatives."[26]

Three decades later, of course, reapportionment became a fiercely debated constitutional question after the U.S. Supreme Court ruled that representative government at all levels must reflect the principle of one man, one vote. At the time Chafee wrote, however, he and other scholars generally agreed that reapportionment was an area in which the judiciary would not intervene because of the principle of separation of powers. The immediate concern of his 1929 article—which is still cited in the literature—was that Congress ensure that a just apportionment be made after the 1930 census either by Congress itself or by the president or some other high official if Congress failed to do so.

When Chafee first addressed the problem, two main mathematical devices for solving it were available. One was the method of major fractions, developed in 1911 by Walter F. Willcox, professor of economics and mathematics at Cornell University; it was used after the 1910 census and embodied in the automatic reapportionment after the 1930 census. The other was the method of equal proportions, devised by Harvard mathematician Edward V. Huntington while conducting in 1921 the first extensive study of the mathematically possible methods. Convinced of the superiority of equal proportions, Chafee, who enjoyed explaining law to laymen, resolved to aid congressmen and others in recognizing its advantages. In this effort he collaborated with Huntington and at times sought to gain leverage in Washington through his uncle Jesse H. Metcalf, a Rhode Island senator.

The key question in apportionment is this: Given the fact that each state is entitled to one representative regardless of population, how are additional seats to be assigned when population is taken into account? Briefly put, the major fractions method of solving the problem employs divisors that use the arithmetic mean (the average of the sum of two numbers; for example, $1 + 2 = 3 \div 2 = 1\frac{1}{2}$). Those divisors are slightly larger than those of the equal proportions method, which are smaller because they use the geometric mean (the square root of the product of two numbers; for instance, $1 \times 2 = \sqrt{2} = 1.414214$). When the necessary computations are done using major fractions, the big states end up with larger quotients and thus with more congressmen representing fewer constituents in comparison with smaller states. Those advantages are deemed proper by major fractions proponents who argue that the smaller states have an advantage in the Senate as a result of having the same number of senators as the larger states. However, the smaller divisors of the equal proportions method take away the big states' advantage in the House and apportion seats so that the average population per representative has the least variation between one state and another.

When he started writing on reapportionment, Chafee was optimistic that his contemporaries, notably congressmen, were "capable of grasping the superior fairness of Huntington's plan." The message did register on Capitol Hill, where the method of equal proportions was adopted after the 1940 census. For Chafee, it meant "the pleasure of seeing my mathematical ideas on reapportionment . . . embodied in an Act of Congress."[27]

There is no better example of Chafee's wide-ranging intellect and diverse contributions to the law than his work on reapportionment. Undoubtedly, he would have achieved more in nonspeech areas had not the image of "Free Speech" Chafee fastened itself upon him at the start of his career. Try though he might to shake free of it, he never succeeded. A sure sign that the muse of the First Amendment dominated his destiny is the fact that just a few weeks after the equal proportions bill became law on 15 November 1941, President Franklin Roosevelt asked Congress to declare war because of the Japanese attack on Pearl Harbor. Civil liberties issues arising from World War II and the ensuing Cold War ensured that Chafee would never be far from the free speech firing line that he had first occupied, along with a handful of other civil libertarians, at the time of the First World War.[28]

How he got there and what he accomplished in nonspeech sectors while defending the First Amendment are an important part of the story told in these pages.

CHAPTER 1

The Early Years with Freedom of Speech

On 7 December 1941, while pilots of the Japanese air force were destroying the American fleet at Pearl Harbor, Zechariah Chafee, Jr., the Langdell professor of law at Harvard University, was celebrating a joint birthday with his daughter Anne, or Nancy as the family called her. It was his fifty-sixth birthday and her twenty-fifth, and the occasions were marked in the Chafee's three-story frame house at 26 Elmwood Avenue in Cambridge, about a mile from Harvard Square. The location was well suited to the nature of the household's master, the nation's foremost authority on free expression: the house itself stood on the site of the Watertown Meeting, the first protest in the colonies against taxation without representation; and it was across the street from the home of James Russell Lowell, the outspoken poet and Harvard Law School graduate whose excoriation of the federal government during the Mexican War (he defined war as murder) almost certainly would have led to his jailing had sedition laws like those in effect during World War I existed at the time.

Chafee's writings about those laws and the hundreds of federal prosecutions under them culminated in his 1920 book, *Freedom of Speech*. Aimed primarily at lawyers grappling with nebulous questions in the emerging field of First Amendment law, the book quickly became their bible. So shaken was Chafee by repressions under the federal Espionage Act of 1917 that he was convinced that during "the next war," when the statute presumably would again be in force, free expression would be irreparably damaged. In an article printed in 1926 he used italics to emphasize his conviction that *"All genuine discussion among civilians of the justice and wisdom of continuing the next war will . . . become perilous."*[1]

Thus with the approach of World War II, Chafee was understandably receptive when the Harvard University Press Board of Syndics, of which he was a member, suggested that he update his 1920 book. Viewing the suggestion as an opportunity to enlighten his countrymen about the importance of civil liberties during wartime, he decided to aim the new volume primarily at the general public rather than lawyers. He started work on the revisions in December 1940, hopeful that the book would appear during 1941—the 150th anniversary of the Bill of Rights. The book was published on 1 October 1941, only two months before Pearl Harbor, under the title *Free Speech in the United States*. From start to finish, it was prepared in about nine months, a period during which much of his time and energy were taken up by bittersweet family matters—the suicide of his younger son, Robert, and the wedding plans of his older son, Zechariah III.

It was also a demanding period in his professional life: he was named adviser to law students having questions about the draft, a task prompting him to say that he could not write even a short letter without four or five interruptions; he had to teach a new course; he supervised the writing of at least a dozen theses required of third-year students; he graded the hundreds of examinations that customarily occupy many weeks of a law professor's year; and he struggled to find time for research on a comprehensive history of Anglo-American freedom of speech, a project for which he received generous monthly stipends from the Commonwealth Fund of Boston, whose activities included supporting scholarly research.

Although Chafee has been described by Erwin N. Griswold, the last law school dean he worked for, as a faculty member who had the capacity to finish what he started, he never completed the history. In fact, he had done relatively little work on it by the time the Commonwealth Fund's directors voted to discontinue legal-research projects almost five years after asking him to take on the history, which they originally believed could be finished in eighteen months. His letters to the fund from December 1938 to October 1943 reveal the frustrations of a law professor trying to do serious research while teaching, preparing and updating casebooks, carrying on public service, and, in Chafee's case, trying to avoid typecasting because of the reputation he acquired as the author of *the* book on free speech. In an early letter to a fund official, dated 12 December 1938, he wrote:

> I have seen some of my professional friends devote most of their lives to expanding and contracting one book on the Middle Ages or some other single subject. Sometimes it appeared as a textbook for high schools, sometimes as a textbook for colleges, and then again as a popular exposition. But it was always the same old turkey, whether it was hash or soup. I confess to some reluctance [to write the history] because of the fear that my young colleagues will regard me as "single free speech Chafee." Perhaps this is not a very noble attitude and it would be presumptuous to compare myself with John Stuart Mill, but I have sometimes had the hope that I might make substantial contributions of a semi-permanent nature in more than one section of knowledge.

Two years later, with no work on the book yet accomplished, he explained to the fund: "The situation is getting so bad that I am drafting (pause for interruption by student) a remonstrance to the Dean on the subject. I am thinking of applying for leave of absence so that I can go to Yale Law School for two months and do some research." On 26 October 1943, after being notified of the fund's decision to stop supporting legal research, he wrote that he hoped to justify the payments he had received by completing on his own at least a portion of the study, perhaps something on freedom of legislative debate. He was confident that a publisher could be found, and "when the book does appear I shall acknowledge the help which the Commonwealth Fund has given me." And in a postscript he said: "Although it is not quite what you asked for, your help has made possible a good deal of scholarly research in the field of free speech. The resulting relief from financial worry enabled me to do a great deal of work on several briefs in this field for the Bill of Rights Committee of the American Bar Association, and with your kind consent I felt justified in giving the time to my *Free Speech in the United States*, without getting any royalties."[2]

Actually, he did receive royalties. But he had Harvard University Press price the book as low as possible and in return took a smaller royalty because he was less interested in profits than in a large circulation so as to do "all I can to prevent a recurrence of the suppressions of the last war."

When those repressions began soon after Chafee joined the Harvard Law School faculty in 1916, he quickly recognized that they represented an important area of law in the making. Primarily a teacher of commercial law subjects at the outset, he also taught a course in equity that compelled him to do some research on freedom of the press—specifically on the use of injunctions as a prior restraint on publication—and he found the literature limited. He had longed to be a writer, and the uncharted terrain of the First Amendment clearly offered a young legal scholar many opportunities to write. The literature was scanty, mainly because Congress had enacted no laws restricting expression since the Alien and Sedition Acts of 1798, and therefore federal judges had handled little litigation forcing them to ponder what the First Amendment means by "Congress shall make no law . . . abridging the freedom of speech or of the press." As for questions of whether or not state laws may infringe the federal free expression guarantee, they were infrequently entertained by federal courts until after 1925 when the U.S. Supreme Court held that the due process clause of the Fourteenth Amendment applies the First Amendment's speech and press guarantees to abridgments by state governments.[3] Of course, state and local courts had been confronted with questions arising under the speech and press guarantees of state constitutions.

Partly because Chafee, the nation's first great scholar of free speech, concentrated on federal laws and cases, the impression arose that the formative period of First Amendment theory coincided with World War I. Later scholarship has pushed the formative era back to the post–Civil War years, and Chafee has been criticized for slighting the earlier state materials.[4] However, he understandably focused on the federal level for at least one compelling reason: that was where most of the action was at the time he started to explore First Amendment issues. Commenting on the dearth of First Amendment materials, he said in his first law journal article on speech:

"The gradual process of judicial inclusion and exclusion," which has served so well to define other clauses in the federal Constitution by blocking out concrete situations on each side of the line until the line itself becomes increasingly plain, has as yet been of very little use for the First

Amendment. The cases are too few, too varied in their character, and often too easily solved, to develop any definite boundary between lawful and unlawful speech ... Nearly every free speech decision, outside such hotly litigated portions as privilege and fair comment in defamation, appears to have been decided largely by intuition.[5]

Elsewhere, Chafee made the point that "it would be foolish for a scholar in this field to limit himself to old authorities while new law was in the making," and he referred to his research as "only one part of my endeavors to master the law and reduce it to reason."[6] In the process he tended to de-emphasize a prewar tradition of judicial hostility toward speech—perhaps dismissing it as a manifestation of irrationality in his eagerness to give the First Amendment a rational interpretation.[7]

Chafee's first article on free speech appeared in the *New Republic* of 16 November 1918—about two years after he initially lectured on the subject in his equity course for third-year law students. At that time, he noted in his diary for the course, "All hour on *Brandreth v. Lance* and freedom of the press." The case concerned the question of whether or not it was constitutional for a court to issue an injunction to prevent publication of a libelous statement.[8] The invitation to write the *New Republic* piece came in late September 1918 from editor Herbert Croly, who had been told by Harold J. Laski, the English political scientist then teaching at Harvard, that Chafee had spent the summer examining Espionage Act cases preparatory to doing an article for the *Harvard Law Review*. Entitled "Freedom of Speech," the piece for Croly amounted to a short, popularized version of "Freedom of Speech in War Time," printed in the *Review* in June 1919.

When Chafee started writing about speech, there was just a scattering of prewar scholarship from which he could get some direction. It included works by Thomas M. Cooley, professor of law at the University of Michigan; Ernst Freund, professor of law at the University of Chicago; Roscoe Pound, Chafee's dean at Harvard; Henry Schofield, professor of law at Northwestern University; and Theodore Schroeder, prime mover of the Free Speech League.[9] Chafee made direct use of some of these writings, and in *Freedom of Speech* he called Cooley's casebook on constitutional law "by far the best textbook" on speech and other civil rights and Schofield's article "the best discussion of the legal meaning" of press freedom. He regarded Dean Pound as a great influence in his life, and the use he made of Pound's balancing-of-interests concept is discussed in Chapter 4. Chafee particularly liked a pamphlet that came out during the war—*Espionage Act Cases* by Walter Nelles, counsel for the National Civil Liberties Bureau, which in 1920 became the American Civil Liberties Union. Writing to Nelles in 1925, he said: "I have always considered it a remarkable achievement, when you had nothing to guide you. It considered several points that I never took up at all, and I was able to write with the benefit of all you had done."[10] Nelles's reasoning, in Chafee's opinion, laid the foundation for Justice Holmes's famous clear and present danger test, a test that Nelles himself did not like.

Anyone inquiring into the meaning of the First Amendment, which is seemingly cast in absolute terms, faces—or should face up to—an even more basic question: What is meant by "meaning"?[11] One may approach the answer from a historical perspective, examining the original understanding of the amendment and the issues in England and colonial America that made such a constitutional provision seem desirable. Chafee recognized the importance of such analytical problems, but his historical research was rather limited and his interpretation of the data has been seriously challenged.

Two principal governmental controls over the press had made a constitutional guarantee of free expression appear essential to many citizens of the new American nation: prior restraints on publication in the form of licensing, which had been much more of a problem in England than in colonial America; and criminal prosecutions for seditious libel under the common law.[12] Historically, one way of viewing press freedom is as meaning simply that while the government could not restrain (that is, license) the press prior to publication, it could inflict punishments after words appeared in print. Another interpretation holds that there could be neither prior restraints nor common law prosecutions for seditious libel. Or it could be argued that the First Amendment meant that prosecutions for seditious libel were all right if (1) truth could be used as a defense and (2) the jury was empowered to bring in a general verdict of not guilty rather than, as had been traditional, having its decision-making power restricted to the narrow question of whether or not the accused published the offending item. Both points had been advocated by proponents of press freedom and were made part of the 1798 federal Sedition Act.

The argument that the First Amendment was designed simply to bar prior restraints was derived from Sir William Blackstone, a British jurist who wrote in his influential *Commentaries on the Common Law of England:* "The liberty of the press . . . consists of laying no *previous* restraints upon publication and not in freedom from censure for criminal matter when published." Asserting that Blackstone's doctrine ought to be "knocked on the head once for all," Chafee criticized it, as had some scholars before him, for going too far as well as not far enough. Too far, for example, by not allowing the government to suspend a newspaper for repeatedly furnishing to the enemy military information such as sailing dates of troop ships; and not far enough because the threat of harsh punishment for sedition, or some other offense, may prove as effective as prior censorship in stifling political discussion.

"Since Blackstone's definition was really just a statement of the objectionable English law of seditious publications," Chafee declared in his *New Republic* article,

> it throws no light on the meaning of free speech clauses in our Federal and State Constitutions. Those clauses were written by men . . . who intended to make prosecutions for seditious utterances impossible in this country. This is shown plainly by events soon after the First Amendment. When Congress enacted the Sedition Law of 1798, punishing "writings against the government of the United States and the President," Jefferson treated it as unconstitutional, while Hamilton a few years later defended a Federalist editor from prosecution in the name of the liberty of the press. Thus we have testimony from the leaders of both parties.[13]

Chafee repeated this belief, derived partly from an article by Professor Schofield, in his 1919 *Harvard Law Review* article and in his 1920 book, although he hedged his conclusion by adding qualifications such as "the meaning of the First Amendment did not crystallize in 1791."[14]

Other insights into his notion of the framers' original understanding of press freedom appear in letters written during 1920–21 to Edward S. Corwin, an eminent constitutional scholar at Princeton University. Noting that Corwin had shown that the founders had a strong "persecuting instinct," nonetheless he said he did not think that "this yielding to temptation in weaker moments prevents their wishing to carry out the principle of very wide discussion in the Constitution. A man's thoughts may be much better than his acts." But he also expressed his belief that "people in general at the time these guarantees were framed had no very definite idea of what they meant, and so were frequently swayed by the passion of the moment or by English precedents, which should have had no application to American conditions. In order to give the Constitution real meaning, it is necessary to look at the functional value of freedom of speech and not merely at contemporary practice."[15]

It is interesting that forty years after Corwin argued that the First Amendment was not intended to bar seditious libel prosecutions but was intended to give the states exclusive jurisdiction over sedition, much the same argument was put forth by a historian named Leonard W. Levy. His book *Legacy of Suppression*, published three years after Chafee's death in 1957, clearly reflected more historical research than Chafee had done and was widely acclaimed, partly because it was seen as a refutation of Chafee's view that the First Amendment proscribed seditious libel. Levy himself declared that Chafee, along with Schofield and others, had, "in Mrs. Malaprop's phrase, 'anticipated the past' by succumbing to an impulse to re-create it so that its image may be seen in a manner consistent with our rhetorical tradition of freedom, thereby yielding a message which will instruct the present. The evidence suggests that the proposition is more presuppositious than plausible, or if plausible, unprovable."[16]

In addition to presenting his central thesis that the framers merely intended for the First Amendment to incorporate Blackstone's conception of press freedom, Levy contended that a broad libertarian theory of press freedom came into existence only in response to enactment of the federal Sedition Act of 1798, whereas Chafee saw the critical reaction to that law as proof that the First Amendment's authors had themselves sought to destroy seditious libel.[17] Both positions continue to have their supporters and detractors, and it is probably impossible in any event to prove what the framers meant. Maybe they did not know what they meant; or perhaps they intended to allow the First Amendment and the rest of the Constitution to be interpreted and reinterpreted as times and circumstances changed. In somewhat different ways both Chafee and Levy accepted that view, as have other scholars. Because the U.S. Supreme Court is the paramount interpreter of the Constitution, it is safe to say that the First Amendment means what the court says it means. And that tribunal, in its unanimous decision in the 1964 case of *New York Times v. Sullivan*, settled as a matter of modern constitutional law the major point of contention between Chafee and Levy. In an opinion by Justice William J. Brennan the court said that the outlawing of seditious libel constituted "the central meaning of the First Amendment." Reaching that conclusion by relying on the historical events of 1798 rather than of 1791, Brennan declared: "Although the Sedition Act [of 1798] was never tested in this Court, the attack upon its validity has carried the day in the court of history."[18]

In his 1919 article Chafee noted that Blackstone's concept of no prior restraint "was adopted by American judges in several early prosecutions for libel, one of which was in Massachusetts, whence Justice Holmes carried it into the United States Supreme Court [in *Patterson v. Colorado* in 1907]. Fortunately he has now [in the 1919 case of *Schenck v. United States*] repudiated this interpretation of freedom of speech, but not until his dictum had had considerable influence, particularly in Espionage Act cases. Of course if the First Amendment does not prevent prosecution and punishment of utterances, the Espionage Act is unquestionably constitutional."[19]

When the U.S. Supreme Court in 1931 squarely considered for the first time the relevance of Blackstone's doctrine to the First Amendment, it struck down a Minnesota statute calling for the outright suppression of "malicious, scandalous, and defamatory" publications. Writing for the majority in *Near v. Minnesota*, Chief Justice Charles Evans Hughes emphasized Blackstone's statement that "the liberty of the press consists in laying no *previous* restraints upon publication." But he also carefully noted the risks in equating free expression with that doctrine. Without referring to Chafee by name, Hughes echoed his criticism of Blackstone and, as Chafee had done, quoted Cooley's *Constitutional Limitations* to the effect that "mere exemption from previous restraints" is not enough to ensure constitutional free expression. Hughes did cite Chafee's point concerning publication of troop-ship sailing dates.[20] Having observed in 1919 that Blackstone's doctrine "dies hard," Chafee later said he "fondly supposed that the acceptance of the views of my first chapter [of *Freedom of Speech*] by Chief Justice Hughes effectively disposed of this notion." The comment came a decade after the *Near* decision in a critique for the *Harvard Law Review* of a manuscript stating that "the Blackstonian test of free speech is said to be 'generally agreed.' " Faced with this assertion that Blackstone was alive and well in the United States in 1942, he complained: "I suppose I may as well retire into a rat hole."[21]

When Chafee set out in 1918–19 to clarify the language of the First Amendment, he did not view its "no law" commandment as an absolute; rather, he thought the basic question was where to draw the line between permissible and punishable speech. His thinking was permanently influenced by the ideas—related yet different—articulated by judges Learned Hand and Oliver Wendell Holmes, Jr., both Harvard law graduates, in two important cases arising under the 1917 Espionage Act. That law, despite its name, amounted to a sedition statute. But for good measure, Congress amended it in 1918 by adding a specific Sedition Act.[22]

It is true that portions of the 1917 law dealt with actual espionage as well as protection of military secrets and enforcement of neutrality between other nations in future conflicts. But section 3 of title I created these new offenses (I have added the numerals): "(1) Whoever, when the United States is at war, shall willfully make or convey false reports or false statements with intent to interfere with the operation or success of the military or naval forces of the United States or to promote the success of its enemies (2) and whoever, when the United States is at war, shall willfully cause or attempt to cause insubordination, disloyalty, mutiny, or refusal of duty, in the military or naval forces of the United States, (3) or shall willfully obstruct the recruiting or enlistment service of the United States, to the injury of the service or of the United States, shall be punished by a fine of not more than $10,000 or imprisonment for not more than twenty years, or both."

One other section of the act should be noted here: title XII made nonmailable any matter violating the act, or advocating treason, insurrection, or forcible resistance to any law of the United States. And the 1918 sedition amendment went further, inserting "attempts to obstruct" in the third of the original offenses; adding nine more offenses, including derisive utterances about the U.S. government, the constitution, the flag, and military uniforms, and utterances urging curtailment of materiel production with intent to hinder the war effort; and making the nonmailable provision harsher by allowing the postmaster general to stop delivery of even innocent mail addressed to a sender who he thought had committed any of the twelve offenses.

In deciding the case of *Masses Publishing Co. v. Patten* in the summer of 1917, Hand, then a federal district judge, formulated a direct incitement test in deciding that criticisms of President Wilson and the war effort in the radical *Masses* magazine did not fall under the Espionage Act's postal provisions.[23] Differentiating between words as "keys of persuasion" that are protected under the First Amendment and words as "triggers of action" that are unprotected, he emphasized that words having "no purport but to counsel the violation of law" are punishable. Holmes's test became much better known than Hand's after he formulated it in the spring of 1919 in *Schenck v. United States*, the first case under the 1917 Espionage Act to reach the Supreme Court.[24] Writing for a unanimous court in upholding the convictions of Charles Schenck and others for urging men to resist induction into the army, Holmes wrote: "The question in every case is whether the words used are used in such circumstances and are of such a nature as to create a clear and present danger that they will bring about the substantive evils that Congress has a right to prevent. It is a question of proximity and degree."

Superficially, at least, Hand's direct incitement test (some scholars call it the objective standard test) is appealing because it appears to be easy to administer as well as quite protective of speech. No consideration is given to the rather slippery question of the likely harm that words may cause; instead, it focuses on the nature or content of words (for this reason Hand called it a qualitative standard) and establishes a category of punishable speech—the kind that urges people to break the law. What could be more clear-cut? In concrete instances, however, the test may yield some highly unsatisfactory results. Particularly troublesome is the so-called Marc Anthony problem (Chafee used it to twit Hand) in which words that do not directly incite nevertheless lead to incitement because of the context. Similarly bothersome is a hostile-audience situation in which an innocuous speaker may produce a real or potential breach of the peace, not because he has directly urged the listeners to break the law but because they do not like his message. Conversely, Hand's test allows words to be punished for direct incitement even though in context they are harmless or hyperbolic.[25]

Holmes's clear and present danger test also has a surface attractiveness. Although it takes into account the tricky question of the likely harm of words, it does call for close linkage between words and harm. And it also considers the circumstances or context of words so that the same words that are punishable in one context (wartime, for instance) are protected in another (peacetime, by contrast). But this test, too, has its drawbacks. For example, it may allow police to punish rather than protect a political agitator whose message so angers listeners that they become hostile toward the speaker. In the oft-quoted words of Paul Freund:

> Even where it is appropriate, the clear-and-present-danger test is an oversimplified judgment unless it takes account also of a number of other factors: the relative seriousness of the danger in comparison with the value of the occasion for speech or political activity; the availability of more moderate controls than those the state has imposed; and perhaps the specific intent with which the speech or activity is launched. No matter how rapidly we utter the phrase "clear and present danger," or how closely we hyphenate the words, they are not a substitute for the weighing of values. They tend to convey a delusion of certitude when what is most certain is the complexity of the strands in the web of freedoms which the judge must disentangle.[26]

Chafee saw strengths and weaknesses in both the Hand and Holmes formulations, and in a 1920 letter to Judge Hand he characteristically—for his personality dictated a middle position on most questions—raised the possibility of combining the two tests. Referring to Hand's distinction between (1) political agitation and (2) incitement to resistance to law or violation of law, he said "the right view as a matter of expediency" seemed to be that "(1) can never be punished; (2) can be punished only if it satisfies the danger test."[27] Hand's reply did not mention Chafee's proposed compound test, which in a sense anticipated a formula used much later by the U.S. Supreme Court in the 1969 case of *Brandenburg v. Ohio*.[28] In the abstract, at least, Chafee's proposal undoubtedly represented an improvement over either test taken alone. But in concrete instances the previously described problems of each could be compounded in the combined test, and there is the added problem, not mentioned heretofore, of distinguishing clearly between agitation and incitement. As Holmes himself once remarked, "Every idea is an incitement."[29]

In any event, the letter containing Chafee's proposal forms one part of a series of correspondence between himself, Hand, and Holmes during the years 1918–1921 that illuminates their various labors on determining the boundary of free expression.[30] Some letters show Hand touting his test as offering the surest protection of expression, because it emphasizes language (the nature or content of words) rather than its likely harm, and trying to convince Holmes of its merits; others reveal Holmes arguing that his test and Hand's amount to the same thing while reflecting a callousness toward free speech. Such an attitude was consistent with his opinions for the Supreme Court in the *Schenck* case, where the danger test was used to uphold Espionage Act convictions, and, a week later, in *Frohwerk v. United States* and *Debs v. United States*, where Holmes cited *Schenck* as dispositive in upholding other convictions under the statute.[31]

About eight months after those cases were decided in the spring of 1919, the leading case under the 1918 Sedition Act was decided by the court. This was *Abrams v. United States*, in which the court upheld the convictions of five Russian aliens, including one woman, and the harsh prison sentences they had been given.[32] For his published criticisms of this political trial, Chafee himself was put on trial before a law school committee at the instigation of angry alumni. That incident is related in the next chapter; for now, it is important to stress that Holmes in a dissenting opinion in *Abrams*, joined by Louis D. Brandeis, elaborated the danger test in a way that showed he had become much more sensitive to the importance of expression. But while Holmes's dissent reflects an appreciation of the value of expression such as Hand urged upon him, Gerald Gunther has noted that it says little—apart from adding an element of immediacy to the danger doctrine—about how to protect it.[33]

Holmes's dissent and the majority opinion in *Abrams* were discussed by Chafee and Hand in letters that initiated their correspondence. Chafee wrote Hand to invite him to speak at a Harvard Liberal Club dinner honoring Holmes and Brandeis for their stand on free expression, but it did not take him long to bring up the Sedition Act ruling itself: "I suppose the *Abrams* decision was the same kind of shock to you that it was to me. At all events Holmes' dissent is bound to win against the unreasoning majority opinion as the years go on, and I console myself occasionally with Browning's 'baffled to fight better.' If the Circuit Court of Appeals had only sustained [your *Masses* decision instead of reversing it], one of the worst pages in our history might not have been written."[34]

In reply Hand said that, although he believed the *Abrams* decision might well be justified by the facts, "nothing could be more needed than Justice Holmes's opinion" and "I am delighted that it appeared." However, he wished that "it could have been written with your historical perspective," as displayed in Chafee's piece in the June 1919 *Harvard Law Review*, and he did "not altogether like the way Justice Holmes put the limitation. I myself think it is a little more manageable and quite adequate a distinction to say that there is an absolute and objective test to language. I daresay that it is obstinacy, but I still prefer that which I attempted to state in my first 'Masses' opinion, rather than to say that the connection between the words used and the evil aimed at should be 'immediate and direct.' "[35]

After an exchange of letters in October 1920 in which Chafee received permission to dedicate *Freedom of Speech* to the judge, Hand wrote again in December to thank Chafee for sending him a copy of the book. Noting that the *Masses* decision "cost me something, at least at the time," a reference to his having been passed over for promotion to the federal Court of Appeals, he noted again that his view received practically no professional approval. "I kept up my hopes till Debs' case and when the whole court affirmed that without laying down anything like what I thought was the rule, I confess I began to wonder whether I had not got some kind of wrong squint on the subject." He continued:

> Later things turned a little the other way [with Holmes's dissent in *Abrams*], but your very generous, and, I must believe, exaggerated, recognition of my views has been by far the most whole-hearted support I have ever got. It may interest you to know that when I was suddenly faced with the decision, I looked back with the greatest regret at my wasted days. "Here," I thought, "if you only knew enough, there is a place to state correctly, based on scholarship, what is the right rule. You don't know your job; you don't know anything about the history of the subject, and you must fire

off your own funny ideas about what ought or oughtn't to be."[36]

Was Chafee, who conducted extensive scholarship on the subject, able to state "the right rule"? In his June 1919 *Harvard Law Review* article he confidently announced his solution to the problem of finding the free speech boundary line. Ironically, his early writings leaned on the "funny ideas" of Hand, who, while certain that his test was better than Holmes's, believed his lack of scholarship kept him from finding the correct rule.

In a paragraph that he called the key passage of *Freedom of Speech* (it also appeared in his 1918 and 1919 articles), Chafee stated:

> The true meaning of freedom of speech seems to be this. One of the most important purposes of society and government is the discovery and spread of truth on subjects of general concern. This is possible only through absolutely unlimited discussion, for, as Bagehot points out, once force is thrown into the argument, it becomes a matter of chance whether it is thrown on the false side or the true, and truth loses all its natural advantage in the contest. Nevertheless, there are other purposes of government, such as order, the training of the young, protection against external aggression. Unlimited discussion sometimes interferes with these purposes, which must then be balanced against freedom of speech, but freedom of speech ought to weigh very heavily in the scale. The First Amendment gives binding force to this principle of political wisdom.[37]

He emphasized that it is useless to try to define free speech in terms of rights. Deadlock inevitably results because agitators assert their constitutional right to speak, and the government invokes its constitutional right to conduct war. To locate the boundary line of any right, it is necessary to go behind legal rules to human facts. "In our problem," he declared, "we must regard the desires and needs of the individual human being who wants to speak and those of the great group of human beings among whom he speaks. That is, in technical language, there are individual interests and social interests, which must be balanced against each other, if they conflict, in order to determine which interest shall be sacrificed under the circumstances and which shall be protected and become the foundation of a legal right."

Not until Congress and the courts recognized this balancing principle could the true boundary of the First Amendment be fixed. Classifying speech as lawful or unlawful, Chafee argued, involves balancing two vital social interests—public safety and the search for truth. "Every reasonable attempt should be made to maintain both interests unimpaired, and the great interest in free speech should be sacrificed only when the interest in public safety is really imperiled, and not, as most men believe, when it is barely conceivable that it may be slightly affected. In war time, therefore, speech should be unrestricted by the censorship or by punishment, unless it is clearly liable to cause direct and dangerous interference with the conduct of the war."

So there it was: the "problem of locating the boundary line of free speech is solved. It is fixed close to the point where words will give rise to unlawful acts." However, in a remark of considerable significance coming from a professor of commercial law, Chafee immediately noted that free speech, because it involves "much more flexible national policies," does not lend itself to the precise rules of private property law such as the Rule against Perpetuities and the Rule in Shelley's Case.[38] This difference between First Amendment law—where "the right rule" is still to be discovered—and property law frustrated him for the rest of his life.

Chafee's 1919 article also stated that the boundary line of speech punishable under the Espionage Act was "fixed where words come close to injurious conduct by the judge who has given the fullest attention to the meaning of free speech during the war,—Learned Hand, of the Southern District of New York."[39] In the *New Republic* the previous year he praised Hand for stating in the *Masses* case "the proper attitude toward free speech in war time"; now he wrote that "there is no finer judicial statement of the right of free speech" than Hand's opinion; and in 1920, in asking the judge's permission to dedicate *Freedom of Speech* to him, he said: "It was really your opinion in the Masses case that started me on my work. I feel more and more that it was a staggering task to solve the problem as you did at the very outset of the War, with so few precedents and in such pressure and excitement."[40]

Yet Chafee's 1919 article also spoke approvingly of the danger test, albeit the bouquet included brickbats for Holmes. Published after the justice's majority opinion in *Schenck* and before his dissenting opinion in *Abrams*, the article complained: "Justice Holmes in his Espionage Act decisions had a magnificent opportunity to make articulate for us that major premise, under which judges ought to classify words as inside or outside the scope of the First Amendment. He, we hoped, would concentrate his great abilities on fixing the line. Instead, like the other judges, he has told us that certain plainly unlawful utterances are, to be sure, unlawful." In addition, Chafee criticized the justice for not defining more specifically what he meant by substantive evils when he wrote in *Schenck* that "the question in every case is whether the words used are used in such circumstances and are of such a nature as to create a clear and present danger that they will bring about the substantive evils that Congress has a right to prevent." If Holmes meant overt acts interfering with the war, Chafee wrote, then he drew the boundary line "very close to the test of incitement at common law and clearly made the punishment of words for their bad tendency impossible." For Chafee, "the most essential element of free speech is the rejection of bad tendency as the test of a criminal utterance."[41]

Chafee commended Holmes for recognizing the close link between expression and criminal attempts by using in *Schenck* the phrase "it is a question of degree," a phrase earlier used by Holmes in deciding an attempt case while on the Massachusetts Supreme Judicial Court.[42] Chafee's point was that the test of criminal attempts and incitement does not punish bad intention alone; to be punishable, attempts and incitement must come dangerously close to succeeding.[43] "If the Supreme Court test is to mean anything more than a passing observation," Chafee stressed, "it must be used to upset convictions for words when the trial judge did not insist that they must create 'a clear and present danger' of overt acts."[44] Chafee got off one final volley at Holmes, a Union veteran of the Civil War who almost died of combat wounds: "Furthermore, it is regrettable that Justice Holmes did nothing to emphasize the social interest [in truth] behind free speech . . . The last sentence of the passage quoted from the Schenck case ["When a nation is at war many things . . . will not be endured . . . and . . . no Court could regard them as protected by any constitutional right"] seems to mean that the Supreme Court will sanction any restriction of speech that has military force behind it, and reminds us that [Holmes] used to say when he was young, 'that truth was the majority vote of that nation that could lick all others.' "[45] But despite his criticisms of Holmes, he called clear and present danger "a good test for future free speech cases."

Chafee received several complimentary letters about the article—less appreciative were Justice Department officials, whose reaction is described in the next chapter—and the author of one thought it "might have almost stung [Holmes] into a reply." Harold Laski gave Holmes a copy of the piece, then asked Chafee to tea to meet the justice. In the written invitation Laski said he had read the article twice—"I'll go to the stake for every word"—and "we must fight on it." It has been suggested that it was at this meeting that Holmes was converted to the more liberal view of speech expressed in his *Abrams* dissent.[46] But any such conversion was not immediately apparent to Chafee, who wrote Charles F. Amidon, a federal district judge in North Dakota whose handling of expression cases he admired:

> I have talked with Justice Holmes about the article but find that he is inclined to allow a very wide latitude to Congressional discretion in the carrying on of the war. He does not think it possible to draw any limit to the First Amendment but simply to indicate cases on the one side or the other of the line. While I do not anticipate myself that any hard and fast line could be drawn, his failure, it seems to me, is the omission to state the principles by which decisions are to be placed on one side or the other. He further thinks that he could not have gone behind the jury verdict in the Debs case. I am not sure that there is any erroneous passage in that charge on which a reversal could be based. The trouble is that the language is so general that the jury would condemn for a remote tendency. It is too bad that Justice Holmes' decision did not come earlier in the war so that at least his test of clear and present danger might have been laid down in [jury] charges. The greatest pity of all is that Judge Learned Hand was reversed. It is clear from the way Justice Holmes talks that if he had been on the jury in the Debs case he would have voted for acquittal.[47]

Nor did Holmes apparently say anything during the teatime chat to justify Chafee's statement in *Free Speech in the United States,* written two decades later, that the justice "was biding his time until the Court should have before it a conviction so clearly wrong [the *Abrams* case] as to let him speak out his deepest thoughts about the First Amendment."[48] Of course, it seems likely that Holmes's deepest thoughts were to some degree shaped by the criticisms of Hand and Chafee.

If nothing else, Chafee's conversation or his writings apparently persuaded Holmes that the First Amendment did not leave common law sedition in force. In June 1922 Chafee wrote Holmes posing a question he had long intended to ask—whether the definition of free speech formulated in *Schenck* "was at all suggested to you by any writers on the subject or was the result entirely of your reflections. Since you hit the nail, in my opinion, so squarely on the head, I am wondering whether you had been aiming at it for a long while and whether you had learned of others who had at least succeeded in mashing their fingers somewhere in the neighborhood of the nail."[49] Holmes replied:

> The expression that you refer to was not helped by any book that I know of—I think it came without trouble after the later cases (and probably you—I don't remember exactly) had taught me that in the earlier Patterson case, if that was the name of it, I had taken Blackstone and Parker of Mass. as undisputed, wrongly. I simply was ignorant. But I did think hard on the matter of attempts in my Common Law and a Mass. case—later in the Swift case (U.S.)—and I thought it out unhelped. I noted that Bishop made a slight modification of his text after I had printed but without reference to me. I speak from ancient memory. And much later I found an English nisi prius case in which one of the good judges had expressed the notion in a few words. That early effort no doubt made that formula easy if it is good— as I hope.[50]

If Chafee played some part in Holmes's conversion, it is evident that Chafee himself became more committed to the danger test between publication of "Freedom of Speech in War Time" in the summer of 1919 and *Freedom of Speech* in the fall of 1920. No doubt his regard for it grew rapidly after Holmes's elaboration in his *Abrams* dissent; indeed, it is likely that the dissent aroused some feeling of regret in Chafee over his earlier criticisms of the justice. Two marginal comments among annotations he made on a printed copy of his 1919 article point in this direction. He wrote "Soften this" beside the passage containing the criticism that "Justice Holmes . . . , like other judges, . . . has told us that certain plainly unlawful utterances are, to be sure, unlawful." And in his book there is a "softened" version although the quoted phrase is retained. The second marginal note, appearing beside the criticisms of Holmes for not defining substantive evils, said: "Holmes was a bit hurt at this accusation of obscurity, and meant what I suggested. See Abrams case." In the book the point is made this way: "Although 'the substantive evils' are not specifically defined, they mean successful interference with the particular power of Congress that is in question—in this instance, the war power."[51]

Freedom of Speech, although hardly an unqualified paean to Holmes, presents a brief for the danger test—even though Chafee thought so highly of the objective standard test that he dedicated the book to Hand. As Chafee explained it, he wrote the first three chapters "in support of this danger test as marking the true limit of governmental interference with speech and writing."[52]

Hand read Chafee's book with admiration—"it will stand for an indefinite time as the most complete and satisfactory exposition of one of the most baffling subjects in the law"—but he could not share its author's enthusiasm for the danger test: "I am not wholly in love with Holmes's test and the reason is this. Once you admit that the matter is one of degree, while you may put it where it genuinely belongs, you so obviously make it a matter of administration, i.e., you give to Tomdickandharry, D.J., so much latitude [he wrote but deleted "as his own fears may require"] that the jig is at once up. Besides their Ineffabilities, the Nine Elder Statesmen, have not shown themselves wholly immune from the 'herd instinct' and what seems 'immediate and direct' to-day may seem very remote next year even though the circumstances surrounding the utterance be unchanged. I own I should prefer a qualitative formula, hard, conventional, difficult to evade." But he conceded: "You have, I dare say, done well to take what has fallen from Heaven and insist it is manna rather than to set up any independent solution. 'Immediate and direct' is all we have; for God's sake let us not look it in the mouth."[53]

Chafee, who earlier had declared the problem solved, responded that drawing the boundary line in sedition cases "seems to baffle us all" and agreed that in many cases the danger test would "prove unworkable" because juries would go over Holmes's distinction "rough shod." He called Hand's test "surely easier to apply," but added that "our old friend Marc Anthony's speech is continually thrown at me in discussion"—meaning that the direct incitement test is not readily applied to the problem of indirect but purposeful incitement such as Anthony's funeral oration. Chafee closed with a characteristic reference to the importance of education: "After all, we ought to take the best test we can find even though it will sometimes break down, and then prevent its breaking down by using channels outside the law to produce greater tolerance in Judges and jurors and the public at large, so that when the next emergency arises we shall be better prepared."[54]

Two questions arise concerning Chafee's preference for the danger test: Did he clearly understand Hand's objective standard test to be more speech protective than the Holmes formula because it focuses on language and avoids difficult judgments as to their likely harm? If so, why did he persist in championing clear and present danger?

Chafee tried to make clear in *Freedom of Speech* that he considered Hand's test to be more protective than Holmes's: "Justice Holmes interprets the Espionage Act more widely than Judge Hand, in making the nature of the words only one element of danger, and in not requiring that the utterances shall in themselves satisfy an objective standard. Thus he loses the great administrative advantages of Judge Hand's test." But he also pointed out that Holmes had been able to announce the danger test with the backing of a unanimous Supreme Court whereas the Hand formula "unfortunately lacked the weight of binding adjudication" because the *Masses* decision was reversed on appeal.[55] Years later, he observed that "Holmes' inestimable service to free speech consisted in his getting a unanimous Supreme Court to accept his test of guilt, which placed a great area of discussion beyond the reach of the government. At last the First Amendment had been given an informative interpretation by the Supreme Court." Yet he went on to say:

> Perhaps the clear and present danger test is not the best possible formulation of the line between constitutionally protected speech and speech which is punishable if legislatures, prosecutors, and juries so desire. I still like better Judge Learned Hand's phrase in 1917 . . . "direct incitement to violent resistance," or my own suggestion written in

1918: "In wartime, speech should be free, unless it is clearly liable to cause direct and dangerous interference with the conduct of the war." Yet these are only minor variations. The point is that instead of the old line between forbidden previous censorship and wholly permissible subsequent punishment, there is a new line as to punishment. Censorship still remains prohibited by the Constitution, and in addition punishment is prohibited, too, for all words which are not closely connected with dangerous acts.[56]

Chafee was clearly wrong in calling the variations "only minor," as Gunther has stressed in presenting a strong case for the objective standard test's superiority to the clear and present danger test.[57] But for Chafee the most important consideration—"the point"—was to knock Blackstone on the head and get the high court to accept a test that would afford greater protection to speech. In 1949, in a letter to his former colleague Felix Frankfurter, then a Supreme Court justice and no admirer of the danger test despite his adulation of Holmes, he said: "In 1918–19 I was ready to welcome any acceptance of this solution [balancing interests and making the free speech policy weigh heavily] . . . The clear and present danger test is one way of describing the solution and making it vivid. At the time, I preferred the way Learned Hand described it in the *Masses* case, and am still inclined to regard his treatment of the free speech problem as the most satisfactory of all the decisions in those years. But a reversed district judge can't be profitably set up against a unanimous Supreme Court. To quote you and Dr. Johnson . . . 'It was not for me to bandy words with my sovereign.' "[58]

Chafee's eagerness to find a solution to the speech problem in 1918–19 explains why he seized upon the danger test as manna, especially after Holmes's eloquent dissent in *Abrams*. This same eagerness may also help explain why he flatly declared that the bad tendency test had been banished by the First Amendment, only to be revived by the Espionage Act cases, even though his research would have exposed him to judicial decisions to the contrary.[59] To cite evidence that bad tendency enjoyed favor with courts during peacetime would have ill served his contention that the social interest in free expression as a way of discovering truth is especially important in wartime: "Even after war has been declared there is bound to be a confused mixture of good and bad arguments in its support, and a wide difference of opinion as to its objects. Truth can be sifted out from falsehood only if the government is vigorously and constantly cross-examined . . . Legal proceedings prove that an opponent makes the best cross-examiner. Consequently it is a disastrous mistake to limit criticism to those who favor the war."[60]

Although Chafee's early writings on free speech established him as the nation's leading authority on the subject, his scholarship was largely limited to the field of sedition—a relatively small part of the whole speech complex. A quarter-century elapsed before, as a result of his service on the Commission on Freedom of the Press, he produced a work (*Government and Mass Communications,* discussed in Chapter 5) exploring a wide range of legal problems affecting expression. Moreover, it took many years before the ideas he expressed in his early works had any liberalizing influence on majority opinions of the U.S. Supreme Court.

In the meantime, his libertarian convictions together with his championing of clear and present danger as a speech-protective test helped convince Justices Holmes and Brandeis of the importance of free expression in a democracy; in their hands, as they produced a series of dissenting opinions, the original danger test evolved into a more liberal instrument of the type Chafee had envisaged.[61] Chafee himself, between the publication of *Freedom of Speech* in 1920 and *Free Speech in the United States* in 1941, grudgingly continued to restate his First Amendment views while seeking to demonstrate that he could "make substantial contributions of a semi-permanent nature in more than one section of knowledge." But first he had to convince his employer that he was responsible enough to remain on the payroll.

CHAPTER 2

Trials and Tribulations of a Justice Department Critic

In the early spring of 1921, just a few months after *Freedom of Speech* was published, the library in the Boston suburb of Brookline banned the book, and the librarian refused to accept a gift copy from the author. Even in the Boston area, long considered the book-banning capital of the country, it was unusual for the scholarly work of a distinguished Harvard professor to be a victim of censorship. In an important way, though, the incident was symptomatic of more serious personal problems to come. Without Chafee's knowledge, investigators for the U.S. Department of Justice had been building a dossier on him for a year, and a month before the first day of summer, his fitness to teach was put on trial.

What happened to Chafee was all too typical of the climate of repression generated by the controversy over American participation in the war and by the fear of Bolshevism during the immediate postwar period. It was then that the system of federal spying on Americans took root, a system whose ugly methods and wide scope were not fully revealed until the 1970s.[1] Although Chafee died in 1957 without full knowledge of the role federal officials played in his persecution, he would not have been shocked had the whole story been revealed to him, as the following passage in *Freedom of Speech* suggests:

> The very existence of spies . . . is one of the worst evils
> of sedition legislation, whether directed toward prosecution
> or deportation. Espionage goes with an Espionage Act. In-

formers have been the inseparable accompaniment of government action against the expression of opinion since the delators of Tiberius. The state cannot reach such crimes without them. It needs no great force of eavesdroppers to report murders and robberies. The overt act marks the offense, and if a detective is required at all it is either to chase the criminal, to ward off bomb-plots and assassinations, or to discover who is committing especially ingenious thefts. But if political utterances are made criminal, secret police are indispensable to discover that the crime has been committed at all.[2]

The roots of Chafee's Justice Department problems go back to publication of "Freedom of Speech in War Time" in the June 1919 issue of the *Harvard Law Review*. Besides its criticisms of Justice Holmes, it contained some harsh words for Attorney General Thomas Gregory, who (the fortunes of politics being what they are) was soon succeeded by a man who is still remembered for his peacetime persecution of radicals. "Absurd" was Chafee's word for Gregory's complaint that judges like Learned Hand "took the teeth" out of the Espionage Act; maintaining the metaphor, Chafee wrote that "the teeth the government wanted were never there until other judges in an excess of patriotism put in false ones." Other criticisms of the Justice Department appeared toward the end of the article where Chafee, lamenting that "we have censored and punished speech which was very far from direct and dangerous interference with the conduct of the war," said: "The chief responsibility for this must rest, not upon Congress which was content for a long period with the moderate language of the Espionage Act of 1917, but upon the officials of the Department of Justice and the Post-office, who turned that statute into a drag-net for pacifists, and upon the judges who upheld and approved this distortion of law."[3]

Two former assistants to Attorney General Gregory, John Lord O'Brian of Buffalo and Alfred Bettman of Cincinnati, thought "Freedom of Speech in War Time" was too hard on the department in general and Gregory in particular. They believed that Chafee, who wrote that the Espionage Act had been vigorously enforced, had ignored efforts by department officials to hold down the number of prosecutions and had not given sufficient emphasis to the strong community pressures to prosecute. And O'Brian strongly objected to the statement that the department had used the 1917 statute as a dragnet for pacifists. Further, O'Brian complained about Chafee's coupling of the activities of the postmaster general with those of the attorney general. "As a matter of fact," he explained, "the policies of the two departments were opposed and in conflict during the greater part of the War, although for obvious reasons this fact was not public property."[4]

Hearing the views of Bettman and O'Brian did not convert Chafee into an admirer of the Justice Department, but he came to respect the two men and wrote admiringly of them in *Freedom of Speech*, which indeed reflects some of their suggestions. And there is no evidence suggesting that Bettman and O'Brian played any part in his subsequent harassment.

His first indication of trouble came early in 1920 when rumors reached him that Austen G. Fox, an influential law school alumnus, was complaining of inaccuracies in his June 1919 article. A Wall Street lawyer, Fox was a member of Harvard's Board of Overseers and had been among leaders of the opposition to the appointment of Louis D. Brandeis to the U.S. Supreme Court in 1916. Chafee wrote Fox about the rumors and asked for detailed charges; the reply was terse: "I am in correspondence with persons, from whom I hope, soon, to receive information which will enable you to correct the errors of fact in your article of last June—if errors there be."[5]

The two had no more correspondence for four months—until after Chafee had published a controversial article about the case *Abrams v. United States*. Once that piece was off the press, Chafee again wrote Fox to remind him of his offer to point out any inaccuracies in the earlier article. Fox responded by saying that, after hearing from Chafee the first time, he promptly wrote "to the man, who was said to have made, and who undoubtedly did make, the statement that your article did contain inaccurate statements of fact. He has not even acknowledged the receipt of my inquiry."[6] And thus ended the Chafee-Fox correspondence, although Fox was far from finished with the outspoken professor.

In his *Abrams* article, in the *Harvard Law Review* of April 1920, Chafee called "the whole proceeding, from start to finish . . . a disgrace to our law, and none the less a disgrace because our highest court felt powerless to wipe it out."[7] The most disgraceful thing about the case, in Chafee's opinion, was the prejudicial behavior of the trial judge—Henry D. Clayton of Alabama, a former U.S. senator and representative who drafted the Clayton Antitrust Act of 1914. Commenting on Clayton's lack of experience in sedition cases, Chafee wrote in *Freedom of Speech:*

> The position of the defendants could hardly be understood without some acquaintance with the immigrant population of a great city, some knowledge of the ardent thirst of the East Side Jew for the discussion of international affairs. Yet because the New York dockets were crowded the Abrams case was assigned to a judge who had tried no important Espionage Act case [in his article, he had erroneously stated that Clayton had tried no such cases], who was called in from a remote district [in the South] where people were of one mind about the war, where the working class is more conspicuous for a submissive respect for law and order than for the criticism of high officials, where Russians are scarce and Bolshevists unknown.[8]

Chafee expressed two main objections to Clayton's handling of the trial proceedings. First, the judge repeatedly cross-examined witnesses and in the process, as shown by the trial record, displayed prejudice against the defendants. Second—and this was a more serious complaint—the judge had improperly charged the jury and had done it consciously. Clayton had erroneously led the jury to think that pro-Russian sympathies were enough to convict, according to Chafee, whereas correct instructions would have told the jurors that intent to obstruct the war effort against Germany was essential to convict under the 1919 Sedition Act. It was the judge's duty "to warn them explicitly against the Russian theory of guilt, and confine their attention to the pro-German theory," he wrote. "There is no trace of such a warning in the record . . . Therefore, it is very probable that the defendants were convicted on an erroneous theory of guilt, simply because they protested against the dispatch of armed forces to Russia."[9]

The controversy over the *Abrams* case climaxed in May 1921 in the so-called Trial at the Harvard Club, where Chafee's future on the faculty was put on the line. Chafee himself refused to call the proceeding a trial, referring to it instead as a "conference." He also believed that the attack on him "probably had three sources," as he explained to Frederick Lewis Allen of *Harper's* magazine a decade later; the first two he mentioned were fear of Bolshevism and "a hangover" from the Brandeis appointment, which most of the Harvard law faculty had supported. The third probable reason was that

> the United States Attorney's Office [in New York City] felt aggrieved by my account of the Abrams case which they had prosecuted. My account was chiefly based on the printed official record submitted to the Supreme Court. For the rest of the trial proceedings I relied on newspaper accounts [in the *New York Times* and the *New York Call*, official organ of the Socialist Party]. From my inexperience in criminal trials I did not realize that the United States Attorney's Office had a complete stenographic record of the trial, including the portions not printed for the Supreme Court. I also made the mistake of a short call on Mr. [Harry] Weinberger, the counsel for the prisoners, . . . to ask him about two or three minor points. It was one of the foundations of the charges against me that I had used partial sources of information.[10]

Chafee added that talking to the U.S. attorney would not have fundamentally changed his opinion of the trial, but he conceded that failing to do so resulted in "an inference of unfairness" which may not have been wholly unreasonable for persons unfamiliar with the details.

Although Chafee's assessment of the sources of his troubles was mainly correct, there was a more concerted effort to discredit him than he had supposed. Research by Peter H. Irons, drawing upon Justice Department documents that remained secret for more than a half-century, first exposed the extent of the machinations that preceded his "trial."[11] Furthermore, Chafee had done more to antagonize the Justice Department than simply write an article damning the *Abrams* proceedings.

Even before that article appeared, he had signed a petition to President Wilson asking amnesty for the defendants, who had expressed a willingness to be sent back to Russia. The request for his signature came from Weinberger, and Chafee got four of his colleagues to sign as well: Dean Roscoe Pound, Felix Frankfurter, Francis B. Sayre, who was President Wilson's son-in-law and an expert on criminal law, and Edward B. Adams, the law school's librarian. By late April word of the petition had reached J. Edgar Hoover, head of the Justice Department's new General Intelligence Division, who ordered that files be compiled on each of the signers. He also requested information about them from the army's Military Intelligence Division.[12]

At about this time, Chafee learned that a man who was both a former federal prosecutor and *Harvard Law Review* editor was upset by his writings about the Espionage Act cases. The editors of the *Review* showed him a letter from Robert P. Stephenson, a Wall Street lawyer like Fox. Without mentioning that as a special assistant to the attorney general he had handled cases under the act, Stephenson said Weinberger told him of Chafee's upcoming article on *Abrams;* he also complained that Chafee had shown it to Weinberger but not to the prosecutors. Further, Stephenson said Chafee's "Freedom of Speech in War Time," published the previous June, was based on surprising premises and sources, and he advised *Review* editors to publish no more pieces by Chafee without carefully evaluating them.[13] At the top of this letter, Chafee wrote but later partially erased: "This man probably started the whole thing."

Besides Fox and Stephenson, two other New York lawyers were key figures in the plot to get Chafee: Francis G. Caffey, the U.S. attorney whose office handled the *Abrams* case, and John M. Ryan, an assistant attorney who was in charge of the trial. Caffey also chanced to be an Alabamian and friend of Judge Clayton, and both Caffey and Ryan were, like Fox and Stephenson, Harvard law alumni. Stephenson worked closely with the prosecutors in preparing a rebuttal to Chafee's article, and the materials they compiled formed part of Fox's statement to Harvard officials that resulted in the trial at the Harvard Club.[14] Stephenson's ties to Caffey's office became apparent to Chafee when he went there in the latter part of June 1920 to check the files on the *Abrams* trial and found himself confronted by both Ryan and Stephenson.

"I . . . had long conversations with Mr. Ryan and Mr. Stephenson," he recalled in October 1922, "in which I learned of some undoubted small errors in my article, which I took pains to correct in my book, besides modifying my account of the 'third degree' incident. Other points, which they insisted were erroneous, I considered carefully, and decided that I was right. Undoubtedly, they were disappointed when my book appeared that I had not accepted all their objections and [had not] been completely convinced that the convictions and sentences were amply justified. An account of these interviews was afterwards written out by Mr. Ryan and incorporated in Mr. Fox's charges."[15] One of the small errors, which Chafee corrected in the book, has already been referred to: the fact that *Abrams* was not Judge Clayton's first Espionage Act case. Two other small misstatements concerned defendant Lipman's lover, whom Chafee called his wife. The article also stated that the acquittal of one of the six defendants had been directed by the judge, whereas it actually had been voted by the jury. As for the modified account of the third degree incident, it consisted of toning down flat statements about brutal treatment of the defendants.[16]

Unknowingly, Chafee was an all too willing accomplice in the campaign to discredit him; his involvement in two incidents in May 1920 furnished his critics with still further ammunition to use against him. Both incidents—a Boston deportation case and a report by a dozen distinguished lawyers—were related to the red scare that shook the country after the Russian Revolution in 1917. Although the events in Russia posed no immediate threat to American democracy, several crucial developments in this country during 1919 did provide a basis for the national hysteria. First was a series of bombings in May and June. Second was the formation of two Communist parties in the fall. These events, as well as myriad others around the country during 1919–20, including strikes and racial and other riots, are best understood in the context of nativism—the dislike of foreigners, which in its red scare incarnation was directed mainly at immigrants from southern and eastern Europe.[17]

On 1 May 1919, newspaper headlines informed Americans of an assassination plot against three members of the presidential cabinet: Attorney General A. Mitchell Palmer, who had succeeded Thomas Gregory on 5 March; Postmaster General Albert S. Burleson; and Secretary of Labor William B. Wilson. Also said to be targets were Justice Holmes and business leaders John D. Rockefeller and J. P. Morgan. Altogether, thirty-six bombs were mailed in New York City, where postal officials detained about half the packages because of insufficient postage. Most of the others were halted prior to delivery. Justice Department officials concluded that the bombings were meant to trigger a May Day reign of terror.

A month later, shortly before midnight on 2 June, a bomb went off at the attorney general's home in Washington. Within an hour similar bombings blasted public buildings and the homes of government officials and business leaders in eight cities. The Washington explosion heavily damaged Palmer's residence and killed the bomber.

Palmer and his wife were upstairs preparing for bed when the blast showered his head with broken glass. As a U.S. representative from Pennsylvania, Palmer had been devoted to President Wilson's reform program. And although he was as susceptible to nativism as most Americans, during his early months as attorney general he resisted public pressure to go all out in persecuting radicals. It was only after he became alarmed by the bombs and riots during May and June of 1919 that he used more repressive measures.[18]

On 1 August Palmer created the General Intelligence Division (GID) as part of a reorganization of the Justice Department and placed J. Edgar Hoover in charge. An ambitious twenty-four-year-old, Hoover had worked briefly as a cataloger in the Library of Congress and then as a clerk in the department's Enemy Alien Registration Unit, headed by John Lord O'Brian. Drawing upon his library background, he oversaw creation of an index file of more than 200,000 cards on radicalism—leaders, publications, organizations, activities around the country. Thus the GID became known as the department's anti-radical division. Almost immediate confirmation of the need for the division's activities was provided by the Communists themselves, who broke away from the Socialist Party in September to form the Communist Party and the Communist Labor Party.[19]

As early as June 1919 Palmer had decided that deportation was the way to deal with radicals—notably Communists and anarchists, an estimated 90 percent of whom were foreigners, mainly from southern and eastern Europe. Until 1903 the United States had excluded or expelled aliens not for their opinions but rather for reasons such as crime, insanity, and pauperism (and Chinese were excluded simply because of their race). But after the assassination of President McKinley by an anarchist in 1901, Congress passed a law disqualifying aliens for the possession or expression of radical ideas. Later, under the Immigration Act of 1917 as amended in October 1918, six categories of radical aliens, starting with anarchists, were proscribed; included were those advocating the use of violence against property, public officials, or government and those belonging to groups advocating the use of violence. Referring to such legislation, Chafee pointed out in *Freedom of Speech:* "Such aliens are not only refused admission and put out if they succeed in getting in, but if they acquire these views or join these associations after their entry into this country, they are to be deported without any time limit, no matter how long before 1918 they came to the United States."[20]

Interesting is the fact that the Justice Department had no authority under these laws. Arrest warrants could be issued only by the secretary of labor, cases had to be heard by immigration officials, and the actual deportations required signed orders by the secretary of labor. But in the fall of 1919, at Palmer's suggestion, Secretary of Labor Wilson agreed that the two departments should cooperate in enforcing the deportation statutes.[21] These steps were quickly followed by the notorious "Palmer Raids," or "Red Raids," and the "Deportations Delirium," with the offending human cargo sent to Russia aboard the transport ship Buford, commonly called the "Soviet Ark."

On 7 November Justice Department officials raided meetings of the Union of Russian Workers in twelve cities. In New York City some 650 persons were arrested, many without warrants; most were released after questioning, and eventually forty-three members of the Russian Workers were deported. A similar pattern of civil liberties violations occurred in the other cities.[22] But the worst abuses occurred during raids—on the night of 2 January 1920—of meetings of the Communist Party and the Communist Labor Party in dozens of cities. Under the supervision of J. Edgar Hoover in Washington, these operations were carefully planned and coordinated; agents who had developed contacts inside the parties were told to have their informers make sure meetings were held that night. Some 3,000 warrants—many of them blank—were obtained, and approximately 6,000 persons were rounded up that night and in the days that followed. As in November, there were charges of brutality and of overcrowded, unsanitary detention centers. But both the press and the public generally cheered the massive dragnet operation.[23]

Approval was not universal, however. Civil libertarians were understandably upset, and at the Labor Department, Assistant Secretary Louis F. Post emerged as Palmer's nemesis when in March 1920 he took charge of all deportation matters during the illness of Secretary Wilson and immediately began reviewing the records of those arrested in the raids. A slight, seventy-one-year-old lawyer with no use for radicals, Post himself held some unpopular views: he was a single-tax advocate, and he shared the populists' fear of the "money power." More important, he thought aliens ought to be treated like human beings, not just cases.[24]

Before Post took over the deportation responsibilities as acting secretary, Secretary of Labor Wilson made two key rulings; first, on

24 January 1920 that the Communist Party fell under the deportation laws and, second, on 5 May 1920 that the Communist Labor Party was lawful. But at the time of the raids, the secretary had not formally ruled that either of the Communist parties was illegal.[25] J. Edgar Hoover, in his rush to round up as many Communists as possible on 2 January, simply assumed that membership in either group was a deportable offense. By 10 April Post had reviewed 1,600 cases and canceled the arrest warrants in 1,141 of them. In addition, he ordered the release of many other prisoners arrested without warrants, and in still other cases he reduced the amount of bail. Palmer and Hoover were outraged, and there ensued an unsuccessful effort to impeach Post.[26]

In March 1920, the month that Post became acting secretary, a Labor Department official contacted Lawrence G. Brooks, a Boston lawyer and acquaintance of Chafee, expressing the urgent need for a test case on deportation before a sympathetic judge. The message from this source, whose identity is unknown, seems to have been dictated over the telephone; the caller, who explained that he was acting without the knowledge of the labor secretary or the assistant secretary, told Brooks that "speed [was] of great moment" because efforts were under way by the Justice Department to bring a case "before a judge who would be likely to sustain [Palmer's] extreme position" in favor of deportation.[27] "What the Labor Department official was asking of Brooks was a matter of great delicacy," Peter Irons writes, "since what the Department sought was in fact a *reversal* of Secretary Wilson's earlier determination that, under the law, membership in the Communist . . . Party was grounds for deportation. This was a position urged on Wilson by the Justice Department and one that he hoped would be reversed by the courts. Brooks was informed that ideal clients for a potential test case were awaiting deportation in Boston."[28]

The "clients" were William and Amy Colyer, an "intelligent" English couple arrested in the January raids and both "bona fide members of the Communist Party." The Labor Department official also stressed that it was "very important that this case should be brought to trial before Judge George Anderson." Brooks was asked to "take up the matter with Mr. Chafee and Mr. Frankfurter, who are reported to be interested" in deportation matters. Brooks also received a letter from his friend Judson King, executive secretary of the National Popular Government League, a Washington-based group seeking to improve government. King urged Brooks to join Morris Katzeff, the Colyers' lawyer, in arguing the case because he questioned Katzeff's competence and considered him sympathetic to the couple's radical views. King believed that the participation of respectable lawyers like Brooks was essential both to the liberal movement and to victory in the case.[29]

Judge George W. Anderson did hear the test case of *Colyer v. Skeffington*, involving a total of eighteen aliens arrested during the January raids.[30] The judge was greatly admired by Chafee because while serving as U.S. district attorney in Massachusetts during the war, he had initiated no prosecutions under the Espionage Act. Earlier, in 1916, Anderson had represented Louis D. Brandeis during the Senate hearings on his nomination to the Supreme Court. In that role he tilted with Austen Fox, then representing railroad barons and conservative members of the bar opposed to Brandeis.

A half-century after the *Colyer* case, Brooks recalled assisting Katzeff, conferring with Judge Anderson, whom he knew "pretty well," and preparing habeas corpus writs in behalf of the defendants. The judge came from the same country town in New Hampshire as Brooks's father, John Graham Brooks, a reform-minded sociologist specializing in labor and industrial problems and the first president of the National Consumers' League.[31] Chafee was a good friend of the elder Brooks, of whom he wrote in the preface to *Free Speech in the United States:* "John Graham Brooks, whose age never kept him from living with younger men in the present, taught me out of his long experience that there is no single or easy remedy for any human maladjustment."[32] According to Lawrence Brooks, who went on to become a respected Massachusetts state judge, Anderson "rather engineered the case so it would come into his court," where he "mercilessly questioned" Justice Department lawyers about the illegal blank warrants they used in the raids. Brooks said he and Katzeff did legwork on the case in addition to appearing in court.[33] Chafee and Felix Frankfurter, who was back on the law faculty after wartime government service, joined the defense as amici curiae after Anderson called Frankfurter to say he "very much wanted" him to help out and Frankfurter in turn suggested that he be joined by Chafee.[34]

Once in court, Frankfurter cross-examined Justice Department and immigration officials, and pried vital information out of George E. Kelleher, head of the Boston office of the Justice Department's

Bureau of Investigation.[35] This consisted of the bureau's confidential instructions to the local agents making the arrests, instructions that Chafee said "best showed the character of the raids." Even "a cursory glance at Mr. Palmer's Instructions," he wrote in *Freedom of Speech*, "shows that the character of an individual had absolutely nothing whatever to do with his arrest. The most harmless person was to be seized if suspected of membership in the specified political parties. And although there was no law authorizing the arrest of citizens, these instructions direct that all Communists shall be seized, expressly including citizens. Elsewhere it is ordered that if citizens are arrested 'through error,' they shall be referred to the local authorities. Thus United States officials would arrest American citizens for prosecution under the harsh state anti-anarchy acts."[36]

In his sixty-page opinion in the *Colyer* case, Judge Anderson flayed the Justice Department for the "terrorizing conditions" of the raids. That Chafee's ideas influenced the judge's thinking is shown by his later remark that "the Colyer opinion and my book contain about all I know" about free speech.[37] After carefully surveying the New England raids, Judge Anderson ruled that many of the aliens scheduled for deportation would have to be released because they had not been accorded due process. And on the question of whether, as Secretary Wilson had held, membership in the Communist Party was a deportable offense, Anderson ruled that even those aliens who had been treated fairly would have to be freed because the Communist Party did not advocate force and violence. The judge later was reversed on this second point by a federal appeals court.[38] Of that reversal Chafee wrote to a former law partner in Providence: "I do not worry much about the reversal of Judge Anderson because it affects only the less important part of his decision . . . [which] placed the facts of those outrages before the public, and as a result they never recurred . . . To this restoration of law and order, I feel that our work in the Colyer Case and the report of the twelve lawyers has somewhat contributed."[39]

Before discussing Chafee's connection with this "lawyers' report," it needs to be noted that J. Edgar Hoover's investigation of Chafee and Frankfurter, begun after they signed the *Abrams* amnesty petition, accelerated after the *Colyer* hearings began. An agent was sent to Rhode Island to see what skeletons might be exhumed from Chafee's past, including his undergraduate days at Brown University, where officials granted ready access to his student records. However, the investigator's principal findings were that Chafee came from "a very wealthy family" and that none of his relatives "were ever known to be connected with any radical organizations."[40] Actually, Chafee himself had once belonged to a Providence group known as the Radical Club; if this tidbit was turned up by the agent, he also must have learned that the group, despite its name, was merely "a sedate dining and lecturing society which heard speakers on such varied topics as feudalism, socialism, and—a peculiar concern in its time— oleomargarine legislation."[41] But despite the lack of evidence connecting either Chafee or Frankfurter to radical activities, in Irons's words, "their dossiers were soon filled with gossip and innuendo."[42]

Chafee's participation in the *Colyer* case resulted in an even more public confrontation with the Justice Department when he signed the previously mentioned lawyers' report, published in late May 1920 by the National Popular Government League (NPGL). The idea for this document, formally called the *Report upon the Illegal Practices of the United States Department of Justice*, was born at a joint meeting of the NPGL and the American Civil Liberties Union (ACLU) on 13 April 1920, in Washington. It was agreed to investigate and publicize in pamphlet form the civil liberties violations during the Palmer Raids, in an effort to compel Congress to investigate and possibly even censure the attorney general. Judson King of NPGL supervised the project. Most of the work on the pamphlet was done by Swinburne Hale, a retired Military Intelligence officer and a member of the New York law firm of Hale, Nelles, and Shorr (both Walter Nelles and Isaac Shorr were ACLU counsel), and by Jackson Ralston, Louis Post's lawyer during the impeachment proceedings and a member of the Washington firm of Ralston and Willis.[43] They collected and carefully authenticated information from aliens arrested during the raids. Ten days after the organizational meeting, Ralston wrote Chafee asking him to sign the document upon its completion. Chafee did sign, as did Frankfurter and Dean Pound.

The sixty-seven-page report, including more than fifty pages of affidavits and other exhibits (much of the material dealt with the *Colyer* case even though Judge Anderson's opinion was not formally released until a few weeks later), opened with this statement: "For more than six months we, the undersigned lawyers, whose sworn duty it is to uphold the Constitution and Laws of the United States, have seen with growing apprehension the continued violation of that Constitution and breaking of those Laws by the Department of

Justice of the United States government."[44] The pamphlet then re-cited six specific charges against the department including the al-leged violation of several constitutional amendments: inflicting cruel and unusual punishments in violation of the Eighth Amendment; making arrests without warrants, and conducting unreasonable searches and seizures of homes in violation of the Fourth Amend-ment; and compelling persons to be witnesses against themselves in violation of the Fifth Amendment. The report received wide pub-licity, and an angry A. Mitchell Palmer launched an almost im-mediate counterattack.

A subcommittee of the House Rules Committee, the group that had recently hounded Louis Post, arranged a 1 June session as a vehicle for Palmer's reply.[45] He denied the truth of the charges, which he said rested on false affidavits obtained from arrested aliens. His testimony also contained ad hominem remarks directed at the twelve signers. The next morning Chafee and Frankfurter read in the *Boston Transcript* that Palmer's testimony included this com-ment: "We find several of them [the signers] appearing as counsel for Communists at deportation hearings . . . I have difficulty in re-conciling their attitude with that of men who have sworn to uphold the Constitution of the United States."[46] After conferring, the two professors drafted a lengthy wire to Palmer ending with two ques-tions: "Do you mean that these aliens are not entitled to counsel? Is this your position?" Two days later, Palmer wired back that he had not criticized them for appearing as counsel for aliens but for signing the report. Its charges were based on "palpably false" state-ments by arrested aliens, he averred, and having been confronted by "proof of the undoubted falsity of these charges, you owe it to your-self as well as to the Department of Justice publicly to retract them." This telegraphic exchange ended with Chafee and Frankfurter writ-ing back the same day that they had signed the report chiefly because of their knowledge of the *Colyer* case and that "we are prepared to substantiate these allegations and have so advised Chairman Camp-bell of the Rules Committee. We are prepared to do the same thing before a committee of the American Bar Association consisting, we suggest, of the ex-Attorneys General of the United States."[47]

After Palmer's 1 June appearance before the House subcommittee, Swinburne Hale dispatched a memo to the signers of the report: "For the present . . . I have recommended to Mr. Judson King that we do not make any answer to the Attorney General's defense but that our document continue to stand and speak for itself. It had wide publicity throughout the country, and Palmer's 'refutation' got very little."[48] Early in 1921, however, the NPGL did reply to Palmer's defense after Senator Thomas J. Walsh, a Montana Democrat, revived the controversy by requesting that the lawyers' report be referred to the Judiciary Committee for possible action. At Walsh's invitation, the NPGL prepared a memo for the ensuing hearings. King wired Chafee on 21 January that Walsh wanted him to testify on the twenty-fifth and to focus on undisputed evidence proving illegality or bad public policy. With Chafee scheduled to appear before a Judiciary Committee subcommittee, the Justice Department dug out its dossier on him. Francis G. Caffey and John M. Ryan, the *Abrams* prosecutors, furnished Robert P. Stewart, assistant attorney general in charge of the criminal division, with Chafee's admitted misstatements in his *Abrams* article. And Ryan advised Stewart that "a vigorous cross-examiner" using these materials "could easily break down his testimony before the Committee."[49] Chafee, however, concluded his day-long testimony without being asked one question about his article.[50]

Chafee's testimony before the committee served mainly to renew Austen Fox's attack against him. Not long after he testified, Harvard President A. Lawrence Lowell learned that Fox was drawing up charges against Chafee. Lowell and Fox had been on the same side five years earlier in the fight over the Brandeis nomination to the Supreme Court. An 1880 graduate of Harvard Law School, Lowell was a staunch conservative and had been among fifty-five lawyers signing a petition against Brandeis. It was Fox who officially presented it to the Senate Judiciary Committee. Nonetheless, Lowell regarded himself as "an old-fashioned believer in the constitutional protection to individual rights," as he put it in a letter to Fox, and he was determined to avert intramural fighting that might harm Harvard's reputation or rend the faculty into factions. When Fox was finished "looking up the accuracy of some points in Professor Chafee's article" about *Abrams*, Lowell wrote, "I should like very much to talk with you about the matter."[51]

The day after Lowell wrote to Fox, the latter queried Francis P. Garvan of the Justice Department about getting "copies of any letters or petitions in the Department . . . that show Mr. Chafee's close association, or sympathy with anarchistic 'Reds.' " Garvan relayed the request to J. Edgar Hoover, who sent Fox a copy of Chafee's

testimony before the Senate subcommittee.[52] Fox got more significant help from *Abrams* prosecutor Ryan, who with Robert P. Stephenson wrote a memo reviewing their discussions with Chafee and
enumerating the misstatements in his article. Ryan noted that he
had told Chafee his article "sounded more like a summation for the
defense than a scholarly discussion of the case," and that Chafee
replied, "I don't know how I came to make that mistake."[53]

On 9 May 1921 Fox submitted to Harvard's Board of Overseers a
thirty-two-page document containing his charges.[54] Most of the complaints concerned the *Abrams* article and Chafee's failure to publish
corrections in the *Harvard Law Review*. But some charges also centered on the amnesty petition signed by him, Frankfurter, Pound,
Sayre, and librarian Adams. The "indictment" was prefaced by the
Ryan-Stephenson memo and correspondence between Caffey and
Chafee concerning the latter's June 1920 visit to New York. Fox's
statement added little if anything to the alleged errors pointed up
during the conversation among Chafee, Ryan, and Stephenson.

After Fox presented his charges to the overseers, Chafee later
recounted: "I am told by men present that Mr. Lowell made a determined speech. He said that the time had come for him to make
a confession of faith . . . What he had said in [an important 1916
statement on academic freedom] must be steadfastly maintained.
The teaching at Harvard could not be controlled from Wall St."[55]

The overseers voted to refer the charges to the standing Committee to Visit the Law School comprising fourteen prominent lawyers and judges. The chairman was Francis J. Swayze of the New
Jersey Supreme Court, who set 22 May for a hearing. The committee
included Benjamin N. Cardozo of the New York Court of Appeals,
Augustus N. Hand and Julian Mack of the federal bench in New
York, James M. Morton, a federal judge in Boston, three Massachusetts state judges, and several lawyers including Henry L. Stimson
of New York.[56]

After the overseers' meeting, Lowell and Chafee conferred. Lowell
"described the charges as trivial," Chafee recalled, and explained his
policy: whenever large numbers of alumni complained about something in the university, no matter how baseless the complaint seemed,
they were entitled to have it investigated and be given a chance to
be heard. Together, the president and Chafee carefully went over
Fox's charges and discussed how each ought to be met. After Lowell
emphasized that Fox was guilty of a serious misstatement concern-

ing the amnesty petition, Chafee prepared for him a copy of what he and the others had actually signed for comparison with what Fox alleged they had signed.[57]

As the hearing approached, Chafee prepared a detailed memo to serve as the basis of his oral rebuttal on the twenty-second.[58] "I was dictating one afternoon to my red-headed secretary . . . ," he later explained, when "suddenly she stopped and said, 'Who is this Mr. Fox that we are spending so much time on him?' This question of hers cleared the air and reduced everything to its proper proportions."[59] But it did not reduce the length of his statement—brevity was not among his virtues as a writer—and its bulk bothered his friend and then acting dean, Edward H. Warren, who warned that Chafee was protesting too much.[60]

While Chafee drafted his reply and sent a copy of his *Abrams* article to each member of the visiting committee, President Lowell was also thinking ahead to the meeting. At first he thought he would not attend, but reading Fox's statement angered him because of its own inaccuracies—a fact that he made a crucial part of Chafee's trial.[61] And Frankfurter, who later became legendary for his behind-the-scenes political maneuverings, was busy as well. To Chafee he sent a note ("This is what the Abrams record did to me . . . Good luck!") along with a copy of a letter he had sent to Judge Mack urging him to read the record by 22 May ("I'll miss my guess if it doesn't make your blood boil . . . I have no hesitation in saying that it is the most disgraceful record of a criminal case I have ever read in the Federal Courts") and suggesting that he get both Cardozo and Augustus Hand to do likewise.[62]

The Trial at the Harvard Club, situated on Commonwealth Avenue about a mile from the Boston Common and Public Garden, began at 10:00 A.M. on the twenty-second, a "sizzling hot" Sunday. The description comes from Frankfurter, who attended along with Chafee, Adams, Pound, and Sayre, who had to leave at noon.[63] Others present, besides Fox and all but three members of the visiting committee, included Caffey, Ryan, Stephenson, three signers of the Fox statement, President Lowell, Frank W. Grinnell, secretary of the Harvard Law School Association of alumni, and a stenographer.[64] The presence of Caffey, Ryan, and Stephenson, as Irons has written, "revealed the real alignment of the disputants: the law school faculty on one side and the Department of Justice on the other."[65] Chafee himself later remarked that Stephenson "appeared . . . in no defined capacity, and acted as if he had some claim to ask questions of me. I infer that he was liaison officer between Fox and the U.S. Attorney's Office."[66]

Despite the presence of a stenographer, no transcript of the proceedings is known to exist. But details of what happened appear in a letter from Chafee to Upton Sinclair, written the following year to correct errors in Sinclair's forthcoming book *The Goose-step*. One change Chafee called for concerned the president's role at the hearing: "It is not correct to say that Mr. Lowell acted as my counsel,— the whole proceeding was informal, but from the start I felt that I had his strong support and the benefit of his advice."[67] Nonetheless, Lowell functioned very much like a lawyer for the defense, taking the offensive right after Fox told the group that he would rest on his printed statement rather than presenting the charges orally. Lowell criticized Fox for submitting his charges without first discussing them with him, and then accused Fox of inaccuracies in his statement.

After a member of the visiting committee had read a list of the charges from Fox's "rambling pamphlet," as Chafee called it, Lowell bore in on the most serious inaccuracy. This concerned the amnesty petition signed by Chafee and the other four faculty members. Fox had charged that the petition contained misleading statements of fact, whereas the misstatements were in a circular prepared by Harry Weinberger, the defendants' lawyer, as a promotional device aimed at getting more signatures for the pardon request. Lowell had seized upon this error in Fox's charges almost as soon as they were submitted to the overseers and, as noted earlier, had discussed it with Chafee. After photostatic copies of the amnesty petition signed by the five were circulated among the committee members, Fox was forced to drop this charge. Thus he was discredited on a major point early in the proceedings.

When the time came for Chafee to present his rebuttal, he spoke for about two hours. He described how he had become interested in free speech, he reviewed Fox's charges and admitted making "a few slight unintentional mistakes," and he asserted that "on the main contentions of my article I was not only honest but right." After studying the *Abrams* trial he told the visiting committee, "I was so thoroughly convinced of the injustice done to the prisoners, that as I walked through the streets I kept thinking all the time that while I was enjoying the sunlight, these men and this woman were in prison for a large portion of their lives. I made up my mind that I would set down the truth about this trial for all time, so that others might realize the great wrong that had been done." His closing remarks, which Frankfurter called one of the most impressive statements he ever heard, were: "Gentlemen, I had no sympathy with the political and economic doctrines of these prisoners. I can hardly imagine any persons with whom I should get along worse than with Abrams and his associates. My sympathies and all my associations are with the men who save, who manage and produce. But I want my side to fight fair. And I regard this Abrams trial as a distinctly unfair piece of fighting, that I determined to record accurately and permanently."

Once Chafee was finished, Fox called on Ryan who gave his views of the *Abrams* case, described Chafee's visits to New York, and cast further doubt on a point about which Chafee already had admitted error—the marital status of defendant Lipman. After Ryan stopped speaking, Chafee recalled, "Mr. Lowell asked whether anybody in the room thought that Judge Clayton had given the prisoners a fair trial. Nobody spoke. Then he asked Mr. Ryan, who replied that he did not want to criticize a judge. This was an effective stroke for my case." At this point Judge Swayze said he had received letters from persons asking the visiting committee to look into "the radical teachings of professors at the Law School." And a signer of the Fox statement raised a question about "outside activities of professors"—a veiled reference to Chafee and Frankfurter's work on the *Colyer* case. Lowell objected to both points on the grounds that they were not germane to the charges being heard.

After some discussion about who should speak for Chafee, Lowell said he would. He conceded that Chafee's article included a few unintentional errors that were later corrected in *Freedom of Speech*, although an exception might be his analysis of the judge's charge to the jury. This concerned the question of whether Clayton had given "no warning at all" concerning pro-Russian sympathies, as Chafee stated, or "a very slight warning," a point that Chafee recognized as possibly ambiguous. When his turn came, Fox exploded. To Lowell, whose commitment to his faculty and its academic freedom he apparently underestimated because of their previous alliance in the fight against Brandeis, he complained: "When Joseph Story died, Daniel Webster said that the judicial ermine which fell upon his shoulders touched nothing less spotless than itself. I am astonished to hear the President of this University advocating a lower standard for a teacher in its law school. And I am astonished to hear him express his personal confidence in the innocence of his client, a thing that no lawyer is ever known to do." It was late afternoon when the proceedings ended.

The visiting committee deliberated on into the evening, eventually reaching unanimous agreement that "Professor Chafee made no statements in his article which were consciously erroneous." But concerning Fox's complaint that the erroneous statements should have been corrected in the *Harvard Law Review*, Chafee was narrowly sustained, 6 to 5, with Judge Cardozo casting the deciding vote. Lowell did not tell Chafee of the closeness of the vote when he called him at home that night to report the "verdict," saying only that the committee had unanimously reported that no action should be taken. In fact, eighteen years passed before Lowell told him "that there was only a majority of one." Having finally learned of the close call, Chafee said, "As the minority recommended no action, I don't hold anything against them. In a way I agree with them now, although I am glad that I gave Clayton what he deserved."[68]

As he prepared to leave the Harvard Club at the end of that scorching Sunday in May 1921, he bumped into Caffey, "who was evidently hurt because I had not corrected my mistakes in the Review itself." He told Caffey that he did not object to making the same corrections in the *Review* that he had made in his book, and he later did so. However, this material did not appear until after Lowell and Chafee had reversed their positions on the question of publishing the visiting committee's report and Chafee's corrections; originally, Chafee was for and Lowell against. The issue was forced in July when the *Boston Sunday Herald* ran a sensational story that upset Lowell with its talk of how the university had to "deal with [the five law faculty] summarily for the suppression of incipient anarchism and 'parlor bolshevism' at Harvard."[69] By this time Chafee was less concerned about the *Herald's* sloppy reporting than about the possible effects of admitting his errors publicly.

Lowell and Chafee finally reached an agreement that produced a short "article" in the November 1921 issue of the *Review* consisting of both the report of the visiting committee and a listing of eight "corrections and statements" about his *Abrams* piece.[70] Chafee's portion of this material, he explained, "was really drafted by [Edward

H.] Warren who was acting Dean at that time and tremendously helpful. He was anxious to allay resentment among the graduates. After we had worked out the statement together, he took it down to a luncheon in New York of all the signers except Fox, whom Ed refused to meet because of his garbling of the charge about the pardon petition. It must have been a good luncheon, because everybody there expressed perfect satisfaction with me and I have been on very cordial terms with some of them since."[71] On another occasion, in recounting Warren's mission to New York, he gave a few more details: "When he left the signers . . . they were expressing satisfaction with the school, cursing out Fox, and disputing among themselves who was to blame for their inaccuracies about the pardon petition."[72]

Except for the fact that he may have protested too much in his rebuttal at the Harvard Club, Chafee kept his head throughout the trial—as he had during the war.[73] It is interesting that he believed that he was "something of a pretext" for the Fox attack and that "the real game in the School was higher up."[74] Yet the evidence in the Justice Department's files leaves little doubt that he was the principal target.

What if the trial had turned out differently? "Since I could have returned to practice in Providence," he explained in his letter to Sinclair, "I didn't have much at stake financially, though I should be very sorry to give up my teaching, but I know what it means to some teachers to run the risk of losing their positions for what they say, and I know what it means to many men on the Harvard faculty that there is nothing of that at Harvard." He hoped that Sinclair would include these words verbatim in his forthcoming book:

> During the excitement of the war and the years following, when discussion and the expression of opinion were curbed in many schools and universities, the authorities of Harvard enabled every member of the Faculty to feel that he could teach, write, and say what he believed to be the truth. The only requirement was that he should act like a gentleman and a scholar. Nobody could breathe the air of Harvard and not be free. The declaration of this policy and its maintenance through some stormy criticism by alumni came because of the wisdom and courage of President Lowell.

The fact that Sinclair did not use that passage in *The Goose-step* helps explain why Chafee was displeased with the book's depiction of Lowell although he was satisfied with Sinclair's overall account of the hearing. It also helps explain why Chafee used some of the same language in dedicating to Lowell *Free Speech in the United States*, of which the 1920 version was dedicated to Learned Hand.[75] That Chafee remained forever in Lowell's debt was demonstrated a week before Chafee died when he referred to him as the greatest man he had known.

Besides the sheer vindication of Chafee's fitness to teach, the trial had several other consequences. Although Lowell had issued a strong statement supporting academic freedom in 1916, it is undoubtedly true, as Erwin N. Griswold has written, that "Harvard crystallized much of its thinking" on that subject as a result of the attack on Chafee.[76] For Chafee personally, his confrontation with those who would censure another person for saying things they dislike made it hard for him to stay out of free speech fights later on, even though getting involved often pulled him away from projects of greater interest to him. But he may have found it hard to stay out of them in any event. After all, he came from Rhode Island where, as he often pointed out, he had been "steeped in the Roger Williams tradition."

CHAPTER 3

A Rhode Island Man

On the wall of Chafee's office at Harvard Law School hung a colored print of Thomas W. Dorr, who led the nineteenth-century political struggle known as the Dorr Rebellion. This movement, covering the period 1833–1849 but highlighted by armed revolt in 1842, sought to establish a People's Constitution and broaden the suffrage in Rhode Island. After the armed insurrection failed, Dorr was convicted of treason and spent twenty months in jail.

Obviously, Chafee admired Dorr. As well as keeping a portrait of him in his office, he gave the name of "Dorr Pamphlets" to a series of tracts about Rhode Island affairs he published privately during the 1930s and early 1940s. Each pamphlet bore this quotation from Dorr's speech to the jury at his trial: "I am no stranger in this State. I am a native citizen of Rhode Island, descended from Rhode Island ancestors, and inheriting Rhode Island principles and feelings. By birth, by blood, and by education, I am a Rhode Island man." But Chafee was also critical of Dorr, lamenting that "like many enterprising reformers, he lacked patience and judgment. If he had only been content to compromise on non-essential matters, the reforms he desired would have been peacefully granted. He would have been the first governor under the new Constitution instead of languishing in jail and ruining his health."[1]

As a Rhode Island man, Chafee had been influenced by the Roger Williams tradition; he was, in fact, descended from Williams through his mother. He was also steeped in Providence's manufacturing tradition. Both sides of his family were industrialists, and he said both of his grandfathers "made a deep impression on me." He was born in Providence on 7 December 1885, the eldest of six children of

Zechariah and Mary Dexter (Sharpe) Chafee. A ninth generation American, he was the fourth successive Zechariah descended from Thomas Chaffe, who arrived from England in 1635 and settled in Hingham, Massachusetts, near Providence. That the family had a modest beginning in this country Chafee humorously acknowledged in responding to a query about a Chafee coat of arms: "It is my opinion that if the family did sport a coat of arms, it would have acquired the same by false pretenses. The original ancestor . . . did not know how to write his name. Consequently, I suspect that he was not a member of the British nobility."[2]

As for the name Zechariah Chafee, it was the source of both amusement and exasperation. Chafee's father, who ran the family iron foundry in Providence, once prepared a letter about misspellings of his name and sent it to commercial correspondents. "I appreciate that my first name (Zechariah) is today very uncommon," he wrote, "and that my family name (Chafee) is spelled in different ways by different branches of the family; and to write my full name (Zechariah Chafee), correctly, requires a moment of thought, and some care. If it were correctly spelled our amusement might be somewhat lessened, but here are some of the ways in which it comes to me." There followed a two-column listing of thirty-four misspellings of either or both names. A few of the choicer specimens: Jechuriah Chafer, Zebriah Chafee, Zenas Chafee, Ziehzien Chafee, Zarhariah Chaffee.[3]

Zechariah Chafee, Jr.—the kind of name "borne by American millionaires in English musical comedies," H. L. Mencken wrote in a column praising *Freedom of Speech*—was more resigned to such misspellings. "This is one of the incidents of an unusual appellation," he told a magazine editor who apologized for getting his name wrong. The name provided still other light moments. In the spring of 1920 as the nation was recovering from the red scare, his friend Calvert Magruder, whose career included service on the Harvard Law School faculty and on the federal bench, wrote: "My stenographer first spelled your name Zach & when I corrected it to Zech she informed me that both are biblical—the former a King, the latter a Prophet. I'm sure, in these days, you prefer the Prophet to the King."[4] As a way of saving time and energy, Chafee usually signed his correspondence "Z. Chafee, Jr."

Despite the problems the name caused him, he thought well enough of it to be mildly disappointed when the wife of his only surviving son, Zechariah Chafee III, chose another name for their son, but he tried to be philosophical about it: "I had some wishes that my own grandson might have borne [the] name, but my daughter-in-law wanted to call him after her own father and that settled the matter for me because I think the mother does the work and ought to be absolutely free to chose the name."[5] Naturally, he was delighted when a grand-nephew, the son of John H. Chafee, who has been Rhode Island governor and a U.S. senator, was christened Zechariah in 1951.

Zechariah, Jr., was in a sense a Chafee twice over. Both his parents, who were sixth cousins, could trace their bloodlines back to the original Thomas Chaffe. (Other spellings include Chaphe and Chaf-fee.)[6] The line that descended on his father's side, Chafee liked to note, always lived within about a fifty-mile radius of Swansea— except for a period when his grandfather Zechariah worked in Pitts-burgh. The grandfather, born the son of a stone mason in 1815, had begun working at the age of eleven; at seventeen, perhaps reflecting the Roger Williams spirit of the independent man, he went to Pitts-burgh, where he spent two decades in the flour business, starting as a clerk. In 1845, prior to returning to Rhode Island permanently in 1852, he married a young woman from Providence named Mary Frances Buffington and started a family.

Back in Providence—a move made primarily because Mary dis-liked living in Pennsylvania—Zechariah acquired the High Street Foundry. After changing the name to Builders Iron Foundry, he built it into a solid business producing structural iron work prior to the development of steel-making processes; the firm also made castings for textile manufacturers and cannon for the Union Army during the Civil War. He became a member of several bank boards and of the Rhode Island Hospital Trust Company, and from time to time he was called upon to untangle the financial affairs of small busi-nesses. Things went well for the Chafee family until the nation's financial structure was shaken during the panic of 1873.[7]

This crisis, brought on by wild speculation in railroad construc-tion and by business and agricultural overexpansions, toppled the powerful banking house of Jay Cooke in September. The Cooke collapse caused a drop in security prices, diminishing national in-come and resulting in considerable unemployment. Rhode Island's economy in particular was imperiled by the failure of the A. and W. Sprague textile empire whose assets totaled $19 million. How to prop up the tottering company was obviously a matter of statewide concern. The task would have been easier if there had been a federal law like the present-day one making it possible to reorganize financially troubled businesses. The eventual attempt at a solution, to simplify a complex story, consisted of naming Zechariah Chafee as the sole trustee of the Sprague estate. He insisted on this arrangement despite the fact that he knew nothing about the textile business and that his own company was a comparative dwarf, being capitalized at $150,000. For a time it appeared that he might be able to turn things around; but it was not to be, and ultimately the properties had to be sold piecemeal with creditors gradually paid off at about thirty cents on the dollar.

Although Chafee was never convicted of any wrongdoing, his role as Sprague trustee got him into various legal difficulties. For one thing, he bought up some of the claims against the company; this constituted speculation by a trustee in the trust property and caused him to be censured by the Rhode Island Supreme Court. And he was periodically taken to court by critics of his handling of the trust.[8]

Partly because so much of his time was taken up by Sprague affairs, he asked his son to take charge at Builders Iron Foundry (BIF). This meant a change in the career plans of the man who became the father of Zechariah, Jr., for he had hoped to go west and become a banker. He ended up as president of the foundry upon his father's death in 1889.[9] Besides altering his occupational plans, the Sprague affair made him somewhat distrustful of the legal profession because he blamed lawyers for at least some of his father's difficulties. And, according to some family members, this helps explain his later lack of enthusiasm for his namesake's decision to study law.[10]

Although he would have preferred to be a banker, young Zechariah applied himself to improving the foundry. Under his leadership the firm added new lines, including components for the Venturi Meter, a fluid-measuring device used by municipal water works. Later, comparable devices were produced to measure steam, gas, and oil. During World War I, BIF made mortars, rifling machines, and shell casings for the government. At its peak the foundry had some 300 employees, many of them Italians. Wages were not exceptional—it was an open shop—but it was Chafee's policy to try to provide steady employment. The plant was considered a good place to work, and many employees encouraged members of their families also to seek jobs there. BIF was an important part of Providence's economy—but never as important as the much larger Brown and Sharpe Manufacturing Company owned by the family of Chafee's wife.[11]

After his marriage to Mary Dexter Sharpe on 10 February 1885, Zechariah, Sr., was associated with Brown and Sharpe for a decade, including service as its secretary, while continuing to operate the foundry. Mary's father was Lucian Sharpe, son of Wilkes Sharpe, a Providence livery stable proprietor, and Sarah (Sally) Adams Chafee, another descendant of Thomas Chaffe. Lucian Sharpe and Joseph Brown started Brown and Sharpe as a partnership in 1853 after Lucian had served an apprenticeship with Joseph, a clock and watchmaker and general tinkerer. As befits one trained as a watchmaker, Lucian Sharpe was meticulously organized—a trait inherited by his daughter Mary.

The oldest of six children of Lucian and Louisa (Dexter) Sharpe, Mary Sharpe worked in her family's machine-tool business as a young woman; she maintained an interest in its affairs until her death in 1934, and at times was expected to resolve family differences within the company. As related by some members of the Chafee family, one such incident put her under great pressure. It involved a struggle between her brothers Lucian and Henry for control of the company. She had promised the older, Lucian, a brilliant eccentric generally considered unfit to run a large concern, that he would be granted the presidency originally denied him. Her inability to fulfill that pledge drained her emotionally and apparently contributed to her somewhat frail condition. An angry Lucian went to Paris and remained there in exile, while Henry had a long tenure as head of the firm.[12]

A 1904 graduate of Brown University, Henry Sharpe became one of its illustrious alumni and served from 1932 to 1952 as its chancellor, or chairman of the Board of Trustees. A bachelor until his late forties, he was like an older brother to his nephew Zechariah, Jr., who was just a few years younger. They enjoyed one another's company and took trips together, journeying as far as Alaska in 1902 when Zech was sixteen. Later, they had sharp political disagreements, and Chafee's writings defending free speech for radicals were thought by Uncle Henry to be little short of treasonous. Yet they were always close friends and, apart from politics, greatly respected each other.

Zechariah Chafee, Jr., spent his early years on Hope Street on

Providence's East Side in a house that was a wedding gift from Lucian Sharpe; not far away were Brown University and hilly streets lined with historical homes and churches. He was the first child in what amounted to two families of three children each, separated by a seven-year interval. Besides Zechariah, Jr., there were Henry, born in 1887, Elisabeth in 1889, John in 1896, Mary in 1897, and Francis in 1903. (After much teasing from his siblings about being "an accident," Francis asked his parents if this was true, to which they answered, "You're the only child who wasn't.") By the time of Mary's birth in 1897 the family had outgrown the Hope Street house; thus when Grandmother Chafee gave up her home in 1900, a year before she died, and moved to Boston to be closer to two daughters, Zechariah, Sr., moved his family to the house at 5 Cooke Street, also on the East Side, where he had been born. There he remained until his death in 1943.

The immediate neighborhood of 5 Cooke Street, whose spacious grounds had wisteria, a grape arbor, and a garden that provided fresh vegetables, was quiet but not elegant. A professor at Brown lived next door, another manufacturing family lived across the unpaved street, and two former Rhode Island governors had homes nearby. Beyond the immediate neighborhood lay the "high-rent district" to the north and a large Irish Catholic working-class parish to the south.

A three-story frame structure, the new home provided ample space for the children plus rooms for several servants. A cook and waitress were almost always in attendance, and at times there might be an upstairs maid as well as a nurse. For the three younger children, there was a governess. In a 1952 reminiscence Zechariah, Jr., noted that during his childhood the cook and waitress were both Irish Catholics and that a black nurse was among his earliest memories: "Her devotion and that later on of my [Chafee] grandmother's cook, who had been born a slave, make me feel I can never do enough to repay my debts to the [black] race."[13]

The household furnishings, of the period but not elaborately Victorian, included two pianos—a grand on the first floor and an upright on the second. Both were Steinways because Mrs. Chafee, who had been taught by her father to buy merchandise of quality, thought they were the best; she enjoyed playing and singing herself, and insisted that both Elisabeth and Mary take piano lessons. She also bought one of the first Victrolas and had many recordings, all classical and operatic except for a few by Harry Lauder, the popular

English music hall singer. There was a telephone, although Zechariah, Jr., recalled a time during his boyhood when his parents "felt so hard up" that they had it removed.

The family's first automobile belonged to son Henry, who got it around 1909 after graduating from Brown. When a few years later his mother decided the time had come to have a car, she again opted for quality and chose a Pierce Arrow which she had a chauffeur drive. Later, there were a Model T and a Hupmobile for general family use. Unlike some of her friends, Mary received no Stutz upon becoming a debutante. In 1924 Zechariah, Sr., who disliked speed and walked to work most of the time, acquired an open Pierce Arrow (nicknamed "Red Wing" because of its striping), which he drove at a sedate speed and retained until his death two decades later.

Father Chafee's disdain for speed may also help explain why sailing was one of his favorite diversions. "I think I have sailed more hours and fewer miles than anybody in the United States," he used to say of his summers spent on the waters of Frenchman's Bay at Sorrento, Maine, across from Bar Harbor. Zechariah, Jr., became a somewhat more accomplished skipper, doing well enough to go cruising with old salts like Samuel Eliot Morison (who called him "a good Corinthian sailor") and Lincoln Colcord, who had been born at sea rounding Cape Horn (his father was the captain) and who became a journalist and confidant of Colonel Edward House, adviser to President Wilson.

The Chafee family started spending summers in Maine in 1896, when the parents rented a cottage at Sorrento. Within a few years they acquired a farm house there along with about 150 acres of pasture and woodland, christening the place Weir Haven Farm because of the herring weirs visible from the front porch. As Zech and his siblings grew up and married, their father encouraged them to build their own summer homes on the property with the result that the farm became a family compound. Zech's house, completed in 1916, was dubbed "Red Roof" after President W. H. P. Faunce of Brown, upon seeing it for the first time, exclaimed: "What a magnificent expanse of red roof!"

But despite their numerous privileges, the Chafee children did not grow up thinking of themselves as wealthy—perhaps partly because their parents seldom discussed money. Zechariah, Sr., according to son John, never thought the foundry had even one outstanding financial year; to the extent that he spoke of its revenues at all, it was usually in terms of a year as having been "pretty good" or "a little better than last year." His wife was considerably wealthier after her parents died (the father in 1899, the mother two years later) than before, but her inheritance brought no visible change in the Chafees' lifestyle. While permitting his wife to buy a few extras, Zechariah, Sr., insisted that he provide the home and support the family. So she saved her money and annually gave at least a tenth of her income to charities and needy individuals.

Mrs. Chafee, described by Zechariah, Jr., as "an earnest reformer and constant reader of the *New York Evening Post*" under E. L. Godkin's editorship, was a woman of varied philanthropies. Although she was diabetic and required special care, she was very active in charitable work from 1918 to 1932; she died of leukemia in 1934. Possessing a particular concern for health and nutrition, she was instrumental in starting a district nursing system in Providence as well as in the region around Sorrento. She bought false teeth for many people who otherwise would have had none. And she hired a black woman to do public nursing in Virginia, where the Hampton Institute attracted her interest because daughter Mary's governess had taught there. She gave money to the institute and at times sponsored its choir on tours to Providence or Sorrento, where some residents were aghast the first time they saw blacks swimming in the community pool.

Part of her interest in helping others no doubt resulted from her own experience of hard times, including the depression of the 1870s. Her recollection of financial distress also manifested itself in various economies she practiced. She dressed simply at home and regularly did some of her own sewing and mending. And, while seeing to it that the children were fed ample and nutritious meals, she insisted that the cream be thinned prior to being put on the table.

Through allowances they started receiving at a fairly early age, the children learned the virtues of both saving and giving. Mary Chafee Andrews recalled that her allowance at the age of thirteen was $12.50 a month; from it she had to buy shoes, gloves, underwear, stockings, and probably shirtwaists, using the remainder for spending money. As the children grew older and received larger allowances, they were required to start saving for college expenses. At least a small amount of each child's allowance had to be set aside for charity. "Mother got across the feeling that we had a duty to help others," Francis Chafee observed, "as well as the feeling that money meant work—it wasn't something to throw away. We were the stewards of it for our generation." And from their father came the repeated admonition to "do your share."

Despite Mrs. Chafee's numerous public interests and causes, she was somewhat shy and introverted. Her husband was the extrovert—a man who stopped people on the street to chat as he strolled around Providence and who was remembered by his children for his habit of conversing with streetcar conductors. His happiest moments, Elisabeth Chafee Gamble related, were his associations with Brown University. He served perpetually as secretary of the class of 1880, was chosen as an alumni trustee in 1915, and became a member of the Board of Fellows in 1929. A book collector himself, he was keenly interested in the university's library, and benefactions to Brown by various Chafees have often included gifts to the library.

Religion, too, was an important part of growing up a Chafee. Both parents were dedicated Episcopalians, and the children's presence in church was obligatory. Father was a member of the Episcopal Diocesan Convention and its committee on churches and glebes; he also helped found St. Andrews School in Barrington, an industrial-arts institution. Regular visitors at 5 Cooke Street, according to Elisabeth, were numerous ministers, "all of whom mother adored." Perhaps partly because of the religious atmosphere in the home, the children required little disciplining. Corporal punishment was virtually nonexistent, although father would slap the youngsters if they sassed their mother. The parents looked upon Zech as a model child. He was—except for the time he accidentally broke Elisabeth's nose. The deviant act occurred when he pushed her face into the telephone after hearing her speak derisively about his girlfriend.

In addition to seeing after the youngsters' moral development, the parents guided their intellectual improvement. Conversations at table were almost always about significant topics—politics, economics, music—with the children encouraged to join in and express their views. Listening to father, a wit and raconteur, was educational in itself. "He had a great mind," Elisabeth noted, "and should have been a professor."

Father read aloud most evenings, and as a result, Mary Chafee Andrews related, "everyone read. It was not pushed; we just did. I found I could read before I started school . . . I recall Zech, at 14 or 15, one summer, talking of Spenser's *Fairie Queene* which he was then reading. As babysitter to John and me, when we were three or

four, he'd read us *Pilgrim's Progress*. He read amusing material, too."
Looking back on his parents' influence on him, Zechariah, Jr., recalled that his mother taught him to read, at age five, and his father
taught him how to write: "I do not mean the formation of letters,
but the importance of aiming at persons who are to be persuaded,
and thinking how best to persuade them. 'Suit your oration to your
audience.' "[14] To the end of his life, Zechariah, Sr., maintained an
interest in his namesake's writing, often sending off letters of rep-
rimand when he thought an article lacked balance or was not well
reasoned or might merely reinforce readers' views instead of enlightening them or changing their minds.

At the age of ten, Zech enrolled in the University Grammar School,
a small private boys' school that his father had attended. This followed an eventful summer at camp at Squam Lake, near Holderness,
New Hampshire, where he formed what he always looked upon as
his oldest friendship—with Harry Dana (Henry Wadsworth Longfellow Dana), then fifteen years old. It must have been an instance
of friendship at first sight owing to similarities in character and
temperament. Both had solid Yankee backgrounds—Dana's grandfathers were Richard Henry Dana, author of *Two Years Before the
Mast*, and Henry Wadsworth Longfellow—and both were to become
troubled by the fact that they enjoyed special privileges. And after
both had become university professors, their outspokenness got them
into trouble. In Dana's case it meant being fired from the Columbia
University English Department in the fall of 1917 because of his
pacifist activities.[15] Chafee said he owed to Dana one of his key
ideas, which he stated thus in *Free Speech in the United States:*
"The real value of freedom of speech is not to the minority that
wants to talk, but to the majority that does not want to listen."[16]

Two years later, in September 1898, Zech entered Hope Street
High School on the day it opened. With a student body representing
a cross-section of the community, the school had excellent teachers
drawn from defunct private schools as well as from the public system. His first teacher was Alice W. Hunt, who went on to head the
Consumers' League of Rhode Island and to campaign for shorter
hours for working women; the two corresponded for years about
important social questions. The principal was Charles E. Dennis,
whom he had for Latin and Greek. Of the instruction he received
in the classical curriculum, he said, "What was learned there was
'for keeps' and I cannot conceive of a solider foundation for col-

lege."[17] Schoolmates included two who became lifelong friends: George Hurley, who combined legal practice and Democratic politics in Providence after attending Oxford University, and Claude Branch, who practiced law in Providence and Boston with time out for service as special assistant to the U.S. attorney general in the Hoover administration.

Always bookish and somewhat frail, as well as lacking in physical dexterity, Zech was taken out of school in January 1900 for some outdoor seasoning. In the care of a "congenial couple," Mr. and Mrs. James Otis, Zech along with brother Henry journeyed first to southern California, where they stayed at Las Casitas Villa, about five miles from Pasadena. There he became somewhat smitten with one of the guests, a young violinist named June Reed, and met Mrs. C. P. Stetson, a feminist author of whom he wrote in his diary: "She's very jolly and one would not think she was a theorist."[18] He rode horses, did some mountain climbing, and took drawing lessons in Pasadena, sometimes making the roundtrip on foot. But of course there was always time for books, as he later recalled in an essay, "Confessions of a Book Worm," printed in the Brown University literary magazine: "My head has been befuddled with books since I learned to read. My friends make vain attempts to cure me. One of them frequently tries to alarm me by saying that I know absolutely nothing except what I have gained from books. It is of no use; I am incurable. I swore off [once], and went out West for a horseback trip. On my return I found that among other books I had read a volume of De Quincy, an anthology of English poetry, half of a play of Moilière's, three books of 'Paradise Lost,' and 'Childe Harold.' "[19]

The California sojourn progressed from Pasadena to Montecito, near Santa Barbara, where he learned from a reader of tea leaves that he would be rich, famous, and well traveled—and "best of all" would marry the Providence girl who then appealed to him most. After Montecito, they visited Yosemite Valley and San Francisco before returning by train through Nebraska where "I really formed my Bryanite opinions." The summer of 1900 was spent in and around Providence, but then he and Henry were off again—to northern Maine, where during the autumn they helped a farmer and went to corn huskings with country boys and girls before resuming their studies.

During his career at Hope Street High he was best known for scholarship.[20] He was on the football second team but his father would not let him play in games. As he wearied of being a model offspring, his deportment at times dipped below the norm. Once, after conspiring with most members of his Greek class to answer "unprepared" when called on, he was even kept after school. This event he gleefully chronicled as "The Greek Conspiracy," a narrative launched in a style like that of the Roman historian Sallust but later changed to "a very grandiloquent style like Gibbon's." And in the best Samuel Johnson tradition he sold typed copies of the narrative for fifteen cents each. A diary entry about this publishing venture, however, makes no mention of Johnson's dictum about writing for money.

Outside the classroom he displayed the outspokenness that made him a controversial figure during much of his career. On one occasion he took part in a lunchroom boycott—a fiasco anticipating lost causes to come; on another he campaigned for outdoor recess— a crusade resulting in his first personal encounter with censorship when, in the fall of his senior year, school officials forbade him to speak on the subject.

But there were triumphs, too. He won a medal for a reading called "The Hero of the Play 'Julius Caesar,' " in which he said of Brutus: "Though he errs often and acts wrongly and unwisely, he never does what he believes to be wrong; he is always true to his principles."[21] With Chafee, sticking to one's principles was always regarded as "a very fruitful quality." And, despite C grades in declamation, he was valedictorian of the class of 1903. His commencement speech, opposing an alliance with England, concluded with a portent of the mature Chafee's view of America's role in the world: "Let us throw open our ports to all the world. Let us no longer think of enemies, but regard every nation as our friend. When we act 'with malice toward none, with charity for all' we shall be a people truly great, realizing the ideals of those who founded the Republic."[22]

During his years at Hope Street High his diary became a confessional of the pangs and preoccupations of a typical teenager: having teeth straightened, flirting with girls, expressing doubts about the future, almost ceaselessly indulging in introspection. In the fall of 1901: "Mine is a life of ideals; shatter an ideal, and depression ensues; but soon a new ideal replaces that destroyed and all goes well." In the fall of 1902: "I confess it was rather a disappointment to me that I was not chosen [yearbook] editor-in-chief [his friend Hurley was]. Still, perhaps I lack the requisite executive ability."

And in the summer of 1903, as he prepared to enter Brown, he told his diary: "Father gave me a long talk this morning on my general conduct in college, the sum of it all being, to keep my mouth shut. Very much needed advice. I have decided, on his advice, to try for only two [prizes for entrance] examinations, Latin & Math. He says he does not care how many I try for as long as I don't get them, but I don't think I will waste my time preparing for exams I don't expect to get. His idea is that it is not well to start in with a big reputation, and that entrance prizes merely show excellence for preparation, not like other prizes for excellence in college work." But after changing his mind, he took three exams, in Greek as well as in Latin and math, and won a first prize for each. Consequently, the announcement of the awards by President Faunce at a convocation in the fall of 1903 was, in the words of Zech's friend Branch, "pretty monotonous."

At the time, Brown University had recently been made into a modern institution under the presidency of E. Benjamin Andrews, a fiery economist. He had quadrupled the faculty size, introduced many new courses, created a women's college (Pembroke), and put the graduate school on solid footing. He resigned in 1897 because the trustees had criticized his advocacy of free silver but soon withdrew the resignation. He left Brown, however, the next year, and after two years as superintendent of the Chicago schools became chancellor at the University of Nebraska. There, his dynamic leadership facilitated the efforts of Roscoe Pound, the head of the law school, to transform legal education, and he recruited E. A. Ross, a founder of American sociology, whose ideas about law helped shape the philosophy of law Pound later developed at Harvard.[23] Pound's philosophy, described in the next chapter, also was influenced by another pioneer sociologist—Lester F. Ward, who was on the Brown faculty when Chafee was studying there. Ward, who believed that man could use his mind and spirit to direct the laws of evolution to which all nature and all forms of life are subject, used the phrase "efficacy of effort" in referring to what an intelligent man could accomplish. Although Chafee took no course from Ward, later at Harvard he heard a great deal about efficacy of effort from his mentor Pound.

Also overlapping Chafee's undergraduate years at Brown was Alexander Meiklejohn, the dean of the university. Later, Meiklejohn became an innovative and controversial college president, who was fired by Amherst and subsequently headed an experimental college (dubbed "the Athens of the West") at the University of Wisconsin. Late in his long life he emerged as a First Amendment theorist whose book *Free Speech and Its Relation to Self-Government* Chafee criticized. Much more to the mature Chafee's liking was the First Amendment work of one of Brown's most distinguished alumni— Chief Justice Charles Evans Hughes, whose thinking about free speech was influenced by Chafee's writings.

As a Brown undergraduate, Zech again concentrated on the classics, and came to revere one of his teachers—James Irving Manatt, who had been chancellor of the University of Nebraska when Roscoe Pound was a brilliant student of the classics as an undergraduate there. His interest in the classics was ignited early, as he related in an English composition written in 1904. During summers in the country when he was seven, he and his mother read from a book called *Stories of the Old World*. After they had finished reading about the Trojan War, he played with pointed sticks representing javelins: "Sometimes I was Patroclus, and would wage a long hand to hand combat with Sarpedon, a maple tree on the lawn. Sometimes I was Agamemnon or Ulysses. Most of all, I loved to be the swift-footed Achilles, son of Peleus. Shouting my war-cry, I would pursue an imaginary Hector around the walls of an imaginary Troy, until at last the javelin flew from my hands and quivered in the bark of some convenient tree."[24]

In general, his freshman English compositions showed little of the delightful style that marked his mature writings, although he made some use of a construction ("on the one hand . . . on the other hand") that became characteristic of his prose. The theme "Small Boat Sailing" drew these professorial criticisms: "Except for slight incoherence in one paragraph, and for some colloquial phrases and misspelled words, this is clear and correct. But your style is rather plain and unliterary."[25]

He cared about his writing—in fact, he longed to be a poet or novelist until he realized at Brown that he did not have much to write about—and strove to improve it. By the time of his graduation Brown publications had printed several informed and polished essays by him such as "Literary Conditions in the United States" and "Burton's 'Anatomy of Melancholy.' " Their originality, however, may be questionable; in donating various of his college papers, including English compositions, to the Brown University Archives in 1952, he told a librarian: "I blush now to think of the use that I made of some sort of encyclopedia of criticism, which was possessed by the old polygonal library. I fear there is more of this English in these papers than accords with my present views of the Law of Copyright."[26]

As a freshman, he received two H's (honors) in English, as well as in French, Greek, Latin, and mathematics. Only in gym did he earn a gentlemanly C. But, despite his campus reputation as a brain and a bookworn, he did not spend all his time reading. He enjoyed going to football games and sometimes took brother John, ten years his junior, with him; he was proud of being the author of the official class yell; he delighted in explaining that the class motto (from the Roman poet Tibullus), "Non festa luce madere est rubor," translated freely as, "It's no crime to get drunk when you beat Dartmouth."

He also pledged his father's fraternity, Alpha Delta Phi. Thanks to an agreement Zechariah, Sr., worked out with the fraternity's officers, Junior was spared the kind of hazing usually inflicted on pledges. But fraternity life was not always smooth; he found himself virtually alone in opposing his brothers' support of a new university rule permitting professionals to play on the varsity baseball team. The issue was hotly batted about in campus publications and at mass meetings after the Athletic Board voted in early February 1904, with only Meiklejohn and another professor dissenting, to repeal the amateur-athletics rule excluding from varsity competition athletes who played for pay in the summer. Zech's outspoken opposition to the rule change, Branch related, was "not appreciated" on the Brown campus: "Most of us cared more about a winning team than about amateur standing. He thought the professionals should be disqualified and eventually they were. It was an early example of his integrity."[27] In a revealing diary entry Zech said of the incident: "I suppose I shall always be a minority man. It makes me rather lonely, though I am right . . . I have Father and my own convictions to give me courage."

Perhaps the extracurricular activity that gave him the most pleasure was his membership in The Sphinx, a recently formed intellectual society. He was chosen "to hear the Sphinx' riddles" in June 1905 when Arthur Upham Pope was president. A lifelong friend, Pope became executive secretary of the League of Oppressed People, went on photographic expeditions to Iran, and published A Survey of Persian Art and a biography of Maxim Litvinov, Soviet foreign commissar from 1930 to 1939, who advocated cooperation with the Western powers. "I had many delightful evenings as a member of this noble organization during my last two years at Brown," he recalled in 1955, "and consumed a great deal of Italian wine at an unlicensed restaurant in the Italian district. Fortunately the police did not raid the place while The Sphinx was meeting and eating."[28]

At commencement in 1907 Zech closed out his undergraduate career by giving a speech entitled "The Future of American Poetry." He had not been nominated as a speaker, but President Faunce intervened and made sure the son of Zechariah, Sr., who had been a classmate at Brown, was part of the program. While his undergraduate record did not live up to the promise of the three entrance awards he won, he had accomplished a lot both in class and out. He made Phi Beta Kappa and received one scholarship prize, he contributed to campus publications and served as campus correspondent for the *New York Evening Post*, he was on the class debating team for two years and was president of the Civics Club and the Chess Club during his last year. Not winning a Rhodes Scholarship to Oxford was a major disappointment; that honor went to his friend Hurley. Of the academic assets he carried away from Brown, two proved to be of particular value: the facility to deal with general concepts acquired in a history of philosophy course; and "an everlasting source of delight" in the classics.

The summer after commencement he did go to Oxford—as part of a European trip. And then, fulfilling the role of obedient eldest son, he went to work at the foundry ("the family graveyard," he called it), where, he grudgingly recalled years later. he received some badly needed case hardening. Although there can be no doubt that his father would have wished for him to run the business eventually, Zechariah, Sr., believed that even a few years spent in the foundry might save his namesake from becoming hopelessly pompous. His deep concern about his son's future he expressed in a letter to a family friend, written in early 1909 during Zech's second year at BIF:

As a child he was ever unconscious of any superiority in school over his fellows but the last two years in college he began to look upon himself as a scholar and to be a bit vain . . . As one of my friends says . . . it is quite an injury to a man when he manifests any consciousness of intellectual superiority, and we felt that . . . if [Zech] kept in books the way he was doing, there was danger of that defect in his character . . . I also felt that it is a great misfortune for any one [not to] . . . master or enjoy any form of work which comes in their way. Not to do this, it seems to me, is unmanly or un-American . . .

. . . With his temperament (he is pre-eminently trustworthy) and with some capacity and experience for practical affairs, I think very high positions are open to him . . . But, having had some practical experience, he must decide for himself. At present he is drifting towards law, which might not be a bad thing, although I think at present he is not strong enough for the study.[29]

No single event—no blowup with his father, for example—precipated Zech's decision to leave the family business and become a lawyer. If his father had not virtually commanded him to do so, he would not have worked for BIF in the first place. Once there, he tried to perform conscientiously the tasks assigned him, ranging from common laborer to company secretary. He also had a chance to write his first "book"—a catalog of the firms' products. But grinding out an occasional foundry price list could not end the frustration he felt as an intellectual who wanted to write but was convinced that he had nothing to write about. Conversations with his friend Branch, who was studying law at Harvard, contributed to his consideration of a legal career, and after three years at BIF he convinced his father that he should be allowed to follow Branch down the path of the law. "The study of law," he liked to say, "gave me something to write about."[30] Although his father never quite forgave him for leaving the foundry, especially since he did so in favor of a profession whose integrity Zechariah, Sr., questioned, in an important sense Zechariah, Jr., never left. For he continued to be associated with BIF even after joining the Harvard law faculty, serving as a director and from 1944 to 1954 as chairman of the board.

After graduating in 1913 from Harvard Law School, where he finished second in his class (a fraction of a point behind Robert A. Taft), Chafee returned to Providence and practiced for three years with Tillinghast and Collins, a leading firm whose principal client was the Rhode Island Hospital Trust Company. The senior partners were William R. Tillinghast, a college friend of Chafee's father and a member of the BIF board until his death in the early 1930s, and James C. Collins, who, Chafee quipped, would turn down any job applicant who "lacked a Mayflower ticket." More than once after he became a professor, Chafee saw former students he had recommended get rejected by his old firm simply because they were not of old Yankee stock. Chafee had the right credentials, of course, and he was well liked by the senior partners. He looked upon Tillinghast as "always the ideal lawyer" and a man to whom he owed "a great debt," including the fact that Tillinghast had originally stimulated his interest in interpleader. And he maintained a close relationship with Collins until the latter's death in the early 1950s. Another good friend with the firm was Harold B. Tanner, who was made a partner at the same time as Chafee early in 1916. A few months later, Chafee left to start teaching, but the mails kept him in regular touch with his former associates, and for years some of his happiest times were weekends spent at Ninigret Lodge, situated on a pond in the woods of northern Rhode Island, with Collins, Tanner, Branch, and others, including Harvard faculty occasionally invited by Chafee. As well as good food and stimulating conversation, the group enjoyed long walks and, in winter, skating on the pond. Chafee, while others were drinking and playing cards, liked to just sit and read the *Atlantic Monthly*.

During his years with the firm, which he said paid its young men well and did not require them to work nights or Sundays except in major emergencies, Chafee never tried a case before a jury, handling instead mainly appellate cases. But his brief career as a working lawyer did not lack diversity. Cases he worked on alone or with others ranged from cruelty to animals to challenges to the will of a Newport multimillionaire, Theodore M. Davis; in the latter litigation, which engaged him off and on for almost a decade after he started teaching, he helped save Davis's famous Egyptian collection for the Metropolitan Museum in New York. Outside the firm, as a member of the Rhode Island Bar Association's Committee on Amendment of the Law, he was instrumental in drafting an intestacy statute but unsuccessful in trying to end imprisonment for debtors.

While in practice, he also was an unsuccessful Democratic candidate for the Providence City Council—a race he ran without consulting his father, who felt the outcome might have been different had he known of his son's intention and thus been able to line up support among his numerous community contacts. Certainly there was a need in Rhode Island for someone of Zechariah, Jr.'s, integrity. The worst kind of political corruption continued to infect the state long after the Dorr Rebellion, which did result in some constitutional reforms.[31] Led by "the Blind Boss," Charles R. Brayton, the Republicans bought elections for decades, while Democratic desires for reform were thwarted by gross malapportionment. Conditions received national publicity in 1905, when Lincoln Steffens published an article in *McClure's Magazine* called "Rhode Island: A State for Sale."

During the 1930s Chafee, from his prestigious chair at Harvard Law School, published a series of articles in the *Providence Journal* and the *Evening Bulletin* in an effort to persuade Rhode Islanders of the need for a constitutional convention.[32] His efforts ended up merely as one entry in his mental file of lost causes with which he was identified. Still, he always remained a loyal son of Rhode Island, a city-state like those of ancient Greece, for whose culture he felt such an affinity. His vision of what the state might become he expressed in a letter to Sinclair Lewis, written in 1942: "I have always felt that a city-state like Rhode Island offered unusual opportunities for an integrated community, something like Attica, but I am afraid that these opportunities have not yet been realized. One of the great advantages of Rhode Island is that the state is so small that everybody who counts can easily get to know everybody else who counts. It would also be possible for an enlightened citizen to get to understand the principal needs of the state and the claims of all the different groups. Jefferson had such an understanding of Virginia when he wrote his *Notes* at the end of the eighteenth century."[33]

CHAPTER 4

Interest Jurisprudence and the First Amendment

Not long before he joined the Harvard law faculty in 1916, Chafee reviewed at a Providence literary club meeting two books by Thomas Nixon Carver, a Harvard political economist. Describing Carver as "a prophet among professors," Chafee praised him for representing a middle ground between plutocracy and socialism. In his review of Carver's *Essays in Social Justice* and *The Religion Worth Having*, he noted "the tremendous changes" that had taken place during the two decades since the presidential election of 1896. "The familiar events of this external transformation," he said, "mark a much more far-reaching change under the surface of events, the growth of a new attitude toward private property. This is often described as the passage from individualism to collectivism."[1]

This shift from individualism to collectivism, which is still under way, formed an important part of the broad social milieu in which Chafee grew up and formed his ideas about law and the free speech guarantee of the First Amendment. In Chapter 3 I examined community and family influences on Chafee; now it is time to consider his intellectual development in relation to the larger milieu of major philosophical, economic, and political phenomena.[2]

By the time of Chafee's birth in late 1885 the newspapers in Providence were starting to reflect the socioeconomic stirrings that grew in importance as the old century waned and the new one waxed.[3] On the day of his birth, 7 December, the *Daily Journal* printed the text of a speech by the Reverend Dr. Brown, pastor of the Providence First Baptist Church, as part of a series of lectures on "the social problem." The tone was struck in this sentence: "Few more perplexing questions confront modern society, as represented by the State, than the question as to how to deal with immense and increasing fortunes and with huge and growing monopolies." In addition to calling upon the government to prevent "the tyranny of the railroad pool," the speaker discussed "the grievances of labor," including child labor.

Other issues of the *Journal* reported that Congress was considering a measure aimed at the railroads—the Interstate Commerce Bill—and that disgruntled laborers had begun acting on their grievances, sometimes in violent ways. Editorializing about a Socialist meeting in Chicago in January 1885, the paper commented: "This is a new era. Assassination has become a political doctrine. Conspiracy permeates the most enlightened and free peoples of the world. Socialism threatens not governments alone, but all property and all persons objectionable to the Communists."

Another sixteen years passed before an American president was killed by an anarchist's bullet, but the fear of anarchism spread rapidly after the Haymarket massacre of 7 May 1886, in Chicago. Indeed, 1886 was, in the words of a *Journal* editorial on 3 January 1887, a year of "unprecedented disturbance of relations between capital and labor" and, above all, of industrial wars. Violence and some bloodshed, the paper noted, had accompanied the 3,500 strikes during the year—some of which lasted as long as six months and involved 150,000 persons. The next day, the paper reported the death of Charles Werner Zadick, identified as one of New York's most active and dangerous anarchists. Known as "Powder Charley," he was accidentally blown up along with some of his nitroglycerine.

During Chafee's boyhood there were also various signs in press reports that conservative forces were rallying in defense of the status quo. Lawyers in the District of Columbia, to cite one example, were proposing that a national association be formed to weld local bar groups together into a unified professional phalanx. This National Bar Association (NBA) was formed in 1887 as a rival to the American Bar Associaton (ABA) which since its founding in 1878 had functioned mainly as an elite social group providing no strong national voice for the legal profession. Although the NBA proved ephemeral (the name National Bar Association was revived in 1925 by an organization composed of black lawyers), the ABA got the message and slowly emerged as a powerful conservative force in American political life.[4] And, to cite another example, the Interstate Commerce Commission, created by Congress through the Interstate Commerce Act of 1887 as a means of controlling railroad rates, was quickly reduced to a largely symbolic role by a series of U.S. Supreme Court decisions curbing its regulatory powers.[5] In so ruling, the justices were characteristically reflecting the zeitgeist—in this instance, the spirit of laissez-faire attending the postbellum industrial boom.[6]

And in a small but significant harbinger of the kind of legislative fervor that later stirred Chafee to begin writing about free speech, several members of the U.S. Senate declared in March 1890 that journalists filing dispatches about confidential information obtained from senators were guilty of sedition. In the hope of buttressing this contention, one senator read aloud on the floor the Webster's dictionary definition of the word. In an editorial the *Providence Journal* said if anyone should be prosecuted for sedition, it was the editors who printed such information—although it called the whole idea absurd. For good measure, the paper reviewed the nation's unhappy experience with the Alien and Sedition Acts of 1798, and noted that there currently was no federal sedition law on the books.

But that situation soon changed. World War I, of course, produced far-reaching federal laws aimed at stifling discussion that might somehow interfere with the war effort, but state sedition laws directed at anarchy and syndicalism also became common as a means of trying to maintain order during peacetime. The period that produced such legislation was a time when, as Chafee expressed it, "the same impulse, entirely alien to the principles of Benthamite individualism, namely, an increasing insistence on the interests of the community and on their protection by the state," gave rise to both "the legal restrictions on business and wealth enacted by collectivists at the opening of the twentieth century and the sedition laws enacted against collectivists."[7]

In approaching the free speech problem Chafee opted for a middle position much as Thomas Nixon Carver represented a middle ground between plutocracy and socialism. Chafee's middle ground took the form of a balancing-of-interests approach, which he considered the answer to most legal questions and which he borrowed from a German social utilitarian, Rudolf von Jhering, by way of Roscoe Pound's legal philosophy. How Chafee's balancing test for speech represents a compromise between individualist and collectivist views becomes

clear when it is examined in the context of three related developments in American social thought roughly between 1860 and 1920,
the year *Freedom of Speech* was published. These are the so-called
crisis in liberalism, the revolt against formalism, and the quest for
community.[8]

The crisis in liberalism refers to the shift from classical liberalism,
an economics of individualism grounded in the laissez-faire concepts
of Adam Smith, to neo-liberalism, with its collectivist emphasis,
which calls for the government to play a large role in economic
planning and in providing for individuals who are unable to help
themselves. Popular terms used in referring to neo-liberalism are
the welfare state, the social-service state, and state paternalism. In
the United States the need for the state to intervene on behalf of
individuals became evident after the Civil War as they appeared ever
more helpless vis-à-vis large industrial and business units.

In respect to American political administrations, the second term
of Grover Cleveland (1893–1897) is usually thought of as the divid-
ing line between state nonintervention and intervention. Cleveland
has been called "the last purely negative President, who felt his duty
was to prevent bad things from happening, but not to make good
things happen."[9] The new liberalism was beginning to get a wide
hearing in the progressive movement as Chafee—who, like his father,
referred to himself as a Cleveland Democrat—started studying law
in 1910. The three-way presidential race of 1912 symbolized the fork
in the liberal road: to the left lay the progressivism of Theodore
Roosevelt's New Nationalism, while the path dead ahead led to the
progressivism of Woodrow Wilson's New Freedom. (Down the right-
hand road loomed the ultraconservative figure of William Howard
Taft.)[10] Whereas Wilson's philosophy was merely a restatement of
Jeffersonian ideas such as individualism, which had been a basic part
of traditional liberalism, Roosevelt's philosophy was a novel effort
to infuse liberalism with Hamiltonian ideas of a strong national
state.

Two years after Roosevelt's defeat in the 1912 election, three
progressive publicists who had backed him against the Wilson faction founded a journal of opinion to spread the new liberal doctrine.
As Herbert Croly, Walter Weyl, and Walter Lippmann prepared to
start publishing the *New Republic*, Croly tried to persuade his longtime friend Learned Hand to give up his federal judgeship and join
the magazine. Hand declined, preferring to remain on the bench

where a few years later he formulated the test for deciding free speech cases that influenced Chafee's thinking. But the judge did put Croly in touch with Felix Frankfurter, who early in 1914 was about to leave a government job in Washington and become a law professor at Harvard. Although Frankfurter was never on the magazine's staff, he was actively involved in its planning and later became a regular contributor.[11] After Chafee joined the law school faculty in 1916, he became both a friend of Frankfurter and a contributor to the *New Republic*.

The *New Republic* served as an organ of both progressivism and pragmatism, the philosophy that constituted an important part of the so-called revolt against formalism paralleling the development of the new liberalism. In a classic study Morton White has described this revolt against the abstract, deductive, and static nature of American thought by analyzing the works of five American intellectuals, including the jurisprudence of Justice Holmes. The common theme of their revolt, occurring roughly between 1880 and 1930, was an insistence on "coming to grips with life, experience, process, growth, context, function."[12] And the common enemy of four of these five intellectuals was Benthamite utilitarianism, which Jhering also had rejected.

As the importance of social phenomena achieved greater recognition in American life, the significance of the individual suffered a corresponding decline. Having discerned the haplessness of the isolated human being, intellectuals sought a concept that would furnish individuals protective membership in a social community. This "quest for community" became a concern of intellectuals in disparate fields, and a common aspect of it consisted of seeking balance between the individual and society.

The quest for community was a leading concern of E. A. Ross, a progressive himself and a pioneer American sociologist. It has been remarked that American sociology developed in response to industrialism; but it also emerged as a rebellion against what Ross referred to as "abstract political economy, . . . unhistorical jurisprudence, . . . a priori ethics and the speculative politics" of nineteenth-century scholarship.[13]

Ross gained national prominence with the publication in 1901 of *Social Control*, a book that is "both anti- and pro-individualistic. It opposes economic individualism and argues for the restraint of individual deviations that it believes could threaten the welfare of society. However, it also declares that the 'only welfare there is is the welfare of [concrete, individual] persons present or to come.' "[14] In Ross's view one of the urgent needs of the emerging urban society—whose impersonal cities did "not fit people to deal kindly and honestly by one another"—was for a new morality. And Ross the progressive believed that the needed morality could be found in the Social Gospel movement, in progressive education together with an informed public opinion, and in what became known as sociological jurisprudence. Ross derived his notion of law partly from Jhering, whose *Law as a Means to an End* he read while doing research in Europe in 1898–99.[15] Ross believed that the law could put rationality and planning into social order and social control simultaneously. Through law, he believed, slow, orderly, and gradual change could be accomplished.

The admirers of *Social Control* included two men whose ideas about law and free expression influenced Chafee: Justice Holmes and Pound, who became "modern America's foremost legal scholar."[16] Twenty years before Ross's book came out, Holmes had published *The Common Law*, an early landmark in the revolt against formalism. Its tone was struck in this widely quoted line in the first paragraph: "The life of the law has not been logic: it has been experience."[17] And in an 1897 lecture entitled "The Path of the Law," Holmes declared that "the prophecies of what the courts will do in fact, and nothing more pretentious, are what I mean by the Law."[18]

Pound, the son of a judge in Lincoln, Nebraska, studied law at Harvard for one year before returning in 1890 to help with his ailing father's legal practice. As an undergraduate at the University of Nebraska, he had been interested in botany, and he renewed this interest by enrolling as a graduate student at the university while continuing to practice law. So expert at botany was he that he completed a doctorate in the field, and in 1898 he and a colleague, Frederic Clements, published the *Phytogeography of Nebraska* based on the dissertation they jointly produced. The book was written during a time of tension in the botanical field as the newer Darwinian theory and the older concept of a Great Chain of Being competed with one another. As often happens during such periods, there was a tendency toward compromise, or balance, between the two modes of thought, and such was the approach taken in Pound and Clements's *Phytogeography*.[19]

In June 1903, after serving several years as a commissioner of his state's supreme court—his role was to help clear the caseload, and several of the opinions bearing his name were learned enough to be printed in student casebooks—Pound was chosen to be dean of the University of Nebraska College of Law. Two years earlier, Ross had become a professor of sociology at Lincoln. During meetings of a dining club, the two often debated the worth of the existing system of law, of which Ross was an arch critic. In his autobiography Ross recounts how Pound, a "champion of judges and courts, . . . pounced on me whenever I swung at the current administration of justice."[20] Although Ross did not think he was getting through to his lawyer friend, Pound was actually moving toward the view that law is a function of social forces and philosophies, and that courts, as part of society, must insure that law is adapted to changing social needs. In November 1906, after Ross had gone to the University of Wisconsin, Pound wrote him that "I believe you have set me in the path the world is moving in." A year later, after having joined the Northwestern faculty, he told Ross that if he (Pound) succeeded in formulating a genuinely modern legal philosopy, he would "not fail to state from whom all my inspiration has come."[21]

Pound remained at Northwestern for two years; he then spent one year at the University of Chicago, and in 1910 moved on to Harvard, where he did formulate "a genuinely modern legal philosophy." Harvard was the perfect place for the development of Pound's sociological jurisprudence, a pragmatic legal philosophy, because American pragmatism took shape in Cambridge. In Pound's own words, "The sociological movement in jurisprudence is a movement for pragmatism as a philosophy of law; for the adjustment of principles and doctrines to the human conditions they are to govern rather than to assumed first principles; for putting the human factor in the central place and relegating logic to its true position as an instrument."[22]

It is significant that pragmatism was linked to law from the start. Max Fisch, in suggesting that the methods of the practicing lawyer had a great deal to do with pragmatism's development by Charles Peirce, notes that "Peirce in fact professed to have done no more than follow the lead of . . . [the lawyer] Nicholas Green."[23] During the early 1870s Nicholas St. John Green and Oliver Wendell Holmes, Jr., along with several other lawyers plus Peirce and William James, belonged to the Metaphysical Club of Cambridge. It was at sessions of this group, according to Peirce, that "pragmatism saw the light of day." Although Peirce's assertion has been questioned, there can be no doubt that the club nurtured the development of pragmatic philosophy. One common bond among members was their concern for the far-reaching implications of Darwinism, in which the revolt against formalism was rooted. The response of club members and many other intellectuals to evolutionism consisted of trying to make social thought more scientific but in a way that took account of the changing needs of an evolving society.

Having been forced as a young botanist to come to grips with Darwinism, Pound was an almost perfect person to articulate a legal theory consonant with both the old tradition of law and the new dogma of evolutionism. Within a few months after returning to Harvard he was "molding the gropings of a decade into a comprehensive legal philosophy."[24]

One source Pound drew upon was the new science of sociology—specifically Ross's notion of social control in relation to sociological jurisprudence and Lester F. Ward's concept of the efficacy of effort in achieving ends. Pound envisaged law as a science of social engineering for maximizing the satisfaction of human wants. His philosophy represents a fusion of social science and pragmatism, especially the pragmatism developed by John Dewey, which regards ideas as instruments for reshaping the environment. It is surely significant that Pound spent three years in Chicago at about the time a Chicago school of pragmatism was evolving under Dewey's leadership. This Chicago school, as Charles Morris has written, had "a distinctive social and ethical emphasis different from the individualistic oriented pragmatism of James."[25]

Moreover, it was also natural for Pound, who had once profited from the study of German botanists, to turn again to German scholarship for help. He was particularly impressed by the ideas of Jhering, the "godfather" of sociological jurisprudence and Germany's most important jurist during the latter nineteenth century. Because Jhering's central idea of balance is as American as pragmatism and apple pie, his philosophy had a natural appeal for the American botanist-turned-lawyer seeking to germinate his own legal philosophy. In much the same way that Bentham reacted against Blackstone's legal doctrine—which, with its emphasis on contract theory perpetuated the status quo under English common law—Jhering reacted against historical jurisprudence, in which he had been trained, and which he wryly referred to as "a heaven of juristic concepts." On this side of the Atlantic, of course, the reaction against conceptualism was the revolt against formalism.

The fact that Jhering, in contrast to Bentham did his major work after the Darwinian revolution and the rise of collectivism largely explains why his utilitarianism is social rather than individualist. Jhering rejected the idea that law is merely a development that men could observe and from which they could devise workable principles based on their observations; instead, he believed that law is primarily the realization of a purpose attainable only through a kind of Darwinian struggle. Moreover, that purpose is social in nature: "Law is not the highest thing in the world, not an end in itself; but merely a means to an end, the final end being the existence of society."[26] Using "purposes" and "interests" interchangeably, Jhering emphasized the interests secured by the legal system rather than the rights by which it secures them. And he postulated three basic categories of interests—those of the individual, state, and society. The worth of the legal system was to be measured by the extent to which it struck a proper balance between competing social and individual interests.

Drawing upon Jhering's ideas in various ways, Pound contended that the law is the source of societal rules and is shaped by the needs, desires, and interests of society. In this shaping process the law must assign priorities to conflicting interests, which he classified into three groups: individual, public, and social. An important function of the law consists in weighing and balancing conflicting interests to determine how much effect a particular interest is to be given. Pound also stressed the need to know for what purpose and to what end the law has been developed. In a *Harvard Law Review* article published in 1911, the year after he returned to Harvard, he explained an important consequence of Jhering's teleological method. "Prior to Jhering," he declared, "the theory of law had been individualist. The purpose of law was held to be a harmonizing of individual wills in such a way as to leave to each the greatest possible scope for free action . . . Jhering's, on the other hand, is a social theory of law. The eighteenth century conceived of law as something which the individual invoked against society, an idea which is behind our American bill of rights. Jhering taught that it was something created by society through which the individual found a means of securing his interests, so far as society recognized them."[27]

The implications of this shift in thinking for free expression were touched upon by Pound in "Interests of Personality," the second of two articles printed in the *Harvard Law Review* in 1915, shortly before World War I sedition laws raised urgent First Amendment questions. Freedom of belief and freedom of expression, he wrote, are invested with both an individual and a social interest. However, "the individual interest in free belief and opinion must always be balanced with the social interest . . . of the state in its personality." Beliefs and opinions resulting in action may be restricted under the same laws that apply to actions. "As the law is a practical institution," he concluded, "it can deal only with acting, not with subjective states in and of themselves. But the manifestations of belief, as, for instance, in the case of political opinions adverse to the right of the federal government during our Civil War to coerce the states in rebellion, may so affect that activities of the state necessary to its preservation as to outweigh the individual interest or even the social interest in free belief and free speech."[28]

About a year after Pound started teaching at Harvard, Chafee had his first opportunity to observe him in action. During his second year at law school, 1911–12, he sat in on several of Pound's lectures in a graduate course in legal theory and was "so thrilled" that he attended the class regularly. More than four decades later, as he was preparing to retire, he still regarded the course as "one of the decisive influences on my life because it excited me about the possibilities of doing something to make the law better."[29] In addition to the specific influence of Pound, Harvard Law School's greatest impact on Chafee came from its general pedagogical attitude, which he described as an "attitude . . . of realizing that there is often much to be said on both sides of a question and endeavoring to hear both sides and judge calmly between them."[30]

Throughout his four decades of First Amendment scholarship, Chafee was unwavering in his commitment to the concept of balancing interests. For example, in his first article on the subject, he said: "Unlimited discussion sometimes interferes with [other governmental] purposes, which must then be balanced against freedom of speech, but freedom of speech ought to weigh very heavily in the scale. The First Amendment gives binding force to this principle of political wisdom." And in a book published during the last year of his life he was still maintaining that "no free speech problems can be satisfactorily solved by men who think only of the risks from open discussion. It is indispensable to balance against those risks the deeply felt realization that one of the most important purposes of society and government is the discovery and spread of true facts and sound judgments on subjects of general concern."[31]

"Balance" not only describes Chafee's approach to the free speech problem; it is also a perfect metaphor to characterize his temperament and overall legal scholarship. Like Thomas Macaulay, whom he admired, he is an example of "middlingness," the golden mean existing between two extremes, and this is true in respect to both the form and the substance of his writings. As Macaulay's middlingness is stylistically suggested through the repeated use of the antithetical construction, Chafee's is manifested in the repeated use of an "on the one hand . . . on the other hand" construction. And as in Macaulay's case, the style undoubtedly mirrors the background and personal qualities of the man himself.[32] Perhaps the most literal instance of this in respect to Chafee's style concerns his love of Greek, which "tends toward a form of expression which is translated only clumsily as 'on the one hand . . . on the other.' "[33]

In terms of substance, Chafee's writing exhibited balance as early as his 1913 Harvard commencement address, in which he stated: "Rules without discretion become mechanical and antiquated. Discretion without rules means chaos. The problem is to combine the two methods in proper proportions."[34] In the first book review he did for the *Harvard Law Review*—in 1917, the year after he started teaching—he described how a "scientific legal treatise" should be prepared: gathering decisions would be the first step; then would come classifying the reasons for and against proposed methods of handling the situation; after that would follow the weighing and balancing of these reasons pro and con to get a proper rule; the final step would involve correlating the rules, so far as possible, into a system of principles governing the subject.[35] Thirty years later, in an article called "Do Judges Make or Discover Law?" he wrote that "it is legitimate to reconcile the two sides of this centuries-old controversy by saying that the judges make law out of what they discover, and that law is the will of the Justices trying to do that which is right."[36]

One particularly interesting display of middlingness appears in *Free Speech in the United States,* where he classifies lawyers in terms of their attitudes toward social and economic problems. Group one consists of men "who are satisfied with the existing situation and anxious to keep things as they are. Since they see their path straight ahead, they are likely to succeed in practice and they often fill the higher places on the bench." The second group represents the opposite extreme, "lawyers who are very much dissatisfied with existing conditions and anxious to change them. Such men are not likely to become judges. The legislature or some executive position offers them much greater opportunities for putting their ideas into action, although an occasional member of this group like Brandeis may care for judicial work."

And then of course there is an intermediate group between the two extremes, "lawyers who, though reasonably comfortable themselves, are nevertheless troubled by inequalities in power and fortune and are skeptical as to the external merits of the present rules of the game. Perhaps they would not do much themselves to change the existing situation, for example, if they were legislators. Yet they are reluctant to stop other men from trying to make things better. They are not sure enough of their own ideas to be certain that the reformers are wrong. Hence these lawyers on becoming judges are willing to let men whose minds put them in my second class go considerably farther than they would themselves." Unsurprisingly, Chafee considered himself a member of this middle group, although he does not say so in the book (which does include Holmes in this category).[37]

His middlingness also is evident in his first law journal article on free speech, where he sought "to find the basis of reconciliation between order and freedom" in determining "the nature and scope of the policy which finds expression in the First Amendment to the United States Constitution and the similar clauses of all the state constitutions, and . . . the place of that policy in the conduct of war." He rejected "at the outset . . . two extreme views" because it was "plain that the true solution lies between these two extreme views"— that the Bill of Rights may be ignored in wartime, or that all speech is free and only action can be punished.[38]

Writing under the influence of Jhering and Pound, he downplayed the importance of rights, emphasized the nature and role of both individual and social interests, and argued that the interests must be balanced in deciding free speech questions. It is "useless to define free speech" by discussing rights, because "the agitator asserts his constitutional right to speak, the government asserts its constitutional right to wage war. The result is a deadlock." Pound's ideas about free expression are directly reflected in Chafee's declaration that the First Amendment protects two kinds of interests in speech: first, an individual one—men's need to state opinions on matters that vitally concern them if life is to be worth living; and second, a social one—the nation's need for the truth if it is to take the wisest course of action.[39] The social interest, as explained in Chapter 1, is particularly important in wartime, when the government needs to be rigorously cross-examined to distinguish truth from falsehood.

Chafee's middlingness also helps account for his fondness for the clear and present danger test. Although he justified his preference for it over Hand's objective standard test by pointing out that the danger test was launched with the backing of a unanimous court, Holmes's formula undoubtedly appealed to him because it represents a middle ground between Hand's protective incitement test and the repressive bad tendency test. (On one occasion Chafee described the danger test as a compromise between an unworkable absolute test, on the one hand, and the lack of any protection against legislation, on the other.)[40]

At times, his devotion to the danger test drew criticism from friends. For example, after reading *Free Speech in the United States*, his colleague Edward H. Warren accused him of worshiping its originator. "I did not intend to give the impression of hero worship with regard to Holmes," Chafee explained,

> but I can understand why you received it because I do strongly admire his position on free speech questions. I suppose that he was a philosopher rather than a lawyer, but as you say . . . the issue is not really a matter of legal reasoning . . . From the viewpoint of the practicing lawyer [who needs] to know just what a decision stands for, Holmes is a pretty unsatisfactory judge. For this purpose the judge who builds up his opinion stone by stone, so that one always knows just where he is, must be accounted much more desirable . . . Now if Holmes had satisfied the practitioner by being this sort of judge, he would have been one more in a fairly large group. As he actually is, there is nobody like him. Who else has his flashes of insight? He may go wrong at times, but very often he glimpses the future much

farther ahead than his contemporaries . . . I certainly should
not want a whole bench made up of Holmeses, but I am
thankful to have had one of them in my lifetime.[41]

But a few years later when Alexander Meiklejohn, whom he had
known since he was a Brown undergraduate, published a book ex-
pounding his First Amendment views, Chafee was critical of Meiklejohn for being a philosopher and not a lawyer.

After writing a review of Meiklejohn's *Free Speech and Its Relation to Self-Government* for the *Harvard Law Review,* Chafee told
Felix Frankfurter (who after reading the review criticized Chafee for
defending Holmes's danger test): "The book has more errors of law
per page than about any I ever read, but long acquaintance, his great
work [as president of] Amherst, and the location of his heart in the
right place led me to write as I did. One interesting point about the
book is its love for the privileges and immunities clause. This seems
characteristic of laymen who write about constitutional law . . . [They]
seem wholly unaware of the perplexities which your Court has,
quite naturally, been caused by 'privileges and immunities.' "[42]

"Write as I did" refers to the fact that Chafee's review, although
critical in content, was gentle in tone. His main problem in doing
the review, he told Frankfurter, was one of "painless dentistry. He
doesn't yet know he's lost most of his molars!" He also sent Meiklejohn a manuscript copy of it together with a long letter inviting
him to let Chafee know if he found any statement unfair so that he
could reconsider it while reading galley proofs. Noting that "lawyers
are tempted to be arrogant toward laymen who speak or write on
legal questions," he said he had always found that attitude wrong
but feared he might have succumbed to it in the review.

He thought Meiklejohn would have had greater awareness of the
difficulties involved in his (Meiklejohn's) position if he had first read
more widely in the legal materials; he stayed away from this criticism in the review, he explained, but in the letter he was venturing
to suggest some relevant sources. Many of them concerned Holmes's
formulation of the danger test, which Meiklejohn condemned as
repressive, and its relation to the law of criminal attempts; the letter
also ritualistically recounted Chafee's ambivalence toward clear and
present danger vis-à-vis Hand's test and noted the latter's difficulty
in "taking care of the Mark Anthony problem."[43] The final paragraphs of the review as published also presented a stout defense of

Holmes, including a passage of particular interest in light of one comment in the aforementioned letter to Edward Warren: "A judge who is trying to establish a doctrine which the Supreme Court will promulgate as law cannot write like a solitary philosopher. He has to convince at least four men in a specific group and convince them very soon."[44]

The aspect of Meiklejohn's First Amendment philosophy that has been most criticized concerns his distinction between public and private speech.[45] Arguing that the basic justification for free speech is that it enables the people to govern themselves, he distinguishes between public speech that is absolutely protected under the First Amendment because it deals with the governing process and private speech that may be regulated under the due process clause of the Fifth Amendment. Some critics have objected that Meiklejohn posits "pure" or disinterested speech in contrast to the self-interested speech of political candidates, labor organizers, and others with highly personal axes to grind. Similarly, it has been said that Meiklejohn's First Amendment views focus too much on the intellectual and rational aspect of expression and ignore its emotive aspect, which plays an important role in individual and group protests.[46]

As for Chafee's criticisms of Meiklejohn, he called the distinction between public and private speech the "most serious weakness" because the line between them is "extremely blurred." Pointing out that just about every subject has its public aspects, Chafee wondered why Meiklejohn seemed to relegate scholarship, art, and literature to the lesser protection of the Fifth Amendment instead of including them with public speech under the absolute protection of the First.[47] In response to this criticism of Chafee and others, Meiklejohn made clear that he would protect those forms of expression as part of public speech. But his clarification gave rise to still other objections that the concept of public speech is as meaningless when stretched to include everything as it is when limited to speech explicitly about governance.[48]

Concerning Meiklejohn's belief that public speech deserves absolute protection because it makes self-government possible, Chafee said: "Valuable as self-government is, it is in itself only a small part of our lives. That a philosopher should subordinate all other activities to it is indeed surprising."[49] Still, the best thing about the book, in Chafee's mind, was its emphasis on the interest of self-government. It may be, he wrote, that an account of the balancing process—

for whose advocacy Meiklejohn criticized him because "balancing" is not mentioned in the Constitution and because the logic of self-government rejects it—"should give more attention to self-government than is sometimes done." Referring to Meiklejohn's "badly misdirected" critique of the danger test, he conceded that it "will be interesting to legal scholars who do not regard that test as by any means the last word on the whole of free speech in spite of its great value where war and radicalism are concerned."[50]

Although Chafee always considered the danger test to be a fundamentally sound form of balancing, he tried in 1947 "to sketch out a more inclusive statement" of it to take into account the emergence of new problems. (The review of Meiklejohn's book included a footnote referring readers to "some of the recent thinking on this test" as presented in Chafee's *Government and Mass Communications*.) Chafee began his re-examination of the danger test by noting that it consists of two parts—(1) a substantial evil, and (2) a nearness in time—and that the first part had been "commonly accepted as satisfactory." The criticisms of the test that were "worth hearing" concerned the second part, and here he referred to a review of *Free Speech in the United States* by Mark DeWolfe Howe, who joined the Harvard law faculty after that book came out and later became Holmes's biographer.[51]

Howe had expressed concern that "the threat of a diseased morale" was immediate even though there may have been "no clear and present danger of violent revolution," and had wondered if it was "not quite possible that statutes clearly invalid in the terms in which Holmes considered them, and in which they have been enacted, namely in terms of the danger of immediate violence, may have acquired a new constitutional justification." But to abandon the second part of the test, according to Chafee, would be tantamount to reviving the odious bad tendency test. Thus, instead of scrapping the second part, Chafee undertook to rephrase it: "As Holmes stated the test, it demands a close *chronological* connection—'present' . . . this nearness in time is not altogether a satisfactory requirement in the control of obscenity. It seems sensible for us to retain the element of close connection by recognizing it as *causal* rather than chronological for obscenity and some other situations. The test thus becomes clear and probable danger."[52]

Sedition was not one of the "other situations" Chafee had in mind. But within a few years, the U.S. Supreme Court in the 1951 case of

Dennis v. United States used such a clear and probable danger test to uphold the constitutionality of the Smith Act of 1940.[53] This legislation represented the first peacetime federal sedition law enacted in a century and a half, and, ironically, Chafee had devoted a whole chapter of his 1941 book to mercilessly criticizing it.[54] What is more, a key part of the court's opinion by Chief Justice Fred Vinson—a passage arguing that punishment of speech is justified when a substantial interest is at stake, even though there is no imminent danger—confirmed a prescient comment Chafee had made in the section of *Government and Mass Communications* devoted to revising the danger test: "If the evil is found to be substantial, [a law aimed at speech] seems likely to be upheld regardless of the unlikelihood that the evil will ever come to pass."[55]

As some scholars have pointed out, the clear and probable danger test as used by the Supreme Court in *Dennis* resembled the old bad tendency test that Chafee abhorred. Thus it is of more than passing interest that the test used by Vinson had been formulated in the appeals court below by Learned Hand, who more than three decades earlier had enunciated the speech-protective objective standard test that Chafee admired enough to dedicate *Freedom of Speech* to the judge.[56] In endorsing Hand's newer and much more restrictive formula, the high court's *Dennis* ruling served to clear the way for a period when the justices used a balancing test that ignored the social interest in discovering the truth through speech, which Chafee had always stressed, and tipped the scales automatically in favor of the weighty governmental interest in the national security.[57]

It is not known whether Chafee recognized any link between his modification of the danger test and the clear and probable danger test Hand formulated in *Dennis;* there is no correspondence between them suggesting such recognition. What is certain is that Chafee suffered considerable anguish during his last years and that the source of much of it lay in the fact that the unbalanced political mentality of the cold war and McCarthy era was hostile to the balanced views he had advocated for some forty years. From the *Dennis* decision in 1951 until his death in 1957, Chafee's chagrin was articulated in a lament that became almost a litany: "The First Amendment now means that 'Congress shall make no law abridging the freedom of speech and of the press unless Congress does make a law abridging the freedom of speech and of the press.' "[58]

CHAPTER 5

A Public Service Theory
of the Press

As a lawyer, Chafee understandably emphasized the legal meaning of the First Amendment. But he did not think philosophical aspects of expression were unimportant, as his criticisms of Meiklejohn may suggest. In the bibliography of his 1920 book he said: "The legal meaning of freedom of speech cannot properly be determined without a knowledge of the political and philosophical basis of such freedom."[1] And a dozen years later he made this point: "Free speech means much more than the right of the jury to pass on criminality of a writing or a speech. The [U.S. and state]constitutions also involve broader questions of the essential need of open discussion, unchecked by either judge or jury—such questions as were discussed in the Apology of Socrates and the Areopagitica of Milton. Similarly . . . the free speech clauses . . . must be interpreted in the light of subsequent reasoning in Mill's Liberty, and so on."[2]

Chafee's mention of John Stuart Mill is particularly noteworthy because "the tension between [classical liberalism and modern liberalism] is unusually explicit in his work."[3] It terms of theories about what the role of the press in society should be, Mill's writings on expression, along with Milton's, are identified with libertarian theory—the concept, derived from the classical liberal weltanschauung, that government should keep its hands off the intellectual marketplace, where rational individuals will discover the truth in the open clash of ideas.[4] Yet Mill's view of expression also represented a shift toward collectivist thinking; for while he was a leading proponent of individualism, he sought to balance individual and social interests ("the practical question [is] where to place the line—how to make the fitting adjustment between individual independence and social control") and anticipated the clear and present danger test by distinguishing between "other-regarding" actions that the state may regulate and "self-regarding" ones that it may not. In the literature on press theory Holmes's danger test is referred to as the first important modification of the libertarian thinking that slowly crystallized in England after the Glorious Revolution of 1688 and later in this country.

The passage from individualism to collectivism, described in Chapter 4, is reflected in the newer social responsibility theory of the press, which tends to stand astride of libertarian theory and collectivist press theory such as that of the Soviet Union.[5] On the one hand, social responsibility theory retains the libertarian belief that government controls over the marketplace of ideas should be minimal; on the other, it reflects contemporary doubts about man's rationality and ability to discover the truth and expresses concern over the dwindling number of voices in the market due to media mergers, monopolies, and common ownerships of print and broadcast media. By stopping short of advocating government ownership of media and by calling instead for the media to carry diverse views and thus be responsible to the whole society, the new theory strikes a balance between individualism and collectivism.

Because Chafee recognized the philosophical aspects of free speech, his First Amendment ideas need to be considered not just from the standpoint of law but from the perspective of press theory as well. From this perspective, his thinking is seen to contain strands of both libertarianism and social responsibility. And both strands were present practically from the beginning of his writings on speech, although the latter became more pronounced later on. Like Milton, who argued that the exchange of ideas should be free so that the truth can be uncovered, Chafee believed that free speech is important because it leads to truth; but he also stressed that there is a strong social as well as individual interest in truth. And like Mill, he feared government intervention but also recognized a need to draw a boundary between collective and individual interests. He went further than Mill, however, by flatly declaring that free speech requires a positive or affirmative interpretation, not simply the traditional negative one.

As far back as the early 1920s, he asserted that "freedom of opinion is not safe merely through the absence of legal interference: there must exist affirmative channels of expression." A little later, in an essay appearing in a 1928 anthology called *Freedom in the Modern World*, he wrote that "we [should not] be content with adjusting the negative forces which restrain liberty. We should also consider the development of positive forces which will encourage it and remove the sluggishness of thought into which we all easily lapse even without any prohibitions upon opinion. We cannot afford to neglect methods for obtaining livelier oral discussion and places available for it, and for encouraging fuller presentation of all sides of international and industrial controversies in the press and over the radio."[6] In 1941 he crisply expressed his affirmative view in the first sentence of the last chapter of *Free Speech in the United States:* "Speech should be fruitful as well as free." And in 1943 he argued that the Associated Press (AP), then being sued by the federal government in an equity action under the Sherman Anti-Trust Act, "should regard itself as a public service open to all who will pay the price."

Chafee expressed his public service theory as part of a "debate" with Fredrick S. Siebert, a lawyer and director of the University of Illinois School of Journalism, a debate that was published in several major newspapers. They included the *Chicago Tribune,* for which Siebert had done some consulting work on First Amendment questions, and the *Providence Journal,* in which the Chafee family (but not Chafee himself) has had a minority interest since his mother's generation.[7] An AP member, the *Journal* carried a defense of the AP next to Chafee's criticisms of it. The *New York Times,* the *New York Herald Tribune,* and the *Washington Post* all rejected Chafee's statement.[8]

The *Chicago Tribune,* which a few years later began smearing Chafee with a red brush, had a vested interest in the case. The key issue was whether or not the AP, operated as a cooperative, would make its service available to the *Chicago Sun,* the *Tribune's* new competitor in the morning field.[9] The *Sun,* published by the liberal department store magnate Marshall Field, was pledged to support the policies of President Franklin Roosevelt, whose countless newspaper critics included none more strident than the superpatriotic *Tribune's* Colonel Robert R. McCormick. The AP's by-laws made it virtually impossible for a new paper to get the wire service in cities where there was already an AP-member paper; so when Field sought AP service in 1941, the owner of the AP-member *Tribune* blocked his membership application.

In April 1942, as the U.S. Department of Justice was considering a possible anti-trust action against the wire service, AP members voted to slightly liberalize the by-laws. This was mainly a ploy, as shown by the fact that a vote taken at the same time was more than 2 to 1 against admitting the *Chicago Sun.* The following August the government filed suit in federal court in New York's southern district; the defendants were thirty-five AP newspapers and publishers as well as the wire service itself. The litigation presented an interesting role reversal. On one side, standing under the AP umbrella and arguing that to expand the wire service's flow of information would infringe the First Amendment, were the vast majority of daily newspapers—venerable advocates of press freedom.[10] On the other, holding the First Amendment high while endeavoring to open up the channels of news and information, was the federal government—traditional nemesis of that freedom. It is possible that the government's motivations were at least partly political; rumor had it that the Justice Department wanted Field to have AP service because he was a staunch supporter of Roosevelt.[11] In any event, the case was unique because it was the first time the press had been taken to court under the Sherman Act.

While the case was pending before a three-judge court consisting of Learned Hand, his cousin Augustus N. Hand, and Thomas W. Swan, the Chafee-Siebert colloquy appeared in April 1943. Stating that he had no opinion as to whether or not the AP had violated the Sherman Act, Chafee contended that "liberty of the press in the Bill of Rights must mean something much bigger than the right of some newspapers to deprive other newspapers of access to a vital channel of information merely because the insiders got there first. Liberty of the press is not the property of some newspapers or even of all newspapers." The AP's restrictive by-laws caused the greatest harm "not to the excluded newspapers, but to the citizens who are deprived of the chance of getting the best news in those newspapers." Calling the "liberty to hear just one side a poor kind of liberty of the press," he stated that

> the AP should of its own accord adopt the principle of public service and thereby increase the flow of news to all citizens, which is the very essence of liberty of the press.

The new conception of public service brings new responsibilities. Within reasonable limits the public can shape the nature of the service which it receives. Prices, quality, wages paid, conditions of employment, etc., are subjected to regulations. This does not mean that the legislature or some government bureau can or should take over the whole conduct of a business.

Thus there is no warrant for the fear that the present attempt of the government to throw open the AP to all buyers of news is equivalent to putting a New Deal official at every editorial desk.[12]

Siebert, who ended up as associate counsel for the *Tribune* in filing a friend of the court brief when the AP carried the case to the U.S. Supreme Court, dismissed the public service argument: "It is more to the public interest to see that there is lively and vigorous competition between the various news agencies than it is to see that every newspaper gets the same news service . . . In fact, [AP] . . . has fostered the growth of rival news agencies by restricting its own membership."[13]

When the federal district court voted 2 to 1 (Judge Swan dissented) to enjoin the AP restrictions on membership, the opinion by Learned Hand contained a public service theory resembling Chafee's views.[14] Before he had a chance to read the opinion, Chafee heard from his friend Carl Stern, who filed an amicus brief for Field Enterprises on the government's side: "It must be a great satisfaction to you to see how slavishly Learned Hand followed your views of AP and the freedom of the press. I don't know whether he ever saw your letter [apparently a reference to Chafee's statement in the debate with Siebert] but he concurred in both of your views: First, that the opening up of AP was in line with what was protected by the First Amendment. Secondly, he held that there was absolutely nothing to the objection voiced by AP—he definitively blew up the idea that because you restrict a newspaper from hogging a source of news for itself, you interfere with freedom of the press."[15] Hand's opinion included this oft-quoted passage about the First Amendment's function:

Neither exclusively, nor even primarily, are the interests of the newspaper industry conclusive; for that industry serves one of the most vital of all general interests: the dissemination of news from as many different sources, and with as many different facets and colors as is possible. That interest is closely akin to, if indeed it is not the same as, the interest protected by the First Amendment; it presupposes that right conclusions are more likely to be gathered out of a multitude of tongues, than through any kind of authoritative selection. To many this is, and always will be, folly; but we have staked upon it our all.[16]

Because the district court did not decide all issues raised by the case in favor of the government, the Justice Department as well as the AP appealed to the U.S. Supreme Court. The eight sitting justices filed five opinions, with the main one coming from Justice Hugo Black.[17] In the words of Black's biographer, "he almost laughed out of Court the contention of the Associated Press that its First Amendment freedoms included immunity from the Sherman Antitrust Act."[18] However, the justice's reasoning inclined toward a restraint-of-trade, rather than a public service, theory. Justice Frankfurter, friend of both Hand and Chafee, wrote a separate opinion agreeing with Black but deferring more to the public service language of Hand in the court below.

In December 1943, about two months after the district court decision in the AP case, Chafee was appointed to the Commission on Freedom of the Press—popularly known as the Hutchins Commission after its chairman, President (later Chancellor) Robert M. Hutchins of the University of Chicago. The commission was the brainchild of Hutchins's friend and fellow Yale alumnus Henry R. Luce, who, as head of the Time-Life magazine empire in a period of mounting press problems, wished to have produced a substantial restatement of the importance of a free press in America.[19]

What was happening to the press was yet another reflection of the transition from individualism to collectivism. For one thing, newspapers and other media were themselves becoming large organizations, whose growing visibility invited closer public scrutiny and criticism. For another, as government grew, its regulatory role expanded and questions arose as to whether the newspaper business could be controlled like other forms of commerce. Once the New Deal arrived with its raft of reform measures, the battle lines were rather quickly drawn between big government and the press as big business. With litigation inevitable, in 1937 newspapers for the first time were declared to be in interstate commerce and thus subject to some federal control. In a 5 to 4 decision foreshadowing its ruling eight years later in the case involving the *Chicago Sun*, the Supreme Court told the AP that it had to recognize the American Newspaper Guild as a collective bargaining unit. "The business of the Associated Press is not immune from regulation because it is an agency of the press," the court said. "The publisher of a newspaper has no special immunity from the application of the general laws."[20]

The federal government's assertion of some authority over the media strengthened the hand of press critics who, since the progressive period early in the century, had been saying that if the media did not reform themselves, the government would do it for them.[21] As they were increasingly put on the defensive, many newspaper publishers blamed their troubles on President Roosevelt—whom most of them disliked anyway. "But even in the late 1930s," Margaret A. Blanchard writes, "there were some voices within the profession—such as that of William Allen White, president of the American Society of Newspaper Editors (ASNE) in 1939—who refused to blame the profession's problems on someone else and called on the newspaper business to put its own house in order."[22]

Against this background, then, the Hutchins Commission was set up with $200,000 provided by Luce. Neither he nor the University of Chicago, which administered the funds, was to have any control over the commission. The personal background of Hutchins, who picked the commission members and generally ran the show, is as relevant to a consideration of the commission's work as is the politicoeconomic climate of that period.[23] Born in the last year of the nineteenth century, he came from a family of Presbyterian educators. When he graduated from Yale Law School in 1925, he was asked to join its faculty. He did, and two years later became dean. Then in 1929, at the age of thirty, he was inaugurated as the fifth president of the University of Chicago, considered the nation's most dynamic institution of higher learning at the time. In short, young Bob Hutchins—who even managed to abolish intercollegiate football at Chicago—was a supernova in the galaxy of American education.

Controversial partly because of his "boy wonder" reputation, he helped shake up legal education during his brief deanship at Yale by making major curriculum changes and in doing so contributed to a major controversy concerning legal realism. Yale and Columbia were becoming hotbeds of realist jurisprudence, which emphasized the use of empirical methods to illuminate the process of judicial decision making and to facilitate predictions of court decisions.[24] Still a dedicated realist when he left New Haven, Hutchins became disaffected in Chicago. If the law is nothing more than predictions of what courts will do, he now asked himself, then what happens to the ideal of justice?

Helping to speed Hutchins's change in outlook was the influence of the philosopher Mortimer Adler, whom he hired for the Chicago faculty. He came to share Adler's admiration for the "great books," and later commented that this new source of knowledge was "the first education I ever had."[25] As he continued to question his old pragmatic ideas during a period of depression at home and emergent fascism abroad, the metaphysics of the Aristotelian-Thomistic synthesis attracted him. By 1935 he could say that "the law is a body of principles and rules developed in the light of the rational sciences of ethics and politics."[26] The following year, he articulated his new thinking in The Higher Learning in America, an attack on traditional university education for its emphasis on getting jobs and making money and lack of concern for intellectual achievements. According to Hutchins, the modern temper—that is, the skepticism of scientific naturalism—produced "that strangest of modern phenomena, an anti-intellectual university."[27] What could be done? In other times, the solution might be found in religion. But, Hutchins said, he was addressing a faithless generation of Americans who were more like the ancient Greeks for whom metaphysics was the ordering principle. Thus metaphysics, the highest wisdom because it deals with the highest principles and causes, could again serve that purpose in the twentieth century.

Through the late 1930s Hutchins continued his attack on American education. Despite his critics' charges of elitism and authoritarianism, one scholar notes, he "retained his belief in human equality and free government . . . Throughout his career, Hutchins remained committed to the values of democratic society and as president of Chicago emerged as one of the most outspoken defenders of free speech and academic freedom in the United States."[28] Unsurprisingly, Hutchins looked upon the press as an instrument of public education, and in addressing groups of editors he made the point that newspapers were failing to meet society's needs.[29]

When it came time to select members of the Commission on Freedom of the Press, he decided that a more objective appraisal of press performance could be achieved if working journalists were excluded. Instead, he chose current or former academics—a dozen leading figures in the fields of law, economics, history, philosophy, and theology. Counting Hutchins himself, the commission thus consisted of thirteen members—a number that aptly anticipated the unlucky reception given the group's general report. It is significant that ten of the thirteen members are discussed at least briefly in Edward A. Purcell's *The Crisis of Democratic Theory*, a lucid study of the ethical basis of democracy focusing on major ideas shared by many twentieth-century intellectuals.[30]

Two members of the commission—Archibald MacLeish and John Dickinson—were friends of Chafee and, like him, products of Harvard Law School at a time when Roscoe Pound's influence was strong. MacLeish, who deserted law for poetry and was then librarian of Congress, had recently blamed intellectuals for seeking objectivity and forgetting their responsibility for the moral life—a state of mind he considered largely responsible for the rise of fascism. Dickinson, professor of law at the University of Pennsylvania and general counsel for the Pennsylvania Railroad, was an important disciple of Pound, and both he and Chafee were critical of the legal realism that flourished at Yale.[31]

Two commissioners were political scientists who had had affiliations with the University of Chicago: Dean Charles E. Merriam would soon become a professor emeritus, and Harold Lasswell had moved on to Yale. The latter's well known *Politics: Who Gets What, When, How* relied on psychological analysis, and he later added to his renown with his definition of communication: "who says what in which channel to whom with what effect."[32] Two other commissioners, Reinhold Niebuhr and William Ernest Hocking, had long been interested in ethical and moral questions. Niebuhr, with whom Chafee became friendly, was a distinguished theologian perhaps best remembered for his formulation of Protestant neoorthodoxy, which stresses man's sinful nature. His intellectual path roughly paralleled that taken by Hutchins, and he ended up a symbol of the shift in American thought "from confidence and optimism in social scientific rationalism to some form of philosophical or religious transcendentalism."[33] But he also retained a strong element of pragmatic thinking. Hocking, a Harvard professor of philosophy primarily of the idealist school, had written widely on morality and religion. He was also a Harvard pioneer in the field of political philosophy; he had jointly taught a seminar with Pound, and in 1926 had published two important books, *Man and the State* and *The Present Status of the Philosophy of Law and of Rights*. On the Hutchins Commission he proved to be the member most sympathetic to an expanded role for government in the communications field.

It is interesting that Hocking regarded Chafee, who served as the commission's vice chairman, as a direct descendant of natural law thinkers like John Locke and Hugo Grotius.[34] Hocking was wrong about that. Although there have been various strains of natural law, they all partake of the notion that there is an abstract standard of perfect justice by which man-made law may be judged; Holmes had a derisive phrase for it: "the brooding omnipresence in the sky." Chafee, as a disciple of Poundian pragmatism, could not help being skeptical about natural law, "except as I believe that there are some rather nebulous standards by which we ought to test the desirability of the rules of law as they have been administered." For the most part he considered it "a lovely label to be attached to the ideas a particular person would like to have prevail."[35] Yet there were times when he also showed some appreciation for the brooding omnipresence, as when he argued that men obey the law mainly because they recognize its "objective truths and values."[36] So there were limits to his pragmatism, a fact he made clear when he wrote that "I want to be a pragmatist, but I don't want to work very hard."[37] This was a shorthand way of saying that he preferred to solve legal questions by thinking his way through a problem rather than "going around looking up a lot of things in the outside world." That was the voice of the Platonist in Chafee, who once remarked that in assisting the Wickersham Commission's study of lawlessness he had done "all the fact-finding I want to do in my life."[38]

Chafee's pragmatic-Platonic dualism is undoubtedly one more reflection of his middlingness. As a pragmatist, he cared a great deal about keeping the law abreast of changing social conditions. Because of his "eager, continuous quest for improvement of the law," a law school colleague observed, he always saw policy issues as central.[39] But as a Platonist, he liked to formulate policy by putting his reason to work instead of gathering empirical data.

No wonder he considered the Hutchins Commission, concerned as it was with formulating press theory and policy while doing little field research, "the most interesting and enjoyable cooperative enterprise in which I have ever engaged."[40] Similarly, he enjoyed the work because the group's deliberations reminded him of Platonic dialogues. A playful feature of Chafee's *Government and Mass Communications*, a two-volume study he produced as part of his commission work, is verbatim accounts of some of its deliberations printed in the form of dialogues. Instead of using actual names, he gave each discussant the name of an author or historical figure whose views or achievements were similar to those of a commissioner. Hutchins became Plato, of course, and he called himself Wilkes—after John Wilkes, the rakish English editor who was twice jailed for sedition during the reign of George III and for whom Chafee's great-grandfather Wilkes Sharpe was named.[41]

From December 1943 until September 1946, the commission usually met for three days about every six weeks—except for summers, when the intervals were longer.[42] Because there was no stenographer at the early sessions, Chafee kept notes and had them typed and distributed to his colleagues. "It is beyond me," MacLeish remarked, how he managed to take notes while actively participating in the discussions. Later, he also took candid photos of the commissioners at work and gave them prints.

One long session set for Bennington, Vermont, in the summer of 1945 had to be switched to Chicago so that Chairman Hutchins could attend a meeting there about the atomic bomb; its use against Japan had just climaxed the chain reaction achieved by Enrico Fermi a few years earlier at the abandoned University of Chicago football stadium. Chafee missed that session because of his teaching commitments, but he wrote the staff director, Robert D. Leigh, asking if he could receive the customary $300 honorarium anyway because of written work he had been doing. The imminent expense of marrying off one of his daughters, he told Leigh, had made the money for the Bennington conference look "almost as attractive as the scenery." Chicago was the first meeting he had missed since the second session, held in February 1944; he skipped that to attend a meeting of the Builders Iron Foundry directors, who were faced with several important decisions as a result of his father's death the previous summer.

While serving on the Hutchins Commission, Chafee also was an active member of the American Bar Association's Bill of Rights Committee, and the demands of that group at times interfered with his commission responsibilities. During 1944–45, for example, he helped draft a friend of the court brief for a conscientious objector appealing to the U.S. Supreme Court after he was denied admission to the Illinois bar.[43] Apologizing to Leigh for not having sent along comments about a draft of the commission's general report, he explained that the brief was consuming all his time not required by students: "In short, I am so much preoccupied with freedom that I am never free."

His concern for freedom, and more specifically for press freedom in a democratic society, made him somewhat apprehensive during the early months of the commission's life. In a memo to fellow commissioner Harold Lasswell, he voiced concern that "the scope of the inquiries seems to have drifted away from freedom of the press (all media of communication) to asking all about what the press does. The subject is now the use made of freedom rather than the limitations upon freedom alone. The effect of whatever the press does on the public is also proposed for consideration. It may very well be that this shift of emphasis is desirable, but we should be conscious of what we are doing."

Later, in commenting on a draft of the general report, Lasswell in turn complained that "too much prominence [is given] to *legal* argument in place of *policy* statement. What is said about the First Amendment is sufficiently dubious to provide an opportunity for a big, red herring to be drawn across the trail of public consideration of the Report. Policy is primary; if we can clarify the goals of a free society, as related to the mass media, we shall have done our bit. Let the legal arguments rest in peace until the gladiators of the law are paid to stir them up again." Lasswell also raised a question concerning an issue central to the commission's deliberations:

> Don't we want to give "freedom of the press" *both* a *positive* and a *negative* meaning? The present talk of a "right" to "use" (too narrowly confined in any case to independent proprietorship), offset by "responsibilities," seems to perpetuate the negative conception of the freedom of the press as *absence* of control, tempered by admonitions to goodness. It is wiser strategy for the Report to give richer meaning to the phrase from the outset—freedom of the press signifies "freedom from" and "freedom to." I suggest playing down the terminology of "right" and "responsibility,"

and sticking to the language developed by the Commission. Our job is to clarify the conduct on the part of the press that coincides with, or fosters, a free society.

When the commission's general report was issued in March 1947, it did define press freedom in both a negative and positive way: "Freedom of the press means freedom from and freedom for." But the definition was surrounded by the language of rights and responsibilities that Lasswell had objected to. "The complexity of modern industrial society, the critical world situation, and the new menaces to freedom which these imply mean that the time has come for the press to assume a new public responsibility," the report stated. Furthermore, the press "must be accountable to society for meeting the public need and for maintaining the rights of citizens and the almost forgotten rights of speakers who have no press . . . Freedom of the press for the coming period can only continue as an accountable freedom. Its moral right will be conditioned on its acceptance of this accountability. Its legal right will stand unaltered as its moral duty is performed."[44]

Having emphasized that press freedom carries with it a responsibility to society, the commission took up the question of what a free society requires of the media. Its answer consisted in listing standards by which press performance can be gauged, standards not originated by commission members but taken largely from the media professions and practices: "Today our society needs, first, a truthful, comprehensive, and intelligent account of the day's events in a context which gives them meaning; second, a forum for the exchange of comment and criticism; third, a means of projecting the opinions and attitudes of the groups in the society to one another; fourth, a method of presenting and clarifying the goals and values of the society; and, fifth, a way of reaching every member of the society by the currents of information, thought, and feeling which the press supplies."[45]

The report's call for the press to be morally responsible to society as a whole is similar to the public service theory that Chafee had used in his critique of the Associated Press by-laws. In particular, the commission's second social requirement—that the press should regard itself as in effect a common carrier of public discussion—parallels Chafee's belief, expressed in his debate with Siebert, that "the AP should regard itself as a public service open to all who will pay the price."

The commission was criticized on many counts: for holding closed sessions, for including no working newspaper persons in its membership, for defining the press to include radio and the movies, for taking up broad societal concerns, and for advocating government control of the press. The last criticism may have stemmed largely from ambiguous language that made it possible for both those readers favoring more government regulation and those opposing it to conclude that the general report supported their view.[46]

Many journalists—led by the *Tribune's* Colonel McCormick—saw as a call for government-run media the commission's statement that press freedom should be defined in a positive as well as a negative sense. And at the same time, some observers criticized the commission for having failed to advocate government controls. For example, Morris L. Ernst, a prominent civil liberties lawyer who argued in his 1946 book, *The First Freedom*, that media monopolies should be broken up, was unhappy because the commission did not endorse the use of the anti-trust laws.[47] Apparently having assumed that Chafee's public service view of the AP meant that he favored wide use of the anti-trust laws against the media, Ernst told Chafee that he found it "hard to believe that you really agreed with the final document. I should imagine that at the most you would have had to write a footnote, as [Chief Justice John] Marshall did, stating that you have 'acquiesced.' " In reply, Chafee offered this explanation:

> You may be disappointed that the members of the Commission, including myself, have disagreed with your reliance on the Anti-Trust Laws and similar legislation, but I can assure you that a very great deal of thought was given to this whole problem. For my own part, I feel that the use of legal methods is somewhat unified. We cannot expect the government to employ the Anti-Trust Laws extensively and at the same time to be very sparing in legal actions about sedition and obscenity. Once they get going, they will move in many directions.
> ... My own concurrence in the General Report was wholehearted ... I should say that we came as close to una-

nimity as any group with which I have been connected . . . I hope that you will not think of us as giving up any convictions for the sake of log rolling.

Such log rolling there may not have been. But some important differences—including major ones between Chafee and Hocking—had to be resolved. Indeed, so strong was the disagreement between them over one point that a special subcommittee—a kind of conference committee—had to be created during the summer of 1945; its members, besides the two disputants, were Lasswell, Niebuhr, and, as secretary, Llewellyn White, assistant director of the commission's staff. The dispute centered on whether or not the government should punish the press for falsehoods, with Hocking arguing for such a policy and Chafee against.[48] During the last weekend of July 1945, Chafee journeyed to Hocking's farm in the White Mountains of New Hampshire where they clarified their differences. The other committee members visited Hocking later. As a result of these discussions, Chafee related, the general report relied mainly on extragovernmental remedies against falsehoods; the only legal measure recommended was the compulsory correction of errors.[49]

But the work of this subcommittee neither ended all disagreements between Hocking and Chafee nor left all members of the committee feeling equally satisfied. The following summer Hocking complained to Chafee, chairman of the commission's Subcomittee on Law and Government, that a draft document by the latter made it sound as if there was "something wrong" with those arguing for government restrictions on the press. And in December 1946 White, who strongly believed that radio and newspapers should receive equal treatment under the First Amendment, complained in a memo to staff director Robert Leigh that Chafee and Niebuhr had caused Hocking to alter his view of the need for government control of newspapers comparable to that in broadcasting.

The author of a separate book for the commission called *The American Radio*, White believed that the creation of the subcommittee marked a turning point in the evolution of "the Hocking Principles"—that from then on Chafee, backed by Niebuhr, convinced Hocking to take "a more pragmatic view" of what constitutional reformers could do. "At the time, this was rather a blow to me," White related. "I felt that this development marked the beginning of a long retreat by the Commission. I saw the yardstick of unqualifiable social need being discarded for what has always seemed to me to be the familiar "double-talk" of courts and legislatures. Much as I valued then, and do now even more, the personal friendship of the Messrs. Chafee and Niebuhr, and much as I respected, and continue to respect their judgments and their almost symbolic integrity, I regard Mr. Chafee's most persuasive rationalization of the differentiations between the press and radio as a brilliant defense of some accidentally discovered criteria which seem to me to weaken more than they bolster the criterion of social need.

Nonetheless, I had . . . to shape my thinking about [my book] The American Radio to the realization that the Commission was not going to apply the criterion of social need equally as between the press and radio.

White's reference to Chafee's "brilliant defense" of differences between the press and radio was apparently meant to be sarcastic. Because White believed both media should be treated equally under the First Amendment, he was annoyed by Chafee's views—which were actually more conventional than original. In the first place, Chafee believed that licensing of broadcasting is necessary because the number of frequencies is limited and thus the government, acting through the Federal Communications Commission (FCC), must decide who shall be permitted to broadcast and then evaluate each licensee's performance. And second, he thought that the licensing of the print media was both unnecessary, because their number (unlike that of broadcasting stations) is not limited by their physical nature, and undesirable, because of the long tradition of press freedom from such government control. Chafee also asserted that radio, because of its physical nature, was the only medium to which the public service theory could be applied (the AP to which he applied it, is not a medium but a service to media). Noting that the FCC is "the one department of the government which probably has the power to compel broadmindedness" (that is, diverse views), he said that FCC critics "are barking up the wrong tree when they talk about infringement of freedom of the press" because the key question "is whether such action of the FCC is wise."[50]

Returning to the disagreements between Chafee and Hocking, it is clear that the latter strongly objected to Chafee's penchant for balancing. Noting that Chafee called balancing "a compromise solution," Hocking complained that "a compromise solution is not a solution but a practical adjustment," and that "we should like to get beyond that point if possible though I think it is a correct analysis of where legal theory stands as of today." And Chafee was annoyed because he said Hocking blurred the line between law and morals and "constantly referred" to rights and duties without specifying if he meant a moral right or a legal right. His exasperation with Hocking on this point he expressed in a letter to Leigh about a year and a half after the commission began its study: "Frankly, I am getting a little weary of completing his education. He seems to suffer a relapse after every conference." But he persevered in his educational efforts, writing Hocking a few weeks later:

> In this subject of freedom of speech there are at least two reasons why law should not coincide with morals: (1) The usual reason for the distinction between law and morals, that law is a crude instrument, a carving-knife unsuited to the more delicate aspects of personal conduct and group happiness. (2) The special reason that government officials cannot be trusted to take a coercive part in the process of discussion, which directly affects their own beliefs, policies, and continuance in office—the main argument of Milton.
>
> I venture to think that you slide imperceptibly from moral problems into legal problems, or vice versa. The distinction stressed above is not preserved. At any rate, I am often left in doubt whether you are talking about philosophical freedom or about legal freedom, the sort which the First and Fourteenth Amendments protect and which is somewhat limited by statutes and settled judge-made rules.

As a philosopher inclined toward idealism, Hocking may well have been incapable of making the tidy distinction between law and morals that most twentieth-century lawyers draw. In any event, it is clear that central to his thinking about free expression were these twin beliefs: There is a moral right of expression carrying with it an obligation or duty—to the community and to truth—to exercise the right; if the moral duty is used irresponsibly or is rejected, the moral right ceases. The legal right of expression rests on the moral right; if the press does not take seriously its responsibility to enlighten the public, the moral right is forfeited; while this does not result in the immediate forfeiture of the legal right, it weakens the claim to the legal right, which may eventually be lost.[51]

Chafee was not unsympathetic to the general spirit of Hocking's ideas; in fact, after his commission service was over, he often spoke in somewhat comparable terms. For example, in suggesting a theme for a talk to journalists in San Francisco, he said: "In our country there is very little legal responsibility and I strongly believe that such a situation is right and ought to be preserved. This very absence of liability for what one says increases the moral obligation to carry out the purposes of the press . . . Yet there is a great risk that moral irresponsibility will lead to the growth of legal responsibility." But prior to making those observations, he emphasized that "my general thought is to distinguish sharply between legal responsibility and moral responsibility."[52] So Chafee began with the law of expression and went on to consider its implications for morality, while Hocking began with morality and could not conceive of the law of expression apart from it. Since many commissioners, starting with Chairman Hutchins, were predisposed toward moral considerations, Hocking's ideas received more prominence in the general report than Chafee thought wise.

During the drafting of the report in the fall of 1946, he objected to the presence of Hocking's ideas in the first chapter, which he considered the most important in the book (the published report contains six chapters, with the first entitled "The Problem and the Principles"). "Mr. Hocking's material should come out," he argued, adding that "the trouble is not with Hocking's material itself, but we have put about one-hundred measures from the slow movement into the middle of the first movement. Whether our symphony should have a slow movement at all is another question." Chafee did favor including a summary of Hocking's ideas as an appendix to the report, in addition to the publication of a separate volume by Hocking called *Freedom of the Press: A Framework of Principle*. When the general report came out, however, Hocking's ideas appeared in chapter 1 as well as in an appendix.

These differences over law and morals contributed to delays in producing a report on which all commissioners could agree after a line-by-line reading of the text.[53] Originally scheduled for release in the spring of 1946, the report was delayed until fall and then again until the spring of 1947. In the meantime Luce's original $200,000 was exhausted, and the Encyclopaedia Britannica (owned by the University of Chicago) provided a $15,000 bailout. Ultimately, a total of nine drafts was required, with MacLeish writing the early ones and Hutchins himself doing the last several.

As for Chafee's own contributions to the general report, one of the few parts entirely written by him is the passage on page 88 of *A Free and Responsible Press* calling for repeal of laws, including the peacetime sedition clauses of the 1940 Smith Act, against expression advocating the overthrow of the government when there is no clear and present danger. This proved to be the passage that Colonel McCormick found most objectionable. Chafee also wrote the passage from the middle of page 102 through the second paragraph on page 105 justifying recommendations for an independent agency to appraise media performance.[54]

When Chafee's *Government and Mass Communications* came out in October 1947, it was hailed by the *Tribune* and some other papers as a refutation of the general report whose ideas they saw as a threat to press freedom. Once again, he insisted that he had had no reservations about signing the report, which he said represented "an intensive contribution" by all the commissioners and "was extremely free from concessions on substance."[55] The fact that his book, which he considered an expansion of the general report, was seen as a repudiation of the commission's recommendations may have been because he stated the anti-government case with greater clarity and force. He also carefully traced how the commissioners' thinking evolved concerning the question of government controls:

Like many other members of the Commission, I started with the assumption, growing out of the First Amendment, that the less governmental control, the better. Then we kept running into the danger from a few concentrations of power, which inclined us toward the desirability of governmental control in some form . . . For a considerable time, I shared the general feeling that our recommendations would have to rely heavily on the Antitrust Laws and the power of the Federal Communications Commission to prevent undue centralization or regulate it drastically. Yet during the long ensuing discussions . . . this comprehensive program faded away. The members of the Commission could not agree on any specific application of those laws as a solution of our main problem—how can our society get the kind of press it needs?[56]

The commission generally did agree, as Chafee also explained, that governmental controls should be minimal, that free speech problems should be solved by balancing interests, and that the best hope for press improvement lay with the press itself.

In *Government and Mass Communications* Chafee chiefly addresses the question, What should be the future policy regarding the relationship of the government to the media in a society becoming increasingly collectivized? He naturally favors a policy of middlingness, one that takes account of both negative and positive freedom in the marketplace of ideas. He fears that the growing emphasis on how economic pressures distort mass communications might blind Americans to "the evils of a government-controlled press." But he also recognizes that freedom from governmental control is not enough and that the press should be free from private pressures as well. "Yet nobody should fall into the opposite error of assuming that economic obstacles are the only impairments of freedom or that a press which is dominated by the state is free merely because it is dissevered from all capitalistic controls. The meaning which our ancestors gave to liberty of the press, namely, freedom from the will of legislatures and officials, is just as vital today as it was in 1791." Indeed, he refers to the First Amendment as "a gun behind the door which must never be allowed to rust."[57]

Chafee devotes one chapter of the book to squarely considering whether the government could make the press better.[58] Characteristically, he warns against taking "a dogmatic position such as Jeffersonianism or Marxism—to name the two extremes" and refers to "an obligation to mediate between authoritarianism and laissez faire and see whether some guiding principle can be proposed which will help cure the evils of aimless discussion."[59] Then, after examining several proposed governmental remedies (the FCC's 1946 "Blue Book" spelling out program-service factors in license renewals, a Free Press Authority, subsidies, and other fiscal measures), he concludes: "I question whether law can impose more than a low minimum of fairness and decency upon the instrumentalities and frame reasonable regulations for the orderly flow of their output through the channels of communication to citizens. Compulsion cannot stop any tendency toward meaninglessness and vulgarity, and it will do more harm than good as a remedy for the uncertainty that truth will prevail over error. The only direct cure for these evils lies in the internal ideals of the [media] enterprises. Organized outsiders can improve these ideals by persuasion and approval, but not by force or extensive financial support."[60] The best hope, in other words, is for the press to be socially responsible and thus achieve balance between a free and a controlled press.

Chafee considered *Government and Mass Communications* to be his "best book," even though it was "a series of monographs rather than an integrated piece of writing." No doubt he liked it better than his other books on free speech because it was less concerned with facts and more concerned "with the wisdom of various methods of control without regard to the precise formulation of statutes and orders." It was "not a legal treatise to help lawyers write briefs but a series of sketches on various ways in which the law operates upon newspapers and other agencies of communication." His preparation of this series of memos to instruct commission colleagues in legal problems of the media also gave him a chance to update portions of *Free Speech in the United States* and readily resulted in what he called "a book for citizens who are interested in the press."[61]

His Hutchins Commission service also resulted in his appointment, in the spring of 1947, to the United Nations Subcommission on Freedom of Information and of the Press, composed of one representative from each of twelve nations. These activities, described in Chapter 10, brought him into conflict with representatives from the Soviet bloc, reinforced his growing belief in the need for the news media to be morally responsible, and caused him dismay when the American press refused to support United Nations efforts to improve the flow of information around the world. At times like this he referred to himself as "the home of lost causes" and regretted the time and energy devoted to free speech at the expense of other subjects that he cared about. His Hutchins Commission service, for example, meant that he gave less attention to the revision of the Uniform Negotiable Instruments Law.

In a letter explaining that the commission's work would keep him from attending an upcoming conference on the revision, he showed that the project was very much on his mind: "The English rule [on ordinary bank paper] is simple and so is the rule advocated in my old article [on overdue paper, printed in 1918] . . . I now think that there is something more to be said for the English rule than I realized in 1918. Still, if we now get away from my old rule, which was adopted in *Wolfe v. American Trust & Savings Bank*, 214 Fed. 761, I don't think that we shall change to the English rule."[52] Such ruminations are a useful reminder that Chafee was primarily a teacher of equity and, in the beginning, of Insurance and Bills and Notes (a subject regarded by many law professors as dull if not irksome). For Chafee, they were part of the exciting opportunity to assist in the reformation of American law offered by a Harvard professorship.

CHAPTER 6

The View from
the High Citadel

Chafee was practicing law in Providence during the spring of 1916 when Roscoe Pound, who had just become dean of the Harvard Law School after six years on the faculty, wrote to congratulate him on his decision to "cast your lot with us." And he added: "I am sure you will never have any cause to regret this, and confidently look forward to see you achieve great things in legal scholarship."[1] The offer of an assistant professorship had been tendered by Austin W. Scott, who became acting law dean after the drowning suicide of Ezra Ripley Thayer in September 1915 and served until Pound took over in February 1916. "I always thought that one of the most important things that I did [during the academic year 1915–16] was to go down to Providence and ask Chafee if he would come and join our faculty," Scott recalled.[2]

His wife, Betty, was a little hesitant about making the move because she had just refurbished their house on Providence's Hope Street on the assumption that "I was to live there the rest of my days." As for Chafee himself, who was thirty at the time, Scott believed that "he knew, really, that although he enjoyed practicing . . . the scholar's life was the life that he ought to lead." Years later, after her husband's death, Betty wrote "Scotty" that "I will always remember Zech's face and his very evident desire to come to Cambridge and the Law School . . . In Providence those few years I was with him there, he was constantly having to defend his beliefs and had to take very hard criticism from his family and some of his friends. When he came to Cambridge it was wonderful to see his happiness and his freedom from criticism."[3]

An opportunity to join *the* law school, as its alumni call it, comes to few men (and even fewer women), usually those who have demonstrated brilliance in legal scholarship or preeminence in practice—or both. All prestigious schools have come to require such credentials of prospective faculty, plus one other qualification—service on the law review board of their alma mater. Just three years earlier Chafee had graduated from the school with a brilliant record; his third-year average was the highest that year although a *C* in Contracts his first year caused him, as noted earlier, to finish second to Robert A. Taft in the cumulative class standings. And he had a fine albeit brief record with a leading Providence firm. But he had never served on the editorial board of the prestigious *Harvard Law Review*; in fact, he had done the unthinkable by flouting the warnings of his friend Claude Branch and rejecting a bid to join the *Review*. He did so because he earlier had done something else unusual for the time—married while still a student.

Chafee's marriage in 1912, with one year of law school still ahead of him, was unusual in other ways as well. The bride, Bess Frank Searle, was the daughter of Mrs. Bertha A. Searle of Troy, New York—a social worker with no formal training and a Socialist who became an admirer of the Soviet Union after the Revolution in 1917. (During the 1920s, she visited the USSR for a glimpse of "the future" and returned with even greater admiration for it. But like some other American true believers who made the pilgrimage, she was less enthusiastic while in Russia; indeed, as Zechariah Chafee III related, she was greatly annoyed while contending with the inadequate public transportation and lack of sanitation facilities.)[4]

Left a widow with three small children when Bess was two years old, Mrs. Searle gave her daughter to a spinster aunt to raise. Betty (as Bess came to be called) remained with the aunt until she was twelve, when her mother decided it was best for the child to be back with her. The decision infuriated the aunt, who never spoke to Betty again. Recalling her painful childhood after suffering a nervous breakdown in 1937, Betty wrote to her husband: "Aunt Ella didn't help to give me a normal family reaction—she being an 'old maid' always was playing up to men—and while she took care of me—as best she could, she wanted me to love her more than Mother. That started sort of a conflict—and made me rather dissatisfied with what I had and made me think [what] the other feller was having was perhaps better than my lot." The letter continues,

> Then when I did go back home . . . I had to readjust—with two brothers, a grandmother who made me feel I had done a mean thing to leave Aunt Ella—and a mother who was young—trying against terrific odds to keep ahead of poverty—and who was also craving attention and adoration from men without the settled quiet companionship which married life brings. She also wanted us to have things which were beyond our means—or perhaps it is truer to say we children wanted things beyond our means—& what happened you know—we lived in debt all of the time—and I wasn't very cooperative with what was going on. I was selfish—and looking out only for little Betty—I always liked things to go my [way]—and of course used all the feminine wiles I had to attain that end.[5]

Betty met Zech through his sister Elisabeth when both were students at the Garland School in Boston, where Betty was preparing to be a kindergarten teacher and Elisabeth was studying homemaking. When Betty spent some time as Elisabeth's guest in Providence, Mrs. Chafee, impressed with her appearance and manner, asked her to spend the summer of 1911 at Sorrento caring for seven-year-old Francis. "No time was wasted on me," Francis Chafee said in looking back on that summer. "It was 'get the hell in bed' so Betty could spend time with Zech."[6]

Everybody knew what was going on—except Mother Chafee. Nor did her son tell her just how serious his intentions were until after he had proposed. After learning of the proposal and of Betty's belief that they should both think it over before proceeding with wedding plans, Mrs. Chafee told him: "I think Betty's reply to your suit was a most wise and sensible one. You should both of you take plenty of time for such a very important decision. Neither should feel hurt if the other decides in the negative. But if you do hold fast, we shall all welcome Betty, and do our best to make her life among us a happy one."[7]

The wedding ceremony itself was also somewhat unusual. When the Episcopal Bishop of Maine announced that he would not let a minister of Betty's Presbyterian faith perform the wedding in Sorrento's Church of the Redeemer, it was decided to have an outdoor ceremony. So at 4:00 P.M. on Saturday, 20 July 1912, amidst fragrant wildflowers and with the Boston Symphony providing the music, the scion of a prominent Providence family and a kindergarten teacher from Troy went to the altar. After a honeymoon in Canada fishing, camping, and reading [Royce's *The Spirit of Modern Philosophy* and *The Odyssey*, among other books), they set up housekeeping at 16 Traill Street in Cambridge. They had a maid named Priscilla and an airedale named Hoots that was afraid of the maid ("because of her color, I suppose," Chafee informed his mother), and their home became a haven for law students who were invited—usually two at a time—for chafing-dish suppers on Sundays. Not long before commencement the next spring, Zechariah Chafee III arrived at 10:15 A.M. on 21 May 1913. He was "pretty thin," at just over six pounds, Chafee wrote his mother, adding that "Betty says to tell you that 'he' is the living image of my baby pictures."

On commencement day Betty reached the ceremony in time to hear only the last part of her husband's invited speech "The People v. the Law" because she was home nursing Zechie. Chafee's belief that fatherhood was delightful did not lessen his annoyance when the faculty made him cut his speech "down to the part which agreed with them and rejected the part which didn't." Despite this pre-publication censorship, he gave the speech with enthusiasm: "I spoke last, had to make two bows, and launched out with 'It is now some years since the Man with the Hoe was displaced as popular hero by the Man with the Muckrake.' That struck them in the right spot, and after a while I had enough laughs going so that I had to stop and wait for them to stop before I began talking again. It was a great sensation, I can tell you."[8] Rather conventional commencement fare (maybe partly because of the blue-penciling done by the faculty), Chafee's address emphasized the need for both legal rules and judicial discretion—the need for both permanence and change in the law, a view increasingly being expounded by Pound.[9] While Chafee was a student at the school, Pound had published his influential three-part series on sociological jurisprudence arguing that the law is not a static convention but rather a social institution that can be improved through intelligent human effort.[10]

Chafee said Pound's teaching was "a main influence in bringing me back to the school" as a faculty member. "There is a very remarkable group of men at the School," he told his mother-in-law at the time he received the teaching invitation, "and it is a wonderful opportunity to share in the modernizing of American law."[11]

To Chafee's mind, the professorship clearly constituted being in public life, not an alternative to it, as he sought to explain to his father: "You were saying at Sorrento that I might want to go into public life. That recalls the conversation Frankfurter, one of my colleagues, had with a prominent lawyer, when he gave up his work as counsel in Philippine affairs to go on the Law School faculty. The lawyer told him it was a great pity for him to leave public life, and Frankfurter replied, 'I shouldn't go there if I didn't believe I shall still be in public life.' " (Using Frankfurter as an example probably did not reassure Zechariah, Sr.; for, as Elisabeth Chafee Gamble explained, her parents had been upset at the prospect of Chafee's being around Jews at Harvard.) As one who harbored hopes of sitting on the U.S. Supreme Court one day, Chafee did concede to his father that the law school's portals might lead to bigger things: "Don't worry about me. I can see the world through library windows, and I don't intend that all the looking shall be in one direction . . . There is a good chance here to meet older men of importance in national affairs, and if they happen to like my books and should ever need me for work which seems more important than what I'm now doing, well and good. There's more than one road to Washington."[12]

Chafee, of course, never made it to the Supreme Court; that honor went to his friend Frankfurter, the only Harvard professor in the twentieth century to reach the judicial pinnacle.[13] As friends (and spouses) often are, the two professors were an odd couple in some ways: the one a short, immigrant Jew whose first five years in America were spent on New York's lower east side, and the other a much taller Yankee born with the proverbial silver spoon. But they were united by their brilliance as well as their Harvard law degrees, and their political outlook was similar; both had been Bryanites as young men and both became, although not unreservedly, defenders of Woodrow Wilson. (As for the New Deal, which gave Frankfurter a chance to wheel and deal as an adviser to Roosevelt, Chafee was supportive in the beginning but vacillating thereafter; the administration's going off the gold standard and Roosevelt's bid for a third term made him a temporary Republican in 1936 and in 1940.) Most important, perhaps, was their common desire to improve American life by reforming the law. And they were confident that they were in the right place at the right time, for the law school seemed to be entering a new era under Pound's leadership.

During the deanship of Christopher Columbus Langdell from 1870 to 1895, the school had become the preeminent law school in the country.[14] Langdell revolutionized legal education by developing "the case method" of teaching, using casebooks as sourcebooks. He believed his method was scientific because the cases (actually appellate opinions) were scrutinized rather like organisms in a laboratory, and the evolution of doctrine was derived from the process. The casebook replaced the treatise as the basic textbook, and the law professor ceased to be primarily a lecturer and became a modern-day Socrates who through careful questioning helped students find the law. Although the case method was understandably controversial, it not only survived at Harvard but also gained disciples who introduced it at other law schools; by the end of the century, it was firmly entrenched around the country, which it still is, just as it still is controversial. Although the method stands as Langdell's greatest monument, Harvard honored him in 1903 by creating the Langdell professorship, a chair Chafee held starting in 1938, and naming a mausoleumlike building after him in 1906.

Langdell's role in making the school great was not, however, limited to his development of the case method. "During his time," William Twining writes, "a rigorous system of examining was introduced, the foundations of a great library were laid, an outstanding faculty was recruited, and an atmosphere was generated which encouraged scholarly research and writing of a high order."[15] Under Langdell's immediate successors, James Barr Ames and Ezra Ripley Thayer, these gains were consolidated. Ames, one of the great "Harvard chancellors" (teachers of Equity) and an authority on negotiable instruments, was the second Harvard professor to teach with the case method, and ten of his own students became law school deans. After Ames died in 1910, the same year Pound came to Harvard as Story professor and Chafee enrolled as a student, Thayer left practice to head the school.

Thayer was the son of James Bradley Thayer, a Harvard law professor whose advocacy of judicial restraint greatly influenced Frankfurter and others. A brilliant perfectionist filled with self-doubt, the younger Thayer had previously passed up two offers to join the faculty, and, after becoming dean, he often questioned his fitness for academic work. "In hours of depression," the school's historian explains, "he sometimes asked colleagues whether the School really needed him."[16] Like Pound and Chafee, he read Greek, and Pound said of him, "His wit was Greek in its gracefulness and playfulness." Because of his extreme conscientiousness about his administrative duties as well as his teaching, he published little during his short life (his body was found in the Charles River on 14 September 1915). Significantly, he often said that "the central tragedy of life is that there are only twenty-four hours in a day"—a line that Chafee regularly quoted when he felt he was not accomplishing enough.

Although Pound was an innovative legal thinker, as dean he did virtually no tampering with the school's basic program. In fact, important aspects of the program had changed so little by the 1970s that a student could remark that "the resemblances between Dean Pound's first year [as a Harvard law student, in 1889] and mine are striking."[17] As one who believed that law professors should come primarily from the ranks of scholars rather than practitioners, he saw the law school's doctoral work as a training program for teachers. Further, he was convinced that law schools staffed with scholars using the case method of instruction would improve the practice of law.

This emphasis on scholarship, going back to Langdell, undoubtedly mitigated any possible stagnation given the lack of significant change in the school's curriculum and teaching methods. Bright young men like Chafee were recruited for the faculty (and, as in his case, were sometimes seen as prospective teachers while still students), then granted the freedom to pursue their own ideas and interests. The excitement Chafee felt as the 1916–17 academic year began, though tempered by concern for Zechie's health (he was ill and an infantile paralysis epidemic made "every ailment a terror"), is reflected in this diary entry: "At last I am free to pursue ideas unhampered by practical demands, to search out my own problems, and select the work for which I am best fitted."[18] Chafee's starting salary as an assistant professor was $3,000; the five-year appointment, as was customary, provided that, if he did well, after three years he would be advanced to a full professorship and a salary of $5,000. That could rise to $7,500 as a result of annual increments.

Upon returning to Cambridge he was delighted to find in the office he occupied, formerly that of Joseph D. Brannan, the blue books that he and Bob Taft had written in Brannan's Bills and Notes course—

the only exams Brannan had kept. Later, Chafee pasted his exam at the rear of a bound volume of his notes for the course, a volume he gave to the law school library along with similar ones containing notes from the other courses he had taken. These notes—written in his large, upright hand (he called it "childlike"; his friend Samuel Eliot Morison rightly called it "legible to a marked degree")—he had had bound in pigskin at the end of each year he was a student. The notes comprise twenty volumes—two of them for courses not taken for credit, Trusts and Theory of Law. Chafee the neophyte professor was also pleased, and even more amused, to hear rumors that a summary of Bills and Notes—prepared by him as a student and typed by some of his peers for circulation prior to the final exam—was selling for twelve dollars a copy. Referring to these rumors during his opening lecture in that course, he warned the students against parting with cash under false pretenses.[19]

Chafee was fascinated by the rather mundane subject matter of Bills and Notes and never lost interest in it, despite his mastery of public law in respect to free speech and other constitutional rights. He did concede that his "affection" for the material was somewhat cooled by his experience during the 1920s of getting out the fourth edition of the monumental *Brannan's Negotiable Instruments Law.*[20] About this project, "a terrific job" to which he devoted "every spare hour" for two years, he remarked: "I must admit that before I was through, I echoed the doubt Darwin expresses about his monograph on barnacles, that he is not sure it was worth the trouble and time."[21]

Chafee was aware that many students found the study of negotiable instruments to be inherently dreary and that Brannan's classroom preoccupation with case citations had prompted a young poet to produce this quatrain:

> Brannan got up and put on his shoe—
> (Fifty Michigan forty-two).
> He put on his coat and went out the door—
> (Twenty Wisconsin sixty-four).[22]

His concern about making the course interesting appears in notes he wrote himself about preparing a casebook on Bills and Notes. "A casebook is a pedagogical instrument, not a reference book for practitioners," he said. "Many lists of cases swamp the student, cost money and time." Noting that the course was "partly static . . . &

partly dynamic," he called the static part "probably the dullest thing in Harvard Law School. Moreover, coming at the beginning of the B-N course, it depresses it unduly. Obviously, it is inevitable, but the evil can be mitigated." The solution lay in minimizing the number of cases in the early part of the book and the course ("Every case omitted brings the fighting part of the course that much closer") and making the Negotiable Instruments Law (NIL), the uniform statute states began adopting in 1896, the core of the course rather than the common law. The latter should be used to illustrate the principles behind the NIL, the "fighting part" of the course. "All common law doctrines which do not embody a real principle do not deserve a case—e.g., position of anomalous endorser. Many cases should be used on points that the Act leaves unsettled or conflicting."[23]

In addition to demonstrating his desire to make courses as interesting as possible, this decision to give greater emphasis to statutory law may have been a reaction to the school's focus on the work of appellate courts at a time when the legislative function was expanding as one response to social problems caused by the post–Civil War surge in business and industry. In any event, Chafee later had this to say about his early years on the faculty (the comments are in a critique of an autobiographical manuscript by Francis Sayre, an expert in labor law and his former colleage and co-defendant in the Trial at the Harvard Club):

> There is one just adverse criticism which, looking backward, I believe can be made of the teaching in our time. It was too much oriented toward courts and litigation. We trained students almost exclusively to win cases in court or to shape transactions so that later lawyers would win cases if they arose. And when we saw shortcomings in the law, as every teacher often did, we pretty much confined ourselves to hopes that judges could be persuaded to adopt a sounder rule.
>
> The terrible impact of the Great Depression re-enforced the teaching of Pound and others about the usefulness of legislation as a means of changing law.
>
> Take your fields and mine. The Interpleader Act of 1936 [drafted by Chafee] accomplished what judges couldn't have done except with enormous difficulty and gradualness. The

objectionable labor injunctions faded fast because of the Norris-LaGuardia Act and the Wagner Act. Case law was not the way out.[24]

Recalling that the typical exam question ended with "Should A recover?" or "Judgment for whom?" he told Sayre that "I stuck pretty close to the old question, 'Judgment for whom?' right to the end, but I'm glad others are interested in new ways of making good lawyers."

There are several ironies in the fact that Chafee never strayed far from Langdellian orthodoxy. For one thing, the first significant attack on Langdell had been made by one of Chafee's heroes—Oliver Wendell Holmes, Jr., a law school insider in a dual sense because he had both studied and taught there. And Holmes's legal ideas evolved into what came to be called the "realist movement"; its incarnation especially at Columbia and Yale starting in the 1920s posed a major challenge to the Harvard philosophy of legal education. For another, the so-called realists drew much of their original inspiration from the sociological jurisprudence of Chafee's mentor Pound.

To Holmes, who had taught during Langdell's early years, and other realists (philosophically speaking, as Chafee once noted, they were nominalists in contrast to the realism of Plato), Langdell stood for "the enemy"—formalism. In 1880 Holmes criticized Langdell in reviewing a casebook on Contracts prepared by the dean: "Mr. Langdell's ideal in the law, the end of all his striving, is the *elegantia juris* or *logical* integrity of the system as a system. He is, perhaps, the greatest living legal theologian. But as a theologian he is less concerned with his postulates than to show that the conclusions from them hang together."[25] And in a letter to Sir Frederick Pollock, Holmes referred to the dean and his book in even harsher terms: "A more misspent piece of marvellous ingenuity I never read, yet it is most suggestive and instructive . . . He is all for logic and hates any reference to anything outside of it, and his explanations and reconciliations of the cases would have astonished the judges who decided them. But he is a noble old swell whose knowledge, ability and idealist devotion to his work I revere and love."[26] But such criticisms from Holmes, despite the influence he increasingly enjoyed, did nothing to deflect the school from its Langdellian path.

Nor did Pound's development of sociological jurisprudence, which like realism was part of the revolt against formalism and which carried within it the genes of the social sciences, particularly sociology. The kinship between Pound's philosophy and realism was noted by Karl Llewellyn of Columbia, a leading realist, in remarking that "half of the commonplace equipment" of the realism of the 1920s and 1930s had been forged by Pound: the theory of interests, the concept of law as social engineering, the stress on cooperation between law and the social sciences and on the need for data about "the law in action" (in contrast to "the law in books"), and the concern for the nature of judicial discretion.[27]

Yet Pound not only did not make the social sciences an integral part of Harvard's curriculum, he emerged as an arch critic of realism.[28] It has been suggested that if Pound had truly understood realism, he would have approved of it because of its affinity with sociological jurisprudence.[29] Since there have been many strains of realism rather than one distinct species, Pound may well have been confused. However, he understood clearly enough that realists were united by a desire to expose how the law *really* works, in contrast to how it is thought to work or ought to work, and that quite a few of them favored imitating natural-science methods, rather than those of the social sciences, in explicating the law. Pound, by contrast, was interested in what the law ought to be and do in modern industrial society. And what it ought to do he described this way in a well-known lecture delivered in 1921:

> For the purpose of understanding the law of today I am content with a picture of satisfying as much of the whole body of human wants as we may with the least sacrifice. I am content to think of law as a social institution to satisfy social wants—the claims and demands and expectations involved in the existence of civilized society—by giving effect to as much as we may with the least sacrifice, so far as such wants may be satisfied or such claims given effect by an ordering of human conduct through politically organized society.[30]

Moreover, Pound believed that "if the physical sciences have for their function to discover what is, the social sciences have for theirs to discover what ought to be and how to bring it about . . . What-ought-to-be has no place in physical science. It has first place in the social sciences."[31] For Pound, accordingly, it was the method of the social sciences that could be useful in studying the law, even though as dean he did little to incorporate the social sciences into the curriculum. Was he, as William Twining suggests, imperceptive about the implications of his sociological jurisprudence for teaching and research?[32]

Pound was a busy man—much of the time, he had a staff of only two to help with administration; he often taught a heavier load than some regular faculty; he did wide reading and research, including in various foreign languages; he was frequently absent during public service stints such as helping to direct the Wickersham Commission's study of law enforcement. And it may be that he was just too busy to work out his philosophy in a more systematic and effective way. His failure to do so is all the more regrettable because he was not a good administrator.[33]

He found it hard to delegate work despite his small staff, he took any criticism as a criticism of him, he lost his temper easily. ("He once told me," Austin W. Scott related, "that the reason he lost his temper was that as a child he had been left-handed, and his parents tied it behind him—frustrating him and making him angry.") And, as John M. Maguire, who taught Evidence at the school from 1923 to 1957, put it, "he was not above telling the kind of lie that gave him an easy escape. For example, he once told the faculty that a no-smoking rule was necessary because of fire insurance requirements. I did a little checking and found that the university had no fire insurance but was self-insured." The dean did not lack a sense of humor. "He had a jovial side—he liked parties," Scott recounted, "but he had a very complicated character. I did what few did—tried to kid him a little. Once he brought in a commendation from China for work he had done there. It was beautiful, and I said so. Then I said, pointing to one of the Chinese characters, 'But isn't this a misprint?' 'What's that, what's that?' he said. I had to explain that I didn't know Chinese. It was kind of flat when I tried to explain it. I think it shows how he would immediately resent any criticism."[34]

Many of Pound's most volcanic eruptions were set off by Chafee's friend Frankfurter, who, Maguire and Scott agreed, considered all questions from a narrow perspective. "Felix had the irritating habit of treating any question—even how many hours a first-year man should take—as if it were a moral question," Scott said. "If you disagreed with him, he treated you as if you were morally at fault some way. That irritated Pound and some other faculty."

For the most part, Chafee either sided with Pound or remained silent instead of openly expressing disagreement. When Chafee stood alongside the dean in opposing legal realism, this was consistent with his overall admiration for his mentor, of course. But it also reflected his approval of "the entirely new social viewpoint" that Pound, and then Frankfurter, had brought to the school—"making the 'ought' in the 'law as it ought to be' a much richer word."[35] Commenting on an influential 1930 article by Llewellyn, a friendly adversary in the field of commercial law, Chafee objected to the view that empirical investigation of behavior must be carried out to determine if a particular rule actually controlled a case:

> Even after a considerable number of carefully proved instances have been collected, the important question still remains whether those instances are sporadic or represent a prevailing tendency. One wonders how he can make this critical decision until he is sure that he has accumulated somewhere near a majority of all the instances . . . If we professors must supervise such investigations for all the topics in our courses, it is going to be hard to find time to read cases.
>
> . . . I strongly doubt my own capacity for the kind of investigations which you describe. My work in the law library corresponds to my training and inclinations . . . When I contemplate the great change of activities which I should have to make to carry out your program, I feel like the aged clergyman in Maxwell's novel, *Spinster of This Parish*, who said he was too old to change his faith.[36]

If Chafee remained faithful to Harvard's way of teaching, he often wished that there were fewer students to teach. For a considerable period, including much of Pound's deanship, the school took just about anybody who applied.[37] This loose admissions policy coupled with the school's strict grading standards routinely produced a first-year flunkout rate of close to one-third. The faculty member best illustrating this alarming attrition was the legendary Edward H. (Bull) Warren, who ritualistically advised new students to "look at the man on your left and the man on your right because next year one of you won't be here." Scott, noting that "the Bull" was also one of the most ominous practitioners of the Socratic method, recalled with amusement a rare colloquy in which a student, who happened to be Puerto Rican and thus even more apprehensive than his classmates for whom English was their first language, gave Warren an acceptable answer:

> Warren: Would you find for the plaintiff or the defendant?
> Student: For the plaintiff.
> Warren: Right.
> Student: Jesus!

Warren was also given to rendering extreme personal judgments of students in front of their peers. During one class session, for example, he told W. Barton Leach, who later became a member of the faculty, that he was unfit to practice law simply because he gave a wrong answer. "But his pronouncements in class seem not to have had the damaging psychological effect that you might suppose," Scott said. "Most students dismissed his comments with 'Oh, that's just the Bull.' Most students are mature, after all." Although Scott regarded Warren as "a good teacher in some ways," he did not think browbeating students was an appropriate way to get them to work.[38] Chafee was of much the same mind.

And both Chafee and Scott, along with Frankfurter and Maguire, were opposed to the open-admissions-high-flunkout-rate policy, which was perpetuated by Pound. Making matters worse from their standpoint was the fact that the dean actually favored a policy of growth. As a recent Frankfurter biographer has written, Pound "believed that more was better . . . that Harvard could become the General Motors of American law schools."[39]

Frankfurter—who in his reminiscences described Pound as "a scare cat" who "wanted to be all things to all people"[40]—was the most strident critic and voiced strong opposition to Pound's expansionist plans. "There is not the slightest chance of that limitation of numbers [of students] which you and I so deeply care about," he told Chafee who had written Frankfurter from Europe while on sabbatical in 1926: "The physical crowding is bad, but the mental crowding is worse. Every year I am increasingly troubled by the number of men in the class whom I can't get to know by sight and the number of names on exams which are only names. More and more I am grading books, not men . . . To my mind *any* scheme of limitation is better than more numbers."[41]

Yet despite his strong preference for limiting or cutting back enrollment rather than increasing it, in this and other matters Chafee seldom opposed Pound openly. Scott remembered Chafee as one who was "not a great talker" at faculty meetings although he spoke forcefully at times. "He did often make the point that there should be more vacations." As a faculty member, he was "absolutely independent," in Scott's words. "He didn't get involved in politics, not that there ever really were Pound and Frankfurter factions [as the conventional wisdom has held]. There was no clique of any kind as far as Chafee was concerned."[42]

Frankfurter obviously wished that Chafee, who was like-minded on many questions, would have come out of the closet and helped to form a Felix faction. At times, he upbraided Chafee for failing to take a clear stand in opposition to the dean. Perhaps the angriest Frankfurter ever got at Chafee over a law school matter—later, they had heated exchanges over the judiciary versus the legislature as the best guardian of civil liberties—was in connection with a bitter dispute in 1928 over the hiring of a Jew. The man was Nathan Margold, an assistant U.S. attorney, a Frankfurter protégé, and a graduate of the school, who had spent a year on the faculty before being offered a five-year appointment to teach criminal law. After the faculty voted, with two nays, to make that offer, President Lowell kept the nomination from going to the Board of Overseers.

On 10 February 1928, Chafee, Francis Bohlen, and Edmund M. Morgan met with the president to discuss the case. "Mr. Morgan presented the evidence which led the faculty to recommend the appointment of Mr. Margold as instructor last year and as an assistant professor this year," Chafee said in a memo summarizing the meeting, "and in addition evidence of his qualifications secured by attendance of some members of the faculty at lectures since his appointment was recommended." On the crucial question of possible anti-Semitism, he wrote: "When it was mentioned that one member of the faculty had voted against Mr. Margold because he was a Jew, Mr. Lowell said with obvious sincerity: 'That, of course, has nothing to do with the question.' "[43]

Pound stated his view that the president should not be challenged on Margold at an acrimonious faculty meeting in late February. After Chafee voted with the majority in backing Pound's position, he received a reproving note from Frankfurter: "You can have no more doubt than did Maguire, Morgan, Bohlen, Powell, Magruder, Landis, Foster, and Redlich that [Margold] was not rejected on the merits, that the rule of reason did not operate." To Frankfurter, as he put it in another note to Chafee, "the Margold affair raise[d] . . . basic questions of human dignity," and "self-respect & the arbitrary conduct of authority [were] at stake."[44]

Chafee could scarcely be accused of being insensitive to basic questions of human dignity and the abuse of authority. But because he was nothing if not loyal, his offending vote may have been dictated by loyalty more than anything—loyalty to Lowell, who had defended him during his 1921 trial, and loyalty to Pound, who had also stood up for him in 1921 and who had influenced his thinking about the law as well as his decision to enter teaching. Chafee's loyalty to Lowell and Pound may also have had some influence on his thinking about the controversial Sacco-Vanzetti case, which in 1926–27 had become a divisive issue at the school—the more so because of Frankfurter's published criticisms of Judge Webster Thayer's conduct of the trial. Indeed, the effects of that controversy and Frankfurter's role in it lingered on as the faculty deliberated the hiring of Margold and of James M. Landis, another Frankfurter protégé, as the school's first professor of legislation and pondered the enrollment problem and other policy questions.[45]

At least partly because Chafee was in Europe on sabbatical at the peak of the Sacco-Vanzetti controversy, he said relatively little about it at the time. Of course, it is possible that, even if he had been in Cambridge, his sense of loyalty would have prompted him to follow Pound's lead and maintain a posture of public silence. Although Pound said in private that he did not think the defendants had received an impartial trial, he decided, perhaps with the imbroglio over the *Abrams* case in mind, not to risk further criticisms of himself and the school.[46] His decision proved futile anyway because of his nemesis Frankfurter's excoriation of the state's case in the *Atlantic Monthly* and in a small book spun off from the article.[47] Chafee's views of Sacco and Vanzetti and the case against them have been pieced together from correspondence over three decades, starting with his reaction to Frankfurter's published criticisms. Writing Frankfurter from aboard a ship bound for home in August 1927, he said:

> Well, you've made a great fight and I hope you are not too much overwhelmed by failure.
>   Nothing could have been done better than you did. If the same wisdom and restraint had been shown from the start

by the counsel of the accused and particularly by their friends, the chance for pardon might have been better . . . you did at least mitigate the unfairness of the trial somewhat by helping to secure the commission of inquiry [headed by President Lowell; this governor's Advisory Committee is explained in the following text]. That it was appointed is something to the good, though it reported unfavorably. And beyond this, all that can be done is to set ourselves the more earnestly to make the crooked ways straight in the realms of justice. Here's hoping that you and I shall be together for many long years at this task![48]

It is interesting that some weeks before he wrote Frankfurter, Chafee had corresponded with John H. Wigmore, dean of the Northwestern University School of Law and an expert on the law of evidence, who had written a letter to the *Boston Transcript* criticizing Frankfurter's *Atlantic* article.[49] At the time, Chafee had received a letter from his colleague Maguire saying: "The Sacco-Vanzetti controversy has been really harrowing. Wigmore's ungentlemanly and unscrupulous attack on Felix is of course the worst local feature."[50] Despite this verbal assault on his friend Frankfurter, Chafee, who had taught evidence during his early years at Harvard, wrote Wigmore suggesting that he issue a statement on the case. Wigmore was "unable to accede to your very complimentary suggestion" partly because he thought that "Frankfurter's appeal to the public before the [state] Supreme Court has decided [the case] . . . overshadowed the probative problem."[51]

Back in Sorrento after sabbatical and before the start of the 1927–28 academic year, Chafee again wrote Frankfurter, this time reassuring him that there was nothing improper in his commenting on the case while it was on appeal to the Massachusetts Supreme Judicial Court: "Counsel ought not to try their cases [in the press] and others should so write as not to stir a mob against the court, etc., but within 'the limits of fair comment' I know of no canon of legal ethics that applies or of common sense . . . So forget the whole business as much as you can [before classes resume] . . . and have a good loaf."[52]

Although in his first letter to Frankfurter he had referred to "the unfairness of the trial," two decades later he told a Rhode Island friend that he did not think Judge Thayer's handling of the trial was unfair. However, he did regard the judge as "completely unsuited" to deal with motions for a new trial—motions that he rejected, thus helping to clear the way for the eventual executions after an unsuccessful appeal. Nor did Chafee think that this distinction—between the judge's fairness at the trial and his unsuitability to decide if a new trial should be held—was ever grasped by President Lowell as chairman of the Advisory Committee appointed by Governor Alvan T. Fuller to determine if the defendants had received a fair trial.[53] To some observers, the committee's determination that the trial was fair seemed a foregone conclusion because of the Boston Brahmin background of its chairman. As John F. Moors, a Harvard classmate of Lowell's and a member of the Harvard Corporation who later worked with Chafee in raising defense funds for Alger Hiss, put it, "Lawrence Lowell was incapable of seeing that two wops could be right and the Yankee judiciary could be wrong."[54] Chafee also told his Rhode Island friend, an author planning in 1946 to write a poetic account of the case similar to Browning's treatment of a murder trial in *The Ring and the Book*, that he ought to "explore the minds of the different people who were connected with the case, including Half-Boston and the Other-Half Boston . . . [and] to make Lowell a key figure of your poem."[55]

"Whatever conclusion one reaches as to their guilt," Chafee wrote on another occasion, "it will probably be increasingly a cause for regret that an irrevocable punishment should have been inflicted when so much doubt existed."[56] But he did not believe that their deaths in and of themselves resulted in any real loss to society, as he made clear in a letter to Harold J. Laski: "Shortly after my return to America, the death of two prominent Massachusetts citizens was announced in the newspapers and Felix was much depressed at their loss. There were times when I wished that he might drink of the waters of Lethe because I felt that he was endangering his health and I consider his life more valuable than theirs."[57] As a foe of capital punishment, he was pleased that reaction to the executions helped advance the goals of the new Massachusetts Council for the Abolition of the Death Penalty, which he headed for several years.

What seem to have been Chafee's last pronouncements on the Sacco-Vanzetti affair came in the latter 1950s as part of his critique of Frank Sayre's autobiographical manuscript. He upbraided his former colleague for criticizing the faculty's failure to make courses more relevant and to discuss Sacco-Vanzetti, including at faculty meetings. If the case was not aired at meetings, he suggested, the reason was not "intellectual lethargy on the part of the older men" but their unwillingness to turn luncheons into harangues that would do no good, "for how would they alter the court decisions or the governor's decision about commutation? . . . The only practical result would be to divide by bad feeling a group which ought to be carrying on an important intellectual enterprise effectively."[58]

As the scholarly literature demonstrates, the case, particularly Frankfurter's published criticisms of the trial, did distress the faculty and further damaged Pound's deanship. Through it all, Chafee remained openly loyal to Pound until he stepped down as dean upon reaching mandatory retirement age in 1936 and became Harvard's first university professor. But Chafee also continued grumbling to close colleagues about the large numbers of students.

If he was undemonstrative at faculty meetings, he often used letters and memoranda to unburden himself about school conditions that displeased him. And nothing—not even the size of the student body—upset him more than what he called "the normal school." This was the graduate curriculum, which had been greatly expanded by Pound, who (as previously explained) saw it primarily as a program for the training of teachers who would go forth and improve legal education, and the profession, around the nation. Much of Chafee's disdain for graduate education flowed logically from his conviction that the law school's basic mission was to educate practitioners and his corollary belief that the faculty should be mainly a body of teachers, not researchers. "My own feeling is that degrees are just labels which play altogether too large a part in academic life and that a man ought to be big enough to disregard them and do what he wants," he told a former student inquiring about graduate work. "Indeed if I had my own way there would be no graduate degree given here, but merely an opportunity for advanced work. I like to quote in this connection William Watson's lines about Matthew Arnold, 'He kept his eyes upon the gold, not on the prize.' "[59]

Some of his opposition to the graduate program, however, was more self-serving. Although he ranked teaching ahead of research, he believed that professors should do research; thus he resented the fact that faculty mainly involved in graduate work had fewer students and thus more time for research—and leisure—than those like himself, who while teaching hundreds of students also had some graduate-level responsibilities. The depth of his feelings is revealed in a memo he wrote in 1936, near the end of the Pound era, responding to a curriculum committee's recommendations. "Nobody has ventured to suggest that the graduate teachers should teach our classes or correct part of our examinations," he wrote. "We have often had the pleasure of bidding them a fond farewell as they set out for Europe on the first of June or the twentieth of May, locking their offices at the moment when a large bundle of blue books was carried into ours . . . Although I realize the value of improving the level of legal education at Siwash, I care very much less about it than I do about my own unwritten book on 'Unfair Competition' or numerous other projects in which I am interested." He suggested that teachers of undergraduates be given graduate responsibilities only if they asked for them and that the responsibilities be concentrated in those faculty members with a keen interest in that particular kind of legal education. "I recognize that it is valuable just as coal mining is valuable or flying the Atlantic is, but I should be very much happier if I could devote all my time to something else."[60]

But Chafee was a team player, and the following summer, after Pound had stepped down, he told Acting Dean Edmund M. Morgan that he was even willing to serve as chairman of the Graduate Committee "if nobody better" was available because ' so long as we have [the normal school], we must make it as good as possible." Writing from the University of Chicago, where he earned $450 for teaching Equity during the first half of the summer session, he also explained that he would like to get off the Graduate Committee after one more year—a year ahead of the expiration of his four-year term—and he added: "Some times I have thought of applying for a Research Professorship so as to get time to write, but this would throw me all the more with the Normal School men whom I don't care for and take me away from the real fellows who stand up in our regular courses and whom I like intensely. So I am rather puzzled. Perhaps now that I have finished with the worries of carrying two boys through college in a depression, I shall find more time in a day . . . [I] should like to chat with you about it some day next winter."[61] But by then, he was on medical leave recovering from a nervous breakdown.

At the time of Pound's retirement, Chafee's views as to his successor were solicited by James B. Conant, who replaced Lowell as Harvard president in 1933. Chafee's list of possibilities—presented during a personal meeting with Conant and in follow-up memos—

contained the names of teachers at other universities (including Dean Charles E. Clark of Yale and Dean Young B. Smith of Columbia), practicing lawyers, and one judge—Federal District Judge John M. Woolsey of New York ("The only judge who seems to me young enough and good enough to consider"), who had achieved some notoriety a few years earlier by allowing the unexpurgated version of James Joyce's *Ulysses* to be distributed in the United States. Telling Conant that the most important quality was "a sense of adventure in the law," he said he thought that "we can match most of these [possibilities] inside." His top two choices were his colleague Scott and Henry Wolfe Biklé, formerly a part-time professor at the University of Pennsylvania and general counsel for the Pennsylvania Railroad. If neither of them was available, he told Conant, he would prefer James M. Landis, whom he had backed earlier for the appointment as professor of legislation.[62] When Landis was named dean, Chafee, despite his great loyalty to Pound, joined most of his colleages in rejoicing that a long overdue change for the better had come about.

Ironically, Frankfurter had not favored Landis for the deanship and lobbied the president and the faculty against his onetime protégé. Whatever his basic reason for opposing Landis, who had left the school for government service in 1933 and become chairman of the Securities and Exchange Commission two years later, Frankfurter rightly suspected that he would prove too ambitious to stay for very long in one position.[63] Within a few years, he was off again on government service during World War II, and after the war he returned to Cambridge for an even shorter stay. But during his brief stints as dean, he effected enough changes for one scholar to refer to him as the school's first reform dean.[64] Shortly after Landis took over in 1937, Chafee told a former colleague: "[He] is doing a grand job . . . and we are all very happy. It is perfectly plain that there were never really any divisions in the Faculty except *ad hoc*."[65]

Two important changes Landis promptly implemented had been recommended by the faculty before he assumed the deanship. The first was a tightening of admission standards, which a decade earlier had been slightly altered to reject applicants with what Chafee called "spotty" college records. Now the way was cleared to use applicants' college records in tandem with those of recent law students and the latter's grades in the school to predict rates of success and failure. Out of these data emerged minimum averages for different colleges that were used as the crucial entrance requirements; the minimum adopted for Harvard College graduates, for instance, was a C average because experience had shown that those with anything lower had an 84-percent chance of flunking out.[66]

By early 1939 Chafee was able to boast that "our new policy of selecting the men carefully for admission has reduced our mortality rate to twenty percent [from the legendary thirty-three], and we hope to get it still lower."[67] The total number of students was never reduced, however. The law school had about 1,400 students in 1937–38, and more than 1,500 at the time of Chafee's retirement in 1956. In more recent years enrollment has been stabilized at about 1,800. Yale and Stanford, by comparison, have only about one-third that many law students.

The other major change implemented by Landis consisted of a curriculum overhaul, a subject making up most of his first report to the president covering the 1936–37 academic year. (By contrast, the report devoted only one paragraph to admissions and enrollments, but that was enough to help justify the aforementioned changes.) The faculty faced the problem of introducing new material growing out of rapid legal change, the dean explained, and the solution lay in compressing materials during the first two years and in stressing electives along with seminars centered on research and writing during the third year. Specific examples of proposed course changes included combining Bills and Notes with Sales, both formerly one-year courses, to make one course called Commercial Law and reducing Criminal Law, a field few graduates entered, to a half-year course. These changes were to be "experimental" in the beginning.[68]

The report of the school's Curriculum Committee, which gave rise to such reforms, was strongly criticized by Chafee on several counts. "I looked for some discussion of the place that the school and the law ought to take in the life of the nation. Instead I find only the present elements of the life of the school differently arranged and somewhat differently stressed," he said in a memo. "Sometimes I think that our great predecessors bequeathed to us such an admirable classroom method that we are in danger of running along on our own momentum." A more specific objection was that the third-year seminars, with their emphasis on research and writing, would mean additional work for the faculty who would thus have less time for research.[69]

Although Chafee was always somewhat resentful of the time taken up by grading the students' research papers (he complained particularly about the major paper, comparable to a law review article, that became a requirement of all third-year students at this time), he was ever the team player. In the "News-Letter from Zech Chafee, Jr." that he sent to the class of 1913 as its twenty-fifth reunion approached, he spoke glowingly of Landis and of the recent changes while reassuring his classmates that permanence and change were being accorded equal treatment.

"Our true danger," he said, "was not reckless adventure, but complacency and stodginess. By having all sorts of viewpoints on the Faculty, we are avoiding this danger; and we are very fortunate in acquiring a new Dean who has had direct contacts with the work of one of those important administrative bodies, whose activities now require so much attention and study from members of the bar, in addition to the work of judges."[70] Chafee did not note that the Landis deanship had also made it possible for President Conant to stop attending faculty meetings, a practice he had followed during Pound's last years in an effort to maintain peace. "By the mid-1930s," as Landis's biographer explains, the faculty's "warring had become so intense that President Conant decided to preside personally over the law school's weekly faculty meetings, an assemblage he described as 'the most quarrelsome group of men I ever encountered.' "[71]

No doubt the post-Poundian tranquility of faculty meetings alone justified Arthur E. Sutherland's labeling of the Landis deanship as "a pleasant and wholesome era of good feeling." He was speaking only of the brief period before World War II, however. For some faculty felt that the dean had betrayed them and the school by departing for government service after having made such a noble start. And by the time he returned as dean his personal life was in disarray; he was drinking heavily and continuing an affair with a woman who had been his secretary in Cambridge, then in Washington, and once again in Cambridge. When he finally left his wife, Stella, and announced that the separation was irreconcilable, the conservative Cambridge community was stunned and most faculty colleagues sided with Mrs. Landis, who had been a great hit in the role of first lady of the law school. His second stint as dean lasted from January 1945 until April 1946, when he returned to Washington as head of the Civil Aeronautics Board.

Chosen as Landis's successor was Erwin N. Griswold, who had been a student of Chafee's and a member of the faculty since 1934. As Landis had originally been a skillful and innovative administrator in contrast with the irascible and conservative Pound, so Griswold was a man of strong character in contrast to the restless Landis whose increasing erraticism had left the school's administration in a shambles.[72] Aware of his Puritan and Quaker antecedents, Griswold was a teetotaler as opposed to his hard-drinking predecessor. "You never got alcohol at his home," related John Maguire who rated Griswold "damned good" as dean.[73] At the time of his appointment, faculty expectations were obviously high "When the president asked all of us for suggestions [for Landis's successor]," Austin Scott said, "almost everyone put Griswold first. That surprised the president a little, and I was a little surprised myself because his manner wasn't always one that would make you happy."[74] It was that manner that made him, as Joel Seligman writes in *The High Citadel*, "the most forceful personality ever to lead Harvard Law School."[75]

Despite the brevity of his postwar deanship, Landis was back at the school long enough to set in motion still other significant changes in the curriculum. The vehicle was a new Committee on Legal Education that he appointed, with Lon Fuller as chairman. But its proposals became reality under Griswold during Chafee's last decade on the faculty, a period that included what Chafee referred to as "the debacle of Equity at Harvard."[76]

Chafee, as a Brown University senior, 1907.

Bess (Betty) Searle Chafee, shortly before
her marriage in 1912.

Chafee, in 1920, the year *Freedom of Speech*
was published.

Chafee and Walter H. Pollak, colleagues on the Wickersham Commission, 1929–1931. Pollak was a leading civil liberties lawyer.

Robert, Betty, Chafee, Ellen, and Anne (Nancy) at Red Roof, Sorrento, 1940.

Chafee, sailing on Frenchman's Bay, Maine, 1942.

Harvard Law School faculty, 1950. Chafee is at far right, front row. Next to him is Austin W. Scott, who hired Chafee while serving as acting dean in 1916. Directly behind Chafee is John M. Maguire, longtime colleague and friend. Dean Erwin N. Griswold is front row, center.

Chafee, testifying before the U.S. Senate Subcommittee
on Constitutional Rights, 1955

Chafee, in 1956, shortly before his retirement.

Chafee and granddaughter Elizabeth Tillinghast, 1951.

CHAPTER 7

The Last of the Harvard Chancellors

Two years before Chafee's retirement in 1956, a student in a colleague's seminar on legal education asked him about his teaching methods and objectives. He referred the young man to two articles and a book review he had written. And then, demonstrating how annoyed he could get when he thought his time was being unduly trenched upon, especially if there was the slightest connection with the normal-school mentality, he fired off a note to the professor in charge of the offending course:

> This case raises a . . . problem of great importance to legal education, which perhaps deserves another seminar paper under your direction. How are law school professors to be enabled to do their own research and at the same time give proper attention to students? St. Paul tells us to be given to hospitality, and I have always felt that my students had a first lien on my time . . . Remember the story of the man who was asked whether he would rather have $6,000,000 or six daughters, and he said six daughters because "That would be enough." I am all for the seminar system, but it means several hundred third year students writing papers.[1]

He went on to propose several safeguards "to prevent the time for our own research from being exhausted on the researches of students in other men's seminars."

It is significant that all three items to which Chafee referred the student had been written three decades earlier. The two articles became the first and second chapters of his book *The Inquiring Mind*, published in 1928 as a partial updating of *Freedom of Speech*. The first or title chapter had appeared in the August 1924 number of *The American Mercury*—the new magazine of George Jean Nathan and H. L. Mencken (who told Chafee after his piece had gone to the printer, "The cashier will insult you soon")—and originally was a talk given at Brown University for the twentieth anniversary of his old club, The Sphinx. Chapter 2 of *The Inquiring Mind* is called "Give Your Minds Sea Room," from a poem by William Blake that his friend Archibald MacLeish liked to quote. Both "The Inquiring Mind" and "Give Your Minds Sea Room" were subsequently reprinted by other author-editors. Answering a request in 1935 to reprint the former, Chafee noted it had been reprinted four times already and said it apparently appealed to general readers more than anything he had published. And in 1953, twenty-six years after Chafee presented "Give Your Minds Sea Room" as a Brown Honors Day Address, a Northwestern University speech professor praised it while asking to reprint it: "The vitality of this talk and its application to present generations of students are remarkable."[2]

In these two articles Chafee presented his views on education. He started from the assumption that "knowledge is not a series of propositions to be absorbed, but a series of problems to be solved. Or rather I should say, to be partly solved, for all the answers are incomplete and tentative." Outside the field of the three R's, where there are established facts to be learned such as the multiplication tables, there is a wider and more nebulous form of knowledge with which citizens must become acquainted if democratic government is to cope successfully with life in an advanced industrial society. Such knowledge must be acquired by asking and answering questions. Moreover, he insisted that "this way of looking at life as a series of questions" was not just for specialists or the intelligentsia alone, but for everyone whose vision was "not confined to the acquisition of bare subsistence."

The key to an inquiring mind lay in relating learning to individual experience. The lack of responsive inquiring minds, he argued, had "caused some of our most conspicuous national failures of recent years . . . Before the war we accepted freedom of thought as a venerable tradition, and neglected to exert ourselves to define its scope . . . A conception of freedom which had been given no genuine content through general thinking quickly vanished with the advent of war, when free inquiry was most needed. We lapped up propositions like 'the war to end war,' and 'an association of nations,' without caring to ask what they meant . . . Consequently, when we had obtained the victory, we did not know what to do with it, and we patched up a separate peace which made no provision to secure any of the things for which we had so eagerly fought."

The function of institutions of higher learning, which he said were beset by the conflict of "studium v. stadium," was to give students the power of understanding their own social order as well as the universe beyond. "Not only must the student prepare for a complicated world where truth is hard to find," Chafee maintained, "but for a world where the supposed truths of today may no longer hold good for tomorrow. The best kind of education I know was that received by Mark Twain and described in his *Life on the Mississippi*. After he had learned all the points and shoals from St. Louis to New Orleans, he found that many of them had changed. He had to learn them all over again and to be perpetually gathering information from which he could predict those changes."[3] It followed that the role of the teacher was not to impart rigid doctrines—socialism, protectionism, or any other—but to train students to think for themselves.

As for Chafee's philosophy of legal education, it is summed up in the third item to which he referred the inquiring seminar student— a favorable review of Charles and Mary Beard's *The Rise of American Civilization*, published in 1927.[4] Although he was often frustrated by the knowledge gaps in Harvard law students ("any allusion to science, literature, or history is sure to be meaningless to at least half the college graduates in the room"), he did not favor any single prelaw curriculum. At the same time, because no law student ought to be wholly ignorant of economics, political science, psychology, the methods of the natural sciences, and American as well as English history, he thought law school ought to prepare lists of recommended books in those fields. After World War II he and Maguire prepared an extensive reading list for returning veterans that received wide publicity and a generally enthusiastic response. But Professor Fred Rodell of the Yale Law School made fun of it in a review that intensified Chafee's dislike of the New Haven philosophy of legal education.[5]

In 1941 he slightly modified and embellished the views of legal education he had expressed fourteen years earlier.[6] Anticipating what later became a common requirement of law schools, he believed that prospective lawyers should get an undergraduate degree before starting their legal studies. Paralleling this belief was his conviction that college subjects should not be continued in law school. In Chafee's view, a first-year law student should be made to realize that he is "out of the kindergarten at last" and that the law school "means business." "The first year in law school would be a much less satisfactory educational process if the student did not have all his working intellect fixed on law. It is good for him to eat, drink, and dream law just as the medical student lives among corpses and blood cells." Moreover, few law faculties in the country were fit to teach nonlegal subjects: "I know I am not. It takes about all my time to read the federal cases on Interpleader."

He described six kinds of mental equipment that can be aided by prelegal education—six in addition to "the all important element of character, which includes honesty, courage, loyalty, and faith in justice": a capacity for hard work; an ability to communicate ideas; an understanding of the actual environment of English and American law; a capacity for legal reasoning or, more accurately, the types of reasoning characteristic of lawyers and judges; an ability to understand and weigh the forces that mold human life and institutions; and a spirit of adventure. Of the last characteristic, he said: "I envisage a thirst for exploration, a joy in life, the faith that effort can bring accomplishment, the dream that over the Alps lies Italy. Such a spirit can carry the young lawyer through drudgery and discouragement and personal sufferings. It can turn law into more than an intellectual puzzle or a lucrative occupation. It is the quality which has turned many successful lawyers into great public servants." He said one student might get it from poetry, another from novels, yet another from biography, and so on.

In concluding these reflections Chafee cited books worth including in any list of recommended readings for prelaw students. Among them: Acton's *Lectures on the French Revolution* ("probably the most difficult book on my list, with profound discussions of the reasons for the success or failure of human institutions and political devices"); Sumner's *Folkways* ("Sociology, yet sensible. Few books are so well calculated to cure excessive dogmatism"); Dickens's *Pickwick Papers* and *Bleak House* ("the two best novels in English dealing with the effect of law on human beings"); James's *Psychology* and *Pragmatism* ("an exposition of the philosophy which is most influential upon legal thinking of our time"); and Cohen and Nagel's *Introduction to Logic and Scientific Method*.

Because Chafee's own inquiring mind roamed through many extralegal fields, he brought to the classroom a humanistic perspective that enabled students to see the law in a broad cultural setting. Chafee "was outstanding on the faculty . . . in the breadth of his cultivation and intellectual interests," said Paul A. Freund, Harvard law professor emeritus and distinguished constitutional scholar, of his student days at the school. "He was, of course, extremely well read in English literature and managed to bring that into his lectures. Other members of the faculty I am sure were very broadly based in non-legal culture, but somehow it didn't become part of their law school performance. But with Professor Chafee he was always ready with a literary anecdote or historical parallel."[7] Similarly, David F. Cavers, like Freund a former student of Chafee's who later became a colleague at the school, made the point that "I think all of us in the classrooms that he presided over came away feeling that we had something of a course in the humanities as well as in the law of Equity, or whatever the course might have been that he was teaching." And another former student said Chafee might have been "the only person in the world . . . who could make Bills and Notes come alive."[8]

Chafee was able to bring the law alive partly through the exercise of his lively sense of humor, although his wit often had to be repressed because of the deadly serious nature of legal teaching. "The intellectual emphasis [of the school] was enormous and expressed itself in seriousness," related a former student of Chafee's, a man who earned a medical degree after finishing law school. "Seriousness is the essence of law, and that deprives a teacher of being very humorous. Self-reliance was the key thing the student had to learn. The professors didn't give extra help—that wasn't in the nature of things. The whole physical layout of the school was such as to maintain distance between the teachers and the students, including the fact that the professor entered his classroom through a door just behind the dais, where he would sit like a judge. He was supreme. The Harvard Law School was a world within the world, and nobody from outside was supposed to talk about it."[9] Still, Chafee managed to slip a scintilla of wit into these somber surroundings. Typical was his comment about a man who applied for a patent for new corset stays invented by his wife and who was turned down because he had waited too long to apply: "He had slept on his rights" (a double entendre using one of the maxims of equity).[10] And he often brightened classroom presentations with self-effacing references to his experiences in legal practice and business and with homely examples from his beloved Rhode Island.

When it came to the Socratic method, his use of it was humane in contrast to the stern (or, in "Bull" Warren's hands, savage) manner in which it was employed by colleagues.[11] From their perch on the dais, professors bombarded students with questions about a case in a way calculated to give them a taste of how nasty judges can be to young lawyers. If they called on a number of students and found none who had studied the case, they would get angry. Professors were also easily irritated by the idealism of students because ideals can be barriers to learning to think like a lawyer. In the words of the medical doctor who studied under Chafee:

> They [the faculty] were not practicing psychiatry. They were not practicing human relations. They were not interested in the humanity of everyone who came to them. They were all of them quite willing to fail a student out of the school who didn't come up to their standards, and they didn't care who it was. They failed out Adlai Stevenson, whose grandfather was vice president of the United States, and they failed him out for what seems to us a very cruel and silly reason—his father had died and he had to go home for the funeral at a bad time, and that was that . . .
>
> You have to speak up if you're a lawyer, but Chafee was never nasty to students if they weren't demonstrative in class . . . He used the Socratic method in a gentle way. Besides, the method can't be used in every course, especially a course like Equity which involves a great deal of history. Equity is very intellectual.[12]

At lecturing Chafee was adept, even though his classroom career started shakily when, like many a neophyte teacher, he reached the end of the notes for his maiden lecture long before the period ended. Fortunately, he also had brought along notes for his second lecture; unfortunately, by the time he finished going through those, ten minutes of the period still remained. But that was, as he later recalled, "a difficulty I never encountered again." Despite the fact that he was critical of his speaking prowess ("I have never yet felt well satisfied with the way I speak," he noted after he had been teaching for a decade), he was long remembered by students as a memorable lecturer. "You didn't have the feeling of frustration that you had from several of the other faculty members," Francis T. P. Plimpton related. "He made you think that he was not as abstract as several of his brethren were. He was a very good lecturer. He held your attention. Your mind didn't wander."[13]

Students described his classroom manner as relaxed or informal, with lectures usually delivered as he sat on a desk or table. "He used to seem to bounce in his seat when he was teaching," a former student noted. "He had extraordinary vitality; he gave me the feeling that the law, notwithstanding its prosy aspects, is a great calling, not just a grubby, earth-bound profession." Recalling that Chafee's "movements were quick," Dean Erwin N. Griswold said, "he was not a rapid speaker, but, in the classroom and outside, he spoke at a steady pace, always thoughtfully, and without excessive emphasis, either of voice or hands. He was widely read . . . But his lectures and his writings and his conversation were not heavy with learning."

Affecting tweeds over his lean, five-foot-ten frame, he appeared to some students as gaunt and to others as gawky. His blue eyes, encircled by steel-rimmed spectacles, often drifted upward as he paused to think about a problem or to ponder a student's question. "Whereas Pound would toss off any student question with a brusque word," Barton Leach commented, "Zach would knit his brow, ponder the thing carefully, develop both sides of the issue, and make the question look a good deal better than it was. As students we all liked him. Of course none of us, as far as I know, ever even shook his hand, to say nothing of entering his house, for the barrier between faculty and students was nearly complete in those days."[14] Some students, especially if they were Rhode Islanders, did get invited to Chafee's home, but Leach's reference to barriers is a valid generalization.

Chafee seems to have achieved excellent rapport with students early in his career, perhaps partly because he was closer to their age than many of his legendary colleagues. But it is clear that students liked him because of his calm demeanor as well as his genuine concern for them. Regretting that the large student body made it impossible to know students as human beings, he did what he could to be accessible. Scott recalled that Chafee's office door was usually open, and a former student referred to him as "among the more approachable professors who would linger after class and talk to the students as distinguished from some professors who didn't do that and who were relatively unapproachable."[15] Chafee's concern for students also manifested itself in his attitude toward grades and grading.

Attaching more importance to a student's general average, which he viewed as an index to one's mental ability to handle legal matters, than to grades in individual courses, he disagreed with the school's policy of telling students their marks in individual courses. He would have preferred a policy of informing them of individual grades only in cases of failure. "The men should keep their mind on the law and not on the marks," he liked to say. And he never failed a student on the eve of graduation unless he was "really rotten." (Nearly all his references to students are in the masculine gender because the law school did not start admitting women until 1950. He was, however, among the faculty advocates of dropping the sexual barrier.)[16] When it came to giving out A's, which for him meant command of the subject and not just good work, he was stingy, but he considered students with a C average well qualified to practice law. Most of his letters of recommendation pointed out that his evaluation of a graduate rested mainly on grades because the large classes gave him little chance to know students well.

As his outlook on grades was generally humane, so his approach to the grading process was painstaking. Never, apparently, did his resentment over the time and energy required by student papers result in a slapdash evaluation of a student's work; indeed, his thorough and often elegantly written critiques were at times as long as the original papers. Although these lengthy evaluations bear witness to an admirable conscientiousness, they are also symptomatic of Chafee's one serious shortcoming as a writer: despite his sensitivity to matters of style and usage, he tended to overwrite. When he had to, as in the preparation of numerous contributions to the *Dictionary of American Biography*, he could be both brief and stylish.[17] But in writing many journal articles, memos, and letters, he seemed oblivious to considerations of length; or so it appears from his tendency to dispatch to U.S. presidents multiple-paged letters, which were sometimes accompanied by long statements submitted to congressional committees.

But insensitivity alone is too simple an explanation of his long-windedness. Several other characteristics help account for it. In the first place, he not only was widely read but also had a photographic memory (his brother Francis referred to an "ink-blotter memory" as something of a Chafee family trait)—a quality that readily complicates a writer's difficult task of deciding what to leave in and what to leave out. If he was inclined to write a lot because he knew a lot, he may have been further inclined, when faced with the in-or-out dilemma, to "leave it in" because of residual effects of the charges of incompleteness and inaccuracy leveled against his *Abrams* article. Moreover, he did not take criticism well and liked to avoid it even though he was not inclined to run from controversy. Among colleagues and students he had a reputation for fair-mindedness, because in his teaching and much of his writing he conscientiously presented both or all sides of a question. But there was another, and quite different, side of his personality that is less well known. His sister Elisabeth remarked on how angry he became when people disagreed with him, and his correspondence includes letters from his father and adversaries in Congress and the American Bar Association noting the great irony in the intolerance of opposing views shown at times by this champion of free speech.[18]

In his grading of student papers, however, he could scarcely have been more even-handed and concerned about their progress as writers. Such concern was at least partly a reflection of his own keen interest in composition. He explained that he took "a particular pleasure in the possibilities of prose style" because in his youth he had hoped to write poetry but "soon saw that I had to be content with prose." One source of stylistic inspiration was Macaulay, of whom it has been said that you never need to read a sentence twice to know what it means, and he never forgot that Eugene Wambaugh, one of his law professors, had urged his students to write as if they were telling their mothers about the law.

Chafee attached great weight to openings, calling "the first sentence much the most important part of any piece of writing" because it gave an author "a chance to put his biggest strawberries on the top of the basket." The length of words did not particularly concern him, as he explained in a letter to Edward H. Warren commenting on a treatise by the latter: "It may not be the number of long words that spoils [a] man's style so much as the artificial nature of the long words. For instance, a good deal depends on the tense used. The addition of 'ed' can turn one syllable into two without lessening the simplicity of words, or two into three . . . [A] second point is that an occasional long word gives a firmness of texture to the style, even though—to vary the metaphor—short words have the force of hammer blows."[19]

Chafee's prose style also benefited, as Benjamin Kaplan has remarked, from "long experience as a lecturer [which] taught him the dramatic values of the apt sobriquet. It is a sluggish soul who having once read [Chafee's discussion] of them would not recall the 'Strangle-hold,' 'Dismal Swamp,' 'Hot Potato,' and 'Living Tree' policies in the law of associations."[20]

In short, when Chafee sat down to evaluate a piece of student writing he did so as a man who had strong convictions about style. He also believed, specifically in regard to the third-year writing requirement begun in 1937, that careful critiques were owed to the students if there was to be such a requirement at all. But a student's paper, whether written to fulfill the third-year requirement or some other, nearly always received the same thoughtful assessment. To a student guilty of constructing poor paragraphs, he wrote: "The way in which a writer handles paragraphing is an important indication of the way he does his thinking. Does he jumble his ideas together in his head, or does he separate the pertinent issues and deal with each of them from start to finish before he grapples with the next issue?" He gave advice on figures of speech—"The purpose of a metaphor is to make abstract reasoning clearer and not more confusing than if you had no metaphor"—and one critique included terse lessons on antithetical constructions, usage ("I had heard of the 'tenor' of an argument or speech, but how can a so-called deliberative body have a 'tenor'?"), and sentence length: "Avoid a long clause with a participle at the end of a sentence. Two sentences cost you nothing."

Chafee often used his critiques to emphasize the importance of good writing to a practicing lawyer, as illustrated by these comments: "Qualities like bad spelling and a passion for semi-colons irritate some older lawyers. When the time comes for choosing among several law clerks, because the office is not big enough to keep all of them on at higher salaries, such irritations do affect the partners' decision. Similarly, clients will get unfavorable impressions from a long-hand letter with poor spelling. Sometimes no stenographers are at hand, and you have to write a client in a hurry." If a paper gave him particular pleasure, he might send a student a separate note of congratulations, such as this one to Joseph A. Califano, Jr., a future secretary of health, education, and welfare: "Reading a paper like yours is one of the best rewards which can come to a teacher."[21]

The quality of writing on examinations, including the handwriting, frequently moved him to comment. Exams he considered important not because they resulted in a grade, but because of their educational value in forcing students to pull together everything learned during a term and to think fast about concrete problems. "There are some habits which a man ought to form early in life for the sake of his companions," he told one student suffering from poor penmanship. "One is punctuality. Another is not mumbling his words. A third is legible handwriting."[22] A good way to improve their handwriting, he advised students plagued by illegible penmanship, was to keep a diary for several months.

If most students did not bother to acknowledge his constructive criticism, some took the time to write notes of appreciation. Especially grateful were nonlaw students who took courses he taught in Harvard College after becoming a university professor in 1950. Said one: "Your comments indicate that you've given me more individual attention than I've received from any other member of the Harvard faculty in my seven years at Harvard." Another, who complained that most professors put only a grade and a few brief comments on papers, told him: "This is the first time a teacher has been [so] helpful. Perhaps that is one of the reasons why you are such a well-liked professor over at the Law School—you feel an interest in the students."[23] How deep this interest could be is shown by a letter to a law student, written in May 1940:

> Your paper in Equity III, which I have just finished reading, indicates that you are allowing the European situation to disturb you in a way that is fair neither to yourself nor to your family. Last year you did a very creditable job for me in both Equity II and Bills and Notes. This year I have barely been able to pass you . . .
>
> Of course the European situation is very bad. Everybody is much disturbed about it. But suppose that everybody allowed his anxiety and sadness to affect his work in the way you are letting it affect yours. What kind of an appendicitis operation would a surgeon perform? What would you think of a lawyer who prepared a brief like your paper in Equity III?

If you can get hold of a copy of Whittier's poems read the one about "Abraham Davenport" or "The Dark Day." I found it of great help in the last war. For the next two weeks your examinations are the work that is before you . . .

So pull yourself together. Get out into the country for the week-end if you can and start in on Monday with a new determination.[24]

Chafee's concern for students did not end with their graduation. For years while teaching Equity III, he invited students to seek his advice any time concerning knotty problems they might encounter in practice. That a good many of them took up the offer is evident in his extensive correspondence files. Of course, these letters from students also helped him update both his classroom presentations and his writings. His concern for the practicing lawyer as well as for the student is also reflected in his approach to casebooks (their preparation and regular updating may be the most onerous aspect of a law professor's life). Chafee prepared various such tomes, most of them concerned with equitable problems and remedies (the major exception being a casebook on negotiable instruments published in 1919), and their favorable reception by working lawyers, as evidenced by comments in letters to him and in law journal reviews, delighted him.

Although he never produced a treatise on equity (he worried for years that by failing to do so he had not fulfilled the expectations of Pound when he had turned over his Equity courses to Chafee), he did publish a casebook magnum opus on the subject. This was the two-volume *Cases on Equity*, first published in 1934 with Sidney P. Simpson as coeditor; Simpson had begun teaching Equity II with Chafee after joining the faculty in 1931.[25] Each took primary responsibility for certain topics, and while Simpson's total contribution in terms of space was greater than Chafee's, Chafee explained that his own "much longer teaching experience influenced all portions of the book." And Chafee did "the deadly job of indexing."[26]

The elaborate 88-page index, which made the book particularly valuable to practitioners, was one extraordinary feature of this unique casebook. The 1,600-page work surely erred, as the editors said in the preface they hoped it would, "on the side of abundance rather than paucity of materials." Undoubtedly, this was a reflection of Chafee's thorough and careful scholarship. In his teaching of Equity, as David Cavers has remarked, Chafee always "was ready to consider the views of people and courts who disagreed with the people and courts whose views he approved. You didn't go away from the course knowing only the Chafee views and not the contrasting views. Anyone who has looked at the voluminous annotations in his casebooks will have confirmed his readiness to report the other side or sides of a question."[27] The preface also noted the editors' desire to aid working lawyers as well as students and teachers, and explained that the book "included materials on one topic not usually thought of as part of a course in equity—viz., statutory specific enforcement of arbitration contracts."[28] But what made the book truly unique was Chafee's idea of including illustrations of judges, litigants, and maps to help students "get the feel" of equity in action.[29]

The casebook was published to generally favorable reviews (the inclusion of illustrations was almost universally applauded), although one reviewer objected to its length while another noted that the book, despite its length and title, was devoted almost entirely to one aspect of equity (specific performance) at the expense of many others. One laudatory review called it "the finest work that has ever been done in the particular field covered," and more than one reviewer especially praised the book's utility for practitioners.[30]

By early 1935 the book had been adopted at fifteen law schools in addition to Harvard, and the number of adoptions peaked at twenty-five in 1937. Ironically, the book came out at roughly the same time that a movement to drop Equity as a separate course was getting underway in legal-education circles. Still, it is probable that the book would have been even more widely used in law schools if it had been promoted and marketed more professionally.[31] Instead, Chafee and Simpson published the book themselves, and Chafee (who had done the same thing with earlier casebooks) took care of the correspondence and bookwork.

Thus his office in Langdell Hall doubled as a publishing business, a fact that added to the disorder that normally surrounded his work site. His secretary from 1949 to 1956—by which time he had divested himself of his publishing ventures—described him as "not really well organized in his work, although I'm sure he thought he was. His desk was absolutely cluttered. His idea of tidying up consisted of moving things from his desk to a couch that was hidden behind a screen."[32] Chafee occasionally admitted to his messiness, as he did in a letter written early in 1934, the year *Cases on Equity* came out: "Anything is possible on my desk. The other day I found a money order which had lain in an unopened envelope for a month. At all events I cannot find your previous letter."[33]

Exactly why he chose to shoulder the laborious tasks of book publishing on top of his other responsibilities is not clear, but part of the motivation seems to have been linked to his business background and a desire to prove to his father, who never got over his forsaking the foundry for the law, that he could succeed, at least in a limited way, in the world of commerce. Then, too, he undoubtedly wished to keep most of the profits for himself because he and his wife liked to live well and they had four children to educate. Finally, as a man of many interests, he did not immediately settle into the grooves of academe.

While Chafee was quickly establishing himself as a gifted and popular member of the faculty, during his early years in Cambridge he was also finding out that he was ambivalent about teaching—a common enough discovery among those who become academics after having worked in a business or profession. As noted earlier, the Trial at the Harvard Club strengthened his resolve to stay in teaching, but a year later, in 1922, "hard times" led him to return to practice on a part-time basis.[34] He had joined the law school with the understanding that he could continue practicing if it did not interfere with his teaching, and in July 1922, satisfied that he had his courses "well in hand," he received Dean Pound's permission to spend one day a week in Providence working for his old firm, Tillinghast and Collins.[35] He continued this arrangement for three years, working much of the time on problems caused by contracts for yarn and cotton goods that were canceled after a drop in the market. He also did more work on the *Davis* case, involving the donation of Egyptian artifacts to the Metropolitan Museum. By 1925 he believed he had given all he could to the firm and had got all he could from the arrangement, including "the satisfaction of realizing that I definitely preferred teaching to practice."[36] Thereafter, he occasionally supplemented his income by working on private litigation, usually involving estates, but for the most part he focused on teaching and research.

While discovering that he was ambivalent about an academic career, he also found that the move from Providence to Cambridge did not permanently end the criticism from his family referred to by Betty Chafee in a letter quoted in Chapter 6. One source of criticism concerned his decision to remain at Harvard during World War I rather than entering military or government service.

Chafee's family, particularly his father and his Uncle Henry Sharpe, also criticized his outspoken views concerning the war and free speech for radicals. Even before Chafee had published his first article on freedom of speech, in the *New Republic* of 16 November 1918, his father wrote that he was "a little uneasy" and feared that "if you spoke in a crowd as you do at home" about World War I, "you might get into trouble and perhaps bring the school into notoriety."[37]

The day after the May Day bombings of 1919, Zechariah, Sr., sent a letter commenting on those incidents and relating them to free expression: "Unfortunately, freedom of speech, like everything else in human nature, is not a good thing in itself but only good or bad as it is used soberly, discreetly, unselfishly, and in fear of God. Wouldn't it be well if those who advocate freedom of speech should also advocate more at length that it should be so used, and should they not more frequently condemn its abuse? The great right carries with it a corresponding obligation, and that, I cannot help feeling, is too often forgotten." He then went on to criticize more specifically his son's publicly stated views of recent anti-anarchy legislation in Massachusetts, legislation whose drafting Chafee influenced in a way that kept the focus narrowly on direct incitement and eliminated considerations of bad tendency and guilt by association. Where should the line be drawn as a practical matter, his father asked, and then proceeded to answer his own question: "On the whole, in such matters I am inclined to believe that compromise is king, and perhaps even in practical advantages as well as in theoretical discussions, there must be some middle ground."[38]

As earlier chapters have explained, Chafee's post-*Abrams* views of free speech centered on clear and present danger—the middle ground between Hand's protective objective standard test and the repressive bad tendency test. Whether or not his father's views influenced Chafee's evolving admiration for the danger test is impossible to say. Probably not, because by late February 1920—some three months after Justice Holmes's more liberal restatement of the test in his *Abrams* dissent—Zechariah, Sr., told his namesake that the "right note" on freedom of speech had not yet been struck.[39] To Zechariah, Sr., in other words, Holmes's idea of clear and present danger as stated in his *Abrams* dissent would have seemed too liberal. As for family reactions to *Freedom of Speech*, which came off the press in time for Christmas 1920, the harshest words apparently were those of his uncle Henry Sharpe, who told a friend of Chafee's that he had no time for "that kind of rot."

Of course, Chafee had been led to "that rot" through his teaching of the venerable subject of equity, for which he was best known to students during much of his academic career. That was far from being his only course, however; indeed, he taught a total of fifteen different subjects, including several mutations of Equity as the curriculum underwent changes. But Equity was his great love, at least partly because its content resonated with his temperament and intellectual interests. As his colleague and friend E. Merrick Dodd observed, "by reason of its ethical content and the varied human activities with which it deals, [Equity was] well suited to Professor Chafee's view of law as not only a professional technique and a social science but a subject which is integrally related to the whole range of human culture."[40]

More so than other courses, Equity enabled him to indulge his interest in the humanities and in history. At one point during his undergraduate days at Brown, he recalled in a letter to Frankfurter, he had considered becoming a historian, and he said legal teaching and research gave him a chance to do history "on the quarter rather than dead astern." He went on to say that legal research afforded "a splendid opportunity for a man who wants to be a scholar without living in an ivory tower."[41] The statement reflects the fact that Chafee, despite his preference for theory over facts, had a strong practical side, probably owing at least in part to his experience in business. One important indication of his practical-mindedness was his habit of referring to equity as "a kit of tools."

Equity, a kind of judicial sandpaper for smoothing the rough edges of the law, emerged in England to solve disputes for which common law remedies were inadequate. Before a party could go into a common law court, where the proceeding resembled a scientific inquiry into facts, he had to have a recognizable cause of action. Litigation began with the issuance of a writ for a particular form of action; beyond a point, the causes of action became petrified into the various forms, and as the causes thus became limited, there were not enough to deal with every kind of injustice. Despite this fact, the forms of action lingered on in English law until the nineteenth century.[42] Meanwhile, equity arose to remedy injustices that went begging under the common law. Although equity as it is known in this country was first developed in England, it is noteworthy, especially in light of Chafee's devotion to the Greek language and culture, that a characteristic of ancient Greek philosophy and law was the principle of fairness or equity; *epieikeia* is the word the Greeks had for it.

Historically, appeals for equitable relief were taken to the chancellor, the principal aide to the king, but gradually a separate Court of Chancery emerged to handle proceedings in equity. While cases at law ended in an order directing the sheriff to enforce a judgment for damages by attaching and selling the defendant's property, a court of equity would order a defendant to do, or stop doing, certain acts involving, for example, performance of a contract or removal of a nuisance. The order was tailored to the justice of the case and, where appropriate, contingent on the petitioner's fulfillment of certain conditions.

Three important equitable devices used as early as the fourteenth century are the trust, specific performance, and the injunction, sometimes called the characteristic remedy of chancery. In summarizing the versatility of injunctive relief, Chafee described injunctions as "a kit of tools which can be employed effectively in all sorts of ways . . . They are equally helpful against breaches of contract, against most kinds of torts, against abuses of power by government officials and commissions . . . The problem whether an injunction should be phrased in general terms or should tell the defendant just what he may do and mustn't do, is illuminated by cases on nuisances, unfair competition, family law, labor law, pollution of streams and atmosphere, and the enforcement of the Sherman Antitrust Act."[43] Similarly, he defined equity this way: "[It] is a way of looking at the administration of justice; it is a set of effective and flexible remedies admirably adapted to the needs of a complex society; it is a body of substantive rules."[44]

Because of Chafee's advocacy of a balancing test in First Amendment law, it is significant that the central process in equity proceedings is known as "the balance of convenience"—the process in which a court considers the relative hardship to the parties as it "weighs the equities." However, the balance of convenience is not synonymous with the balancing of interests, which as envisaged by Jhering and Pound applies to numerous legal problems other than those in equity.

By the time Chafee became a professor of law, the distinction between law and equity was starting to disappear. In England elimination of separate courts of law and equity had begun in 1873 with passage of the first of the Judicature Acts. In the United States the movement to merge law and equity began with passage of the Code of Civil Procedure—called the Field Code after its draftsman, David Dudley Field—in New York state in 1848. After law and equity courts were merged, judicial relief in some traditional law cases became more flexible; at the same time, Pound and some other scholars contended, the judging in traditional equity cases grew less flexible. Part of the problem was that equity became subjected to a multiplicity of formal rules, a development that Pound in a 1905 article referred to as "the decadence of equity."[45]

But despite the merger of law and equity into a unified court system, lawyers and judges have continued to think of them as distinct systems, and the injunction and other equitable remedies are still in wide use. That would please Chafee, up to a point at least, for he argued in the early 1940s that the principles of equity were more important than ever for two reasons. First, the complex life of modern industrial society had created new conditions calling for specific relief. Second, the flexibility made possible by various qualifications under an equity decree was admirably suited to complex conditions that were likely to change in the future. To Chafee, pollution problems illustrated the kinds of contemporary evils that equity could solve better than suits for monetary damages:

> Suppose that a copper smelter is throwing out sulphurous fumes which injure surrounding vegetation. A jury merely gives damages for the injury to crops and trees which has already occurred. It can give the smelter no guidance as to the future and it cannot protect the plaintiff from the possible need to keep suing over and over as the injuries continue from year to year. By contrast, an injunction can order the smelter to install new machinery and take other steps to reduce the sulphur content. Furthermore, it can provide for periodical reports which will show the effect of a given sulphur content upon the surrounding vegetation . . . Another situation well suited for the flexibility of an equity decree is connected with rivers and streams. Problems of

the division of water among many claimants or of the pollution of water call for court orders which admit of experimentation and modification as time goes on.[46]

Although Chafee maintained that he was not upset by the merger of law and equity and even favored still greater fusion of the two, he was concerned that the balancing process was working less well and that equity's original humanizing influence was being diminished as the proliferating technical rules made the remedy more rigid. It is interesting that Chafee, despite his reputation as a leading authority on equity, did not consider himself an expert on its procedural aspects. The reason, as he explained to his friend Edgar N. Durfee, a law professor at the University of Michigan, was his deeper interest in substance: " . . . you really know about Equity while I get constantly drawn astray by the lures of the substantive law. When I see a bare arm or leg of a fascinating sort coming from behind a case in chancery, I am tempted to take a look at the whole of the lovely lady and not stop long at the procedure which hides her. To learn about the procedure I constantly have to draw on you."[47]

It comes as no surprise, then, that Chafee was also concerned that the substance of equity—the general principles derived from decided cases—suffered from judges' blind adherence to some of the maxims expressing those principles. These maxims are one of the distinctive features of equity, a field Charles Rembar calls rich in imagery. Among them are: Equity suffers no wrong without a remedy. Equity delights to do justice, and not by halves. Equity regards as done that which ought to be done. Equity abhors a multiplicity of suits. Equity will not stoop to pick up pins. Equity will not aid those who slumber on their rights.[48] Although these colorful principles appealed to the litterateur in Chafee, his sense of *epieikeia* was offended by the sight of a litigant failing to get justice because some judge slavishly followed or misapplied a maxim.

He delighted in squashing legal humbugs, as he did in a widely quoted 1926 article called "Does Equity Follow the Law of Torts?"[49] In the second paragraph he said: *"Aequitas sequitur legem*, of all the maxims of equity, is least entitled to be transformed from a concise expression of a tendency of judicial thought into a hard and fast rule. Exceptions to it are so numerous and well known that judges and textwriters state it with great qualifications." And he concluded: "Our single court of law and equity is like a workman with numerous tools lying before him . . . As it is the function of a factory to produce goods, so it is the function of courts to produce justice, and they should feel free to use for that object all or any of the means which long custom and legislation have placed at their disposal."[50]

And in 1949, as part of a series of five lectures given at the University of Michigan, he inveighed against the abuses associated with one of the best known of equity's maxims: He who seeks equity must come with clean hands. Opening the first of two lectures on the clean hands doctrine, he called it "the most amusing maxim of equity," and went on to say: "Although it is a pity to take this beautiful statue off its lofty pedestal, I propose to show that the clean hands doctrine does not definitely govern anything, that it is a rather recent growth ["It may be only a coincidence," he noted later in the lecture, "that extensive judicial insistence on clean hands began after the advent of the modern bathroom"], that it ought not to be called a maxim of equity because it is by no means confined to equity, that its supposed unity is very tenuous and it is really a bundle of rules relating to quite diverse subjects, that insofar as it is a principle it is not very helpful but is at times capable of causing considerable harm."[51]

Later, he conceded to a reviewer of the published version of the lectures that "you are quite right that I do not give much constructive help about the clean hands maxim. There was a good deal of clearing of the ground to be done, and that used up about all the energy I had."[52] He believed that the main contribution to the advancement of law made by his lectures and book was the discussion of representative or class suits, involving joint litigation of several claims raising common questions of law or fact.[53]

As Chafee noted at the start of the first of two lectures on representative suits, such litigation was infrequent prior to 1938. Then the new provisions of rule 23 of the Federal Rules of Civil Procedure and of the Fair Labor Standards Act brought a flood of such cases, a torrent that left him wondering if the world would not be better off without class suits and feeling "too badly puzzled to propose any sure solutions." Because class suits enable some persons to represent others and thus make it unnecessary to join all persons whose claims are involved, a key element of such litigation consists of determining when it is appropriate for some persons to represent others.

In Chafee's view class suits should be permitted if all claims

involve the same issues, but not if independent issues must be litigated. As he was in respect to the field of equity in general, he was
worried about the possibility that technical rules might prevent
justice from being done; specifically, he was concerned that technicalities could preclude a class suit even when that remedy was
both convenient and just. And as one who constantly stressed the
need for simplicity in the law, he feared that the machinery of class
suits was becoming inevitably more complex as the remedy in-
creased in popularity. And so he urged judges to "be cautious in
extending representative suits beyond simple situations where
everybody in the class has about the same interest as everybody
else."[54]

But within a few years after his death, a massive extension of
class suits occurred as black Americans began using the device to
collect damages resulting from discrimination.[55] Similarly, the injunction—that characteristic remedy of chancery—came to be widely
used by courts for managerial or reconstructive purposes, a use somewhat resembling the equity receivership set up for insolvent corporations. Perhaps the most significant managerial use of the
injunction occurred as federal courts sought to implement the Supreme Court's 1954–55 decisions calling for school desegregation.[56]
It was the injunction, especially as used by the judges of the U.S.
Court of Appeals for the Fifth Circuit, that transformed a dual school
system into a unitary, nonracial school system.[57] Backed by the
judicial power to sentence violators for contempt and capable of
being modified as conditions change, the injunction proved an indispensable tool of courts as they issued integration orders and supervised multifaceted school plans over long periods. Once injunctive
relief became commonplace in the racial field, it was used to achieve
other reforms: to reapportion state legislatures, to improve prison
and hospital conditions, and to safeguard the environment.[58]

Would Chafee have approved of all these developments in his
beloved field of equity? It seems likely that the proliferation of class
suits would have troubled him because of its tendency to make the
legal machinery more complex. And, as explained in the Introduction, he lived long enough to express doubts about the early use
made of the injunction to help achieve school integration. Yet despite any reservations he might have had, these new uses of equitable
remedies stand as a monument to equity's adaptability, which he
so often praised. Ironically, he had brooded during his last years on

the faculty that changes in the school's curriculum meant that students were being graduated with an inadequate appreciation of equity as a tool of undiminished versatility in a highly technological society.

For Chafee, the most worrisome curriculum change concerned the elimination of Equity as a separate offering—a development that made him the "Last of the Harvard Chancellors."[59] Equity's demise in American law schools around mid-century had been virtually predestined much earlier by the merger of law and equity in American courts. At Harvard the first tentative moves toward Equity's termination was implicit in the streamlining of the program carried out by Dean Landis during the late 1930s.[60] By the 1940–41 academic year, Equity II and Equity III, both year-long offerings, were gone, replaced by a single course. The following year a course in Equitable Remedies and Unfair Competition, taught by Chafee, was added to the curriculum, and the year after that, 1942–43, the new course was split into two.

During and right after World War II, when the school ran a year-round "accelerated program" with reduced faculty, Chafee found himself teaching the separate courses in Equitable Remedies and Unfair Competition as well as the single course in Equity—plus Banking and Bills and Notes, which lived on despite the proposal in the late 1930s to collapse it along with Sales into a Commercial Law course. The latter did replace Bills and Notes in 1949. In the meantime, Chafee was delighted to be teaching Bills and Notes again for the first time since 1922–23 (with the exception of 1938–39); so pleased was he that despite the hectic wartime schedule he published a pamphlet collection of his articles on the subject, cleverly entitling it *Reissued Notes on Bills and Notes*.[61] Part IV of the pamphlet he called "a collection of curbstone opinions," explaining that: "Each item consists of correspondence with a lawyer or judge about some question of Bills and Notes. Since none of these people saw fit to remunerate me, except for one gentleman who furnished me the funds to buy a Scottish terrier [named Whiskey], I thought that I might as well get something out of all my work."[62]

But Chafee's delight in returning, however briefly, to Bills and Notes was short-lived. Once the war was over, the Committee on Legal Education, appointed by Dean Landis during his brief return to Cambridge, set about revising the curriculum to help meet the legal challenges of postwar America. And after Equity became a leading casualty of the curricular changes approved by the faculty, Chafee said it had been "taken out and shot at sunrise."

Actually, the wide-ranging subject matter of Equity was not annihilated but rather reconstituted as portions of other relevant courses. The diversity of the subject matter is shown in the lengthy index to Chafee and Simpson's casebook. A fascinating document in itself, the index begins with Abandonment or Laches, dealing with delays in bringing suits, and ends with Zoning, covering injunctions against violations of zoning ordinances and other issues. In between, the index includes such topics as Administrative Law, Civil Law, Conflict of Laws, Constitutional Law, Contracts, Evidence, Labor Law, Procedure, Taxation, Torts, and Unfair Competition. From a professional standpoint, equity was unified in the sense that its myriad tools were crammed into one kit. But from an instructional standpoint, sacrificing such unity seemed prudent for the sake of matching up specific tools with their relevant functions in specific subject areas. Thus under the new curricular scheme, injunctions and extraordinary remedies went to Civil Procedure, specific performance to Contracts, and prior restraints to Constitutional Law.

Despite the fact that Chafee thought the new curriculum meant the destruction of Equity, he largely concealed his unhappiness in face-to-face encounters with colleagues. Recalling that Chafee's views on the desirablity of preserving the separate course were voiced in faculty discussions, David F. Cavers noted that his opinions "were always presented with a degree of reasonableness and, you might say, of indulgence toward his colleagues that is not, I think, the predictable response of a professor concerning a course to which he has devoted the greater part of his teaching over a long period of years. That was a rather striking demonstration of the generosity and liberality of Chafee as a man and as a scholar."[63]

His correspondence, however, shows how irked he was about this turn of events. In a 1949 letter to Simpson, who was then teaching on the West Coast, he expressed concern that book sales would suffer from Harvard's having "thrown [Equity] to the wolves" and said he was "very skeptical about the students getting any real knowledge of Equity from all these shreds and patches, but like Oxford, I am a home of lost causes. What makes matters worse for us is that the example of Harvard will probably lead other schools to junk Equity too. Still I hope there will be enough business at least to keep us in cigars for a few years to come."[64]

Yet his correspondence also discloses that his fondness for Harvard, for the law school, and for the principles of both outweighed his disgruntlement over what he called "the debacle of Equity." His institutional loyalty was obviously undiminished when, a few months after posting the bilious letter to Simpson, he wrote President Conant: "You have no idea how deep a satisfaction it is to me to be spending my life in the free atmosphere of Harvard."[65]

As for his devotion to the law school, perhaps the finest expression of the depth of his feeling appears in a 1951 letter to Dean Griswold. Much of it was inspired by a proposal set forth by Professor Cavers in a memo entitled "A Task for Law School Research in the Rearmament Period," which largely dealt with "measures to diminish the social and economic dislocations resulting from atomic attacks on the United States."[66] While conceding that Cavers's proposed project ought to be carried on somewhere, he said he would be "very sorry" to see it done at Harvard Law School. The reasons for his opposition, he told the dean, "lie so deep that it is hard for me to put them into words." But he tried, and the result, as shown by the following excerpt, was a poignant statement of what the school meant to its last chancellor:

> In past wars Harvard Law School has been an island of thought in a sea of troubles. We have carried on as best we could in the time at our disposal with the boys left within our walls while we had them. This policy sometimes looked like standing aside from the turbulent life of most of the nation, but it paid in the end . . . The true task of the School as a whole, in this crisis, is to play the part of the monasteries during the barbarian invasions and the Dark Ages, and keep vigorously alive the best we know—ready for use when order returns.[67]

CHAPTER 8

Pushing a Stone
up Capitol Hill

"Probably the greatest compliment a lawyer can receive from his profession (a compliment never publicized)," Martin Mayer writes in *The Lawyers*, "is an assignment to draft a major law." A statute needs to be well written, as Mayer also explains, in order to make clear "what the judges will have to do in specific cases, diminishing the temptation to take the question to court."[1] The federal Interpleader Act of 1936, which Chafee drafted under the aegis of the American Bar Association, does not qualify as major legislation because it deals with a very narrow legal field: multiple claims for the same debt against insurance companies, banks, storage warehouses, and similar businesses. But the narrowness of the field is no gauge of either its technical complexity or the vexations it caused prior to 1936.

Interpleader had been around for a long time as an equitable remedy used in England and in American state courts to deal with problems such as the following.[2] A savings bank accepts a deposit from a man and gives him a bank book. Upon the depositor's death, an executor is appointed and sues the bank, seeking the amount of deposit. But because the executor does not have the bank book, the bank is reluctant to pay him. Who has the book? The depositor's landlady, who contends that he gave it to her as a deathbed gift and who also sues the bank. Thus the prospect looms of two independent jury trials. The bank as stakeholder, admitting that it owes somebody but not knowing whom, may have to defend two separate suits at considerable expense to itself, with the outcome of one suit having no bearing on the other. The possibility even exists that one jury will decide for the executor on the ground that the book was not legally given to the landlady while the other will find for the landlady on the ground that there was a gift. In that event the bank must pay twice. But it may avoid this double vexation (as the law calls it) by relying on interpleader, an equity proceeding without a jury in which both the executor and the landlady are brought into court. The bank pays the amount of the deposit into court, and then the landlady and the executor fight it out to see who gets the money. Meanwhile, the two lawsuits are enjoined, and the bank, because the controversy is not its fault, is given a discharge and even receives enough money out of the deposit to pay its lawyer for filing the interpleader.

Traditionally in such cases interpleader was a convenient remedy in state courts—as long as the parties claiming the bank deposit (or insurance money or merchandise in a warehouse) lived in the same state. If they lived in different states, a serious problem arose. What would happen if the executor lived in Connecticut and the landlady lived on Long Island, where the depositor was spending the summer at the time he died? The Connecticut court could not force the landlady to come in to the proceeding; if she would not do so voluntarily, the Connecticut writ would have no effect in New York State. And the New York court would be equally powerless to force the executor to come there. Precisely this situation was involved in a leading case decided by the U.S. Supreme Court in 1916, the year that Chafee became a law professor. In *New York Life Insurance Co. v. Dunlevy* the insurer had to pay the same policy to two different claimants—to the beneficiary who lived in California and to a creditor of the policyholder who resided in Pennsylvania. When the case went to the nation's highest court after New York Life tried unsuccessfully to bring an interpleader proceeding in a Pennsylvania court, the Supreme Court ruled that it was impossible for Pennsylvania to bind the California beneficiary or prevent her from getting a judgment against the insurer in her home state.[3]

After the *Dunlevy* decision, New York Life and other insurance companies appealed to Congress to add the following provision to the Judicial Code: Whenever the same policy was claimed by citizens of different states, the insurer could bring an interpleader proceeding to federal court in the state where one of the claimants lived. The court could then compel the other claimant to come in so the dispute could be resolved. This 1917 change in the law resulted in the rapid settlement of numerous claims, and in 1926 casualty companies and surety companies got the statute amended so that it applied to them as well.⁴ Left uncovered, however, were savings banks, railroads, storage warehouses, and comparable businesses that often found themselves in a similar predicament.

Chafee had used the interpleader remedy while practicing law with Tillinghast and Collins in Providence, but his scholarly fascination with it he traced to the interest of William R. Tillinghast, his former senior partner, in the *Dunlevy* case. In 1950 Chafee recalled that Tillinghast

> was firmly convinced that a savings bank should be able to interplead a Rhode Islander and an outsider in the Rhode Island courts when they were both claiming the same deposit. Consequently, he was much disturbed when the Supreme Court decided that the Rhode Island court would not be able to determine the rights of the outsider so long as he refused to appear. I sent W.R.T. a long letter defending the Supreme Court, and this was my first writing on the subject. This letter got expanded into an article in the Yale Law Journal [in 1921]. Mr. Tillinghast's realization of the practical need for relief led me to see if there was not a new path available after the Supreme Court had blocked the path which he liked to take. Hence, my efforts to amend the original Federal Interpleader Act.⁵

Chafee's article for the *Yale Law Journal* was the first in what became a series of interpleader articles he wrote for it over a two-decade period. The second, "Interstate Interpleader," came out in 1924.⁶ Together, these two articles set the agenda for his decade-long labors on modernizing the law of interpleader.

"As a quick and simple way out of a complex situation," Chafee said in the opening paragraph of his 1921 article, interpleader "has an intellectual fascination like the vx method of solving simultaneous quadratic equations. Upon further study of the cases, however, the lawyer's mental reaction changes to intense exasperation. Nowhere else, perhaps, can he encounter technicalities equal to those which hem in this admirable remedy."⁷ Thus his purpose in writing the article was to describe the main restrictions on interpleader's effectiveness and to consider how they might be cleared away. It was mainly the following requirements, "imposed by a multitude of decisions," that had changed interpleader "from a simple and expeditious remedy into a difficult and technical problem":

1. Both (or all) parties against whom relief is sought must claim the same debt, duty or thing. This is called the identity requirement.

2. The parties' adverse titles or claims must all be dependent, or derived from a common source. This requirement is known as privity.

3. The person seeking relief (called the applicant or the complainant) must not have or claim any interest in the debt, duty or thing.

4. The applicant must have incurred no independent liability to either of the claimants; he or she must be merely a stakeholder—the person from whom a debt, duty or thing is sought by two (or more) parties.[8]

The second requirement (privity) had been the most important of the four, but the first (identity) had also caused a good deal of trouble. Calling the identity requirement "an unsuccessful attempt to phrase the principle of mutual exclusiveness" (to be discussed shortly), Chafee contended that the stakeholder should not have to suffer "needless worry and expense just because this single obligation is given a different technical form or a different amount by the various claimants." He called upon courts to reject identity "as too formal a test which refuses relief unless the claims coincide at every point like two superimposed triangles in plane geometry." As for the privity requirement, he said it got into equity by accident, and then the accidental linking of privity with interpleader "was assumed to indicate a basic principle which had to be rigidly maintained, just as a child who has jam on his bread once always insists on bread and jam."[9] Privity should be abolished, he argued; and where it is not abolished, it should be accurately defined to prevent its indiscriminate use in denying interpleader.

The third and fourth requirements caused Chafee less worry, but he favored replacing all four with "the simple test of mutual exclusiveness." Mutual exclusivity exists when two or more claims overlap but only one is right. Such situations are ideally suited to the kind of relief that interpleader is designed to furnish. And if it could just be freed from its technical limitations, interpleader could be routinely granted to applicants faced with mutually exclusive claims.

Under Chafee's test interpleader would be granted "whenever there is multiple vexation but *in substance* only one obligation."[10] The italics helped differentiate his standard from the rigid requirement of identity.

Yet even if its technical limitations were eliminated, interpleader could not be used in many cases where one or more of the claimants lived in a state different from that of the stakeholder. As noted earlier, a state in which an interpleader bill is filed cannot legally require the presence there of a claimant who resides in another state. And with respect to federal district courts as possible alternative sources of relief, a limitation exists in the form of the U.S. Constitution's diversity-of-citizenship requirement in article 3, section 2. This means that persons wishing to bring law suits in U.S. district courts may do so only if the parties involved are residents of different states—a requirement limited still more by a judicial doctrine calling for *complete* diversity between opposing parties. It was the problems associated with interstate interpleader that Chafee took up in his 1924 article, which described the diversity problem and explained how the Insurance Interpleader Act of 1917 dealt with it.

That statute gave U.S. district courts jurisdiction over bills of interpleader by insurance companies if the adverse claimants were citizens of different states; and it did not specifically rule out interpleader when a stakeholder company and one claimant happened to be citizens of the same state—a situation that ordinarily would not satisfy the complete diversity requirement. But since the 1917 act did not explicitly provide for interpleader in cases involving cocitizenship of the stakeholder and one claimant, Chafee hoped that Congress would do so and that such a provision would be ruled constitutional under the Constitution's diversity clause. And of course he also hoped that Congress would expand the 1917 statute so that it applied to all stakeholders and gave U.S. district courts jurisdiction over claimants in other states against whom the stakeholders sought relief.[11]

In May 1924 he sent a copy of his second interpleader piece to Joseph S. Conwell, counsel for Penn Mutual Life Insurance, who had presented a paper on the federal act in May 1920 at a meeting of the Association of Life Insurance Counsel. Noting that his article referred to Conwell's paper, Chafee explained that he was a strong supporter of the statute, that he agreed with Conwell's description of its defects and also favored its extension to other stakeholders, and that he would like to offer his assistance if Conwell was still interested in such legislation.[12] Conwell promptly sent him a copy of a bill to amend the federal statute, a bill that had been introduced by Senator George Wharton Pepper of the leading Philadelphia law firm of Henry, Pepper, Bodine and Stokes, of which Conwell also was a member. An accompanying letter described the composition of the Senate Judiciary Committee, where the bill then reposed, and suggested that Chafee send his article to the committee members and to various life insurance counsel.[13] He did so, and in a letter to Conwell he said: "I hope very much that if your bill becomes law and works well, it may be possible to secure an extension to all stakeholders. My old office is counsel for a large savings bank in Providence which is frequently subjected to claims by non-residents. So far we have been able to persuade the non-resident to come into a Rhode Island interpleader, but sooner or later, one will refuse."[14]

Several years passed—a period that included Chafee's service to the Wickersham Commission—and then early in 1931 events brought him into contact with a law school classmate who also had a keen interest in interpleader legislation. This was J. H. McChord, of Louisville, who with Chafee had been a member of the Story Law Club at Harvard and was then in the legal department of the Louisville and Nashville Railroad. They began corresponding after a letter from McChord to the Harvard Law Review Board—seeking suggestions on how to improve a recently introduced federal bill giving U.S. district courts jurisdiction over proceedings in the nature of bills of interpleader—came to Chafee's attention. He sent McChord several suggestions about the bill, thus initiating a correspondence that significantly influenced enactment of the 1936 legislation.

By January 1932, with his Wickersham service behind him, Chafee, at McChord's suggestion, was writing to Representative Maurice H. Thatcher, who had introduced the bill about which McChord had written to the law review, and to Senator Alben W. Barkley, who in 1931 also had introduced interpleader legislation. And Chafee prepared for McChord a twenty-page, double-spaced memo about Thatcher's bill, noting that the acts of 1917 and 1926

> were not very well drafted although fortunately no serious difficulties of judicial construction have been caused by this fact. I think it would be very desirable that this bill, which is to extend interpleader over a much wider field, should

be prepared with unusually full consideration so that ob-
scurities and other defects will not be present if they can
possibly be avoided. I should particularly emphasize the fact
that the bill concerns procedure in the Federal courts, which
is a rather technical matter with which I have no practical
contact. Doubtless you and your associates have often been
in the United States courts so that you appreciate the phrases
which would enable Federal judges to go ahead without
difficulty. Would it be possible to get the friendly cooperation of an experienced Federal judge?[15]

Within a few days, Chafee also got off a letter to his Uncle Jesse
H. Metcalf, a member of the Senate whom he wrote from time to
time in an effort to enlist support for or opposition to measures that
Chafee either favored or disliked. After noting that he had written
Senator Barkley, he gave his uncle a crash course on interpleader,
explained his contact with McChord and the latter's desire to broaden
the protection of the statute, and described an actual case involving
Louisville and Nashville Railroad promissory notes and claimants
in New York and North Carolina, a case that had the railroad spin-
ning its wheels in an unsuccessful effort to invoke interpleader. And
of course he hoped Uncle Jesse and his colleagues would back the
bill.[16] Chafee sent a copy of the letter to McChord, who, impressed
by this "clear and forceful" discussion of the merits of the proposed
bill, said he wished every member of Congress could have a copy
and asked Chafee's permission to excerpt it, omitting personal references and those to the Louisville and Nashville Railroad litigation.
Chafee agreed.[17]

Although Chafee was pleased by the exposure his ideas on interpleader were getting on Capitol Hill, he was somewhat frustrated
that no court had cited his writings even though he knew it was
not yet common for judges to rely on law journal articles. But then
he discovered that a federal judge had recently referred to his work
in deciding the case of *Marine Midland Trust Co. v. Irving Trust
Co.*[18] The judge was Julian W. Mack, who had sat on the committee
hearing Austen Fox's charges against Chafee a decade earlier. "Although my article on Interpleader in 30 Yale Law Journal is, I think,
the only recent discussion of the general subject of Interpleader"
Chafee wrote Judge Mack, "it has never, so far as I know, been cited
by any court until this case. The problem before you was very in-

teresting and I am gratified that you took such a liberal view of the defenses of privity and interest."[19] As he was still savoring the judge's citation of his work, he heard again from McChord, who suggested that Chafee draft a bill for McChord to forward to "our representatives in Congress, advising them that it meets with our approval as well as yours."[20] Chafee doubted that he would have the time but promised to keep McChord's suggestion in mind.

A month later, in March 1932, McChord queried Chafee about his progress on the draft bill, adding that he had seen Senator Barkley who said that because Congress was focusing on more important matters than interpleaders, there probably would be no progress on the statute during the current session. In reply Chafee said it seemed desirable not to add to the burdens of Congress and explained he was preparing another article for the *Yale Law Journal*—a task that "ought to put me in a better position to go ahead on the redrafting during the early autumn."[21] Then Chafee, demonstrating that his absorption in interpleader had not left him wholly unmindful of civil liberties concerns, lectured his old classmate about conditions in Kentucky's soft coal fields, the scene for more than a year of bloody battles as state officials sought to put down unionization efforts that sometimes involved Communists.[22] Referring to the recent physical ejection of members of the National Student League, who like various literary figures and academics before them had sought to inspect these conditions, he said:

> Cannot you and some of the other enlightened members of the bar of your state create some public opinion against the exclusion of citizens of the United States from Harlan County and Bell County? . . . Any actual disturbances growing out of these visits could easily be prevented, and it would be well worth while if the local officials and citizens took the attitude that there is nothing which they are afraid to have investigated. An editorial in the Boston Herald this morning which I will try to send you, suggested that the visiting students should be received with old-fashioned Southern hospitality and allowed to find out that their sympathies had been misdirected (if that is the case). On the other hand, if there really is injustice and suffering, Kentucky ought to welcome the opportunity to study the evils and work out a cure.[23]

Prior to getting involved in drafting the bill itself, Chafee sought to convince federal judges that wider use should be made of the interpleader remedy. In the 1932 *Yale Law Journal* article, "Interpleader in the United States Courts," he wrote that "one or two liberal interpleader decisions in the United States courts may have a marked influence in removing technicalities from interpleader throughout the entire federal system. Still further improvements of the remedy may be attained through the Federal Equity Rules established by the Supreme Court, and if necessary by act of Congress. Thus there may be situations where a stakeholder would be able to attain in a United States court the much-needed relief from double vexation which would be denied him in any available state court because of its adherence to local precedents hampering the adequate development of interpleader."[24]

In an effort to get his article into the hands of all federal judges, on 1 November 1932—exactly one week before the election that awarded the presidency to Franklin D. Roosevelt—Chafee asked Dean Pound for $100 from the school's publication fund to cover the cost of sending them the two-part piece. Noting that there were 196 federal judges, he told the dean that he would pay the postage himself if the amount requested proved inadequate for both reprinting the article as a pamphlet and mailing it. The lengthy article, he also explained, was the first product of research aided by a grant from Acting Dean Joseph (Gentleman Joe) Warren during Pound's absence in 1929.[25] Because Warren had originally told him no funds were available but later awarded the $200 requested, saying that funds had become available from an outside source, Chafee suspected that "Gentleman Joe" was himself the source.[26] Warren sent him the check on 29 October 1929, the day the stock market collapsed. Chafee's distribution plans for the article had to be altered after the *Yale Law Journal* would let him have only 100 reprints; he sent 70 of those to members of the Supreme Court, to federal district and circuit judges who had written interpleader opinions, and to several other circuit judges. The remaining copies he set aside for key congressmen and some professors of law.

Shortly after the presidential election of 1932, Chafee sent McChord a draft bill along with a memo explaining why certain phraseology was used. He suggested that the memo, with modifications, could be distributed to members of Congress as well as to the business groups affected, and he also emphasized that claimants, not just stakeholders, had an interest in the legislation: "Is there any way in which we could reach organizations that can be considered representative of claimants? I do not see any way to reach life insurance beneficiaries, but how about railroad shippers and warehouse depositors? . . . I should like to make Congress feel that this was not a partisan measure supported only by the crowd at one of the three angles of the interpleader triangle."[27]

McChord handed Chafee's bill on to Hobart S. Weaver, counsel for the Association of Life Insurance Presidents. When no word was forthcoming from Weaver and after identical interpleader bills were introduced by Senator Felix Hebert of Rhode Island and Representative Harold Knutson of Minnesota, Chafee paused on May Day 1933 to write once again to Uncle Jesse Metcalf. "Among the stormy events now occurring in Washington," he said, "my favorite topic of interpleader is just a little violet, but I am begging for a moment's attention just the same." Stressing that he and McChord did not intend to see action on the bill during the current session, he explained that they merely wanted it fully considered by everyone concerned "so that any mistakes on my part can be eliminated and the measure will be in bang-up form for presentation at a future session after you and your associates in the Senate have cleared away all the present difficulties of the country."[28]

Nothing of consequence happened until early 1934, when Chafee received a letter from a valuable potential ally—Arthur T. Vanderbilt, a brilliant Newark, New Jersey, lawyer and professor of law at New York University. Like Chafee, Vanderbilt had an interest in both commercial law and civil liberties. Representing the American Civil Liberties Union before New Jersey's highest court in the 1928 case of *State v. Butterworth*, he won an important victory for the right of assembly involving an ACLU-inspired test meeting held after the famous Paterson textile strike in August 1924.[29] And as an active member of the American Bar Association, he founded and served as the first chairman of its insurance section.[30] It was in this connection that he wrote Chafee, saying that he was "trying to keep a group of [the section's] committees profitably employed" and that the Special Committee on Interpleader Legislation had been "trying to find its way around in the morass of proposed interpleader legislation, but, I judge from their correspondence to me, without any degree of success in gathering even the materials on the subject."[31] And he explained, in a passage that could not have had a more receptive reader, he wanted the committee to pay particular attention to the adoption of a bill expanding the scope of interpleader under the federal law.

By the time Chafee replied to Vanderbilt, he had heard from Weaver via McChord that many life insurance companies favored Chafee's bill over earlier draft bills and, if a few minor changes were made, would approve amending the 1926 Interpleader Act in this manner.[32] Besides suggesting that Vanderbilt get in touch with Weaver, Chafee explained about his cooperation with McChord and listed the main features of his draft. Never much of an admirer of the ABA, he also noted that he was not a member but would "be strongly tempted to dig up the money somewhere if the Association is seriously going to get after this interpleader problem."[33]

Vanderbilt, eager for the ABA to have the benefit of Chafee's expertise, arranged with the interpleader committee chairman, Judge Arthur G. Powell of Atlanta, for him to serve on the committee without first joining the association. (Chafee did become a member, saying in a note to Vanderbilt accompanying the eight-dollar fee that "when it comes to the expense of attending meetings, I am in greater difficulties.") Although Chafee's bill from first draft to final passage underwent relatively few changes, he worried that a suggestion of Judge Powell's could seriously damage his brainchild.

Powell, who was receptive to Chafee's suggestion that the committee print and distribute his draft together with a revision of his original explanatory memo, suggested that those materials be accompanied by copies of other bills. They included one that Chafee had not seen, that of Senator Hebert of Rhode Island. This suggestion did not bother Chafee; what did was the judge's recommendation that bills in the nature of interpleader be made part of Chafee's measure. The difference between a bill of interpleader (or "a strict bill") and a bill in the nature of a bill of interpleader (or a bill in the nature of interpleader) is this: Whereas double vexation is the only reason for equitable jurisdiction over a bill of interpleader, some ground for equitable relief in addition to double vexation is involved in a bill in the nature of interpleader—the stakeholder might be a trustee, for example, or someone seeking cancellation of a check for fraud.

Neither the 1917 interpleader statute nor later amendments to it included bills in the nature of interpleader, and Chafee feared, as he explained to Vanderbilt, that "the courts may insist more vigorously on objections of partial co-citizenship if we depart from strict bills of interpleader."[34] But after considerable discussion and correspondence among Chafee and others concerned, it was agreed that bills in the nature of interpleader should be included. And after the 1936 act was on the books, Chafee wrote a federal district judge in Baltimore that his decision in a case under the statute "abundantly justifies our decision on this matter."[35]

Of the amendments to the 1917 act Chafee referred to, the principal ones had been made in 1926 (after slight changes in 1925). As has been explained, they extended the legislation to include casualty and surety companies as well as life insurance companies. The main purpose of Chafee's bill was to extend the law to still other kinds of businesses such as railroads, warehouses, banks (especially savings banks), and oil companies operating under licenses when ownership of royalties is uncertain or disputed.

But unlike the existing law, his bill did not refer to specific businesses, and thus the interpleader remedy was made generally available to individuals and corporations subjected to claims by residents of two or more states. In many respects Chafee carefully followed the language of the 1926 act. He also sought to preserve the benefits of the existing law for life insurance, surety, and casualty companies while plugging a few chinks in it concerning life insurance litigation. For example, his bill allowed interpleader with respect to the loan value of a life insurance policy, whereas the existing law allowed interpleader only for the face value. And his bill sought to abolish the privity requirement, omit the requirement of absence of interest by stakeholders, permit interpleader to be set up as an equitable defense as well as by a bill in equity, and repeal complicated venue provisions of the 1926 act.[36]

As for differences between Chafee's bill and other bills, the most important may be summarized as follows: Concerning diversity of citizenship, Chafee's bill closely followed the 1926 act by referring to "two or more adverse claimants, citizens of different States," whereas the language of Senator Hebert's bill (hereafter the Hebert-Knutson bill) was less clear: "two or more citizens of different States, and of one or more States who are adverse claimants . . . " Unlike the Hebert-Knutson bill, Chafee's measure expressly abolished privity and included a provision—which he called the most important change from the existing law—giving the court discretion to dispense with the requirement of a deposit under certain conditions.

"Although the disputed subject-matter should ordinarily be deposited in court," Chafee said in his explanatory memo,

> situations sometimes arise where the requirement would prevent just relief. For example, it is obvious that a deposit is impracticable when one claimant to the benefits of life insurance demands one disposition (or option) under the policy and the other claimant demands a very different disposition (or option) . . . Yet it would be harsh to deny interpleader under such circumstances. The claimants are safeguarded because the company must admit its obligation to pay as directed by the decree, and because the court may require proper security, such as a surety bond, in lieu of the deposit.[37]

The memo went on to note that while the Hebert-Knutson bill gave the stakeholder an absolute right to substitute a bond for the deposit of the property, Chafee's bill adopted "the safer course" of making the bond an exceptional privilege requiring a special court order. (Later, however, Chafee yielded to a suggestion from Hebert and modified this section of his bill to include the same kind of bond provision. Eventually, the Chafee bill was substituted for that of the senator, who upon first reading Chafee's considered it generally superior to his own.)

In omitting any requirement of want of interest by stakeholders, Chafee's measure differed from the bills that had been introduced in 1931 by Senator Barkley and Representative Thatcher; they specified as a condition of relief: "Complainant does not have any claim or interest in the thing or fund which is the subject matter of the controversy." (Neither the 1926 act nor the Hebert-Knutson bill contained such a section.) To Chafee, it seemed wiser to leave want of interest out of the bill and to trust that federal courts would, as some had already been doing, take the position that interest goes only to the discretion of the court. This liberal view made interpleader possible even though, for example, there was a stakeholder's interest arising from a small charge for freight, warehouse storage, and so on.

On the matter of venue, Chafee's bill more closely followed the 1926 act as construed than did the Hebert-Knutson Bill. In addition to repealing some of the act's venue provisions Chafee limited venue to the residence of a claimant, whereas the other measure also made it possible for stakeholders to file suit in their own districts. Chafee thought it unlikely that stakeholders would suffer any real hardship if denied the express privilege of suing in their own districts. And since the main dispute in interpleader is between the claimants, he thought it only proper for the dispute to be fought out in a district where one claimant lived. In one other respect he considered his position on venue preferable to Hebert and Knutson's: he left questions of partial cocitizenship to be settled by judicial decisions.

In August 1934 Chafee's bill was formally approved by the ABA's Insurance Law Section at its annual meeting in Milwaukee, where he gave a speech entitled "Extension of Federal Interpleader to All Businesses." By then he had made a few changes in the bill as agreed upon in May, when the section informally endorsed it at a meeting he attended in Washington, D.C. There he met for the first time Senator Hebert and there, too, he was involved in an incident that he and the others present recalled with amusement for years. After a taxi in which he was riding with several ABA members and congressmen almost struck a female pedestrian, she cursed the driver. And when the driver started to swear back at her, Chafee tapped him on the shoulder and said, "Don't you know you're in the presence of a lady?" Not long after his return to Cambridge, he received this compliment from Vanderbilt: "It was a real pleasure to have you with us [in Washington] and I want you to know that the men in the Section, most of whom are rather hard boiled, practical fellows, were delighted at the cooperation which we received from our 'brain trust,' as Judge Powell termed you, and they were not at all displeased to discover that our brain trust had a sense of humor. I don't know why we professors are always suspected of being exempt from this rather necessary ingredient to a comfortable living under modern conditions."[38]

During this period of extensive work in behalf of interpleader reforms, Chafee was also teaching, completing the two-volume *Cases on Equity*, and doing the other things routinely required of a professor, husband, and father of four. Little wonder, then, that—his sense of humor notwithstanding—he began to regard himself as a modern Sisyphus pushing a statutory stone up Capitol Hill when McChord wrote in January 1935 that Senator Barkley had introduced a bill identical to one introduced in the House a few weeks earlier by Representative Knutson. Since these measures corresponded to bills introduced in 1933 by Knutson and Hebert before the latter had accepted Chafee's draft as a substitute for his own, Chafee sent a despairing letter to McChord: "The only thing I can think of is the Greek fable of the chap who spent his time in hell pushing a stone uphill only to have it roll back every few minutes to the exact spot where it was before. Last winter you and I and the bunch put in a lot of time and got our draft substituted for [those earlier] bills . . . Now Senator Barkley and Representative Knutson bring in exactly the same old bill without the slightest indication that they ever heard of our measure or of the amended bill reported from the Senate Judiciary Committee last spring with an extensive report by Senator Hebert."[39] By Valentine's Day Chafee was "beginning to have the feeling that it is not quite appropriate for a scholar to take an active part in promoting legislation."[40]

However, Senator Barkley recommended that his bill be amended so as to revive Chafee's measure, which then cleared the Senate on 1 May 1935. But Congress, still struggling to dig the nation out from beneath the economic rubble of the Great Crash, adjourned without having acted on interpleader. In the meantime, Chafee had been informed that the House Judiciary Committee recommended his bill with only minor changes in the wording of its caption, prompting him to hope that while congressmen were "busy raising my taxes they may find time to put through my pet scheme." That did not happen until the new year arrived, and then on 6 January 1936 the House approved the bill with minor amendments in which the Senate concurred. Two weeks later President Roosevelt signed it. With Sisyphus no longer serviceable as a metaphor, Chafee remarked: "Now that the interpleader bill is out of the way I feel as if, like Othello, my occupation was gone."[41]

His occupation was not gone but his health was going, and by the following fall a nervous breakdown forced him to take a medical leave of absence for the 1936–37 academic year. No doubt the added burden of getting his act through Congress contributed to his illness. Or, as seems more likely, once he was out from under that additional pressure, he succumbed to the tension associated with a series of family stresses that had begun a decade earlier. For Chafee, his wife, and their four children, the period from 1926 to 1941 was difficult indeed—although financially less difficult than it would have been without the generous assistance of his father.

Those who knew the Chafees considered them a beautiful and gifted family. The paterfamilias was brilliant, of course, but also admired by family and friends for his generous spirit and good humor. His colleague John M. Maguire, who had the intimate experience of accompanying Chafee and others on a coastal cruise in 1917 (he served as cook, and Chafee always admired him for his gallant performance in the galley even while seasick), called him "just plain lovable," adding that "I knew of no one who disliked him." And Austin W. Scott, who knew Chafee well from 1916 on said: "He was really a statesman, not just a great scholar and man, and he was basically an optimist . . . He was a fine companion for all kinds of people—a good talker and a good listener."[42]

Chafee, although companionable, was also somewhat aloof. Not so his wife. Betty Chafee was the stereotypical life of any party. A vivacious molasses blonde, she loved the company of men; and men (Chafee's longtime friend Claude Branch seems to have been the only exception) loved her, even after she became increasingly obese. "Somehow, you just didn't notice," related Chafee's brother Francis, who delighted in recalling how Betty used to mix cocktails in "a shaker the size of a fire extinguisher." In Maguire's opinion, "She was just right for Zech; but she would have been right for any man." With a flair for interior decoration, she presided over a home described by Chafee's sister Mary as "always unusual in taste and comfort; everything from the color of the hangings to the arrangement of furniture and objets d'art was the utmost—as was her skill in putting everyone at ease. She provided the perfect setting for the sociability he enjoyed."[43]

Betty also helped liberalize her husband's sense of humor, which had been somewhat puritanical as a result of his strict Episcopal upbringing, and she liberated him further from parental bonds once he had settled on a legal career. "Betty saw to it that he was no longer a 'yes boy,' " his sister Elisabeth commented, "and that bothered our parents. She was a powerhouse. She had a good mind although she was trained only to teach kindergarten. She was quick to size up a situation—aggressive and in the forefront—a natural actress. And she always had an Irish comeback."[44]

As for the Chafee offspring, their sexual distribution was appropriately balanced. Besides the firstborn, Zechariah III, there were Robert, born the following year, in 1914; Anne (Nancy), in 1916; and Ellen, in 1920. In his relations with his children Chafee was more inclined to give them advice than to tell them what to do. Nor was he a disciplinarian. On the rare occasion when a child's mouth needed purifying, it was Betty who applied the soap. He preferred to deal with language problems of a different sort, such as reproving young Zech for saying "like" instead of "as."[45] Seldom did he show anger or raise his voice, which was naturally so loud that a friend described it as "nautical."

For these and other reasons, Chafee's progeny looked back with pleasure upon their childhood. "His thoughtfulness and quiet enthusiasm for us made a lasting impression," Nancy Chafee Brien related. "When with us, he devoted all his attention to us . . . Our interests were his interests: a new pad of paper for a would-be author, the latest postage stamp for the collector, another piece of track for the boys' electric train, or a picture book for the baby." And Zechariah III remembered how his father encouraged his interest in railroads—an interest that led, after graduation from Harvard Business School, to a career in middle management with the freight traffic department of the Pennsylvania Railroad—as well as in more ephemeral topics: "Once when I was interested in state boundaries, he checked relevant books out of [Harvard's] Widener Library and brought them home for me. And when I compiled maps about voting in presidential elections, he bought me a binder to keep them in."[46]

It was during 1926–27, as the family was enjoying a sabbatical year in Europe, that their personal problems began. While the parents traveled extensively on the continent, the boys attended Le Rosey, a school at Rolle on Lake Geneva, and the girls were cared for and tutored by two sisters in Neuchatel, Switzerland. Toward the end of the leave, Nancy fell ill with appendicitis; but the routine surgery disclosed that she also had a small tubercular gland in her abdomen. The parents decided that the girls' governess at Neuchatel, Mlle. Odette Rutschmann, should be with Nancy during her treatment, which was received at a sanitarium in Tucson, Arizona (recommended by Mrs. Chafee's uncle Thomas W. Salmon, a psychiatrist at Columbia University, who was married to her mother's sister Helen). Prior to leaving Europe, Chafee had to wire his father asking to borrow $300. Zechariah, Sr., obliged by sending twice that amount—a response that set a pattern for many similar but larger gifts and loans over the next decade.[47]

In 1928 the Chafees sold their home at 81 Irving Street—they had lived there since 1916, but the corner location had become increasingly unpleasant because of traffic congestion and numerous accidents at the intersection with Kirkland Street—and bought the three-story residence at 26 Elmwood Avenue. It had belonged to Chafee's law school colleague Francis Bohlen, who found Cambridge stuffy and was returning to Philadelphia; thus he was willing to part with it for what he had paid in 1926 when he came to Harvard from the University of Pennsylvania. The sale price included Chafee's assumption of two mortgages totaling $27,000. After the stock market collapsed a year later, the buyer of the Irving Street house defaulted on the mortgage and Chafee had to reassume that obligation.[48]

And the depression had still other financial ramifications for Chafee and his family. His income from teaching—about $10,000 in the early 1930s—and writing had been supplemented by dividends from the two businesses started by his grandfathers as well as from other investments. The cessation of dividends from Brown and Sharpe and Builders Iron Foundry was a particularly heavy blow because for years he had been able to count on that revenue. Moreover, the financial reversals came at a time when the costs of educating the children were starting to rise. The eldest, Zech III, was ready for college the year after the crash. Believing that "children are the only investment that doesn't go down," Chafee invested heavily in his children's education. All four were allowed to attend the college of their choice after graduating from private schools in the Boston area; both Zech III and Bob opted for Harvard, Nancy went to Radcliffe, and Ellen selected Smith. From time to time Chafee got help with educational expenses from his father or from a family holding company called the Young Orchard Company.

In the summer of 1934, after Zech III's graduation from college and Bob's second year at Harvard, a series of emotional problems began. A brilliant and somewhat frail youth who was sensitive to social injustices, Bob suffered a nervous breakdown while spending the summer at Sorrento. Two years later, after finishing college, he broke down again. After Chafee's own nervous collapse during this period, for a time both father and son were under the care of the same psychiatrist, Dr. Lawrence K. Lunt of Boston. Chafee's illness required treatment at two institutions—Valleyhead Sanitarium in Concord and the Institute of the Pennsylvania Hospital in Philadelphia—and in a typical act of kindness after his recovery, he sent gifts to two patients at the Philadelphia facility. To one who enjoyed puzzles he mailed a little book called *Brain Teasers*. Informing the other that he was having an inflatable rubber horse shipped to him, he explained: "Remembering the good times that I used to see you having in the swimming pool, I am sending you a seahorse . . . He resembles another steed called Percy which my sister and her children bestride in their open-air swimming pool on the Maine Coast. I hope very much that you will enjoy him. Do not spur his sides to make him behave as the result might be disastrous. I hope that you will accept this animal as an expression of my gratitude for your kindness last winter in making my stay at the hospital pleasant."[49] After his year of forced seclusion, he remarked to his friend Ernest Angell, a New York lawyer and then chairman of the American Civil Liberties Board: "The trees have never seemed so green."[50]

Before he was fully recovered, however, his wife suffered a far worse breakdown partially as a result of the stress associated with her husband's and son's illnesses. Two years passed before, in 1939, she was declared well enough to go home permanently. During her absence, Nancy ran the house while herself being treated for anorexia nervosa and the weight loss it produces. And Zechariah, Sr., paid most of Betty's medical expenses. But once she was home to stay, he reproved his namesake for having "carried too much steam in work and in spending" prior to his illness: "You had lived beyond your income and you were in debt . . . Betty also carried too much sail and she was irked if restrictions were suggested."[51]

After his illness, Chafee soon discovered "that I could do as good work as I ever did except that I had learned not to drive myself so hard."[52] He worked shorter hours, rested at least briefly most afternoons—and produced several pamphlets and articles, a casebook, and the updated edition of *Freedom of Speech*. He was working on the last phases of *Free Speech in the United States* when Robert, then twenty-six and an Air Corps cadet in meteorology at Mitchell Field, Long Island, committed suicide on 26 June 1941. He slipped away from the base—exactly how was never learned—and went to New Hampshire, whose White Mountains he loved to ski and climb. There, after having studied train timetables, he stepped in front of a night express from Montreal to Boston.

After entering the service, Robert had been sent to the Massachusetts Institute of Technology, where a professor of meteorology considered him the most brilliant student he ever had. But as the time approached to start making forecasts on which lives and military fortunes would depend, his old emotional problems again surfaced. "A beautiful mind, an intense capacity for happiness, a rare power to confer happiness on others, which was his constant desire," his father wrote in a memorial sketch of Robert. "Perhaps it was these very qualities which made him too sensitive, so that life was a little too much for him."[53]

Chafee's courage in times of trouble did not make him immune to the feelings of guilt commonly experienced by relatives of suicide victims. "I blame myself for not knowing how to move faster so as to reach him in time," he commented, "and yet if I had succeeded his unhappiness would have been very great." And he believed that "we shall never be reconciled to our loss."[54] To some members of the family, he never did seem quite the same after that. Still, he had worked hard most of his life, and there was work to be done— starting with the almost completed book manuscript, whose preface is dated 30 June 1941, four days after his son's death. Those six pages include a poignant evocation of deceased civil liberties comrades along with an expression of hope for peace.

Besides completing the book, Chafee kept busy helping with plans for Zechariah III's wedding on 20 September 1941. Addresses and stamps had to be placed on the 972 announcements of his marriage to Curtis Palmer of Lutherville, Maryland, whose Uncle Frank Ober later drafted a controversial Maryland sedition statute known as the Ober Law. "Everything went off happily and legally," Chafee reported to an old Providence friend, "except that the groom did not kiss the bride at the altar. I assume that this part of the ceremony was merely deferred."[55]

By the time he had the pleasure of seeing his only surviving son walk down the aisle, he had been serving for several years on another ABA committee—a new group that reinvigorated his old concern for civil liberties.

CHAPTER 9

Safeguarding the Bill of Rights

In the summer of 1938 the American Bar Association established a committee "for the fundamental purpose of safeguarding the values of American life embodied in our Bill of Rights by promoting regard therefore and knowledge thereof." The idea for the committee was conceived by Grenville Clark, a member of the Harvard law class of 1906, which included Felix Frankfurter. Clark went on to become cofounder, with classmates Elihu Root, Jr., and Francis William Bird, of one of New York's most prestigious firms. Addressing the Nassau County (New York) Bar Association on 11 June 1938 with the speech "Conservatism and Civil Liberty," he said: "We have our committees on many subjects, such as federal legislation, taxation, the revision of the state constitution in New York and on many other public matters . . . Has not the time come when the Bar generally throughout the country should recognize that we are in a period in which the maintenance of civil liberty has become a constant and crucial problem and that, in consequence, the Bar should be prepared through the operation of competent and active committees to bring to bear the influence of the Bar on at least the more serious of these questions?"[1]

When the *New York Times* printed a large portion of the speech, Clark's idea came to the attention of Arthur T. Vanderbilt, then the outgoing president of the ABA, and Frank J. Hogan, the incoming president. They promptly agreed to recommend to the association that a Committee on the Bill of Rights be established, and in no time at all Clark—who later described his committee service as "one of the most absorbing and fruitful things I have ever done"—consented to be chairman with the understanding that he be permitted to pick the members. Clark chose all but one—John Francis Neylan of California, counsel to William Randolph Hearst—who was recommended by Hogan and who proved to be the only dissenter from some of the committee's early decisions.[2]

The original nine-member committee was expanded to twelve in January 1939. At that time the members, in addition to Clark, Chafee, and Neylan, were: Douglas Arant of Alabama, Osmer C. Fitts of Vermont, Lloyd K. Garrison of Wisconsin, George I. Haight of Illinois, Monte M. Lemann (another of Clark's law classmates) of Louisiana, Ross L. Malone of New Mexico, Burton W. Musser of Utah, Joseph A. Padway of Wisconsin, and Charles P. Taft of Ohio. (Ernest A. Green of Missouri, one of the original nine members, died in November 1938.) After agreeing to serve on the committee, Chafee joked in a letter to Clark that "some newspapers evidently expect us to oppose all the policies of the New Deal on the ground that they deprive American citizens of all their rights, the most important of which appears to be the right to be taxed low."[3]

The committee's scope included the "authority to take a staunch and militant stand, after impartially ascertaining the facts, whenever it is found that [the Bill of Rights is] being threatened or impaired, and may otherwise go undefended or lack adequate public presentation."[4] With that authority the committee participated as amicus curiae in several leading civil liberties cases. And although the members followed the general principle of not intervening in a case before it got to the U.S. Supreme Court in order to keep the workload manageable, the first litigation they went into represented an exception to that rule. This was the highly publicized case concerning the repressive measures used by Mayor Frank ("I am the law") Hague in an effort to keep the Committee for Industrial Organization (CIO) out of Jersey City, New Jersey. Chafee, no admirer of either Hague or trade unions, pithily observed that Hague had "fought the closed shop by establishing the closed city."[5] One thing the mayor was particularly keen on preventing was discussions of workers' rights to bargain collectively under the 1935 National Labor Relations Act (the Wagner Act). The city's pivotal act of suppression was its refusal to grant a permit for an open-air meeting, an action that produced the U.S. Supreme Court decision in *Hague v. Committee for Industrial Organization.*[6]

At issue in *Hague* was a 1930 ordinance requiring a permit from the director of public safety for any public assembly in the streets or parks of Jersey City. Because denials of such permits elsewhere in the country had often been upheld by state courts relying on an 1897 Supreme Court decision, the lawyers for the CIO, Morris L. Ernst and Dean Frazer of the Newark Law School, advised against violating the ordinance and appealing the conviction. Instead, they went into U.S. District Court seeking an injunction to prevent the mayor and other Jersey City officials from enforcing the ordinance.[7] It was the right move, for Judge William Clark issued a sweeping injunction backed by an opinion relying on Chafee's *Freedom of Speech* and other authorities.[8]

The day after his decision in the case, Judge Clark wrote Chafee to thank him for some relevant materials he had recently sent and enclosing a copy of his opinion. He said, "I lean upon you most heavily and hope that you will approve some, at least, of the utterances of your judicial disciple . . . I am sure you have been discouraged in the past with the curious tendency on the part of a certain school of liberals to overlook the countervailing considerations of public order. In my opinion I have tried to give them some reasonable scope."[9] Influenced by Chafee's concept of balancing interests, Judge Clark held that while public officials have the power to deny permits in the interest of public safety, Hague and his colleagues had greatly abused the power.

When Hague appealed Judge Clark's ruling, the ABA's new Bill of Rights Committee filed with the U.S. Court of Appeals for the Third Circuit an amicus brief prepared by Grenville Clark and Chafee.[10] Chafee credited Clark with doing "the lion's share" of the work on the brief and described his own role as that of "chief collaborator." The fact that the brief resembled (in Chafee's words) "an Atlantic Monthly essay more than do most briefs" may partially reflect Chafee's concern for language, a concern reflected in a memo he sent Clark after reading galley proofs of the brief: "My college English theme corrector would have made me insert 'also' after 'but' in lines 5, 7, and 10 of [one paragraph]. His theory was that 'not only' should be followed by 'but also.' See also Fowler, Modern English Usage, (1927), page 384, item 6."[11] And the fact that 2,000 copies of the brief were distributed, most of them in response to requests (many other requests could not be filled), may have been due in part to the brief's readability.

Chafee's contributions to the brief were not, however, simply editorial in nature. On his fifty-third birthday, as he was starting his homework in connection with its preparation, he told Clark: "It never rains but it pours. If either Hague or Hitler would behave himself I would have more time to devote to the other member of this precious pair. The Law School Faculty of the University of Amsterdam has invited our Faculty to participate in a protest, and I have been put on a committee to draft the appropriate resolution. Meanwhile . . . I am shocked by the extent to which some courts have gone [in upholding denials of permits for public assembly]. I think that we should give careful study to the DeJonge case, 299 U.S. 353 (1937), to see if it contains helpful language. I hope to get at this tonight and write you more at length tomorrow."[12]

A week later, after proofreading the brief, he again wrote Clark; this time he suggested an appropriate place to insert a statement of the facts in *DeJonge* and a quotation from Chief Justice Charles Evans Hughes's opinion, which voided an Oregon criminal syndicalism statute on the grounds that it violated the constitutional right of assembly. It was the first time the Supreme Court had held that the First Amendment's assembly guarantee applies to the states via the Fourteenth Amendment. "Doubtless the case will be handled by [Morris] Ernst in his brief," he told Clark, "so that the court will know all about it, but it is pretty strong for us and we ought to make the most of it. Furthermore, it will make our brief more effective for public purposes." At the same time, he expressed concern that the appellate court might find "a hole to crawl through" by saying that the case was moot because no requests were then pending for permits to speak.[13]

On 22 December 1938 the committee filed a brief supporting Judge Clark's position. While dealing entirely with the constitutional right of assembly, it gave special emphasis to Jersey City's contention that threats of disorder were a proper excuse for refusing permits to the CIO and other groups such as the ACLU. Arguing against this view, the brief stated that the position taken by Hague and his associates "would place the rights of free speech and assembly in open-air meetings at the mercy of any faction" and that "it is the duty of the officials to prevent or suppress the threatened disorder with a firm hand instead of timidly yielding to threats."

Furthermore, the brief stressed that outdoor meetings are an important medium of public discussion, and that the denial of the right of assembly was a manifestation of intolerance. On the first point, the brief said: "The outdoor meeting is especially well adapted to the promotion of unpopular causes, since such causes are likely to command little financial support and therefore must often be promoted by persons who do not have the financial means to 'hire a hall' or purchase time on the radio." And on the second point, which anticipated an issue whose volatility a few years later so unsettled the Supreme Court that it produced contradictory decisions in two flag salute cases, it contended: "It is because of the striking example of ruthless intolerance afforded by this case that it is so significant for the future of American civil rights. For tolerance is of the essence of the American system and of the American way of life—not only tolerance in matters of religion, but also tolerance in matters of political, economic and social belief; tolerance not only of views that we can approve, but also (as Mr. Justice Holmes said) of views that we hate."

Contrary to Chafee's fears, the appeals court found no hole to crawl through and instead affirmed Judge Clark's decision.[14] Indeed, the court went even further and held that the ordinance was unconstitutional on its face—the same conclusion reached later by the Supreme Court. Right after the appeals court decision, though, the members of the Bill of Rights Committee doubted if the Supreme Court would find the ordinance invalid per se, and they even questioned if such a result should be urged as desirable in their brief to be filed with the high court.[15] On 10 February 1939 Chafee met with Grenville Clark in New York to make minor revisions in the original brief. While leaving open the question of whether or not the ordinance might be constitutional on its face, the brief for the Supreme Court argued that it was essential to conclude that officials can ban a meeting only if doing so is necessary to avert a clear and present danger of a real disorder. And the revised brief placed greater emphasis than the original on the idea that the decree should be flexible enough for cities to establish "Hyde Parks"—outdoor sites set aside for meetings and speeches—as a solution to the whole problem.[16]

By a vote of 5 to 2 (Justices Felix Frankfurter and William O. Douglas, both newly appointed, took no part in the decision), the Supreme Court agreed with the appellate court's view that the ordinance was unconstitutional on its face. But the court also held that Judge Clark had erred in issuing an injunction that enumerated the conditions under which a permit for meetings in city parks could be issued or denied. "The courts cannot rewrite the ordinance, as the decree, in effect, does," Justice Owen Roberts concluded in the main opinion for the Supreme Court.[17] Chafee agreed with Roberts's reasoning on this point even though, as explained in Chapter 7, he liked the injunctive tool's flexibility, which could enable a court to provide, for example, continuous supervision of a polluting factory. "However," he wrote a short time after the *Hague* decision, "the United States courts would be assuming a stupendous and inappropriate task if they undertook a similar supervision of municipalities all over the country. It was much wiser to leave the job of framing park and street ordinances to the city solicitors of the various municipalities . . . The cities of the United States must be governed by themselves and not by the United States courts."[18]

The five justices making up the majority in *Hague* could not agree on a key point: whether reliance should be made on the due process guarantee of the Fourteenth Amendment or on its privileges and immunities clause. The ABA brief favored reliance on the due process guarantee, referred to a series of Supreme Court decisions (starting with *Gitlow v. New York* in 1925) holding that "liberty" in the Fourteenth Amendment's due process clause includes the First Amendment freedoms, and cited *DeJonge*, whose significance Chafee had emphasized, as the decision specifically referring to freedom of assembly. Justices Roberts and Black, however, believed that the speakers had been deprived of their privilege as citizens of the United States to discuss a national question, the position of workers under the Wagner Act, whereas Chief Justice Hughes and Justices Reed and Stone (whom Chafee was then calling his favorite justice) argued that the speakers had been deprived of their liberty as persons to discuss matters of public importance even if they did not concern a national question.

Reaction of press and bar to the Bill of Rights Committee's initial venture into litigation was generally positive, according to the committee's first report, issued some six weeks before the high court decided *Hague*. The report stated: "In numerous editorial comments, both from newspapers usually deemed 'conservative' and others usually deemed 'liberal' or 'radical,' the Association was commended for being willing to stand upon constitutional principles, irrespective of probable disagreement by most members of the Association with the views and policies of the parties whose position was upheld on the constitutional issue. While some difference of opinion on the part of members of the Association as to the advisability of participating in this Hague case has been shown, many favorable comments have been made by members from all parts of the country."[19]

Just about six months before Mayor Hague had begun his campaign to keep Jersey City safe from the CIO, a member of the Jehovah's Witnesses sect went into federal court in Philadelphia and launched what became a minor holy war. His name was Walter Gobitis, and he asked for an injunction against school officials who had expelled two of his children for refusing to salute the American flag. Thus on 3 May 1937 began the case of *Minersville School District v. Gobitis*, the next litigation in which the Bill of Rights Committee intervened and the first civil liberties case of World War II to reach the Supreme Court. It also found Chafee and Grenville Clark lined up in opposition to their friend Frankfurter, whose extreme views on the flag salute issue damaged his credibility with some colleagues on the court early in his judicial career. And one of Chafee's law classmates, Joseph W. Henderson of the Philadelphia firm of Rawle and Henderson, served as counsel for the Pennsylvania school district that expelled the Gobitis children.[20]

What happened to the Gobitis youngsters was part of a broad movement by the Jehovah's Witnesses to resist compulsory flag salutes, a movement accompanied by a growing number of expulsions of their children from public schools. As early as the middle of 1936, estimates were that 120 children had been expelled; by 1939, the number exceeded 200 with Pennsylvania leading the way with more than 100.[21] In some instances parents were also prosecuted for failing to send their children to school.

In an early comment on the flag salute controversy, Chafee wrote his son Robert from Chicago where he was attending a meeting of the Bill of Rights Committee in January 1939: "We may take a crack at the flag-salute laws on behalf of Jehovah's Witnesses, who are in a jam all right. First their children get thrown out of school for not saluting the flag—'bowing down to a graven image' as they look at it and it amounts to something like that with some of these idolatrous patrioteers—and then they get prosecuted for not sending their children to school."[22] Three months later, on 1 April 1939, the committee entered the flag salute controversy for the first time when it filed with the U.S. Supreme Court a Memorandum in Support of Jurisdiction in *Johnson v. Town of Deerfield*, an expulsion case out of Massachusetts. Without going into the merits, the memo asserted that *Johnson* (and a companion case out of California) involved fundamental civil rights questions that it was desirable for the high court to clarify. And it further argued that the issues had not been foreclosed by previous Supreme Court decisions dismissing similar cases for lack of an important federal question.[23] Unimpressed, the justices on 17 April 1939, in a per curiam decision citing the previous dismissals, affirmed the lower court's judgment without hearing oral arguments.[24]

Even before it filed the memo in the *Johnson* case, the committee was considering intervening in the *Gobitis* litigation. The trial was held on 15 February 1938, before District Judge Albert B. Maris, who had been appointed to the federal bench by President Roosevelt in June 1936. "On the basis of a thoughtful opinion, at a preliminary stage," as the Supreme Court later observed, Judge Maris decided the case in favor of the Jehovah's Witnesses on 18 June 1938. "While the salute to our national flag has no religious significance to me," the judge wrote in a key passage, "and while I find it difficult to understand the plaintiffs' point of view, I am nevertheless entirely satisfied that they sincerely believe that the act does have a deep religious meaning and is an act of worship which they can conscientiously render to God alone. Under these circumstances it is not for this court to say that since the act has no religious significance to us it can have no such significance to them."[25]

Judge Maris's decision was upheld in November 1939 by the Third Circuit Court of Appeals, where William Clark, who had issued the original decree in *Hague*, was one of the three judges hearing the case. Judge Maris himself had been promoted to the circuit court by this time; because he could not sit on the appeal from his own decision a district judge substituted for him. From the time it heard oral arguments in November 1938, the court took almost one year to decide the case in an opinion written by Judge Clark. In balancing the interests of the state with those of religion, Judge Clark imported the clear and present danger test from the free speech field and concluded that in this case the spiritual interests outweighed the material.[26] Not long after the circuit court's decision came down, Chafee sent Judge Maris a reprint of an interpleader article and, in a letter commenting on several recent interpleader cases he had decided, he noted: "As a member of the Bill of Rights Committee of the American Bar Association I was very much pleased by your decision in the *Gobitis* case and I am rejoicing on its affirmance on appeal. I do not see how the Supreme Court can crawl out from under this time."[27]

The court did not crawl out from under in the sense of refusing to review the case. But it did not affirm the circuit court's decision, either, thus rejecting the arguments put forth in the next amicus brief filed by the Bill of Rights Committee. In an account prepared years later Grenville Clark told how he and Chafee "wrote together every word of it" in the spring of 1940.[28] Clark's memory seems to have erred here, because correspondence in files of the Bill of Rights Committee shows that at least the first draft of the brief was the work of Clark and Louis Lusky.[29] It was Lusky who, while serving as clerk to Justice Harlan Fiske Stone a few years earlier, had drafted several paragraphs of the justice's famous footnote four—which evolved into the First Amendment doctrine of preferred freedoms—in the case of *United States v. Carolene Products Co.*[30]

Chafee himself said that the *Gobitis* brief was largely Clark's work and that his own contribution consisted of helping to polish it and of writing a good deal of part II. However, as early as January 1939 he was urging Clark—who had written Chafee of his "strong *feeling* for going into that [flag salute] situation"—to let the committee intervene and asking Harvard law colleague George K. Gardner—who taught Contracts and Insurance but had an active interest in civil liberties—to help the committee by preparing a draft brief.[31] Within a few weeks Gardner prepared a lengthy memo headed "The Immediate Question—Should the Committee Ask Leave to Appear as Friends of the Court in the Case of Gobitis v. Minersville School District?" He concluded that it should; the committee agreed, but a year later, after the appeals court decision, it nearly failed to win the approval of the ABA's House of Delegates to file a brief with the Supreme Court.[32] As for Gardner's involvement in the case, he later wrote an amicus brief for the ACLU and took part in the oral arguments before the high court where, in a harbinger of the final outcome, he was badgered by his erstwhile colleague Frankfurter.

Unlike the committee's briefs in *Hague* and the second flag salute case, decided in 1943, its brief in *Gobitis* was filed with the Supreme Court before the justices had agreed to review the case and it included a technical presentation of the reasons why certiorari should be granted. This aspect of the brief Chafee called "a tough job which we shall rarely care to repeat."[33]

After carefully reading a printed draft of the brief prepared by Clark and Lusky, Chafee wrote Clark that it was "a splendid job." He was especially enthusiastic about its third point—arguing that the flag salute infringed the Gobitis children's liberty apart from any religious considerations—for personal reasons. "My own preparation for college was given by a public high school, where I was very happy," he explained. "I am absolutely certain that if a regulation for saluting the flag had been imposed on us when I was in high school, I should have refused to comply and so been deprived of all I owe to the institution. My refusal would not have been based on religious grounds, but only on instinctive dislike for this sort of ceremony when forced on people."[34] Ironically, Chafee's contributions to the brief appeared in a section (part II) devoted to religious freedom—specifically to the question of whether or not there was sufficient public need for the compulsory salute to override the children's religious scruples. This, in the committee's view, represented the pivotal question of law.

In considering "the appropriate standard of judicial scrutiny," the brief expanded on Justice Stone's recently expressed notion of the First Amendment's preferred position by stating the committee's "firm belief that legislation which infringes upon such basic individual liberties as freedom of speech, press, assembly, and religion should be subjected to a more exacting test of validity than legislation which regulates property and business." And then in the following passage, which leaned heavily on but somewhat modified a lengthy paragraph in Chafee's memo to Clark, the brief presented "solid reasons for a distinction in the *judicial approach* in testing the validity of laws in these two general categories":

In the ordinary due process case involving legislation which taxes or otherwise affects property, the Court is dealing merely with a negative provision of the Constitution, which imposes some limits on common types of legislation . . . Accordingly, a presumption may properly be held to run in favor of the validity of this class of legislation. In recognition of this principle, the general rule for such ordinary statutes and regulations is that they will be upheld if there is evidence in the record tending to establish the existence of a state of facts which rational men might consider a basis for governmental action, or if the Court can judicially notice such facts. [A quotation from Justice Stone's opinion in *Carolene Products* is omitted; it had not appeared in Chafee's memo.]

On the other hand, when legislation undertakes to restrict or override religious beliefs it runs head on against a great affirmative principle expressly declared by the First Amendment and embodied in national emotions since the landing of the Pilgrims. So strong is the policy of safeguarding the basic individual liberties—including religious freedom—that the presumption should be against, rather than for, the validity of any statute abridging those liberties. Therefore, we submit that it would not be sufficient for the Court here to accept the mere opinion of other men. We respectfully submit that in a case of this kind the Court should *itself* be convinced of the existence of a public need which is sufficiently urgent to override the great principle of religious freedom in the particular case.[35]

Chafee said he also was "to a considerable extent responsible for" pages 22–24 and 28–29 of the brief. These passages assessed the alleged public need for the compulsory salute and examined other cases where, the committee believed, in contrast to *Gobitis*, courts had properly held that religious liberty must yield to a legal requirement.[36]

In mid-April 1940, as Clark was preparing to revise the brief to include some of Chafee's suggestions, Chafee quipped to Charles Evans Hughes, Jr., that he had "been so busy trying to persuade your Father that the safety of the United States would continue even if a few children did not salute the flag" that he had done little work on a talk the younger Hughes had asked him to give to Harvard law alumni in New York.[37] Chafee may have supposed that Chief Justice Hughes, a Brown man like himself and an admirer of *Freedom of Speech*, would be easily persuaded; if so, he was wrong.[38] In voting to uphold the flag salute, Hughes helped form a majority of eight; and he assigned the writing of the main opinion to Frankfurter. Frankfurter's controversial opinion, with its stirring references to patriotism and the flag as a symbol of national unity, is so well known that it need not be quoted here.[39] It is enough to note that the themes he struck may be seen, at least to some degree, as a reaction to world events: the fall of France, the British evacuation of Dunkirk, the growing Axis threat to American democracy.[40]

Two days after the court's decision on 3 June 1940, Chafee wrote Clark:

> There is much criticism of the Flag Salute decision here. Merrick Dodd has written Felix a long critical letter. It seems to me particularly absurd after the Phonograph case [*Cantwell v. Connecticut,* 310 U.S. 296 (1940), decided by the Supreme Court two weeks before *Gobitis*]. Religious liberty must have sunk pretty far when it ranks below freedom for canned music [the phonograph record in *Cantwell* did not play music but rather a speech by a Jehovah's Witnesses leader attacking the Catholic Church].
>
> Seriously, the court failed like the school superintendents to realize the distinction between a willing expression of patriotism and a compulsory gesture considered to be irreligious by those who are forced to make it. I suppose in the course of twenty-five years the distinction will work its way through the governmental head.[41]

Chafee also sent Clark a copy of a rather heavy-handed spoof of the decision, a two-and-half-page satire he entitled "Tiberius Caesar v. Josephus, Nathaniel, et al." And he sent Frankfurter a copy along with a note saying, "The patriotic implications of your last opinion are so far reaching that I have explored some of them in the enclosed." From Frankfurter came the reply: "I humbly believe that I read your opinion in Caesar v. Josephus with no less understanding than guided you in writing it and perhaps with even more serenity and humor than you felt in composing it. So you see, if one good reader is worth an author's trouble, you have been duly rewarded. I am glad that you continue to prove that law is not a jealous mistress."[42]

It was well that Chafee's little satire afforded his former colleague fleeting serenity, because *Gobitis* and the second flag salute case combined to cause Frankfurter great anxiety during the next few years. His perturbation began while his opinion in *Gobitis* was being circulated among the brethren. The source was the lone dissenter—Harlan Fiske Stone, who became chief justice a year later, after Hughes retired. Frankfurter tried in various ways to dissuade Stone, even writing him a lengthy letter arguing that he was simply following Stone's own views about the need for judicial restraint.[43] But Stone was not to be deflected from the seemingly paradoxical path he had recently embarked on. The paradox was this: In the aftermath of President Roosevelt's unsuccessful efforts to pack the court with justices who would uphold New Deal reform measures, Stone helped to mold a majority that followed a philosophy of restraint in cases involving social and economic legislation. Yet at the same time, starting with his famous footnote in *Carolene Products*, he favored the opposite philosophy in cases involving First Amendment freedoms.[44] During oral arguments in the *Cantwell* case—in their decision on 20 May 1940 the justices struck down a statute requiring permits for door-to-door canvassing—Stone was upset by a remark from Chief Justice Hughes, who hinted from the bench that the Jehovah's Witnesses could not rely on free speech protection because what they said offended Catholics.[45]

Even in the face of his evolving concept of preferred freedoms, Stone might have been expected to join the majority in *Gobitis* because as recently as 17 April 1939 he joined his colleagues in refusing to review the flag salute cases from Massachusetts and California. But when the time came to decide the Pennsylvania case, he was determined to resist. "I am truly sorry not to go along with you," he told Frankfurter. "The case is peculiarly one of the relative weight of imponderables and I cannot overcome the feeling that the Constitution tips the scales in favor of religion."[46] So strong was his feeling that, in a marked departure from a court custom he had helped to establish, he delivered his full opinion orally while "sitting forward in his seat and, in a manner rare for him, reading with fervor and emotion."[47]

To Stone, the action of the Minersville school authorities could not withstand judicial scrutiny because it blatantly destroyed religious freedom and thus tore at the heart of liberty. As for the relationship of the ABA brief to the respective opinions of Frankfurter and Stone, the judgment of David Manwaring is persuasive: whereas Frankfurter tried to rebut the brief's every argument, Stone's analysis of religious freedom seems to have drawn heavily on it.[48] At all events, the triumph of Frankfurter's views soon proved to be a hollow victory, followed as it was by adverse criticism in legal periodicals and by widespread persecution of Jehovah's Witnesses that included beatings and other acts of violence. And then, when the issue reached the justices again just three years later, the court executed a classic volte-face and condemned a comparable compulsory salute in Pennsylvania's neighbor to the south, West Virginia.

West Virginia's salute was part of the fallout from the *Gobitis* decision, having originally been mandated by the state board of education on 9 January 1942, in a resolution quoting at length from Frankfurter's opinion. Again, as in *Gobitis*, Jehovah's Witnesses challenged the requirement, and once more their objections received a sympathetic hearing in federal district court. This time the key judge was John J. Parker, a member of the Fourth Circuit Court of Appeals in Richmond, Virginia, who was summoned to Charleston to round out the special three-judge panel that heard the case.

In 1930 Chafee had opposed President Hoover's efforts to elevate Parker to the U.S. Supreme Court; in an unsigned editorial written for the *New Republic* (and erroneously assumed by some scholars to be the work of Frankfurter), he concluded that the judge's opinions were "usually decisive and solid, leaving no doubt as to what he means." (Chafee had earlier prepared a memo for his law school colleagues summarizing the 140-plus opinions Parker had written since his appointment to the fourth circuit in 1925.) Furthermore, most of the opinions revealed a "satisfactory handling of the ordinary run of litigation, contracts, personal injuries, land titles, patents, bankruptcy." The trouble was that "the Supreme Court nowadays has little to do with such matters. It deals mostly with questions of constitutional law and the application of acts of Congress."[49]

Although Parker, who failed to win Senate confirmation by two votes, was strongly opposed by the American Federation of Labor and the National Association for the Advancement of Colored People, Chafee said nothing about his alleged anti-labor and anti-black sentiments. He did note that "the only indication of his attitude toward civil rights is one opinion declaring a seizure of narcotics invalid." Adding that "the question whether Judge Parker takes a liberal or conservative view on constitutional issues is much less important than his comparative lack of contact with the problems of this nature which come before the Supreme Court," the editorial went on to say: "There would be less cause to doubt his ability to handle those questions with great distinction if his decisions on questions of private law showed an awareness of new currents of thought . . . Satisfactory as he is in his application of sound and settled law, he gives no evidence as yet of a power to adjust the law to important new conditions."[50]

But a dozen years later when the West Virginia Jehovah's Witnesses case came before him, Parker demonstrated that he was sensitive to recent changes in public law and quite capable of bending with the constitutional winds blowing out of Washington. Whereas in the two years following *Gobitis* the Jehovah's Witnesses had lost eight cases on unanimous decisions in the Supreme Court, suddenly on 8 June 1942 this unanimity was fractured by a 5-to-4 vote in *Jones v. Opelika*.[51] By the time this case—really several cases, all dealing with municipal ordinances taxing publications the Jehovah's Witnesses sold door-to-door—reached the high court, Justices Hugo L. Black, William O. Douglas, and Frank Murphy had come to regret their support of the *Gobitis* decision and were resolved to divorce themselves from it. This they did by joining with Stone, now chief justice, to dissent from the majority's *Opelika* opinion, which upheld the tax ordinances. And they also added a separate statement in which they took the unusual step of saying they now believed that the majority opinion they joined in *Gobitis* was wrong. Presently, the four dissenters were joined by the liberal Wiley B. Rutledge (appointed after the resignation of the conservative James F. Byrnes), *Opelika* was reargued, and the Court vacated its earlier judgment.[52]

With the demise of *Opelika*, the days of *Gobitis* were obviously numbered—an eventuality readily recognized by Judge Parker, who wrote the unanimous opinion of the three-judge district court. Although an unreversed U.S. Supreme Court decision traditionally binds lower federal courts, he was convinced that an exception had to be made in the instant case of *Barnette v. West Virginia State Board of Education*.[53] "Of the seven justices now members of the Supreme Court who participated in [the *Gobitis* case]," he wrote, "four have given public expression to the view that it is unsound, the present Chief Justice in his dissenting opinion rendered therein and three other justices in a special dissenting opinion in *Jones v. City of Opelika* . . . The majority of the court in [the latter case], moreover, thought it worth while to distinguish the decision in the Gobitis case, instead of relying upon it as supporting authority. Under such circumstances and believing, as we do, that the flag salute here required is violative of religious liberty when required of persons holding the religious views of the plaintiffs, we feel that we would be recreant to our duty as judges, if through a blind following of a decision which the Supreme Court itself has thus impaired as an authority, we should deny protection to rights which we regard as among the most sacred of those protected by constitutional guaranties."[54]

In dealing with the religious freedom issue, Judge Parker leaned hard on the lower court opinions of Judges Maris and Clark in the *Gobitis* case. Just as Clark had done, he invoked the clear and present danger doctrine: "Religious freedom is no less sacred or important to the future of the Republic than freedom of speech; and if speech tending to the overthrow of the government but not constituting a clear and present danger may not be forbidden because of the guaranty of free speech, it is difficult to see how it can be held that conscientious scruples against giving a flag salute must give way to an educational policy having only indirect relation, at most, to the public safety."[55]

When the Bill of Rights Committee decided to go into the *Barnette* case, most of the drafting of the brief was done by Chafee. One reason was that Grenville Clark was no longer on the committee; Clark did, however, make important suggestions that were followed by Chafee, who also "left out everything in the galley proof to which Grenny objected."[56] At the outset, it was agreed that the brief should be kept relatively short and rely on key portions of the *Gobitis* brief. Clark advised Chafee to have a student comb law reviews since May 1940 for comments on the *Gobitis* decision and related cases, including the June 1942 recantation by Justices Black, Douglas, and Murphy in *Opelika*. Among other sources that Clark said should be consulted was Judge Parker's opinion in *Barnette*. "You know my idea," he told Chafee, "which is to assemble an impressive body of evidence to show that the profession simply revolted at the *Gobitis* decision in an almost unique manner, proving this (a) by a lot of citations from the Law Reviews, which I believe will be found virtually unanimous; and (b) by Court decisions. I doubt if that evidence of disapproval has ever been marshaled in this way and if it is, I believe it would impress any Court."[57]

This strategy helped shape the third and final section of the brief, which in its method of drafting reveals a small but interesting facet of Chafee's personality. Like many people who come from monied backgrounds, he tended to be economical in small things—even if his own funds were not involved—and in preparing lecture notes and in drafting major articles and memoranda, he often wrote in longhand in unused portions of student exam booklets. (His dictation to a secretary consisted mainly of routine letters and similar short items.) This characteristic may reflect the fiscal conservatism of Dean Pound, who urged upon the faculty such economies as using both sides of a sheet of paper for correspondence. In any event, when it came to preparing the *Barnette* brief, Chafee used any scrap of paper that was handy, including the unused pages of a note to him and even the blank spaces on a postcard from the Swiss Colony Cheese Company in Monroe, Wisconsin.

The first two sections of the brief amounted to a restatement of the religious freedom arguments of the *Gobitis* brief; but this time there was no separate section relying on the doctrine of substantive due process. Early in the *Barnette* brief the committee's position was summarized as follows: "[we have] no interest in this litigation save as its outcome will affect the integrity of the basic right to freedom of conscience. Consequently, this brief will not discuss the effect of the Joint Resolution of Congress" (dealing with respect for the flag; this ambiguous and controversial 1942 measure—known as Public Law 623—had been sponsored by the American Legion). Because the constitutional issues were the same as those in *Gobitis*, the committee hoped that the court would, upon reconsideration of that case, decide to follow the opinion of the present chief justice. The two essential reasons for the committee's position were: (1) The flag salute in its application to the plaintiffs and their children should be treated by the court as a religious ceremony. (2) This impairment of religious liberty had no reasonable tendency to promote any public interest.[58]

In elaborating on those themes, Chafee repeated the committee's view that the compulsory salute was justified only if it was both appropriate and necessary to an end sufficiently urgent to outweigh the policy laid down in the First Amendment. Directly attacking Frankfurter's views in *Gobitis*, he urged that all First Amendment freedoms be treated equally. Responding to Frankfurter's growing conviction that the political process not the courts was the place to correct abuses, he commented: "Such a small religious group is very unlikely to attain sufficient voting power to overthrow compulsory flag salute laws. It must obtain protection from the Bill of Rights, or nowhere. Surely the First Amendment was not written to put the religious liberty of small groups at the mercy of legislative majorities and school boards."[59]

The brief's concluding paragraphs are vintage Chafee in at least three respects. First, there is a reference to balancing interests: "We recognize that some interferences with religious liberty are constitutional, for it is not unlimited. The value of religious liberty must be weighed in the scales against the value of the conduct which the law requires. It is a problem of balancing." Second, a favorite biblical passage is quoted: "The law does not require national unity and it could not. National unity is a creation of the spirit, and the wind of the spirit 'bloweth where it listeth,' " from John 3:8: "The wind bloweth where it listeth, and thou hearest the sound thereof, but canst not tell whence it cometh, and whither it goeth: so is everyone that is born of the Spirit." (The first clause is liberally sprinkled through his correspondence.) And, third, there are references to milestones in the nation's history and to one of its great modern poets: "The nation which survived Valley Forge and the dark days of the Civil War without compulsory flag salutes will not go to rack and ruin because a few children fail to participate in this novel ceremony on account of their religious beliefs. We respectfully urge the Court to adopt the view of the present Chief Justice that their absence will not endanger the safety of the nation. Robert Frost, the poet, put this whole case in a nutshell when he recently said in reply to the observation that Mr. Justice Stone's opinion showed no such fears: 'Yes, he knew the flag was all right, any way.' "[50]

One thing not found in the brief is a reference to Judge Parker's opinion—even though Grenville Clark had included it among suggested sources and despite the fact that Chafee followed many of Clark's suggestions. This omission was noted by a St. Louis lawyer who thought Chafee's brief "admirable, except that I wished that your point II had stepped boldly into clear and present danger [instead of mentioning it without elaboration] . . . in Judge Parker's opinion . . . I was gratified by his application of this test to abridgment of religious freedom. In my article last year, which you cite, I had ventured to criticize . . . the continued failure of the Supreme Court to make this application in other cases of religious freedom, long after the test had been fully accepted for freedom of expression."[61] Writing on the day the justices decided *Barnette*—the court symbolically chose Flag Day of 1943 to hand down its decision in favor of the Jehovah's Witnesses—the lawyer also wondered if Justice Robert H. Jackson's opinion for the Court had said anything about the danger test. It had indeed.

In his majority opinion (Justices Stanley F. Reed and Owen J. Roberts dissented along with Frankfurter) expressly overruling *Gobitis* and the earlier per curiam decisions, Jackson coupled the preferred freedoms concept with clear and present danger: "The right of a State to regulate . . . a public utility may well include, so far as the due process test [of the Fourteenth Amendment] is concerned, power to impose all of the restrictions which a legislature may have a 'rational basis' for adopting. But freedoms of speech and of press, of assembly, and of worship may not be infringed on such slender grounds. They are susceptible of restriction only to prevent grave and immediate danger to interests which the State may lawfully protect. It is important to note that while it is the Fourteenth Amendment which bears directly upon the State it is the more specific limiting principles of the First Amendment that finally govern this case."[62]

The outcome—amusingly foretold by a typographical error on the cover of the ABA brief that turned "Friends of the Court" into "Friends on the Court"—brought Chafee various congratulatory messages. Among them was one from Osmer C. Fitts, an original member of the Bill of Rights Committee and then a major with the Army Judge Advocate General's Division: "It was thrilling to be in the Supreme Court this morning and hear your theories before Gobitis prevail in the Barnette case. Congratulations on your good job." And from his colleague George Gardner came this note: " 'Erasmus wins in the end'; but Chafee doesn't have to wait so long. Congratulations on your victory—for I think it is more yours than that of any other one man in these United States." (Earlier, Gardner had said of the typo on the brief's cover: "I think 'Friends on the Court' was a genuine act of God. It is so completely pertinent to what one finds within the covers that I cannot but think it will fetch just the laugh that is so necessary to close this dreadful affair once and for all.")[63]

Although Chafee himself was pleased with the result, he was not exuberant because the committee's arguments had a negligible influence on Justice Jackson. "Well, we certainly put it over on the flag salute case, or somebody did," Chafee told the committee's chairman. "I can't say that Jackson followed our ideas, but perhaps the brief helped some of the other judges to concur with him. The opinion goes far beyond religious objections. Apparently any child who feels that he cannot join wholeheartedly in the ritual can now be excused."[64] And in a note to Chief Justice Stone dealing mainly with interpleader, he said: "I was naturally pleased with the decision in the Barnette case, but I should have liked it better if the Court had simply affirmed the court below on the basis of your opinion in the Gobitis case, which I shall always consider the best statement of the principles which govern this perplexing situation." Stone replied: "Thank you for your comment on my Gobitis opinion. I naturally think there was more in it than some of my brothers seemed to find in it. But they saw *nothing* in it at first. I thought Jackson's opinion powerful and good reading and I was glad I assigned the case to him for writing."[65]

Much of the reaction to the *Barnette* decision concerned Frankfurter's famous dissent, which began, "One who belongs to the most vilified and persecuted minority in history is not likely to be insensible to the freedoms guaranteed by our Constitution."[66] Perhaps because he was on the winning side this time, Chafee composed no spoof of his friend's opinion. And he apparently chose not to comment—at least not in writing—on criticisms of Frankfurter in letters from other friends. "Don't you think Felix was a little long and it was a little too personal for him to say he was a member of a persecuted minority?" asked the distinguished New York lawyer Charles C. Burlingham. "But these things are better said than written; so please tear this letter up." And Carl S. Stern, a collaborator on Wickersham Commission work, thought it "too bad that Felix got autobiographical and race conscious" although he called some parts of the opinion "wise and eloquent."[67]

Frankfurter's views in dissent must have come as no surprise to Chafee and Clark, who had written Chafee in the fall of 1942, at a time roughly midway between *Gobitis* and *Barnette:* "You know Felix really *did* go off the track in [*Gobitis*]. J. W. Henderson [counsel for the Minersville school officials] remarked to me in Indianapolis that he was convinced that if the case had been argued even a few months earlier or later, it would have been decided differently. The reason is clear enough, viz., that Felix, as a foreign-born person, was unduly sensitive to being accused of lack of respect for the flag. But, of course, that is one of those things one can never prove."[68]

What is certain is that the flag salute cases represented the high water mark of the Bill of Rights Committee's work—with the *Gobi-*

tis brief possibly registering a higher mark than the *Barnette* one because it helped prepare the way for the later favorable result. Reminiscing in 1951, Clark said he thought the committee had "a good deal to do with bringing about" the principle of the *Barnette* decision, a principle that he called "one of the main safeguards of American liberties." But even at the time, as well as later, he thought that "its most important act" was filing the brief in *Gobitis*.[69]

After *Barnette* and for the duration of Chafee's committee service, ending in 1947, the group filed no more Supreme Court briefs. Chafee did draft one other brief, however, while serving on the committee. The case was that of Clyde W. Summers, a Methodist conscientious objector who had been denied admission to the Illinois bar because of his views. Then an instructor of law at the University of Toledo, he went on to become a member of the Yale law faculty.

Chafee became deeply interested in Summers's plight for several reasons, including the fact that "after having had to argue in behalf of Jehovah's Witnesses, it is very agreeable to deal with a man whose religious views are sympathetic to me."[70] When Roger N. Baldwin of the ACLU brought the case to his attention some six months after *Barnette*, Chafee outlined the facts in a letter to Burton W. Musser, then chairman of the ABA committee. At first, the committee's thinking was that Summers should be aided by one of the local bill of rights committees that the national committee had fostered soon after its own creation—in this instance, the committee of either the Illinois or the Chicago bar association. But such help was not forthcoming, and so the national committee directed Chafee to prepare a memorandum on the case.

His memo, written in June 1944, ran to thirty-six pages, but it had no immediate impact because evasive tactics by the Illinois Supreme Court made it impossible for Summers to seek relief from the Supreme Court. Besides twice refusing to review the negative recommendation of the Illinois Bar Association's Character and Fitness Committee, the court would not furnish Summers with a record of the case needed to seek review by the court in Washington.[71] Eventually, in what was considered an unprecedented action at the time, the justices in granting certiorari ordered the Illinois Supreme Court—which had upheld the bar committee's negative recommendation—to certify to the high court the record in the proceedings.[72] This was in late 1944; within a few months Chafee was hard at work on an amicus brief to be filed by the American Friends Service

Committee rather than the ABA partly as a result of timing and partly because of the Quakers' vital interest in the conscientious objector issue.

Chafee collaborated with Harold Evans, a Philadelphia lawyer, and characterized his function as that of "the chief cook and bottle washer." "I have no pride of authorship in this matter," he told Evans, "and indeed realize that a good deal of the draft is a memorandum for you rather than a final statement to the Court. I have conscientiously put in everything which seemed of conceivable importance with the idea of saving you the trouble of running down some point which I had left out . . . So please slash and move around and rephrase and do everything else that occurs to you. This is really your brief."[73] Later he was "touched" by Evans's kindness in putting Chafee's name first on the brief, which concentrated on the issue of religious liberty.

Chafee believed the case turned solely on the question of whether or not conscientious objectors generally could be denied admission to a state bar. While working on the brief, he wrote Summers (whom he elsewhere described as "a fine-grained fellow") a letter speculating on the outcome: "Of course nothing is certain in the Supreme Court of the United States especially nowadays, and the biggest obstacle in your case will probably be the disinclination of the Court to take part in questions of the membership of the bar of a state. On the other hand, the Court is very sensitive to denials of religious liberty and so I feel that there is an excellent chance that the disinclination of which I speak will be overcome by the facts of your case."[74]

The disinclination was not overcome, with five of the brethren (including both Jackson and Stone) voting to uphold the Illinois bar examiners.[75] The result gave Chafee yet another opportunity to refer to himself as "the home of lost causes," but in a letter to Evans he tempered his immediate sense of defeat by taking the longer view: "The [decision] must disappoint you as much as it does me, but we have seen things come around our way before if we only waited long enough. If the Dumbarton Oaks machinery [the basis for the United Nations Charter] can be got to work well, I anticipate a more enlightened attitude toward the valuable service which men like Mr. Summers perform in our country."[76]

Despite the important contributions Chafee made to the Bill of Rights Committee's various briefs, he firmly believed that the committee would have served the public better by opposing proposed legislation rather than by intervening in court cases. "Once a bill gets on the statute books," he complained to Grenville Clark in the spring of 1940, "there is very little that can be done about it. Patriotic judges and panic-stricken juries will apply the statute in ways which were wholly unexpected in Congress . . . A brief as amici takes infinitely more time and labor than a memorandum submitted to a congressional committee or if need be a public statement."[77]

His work for the Bill of Rights Committee afforded him one significant opportunity to prepare two statements—one fifty pages long—opposing pending federal legislation. These argued against the Hobbs bill—legislation introduced by Representative Sam F. Hobbs of Alabama and aimed at negating a 1943 U.S. Supreme Court decision on the admissibility of evidence. In *McNabb v. United States* the court had ruled that confessions obtained by police from a person unlawfully kept in custody cannot be used against the defendant at trial.[78] It was in this case that Frankfurter, in his opinion for the court, wrote the oft-quoted line that "the history of liberty has largely been the history of observance of procedural safeguards."[79] Chafee's long memo, which was widely circulated in Washington, prompted Frankfurter to write that he was "delighted to see this new evidence of the vigorous exercise of your great powers." Not all the mail was favorable; from Federal Bureau of Investigation Director J. Edgar Hoover came what Chafee referred to as "the nastiest letter I ever received in my life."[80] Legislative efforts to wipe away the *McNabb* ruling failed, however, and in 1957 the Supreme Court reinforced it with another controversial decision, in *Mallory v. United States*, that also provoked congressional efforts to counteract its effect.[81] They too were unsuccessful.

In 1947 Chafee left the Bill of Rights Committee after being named to the United Nations Subcommission on Freedom of Information and the Press. During his nine years of service the committee had helped not only to safeguard the Bill of Rights but also to nudge the Supreme Court a little more squarely into its newly assumed role of champion of First Amendment freedoms. On matters of race—dragged into full public view by the nation's participation in World War II—the committee unsurprisingly reflected the conservatism of the legal profession and the nation generally.[82]

Concerning the uprooting, relocation, and imprisonment of 110,000

Japanese Americans, for example, the Bill of Rights Committee acknowledged the program with this comment: "At the request of the committee, one of its members, Ross L. Malone, Jr., made an investigation in Washington of the methods followed in evacuating persons of Japanese ancestry from military areas. He recommended that the committee keep in touch with the problems involved in the relocation of such persons and contribute to their solution through urging tolerance and discouraging hysteria, and in such other ways as may from time to time seem feasible and appropriate."[83] As for Chafee's own views of the program, they partook of the conventional wisdom that such measures were "the inevitable hardships of war." But he noted that they posed real dangers of abuse and could become precedents for worse governmental actions in the future; hence the pending judicial review of the measures seemed "to be all to the good."[84] Climaxing the review process was the Supreme Court's acquiescence in the program, which kept tens of thousands of loyal Americans behind barbed wire for the duration of the war.[85]

At the same time that the war caused Japanese Americans to be condemned as disloyal because of their ancestry, it also included long-oppressed members of the black race in the fight for the red, white, and blue—albeit as members of segregated military units. Inevitably, the war produced, as Chafee expressed it, "an emotional drive against racial discrimination." This attitude filtered through the legal profession to the Bill of Rights Committee, whose members briefly considered two questions concerning blacks.

The first, brought to the committee's attention by several members of the ABA, concerned admitting blacks to the association. Because of his reputation as a civil libertarian, Chafee was a logical contact on the committee for lawyers with such concerns. Among them was Harrison Tweed, a leading member of the New York Bar, who wrote: "I am wondering whether you will not think that defense of civil rights, like charity, should begin at home and persuade your Committee to tell the Board of Governors of the American Bar Association that in excluding Negroes they are making the ABA all of the things that you accused the Associated Press of being—and a few more. [The reference is to Chafee's criticisms, discussed in Chapter 5, of the AP's restrictive by-laws.] Seriously, don't you think that it is essential that the ABA reverse its position firmly and promptly? If all of the decent members insist that the admission of Negroes is so obviously proper that no one can possibly object to it, I do not believe that even the poor white trash among the membership will have the courage to protest."[86]

Chafee discussed this question with Grenville Clark and agreed with the latter's view that it was not within the committee's purview. "No law or government action is involved," he explained, "and I do not see how anybody could say that the American Bar Association is infringing the United States Constitution." Chafee offered two other thoughts on admitting blacks: the initiative for such a policy change should come from local bar associations ("I feel pretty sure that we admit them in the Rhode Island Bar Association but do not know much else"); and "it would be very much better . . . if the proposal for the admission of Negroes should be supported in large measure by Southern members of the [ABA]. I should be rather sorry to see the thing carried by a majority consisting only of people from other portions of the country . . . Although I favor the reform myself, I should like [to see] it backed by lawyers from all over the country."[87]

The second question about blacks considered by the committee concerned whether it should intervene in the case of *Smith v. Allwright*, involving white primary elections in the South. Although the committee did not go into the case (apparently time constraints prevented all members from even considering the possibility), Chafee prepared a lengthy memo arguing for intervention. Noting that the continuance of discrimination against blacks was a serious factor in the war, he said he nonetheless believed it would be a mistake to strive for complete racial equality at that time: "Even if it could be temporarily attained, there is danger of a bad backswing after the war, so that much of what is gained will be lost again as it was after Reconstruction. The law should not push ahead of public opinion too fast. On the other hand, public opinion is advancing and the law can properly go somewhat ahead of it, near enough to maintain a position of leadership." After calling the race problem "the biggest Democratic problem which the nation faces," he concluded: "This case offers the opportunity to bring one important phase of the problem nearer solution. The fact that the [ABA] decides to participate in the case ought to make a great many thoughtful Negroes feel that their claims are not neglected. Thus the participation of our committee should do a good deal to allay the resentment among the Negroes which is capable of causing untold harm."[88] With no assistance from the Bill of Rights Committee, the Supreme Court in 1944 declared Texas's white-primary system unconstitutional.[89]

While serving on the committee, Chafee at times referred to the ABA's governing body, the House of Delegates, as "a pusillanimous bunch." Later, as the association became more timid still, he variously referred to the committee itself as the Committee for Narrowing the Bill of Rights or the Committee for the Suppression of Communism. Such word play was symptomatic of the exasperation he experienced during the last decade of his life, which coincided with the second red scare.

CHAPTER 10

Free Speech in the United Nations

Contrary to Chafee's expectations, he considered the nation's civil liberties record during World War II very good if not excellent. Naturally, he was glad to be proved wrong in his belief that "the next war" would bring a repetition of the earlier repressions. As recently as 1939, he had gloomily prophesied that "whatever happened here in the last war would be even more likely to occur again because the pressure for restrictions is likely to be greater in view of the closely knit organization in Germany." While conceding that "the cause of freedom was better off" in one sense because some U.S. Supreme Court decisions since the First World War had given "considerable weight" to the First Amendment, nevertheless he expected "panic-stricken prosecutors and superpatriotic district judges to run wild again." And because no case would be decided on appeal until after the war, it seemed "probable that errors will not be corrected early enough to help free discussion" during hostilities.[1]

As it turned out, there were few World War II criminal prosecutions for anti-war speaking and writing; in one of those, the Supreme Court in a 5-to-4 decision set aside the conviction, and it did so during, not after, the war.[2] Furthermore, only one periodical seems to have been suppressed—*Social Justice*, published by Father Charles E. Coughlin, the demagogic radio priest from Royal Oak, Michigan.[3]

Among the causes of this improved record, as Chafee and others have pointed out, was the enlightened policy of the U.S. Department of Justice under Attorney General Francis Biddle, appointed to succeed Robert H. Jackson in August 1941.[4] It was a policy that reflected the ideas of Chafee, who restated them in *Free Speech in the United States* not long before America entered the war. One week after Congress declared war, he addressed the Chicago Civil Liberties Committee on the 150th anniversary of the Bill of Rights after appearing the previous day on the University of Chicago Round Table of the Air, a popular radio program. Referring to the liberal First Amendment opinions of Justices Holmes and Brandeis and Chief Justice Hughes, he urged tolerance of unpopular ideas: "The liberties which were created by the action of the people a century and a half ago can only remain vital through the vigorous support of the people today . . . Above all, the maintenance of open discussion depends on the great body of unofficial citizens. If they are intolerant and threaten mob violence and demand suppression, then officials are so sensitive to public view that they will confiscate and arrest and prosecute."[5]

A month later, in a radio address to the American people on Sunday night, 11 January 1942, an assistant attorney general of the United States struck a similar theme. In a speech whose title ("Freedom of Speech in Time of War") was inspired by one of Chafee's early articles, Wendell Berge reviewed the repressions of World War I, including the judiciary's use of the bad tendency test, and endorsed the clear and present danger doctrine. He called it "the guiding test," and emphasized the Justice Department's determination to apply it fairly. And he announced that "On December 15, 1941, we issued instructions to all United States Attorneys, directing that prosecutions for alleged seditious utterances and all other alleged violations of laws affecting free speech shall not be instituted without prior authority of the Department of Justice." Approaching the end of his talk, Berge asserted (and reinforced his assertion with a quotation from Chafee) that "the safest and most effective way to counteract the misguided mutterings of the relatively few people who have not joined with us heart and soul in our mighty effort to win this war is by intelligent and vigorous reply to such people's talk, that is, when what they say is important enough to warrant reply."[6]

A copy of the talk was sent to Chafee by a sympathetic lawyer in the Justice Department, who wrote: "It doesn't fall to many people to fight so hard for an idea they believe in and see their efforts so largely prevail. I am glad you are one of the few.'"[7] Later, Chafee wrote Berge: "Let me take this opportunity to express my admiration for [your address] . . . During the last war, I should never have thought it possible that a leading member of the Department of Justice would express the same views as myself. I would certainly have been proud if I could have said it all so well as you did."[8] Less modestly, Chafee had concluded in 1943 that *Free Speech in the United States* "unquestionably had [had] much influence on the policy of the government toward heterodox opinion."[9]

But if Chafee proved a poor prophet of repressions during the Second World War, he accurately anticipated the political ice age that followed the victories in Europe and the Far East. "Fortunately, there has been much more freedom of speech during the war itself," he told Monte Lemann in late 1944, "but I expect some sort of outbreak of fear during the unsettled period before we get back to normal peace conditions."[10] His terminology was well chosen, for the large literature dealing with postwar repressions includes such titles as *Decade of Fear, The Politics of Fear,* and *The Great Fear.*[11]

Just as the fear was not long in coming, so Chafee was determined not to get mixed up in any more civil liberties causes. In November 1947, for example, with his sixty-second birthday less than a month away, he declined to take part in a forum on the free speech tradition even though he was "frightened and appalled" by what was happening: "I have just published Government and Mass Communications and reprinted Free Speech in the United States, so that practically all I know that is worth saying is accessible to readers. I am afraid that this will have to be taken as my performance henceforth of my obligations to the First Amendment. I have spent a large part of my working career pulling asses out of pits. They still fall in. Mr. J. Parnell Thomas [chairman of the U.S. House Committee on Un-American Activities] needs pulling out, but some younger man will have to do the job. I seem to be needed elsewhere."[12]

It was an old story with Chafee, who quit free speech almost as many times as Mark Twain quit smoking. A dozen years earlier he had said much the same thing in trying to get out of a commitment to draft a statement on academic freedom for a committee of the American Association of University Professors:

> I have some trouble rewriting the view that I expressed so fully fifteen years ago in my book on Freedom of Speech . . . Of course the great trouble about Freedom of Speech is that although there is nothing new to be said on the subject, most Americans pay no attention to what has already been

said. Consequently, I suppose that it is necessary to keep going over and over the same arguments . . . In some ways it would be better to have a new man do the restating because he would come fresh to the subject. On the other hand, I am much shocked by the recent spread of intolerance and hate to abstain from the battle.[13]

The time to stop repeating the arguments certainly was not during the cold war; during its early phase, in fact, his service at the United Nations (UN) gave him a new forum for promoting free trade in ideas. For someone like Chafee, who strongly believed in the original concept of the League of Nations, the opportunity to serve the new world organization was especially welcome.[14]

The first word of his appointment to the United Nations Subcommission on Freedom of Information and of the Press came in a late-afternoon phone call in March 1947. The caller was William B. Benton, assistant secretary of state for public affairs and later an adversary in the U.S. Senate of Joseph R. McCarthy. Benton, who had been a vice president of the University of Chicago and chairman of the Encyclopaedia Britannica board, was familiar with Chafee's work for the Hutchins Commission and had checked him out with Hutchins, his classmate at Yale, and with Henry Luce and Secretary of State Dean Acheson, who had been Chafee's student at Harvard. All agreed Chafee was the man for the job, as Benton explained some years later in clarifying for Chafee that, contrary to allegations made by the *Chicago Tribune*, Alger Hiss had had nothing to do with his selection.[15]

The subcommission, comprising one expert from each of twelve countries, including the Soviet Union, was created by the UN's Economic and Social Council in response to a request from its Commission on Human Rights.[16] The subcommission's chairman was G. J. Van Heuven Goedhart, editor of *Het Parool*, begun as an underground paper during the German occupation and then the largest paper in Holland. Goedhart's background included legal training whereas most subcommission members were either lawyers or journalists. Each functioned as an official of the UN, rather than acting under orders from his government. ("While the Sub-Commission met," Chafee explained, "we were citizens of the world.") But of course each received help from his government's foreign affairs officials and respected his government's wishes to a considerable degree. While Chafee was a member, the group met at Lake Success, New York, from 19 May to 5 June 1947, and again from 19 January to 2 February 1948.

At its first session the subcommission was chiefly concerned with planning the International Conference on Freedom of Information, called by a resolution of the General Assembly in the summer of 1946 and held in Geneva from 23 March to 21 April 1948, with Chafee present as one of five American delegates. Besides working on details concerned with invitations, size of delegations, and committee structure, the subcommission members set the conference agenda. It was limited to news problems, including those involving broadcast commentators and newsreels as well as newspapers and magazines. And the focus was on facilitating the flow of news in and out of countries, although domestic problems of freedom of information were not ignored.

"Regardless of some sharp differences of opinion," Chafee recalled, "the Sub-Commission was an admirable and enjoyable working unit. Nothing draws human beings closer to one another than association in difficult tasks—whether it be a rough cruise or marriage or drafting an important legal document. When the Sub-Commission suspended work in June, all of us (including our Soviet colleague) parted with real liking and regret. When we met again in January 1948, it was like coming back to college after summer vacation and rejoining old friends."

The best of friends sometimes fight, however, and the second session proved more quarrelsome than the first as the subcommission undertook to help the Human Rights Commission with the delicate job of drafting several documents on freedom of information inside nations. The commission had set out to frame an international bill of rights similar to the first ten amendments to the U.S. Constitution and to the bill of rights of most state constitutions. Eventually, the commission decided to issue two documents with somewhat different purposes: the Draft International Declaration of Human Rights and the International Covenant on Human Rights.

The subcommission was asked by the commission to draft articles on freedom of information for both the declaration and the covenant. Although the declaration article was adopted rather promptly, the covenant article—officially designated article 17—turned out to be much more stubborn with work on it consuming most of the second session. The principal difficulty, as recounted by Chafee, who served as secretary of the drafting committee, was that the covenant could not properly protect freedom of speech and press as an absolute right; accordingly, the article guaranteeing freedom of information had to specify some exceptions. Seven were eventually agreed upon.

Within days after the session began, Chafee had several well publicized exchanges with Jacob M. Lomakin, the subcommission's delegate from the Soviet Union. The first concerned Lomakin's charges that the "warmongering, imperialist, capitalist" press of Britain and the United States prevented Russia and the West from achieving peace. Chafee, according to a *Time* magazine report characterizing him as "sharp-witted," waited forty minutes for Lomakin to "talk himself out," then "slyly quoted" from secret Nazi documents just released by the State Department concerning the fate of Poland. Chafee charged that "it *is* imperialism for two nations to say of a third: 'The question of whether the interests of both parties [Germany and the Soviet Union] make desirable the maintenance of an independent Polish state and how such a state shall be bounded can only be definitely determined in the course of further political developments.' This is what the representative of Mr. Lomakin's government agreed with Mr. Ribbentrop [Hitler's foreign minister] on August 23, 1939. To agree to kill a nation! Does that not constitute real imperialism?"[17]

A few days later, Chafee again made news when he sought to rebut Lomakin's contention that "wicked ideas" should be labeled and excluded from the market just like poisons. Calling the analogy mistaken, Chafee remarked that while strychnine is strychnine in every country, the trouble with speech is that "what is poison in one country seems to be the chief and favorite dish in another country." Expanding on this theme, he used several first-person references—a rhetorical device that he soon regretted because of possible embarrassment to Harvard at a time when universities were increasingly suspected of being Communist breeding grounds:

> We have a bill, I regret to say, pending in our state legislature that no person who is a member of the Communist Party or who advocates its doctrines shall be permitted to teach in any school or college in Massachusetts, including the institution in which I am a teacher. And if such a person

is permitted, not only can the teacher be put in jail but also the college can be heavily fined and the president of the college can be put in jail.

Now, the arguments that are used in behalf of this bill are that Communism is poison . . . We cannot tell what is poison and what is not poison in advance . . . Whether Communism will turn out to be the wheat or the tare, I don't know; I don't know, but I want to give people an ample chance to find out. In the American press I am accused of being a Communist, and all I want is to have everybody given a fair chance because I believe that we can trust the people to tell what is good and what is bad and only in that way can they tell what is good and what is bad.[18]

The remarks prompted further accusations from press and public. The *Chicago Tribune*, which only a fortnight earlier had praised Chafee's *Government and Mass Communications* for "refuting" the Hutchins Commission's general report, now blasted him for saying Communism should be discussed in schools and for criticizing the proposed Massachusetts statute. Only the UN's "general stupidity," a *Tribune* editorial stated, could explain Chafee's appointment to the subcommission.[19] And among the critical mail he received was this stereotypical (and unsigned) hate letter: "You and Harlow Shapley [a friend of Chafee's and an eminent Harvard astronomer often accused of being a Communist] seem to be trying to outdo each other in showing your disloyalty to the U.S. and to all that Harvard has stood for through the centuries. Its alumni are disgusted with your antics, as they are with the action of the Harvard authorities in permitting a unit of The Young Communist League to operate on its campus for the purpose of making traitors out of its students."

Because of such criticisms, especially those of the *Tribune*, Chafee had second thoughts about his remarks. In a note to Harvard President James B. Conant accompanying copies of UN press releases of his statements of 22 and 27 January, he explained that both were not written out beforehand but were replies to diatribes by Lomakin: "Both . . . were designed to get away from the side issues which he was raising so that we could concentrate on our main and difficult tasks. On the whole they accomplished this purpose. On our last day we adopted several important points by unanimous vote." He was afraid, however, judging from the *Tribune's* reaction, that the second statement might cause the president "some bother": "If I had had the opportunity to revise it before the release was prepared, I should have altered a few passages toward the end and eliminated some of the first person singular. In my efforts to conciliate the Soviet member I gave no thought to the possibility of misunderstanding on the part of some members of the public. Unfortunately, the stencil for the release was made before I saw what the publicity man for our government had taken down." Some years later he explained to an Oregon journalist that his remarks had been made while "trying to persuade my Russian opposite number to go along with the rest of [the subcommission] in adopting, in the Draft Covenant on Human Rights, a broad formulation for freedom of expression. It would hardly [have] helped win him over for me to take a firm position that Communism was wrong. So I thought it more persuasive to be noncommittal on that subject. Very likely my remarks were not phrased in the wisest way, but my mind was concentrating on influencing his mind."[20]

Even though unanimity had been achieved on several important points as the session ended, Chafee explained to Conant, Lomakin refused to go along on the vote recommending the draft article for the covenant. He almost abstained, Chafee told Henry Luce in a letter noting that he and Lomakin got along "very well," and if he had, "our main work [would have been] unanimous"; however, "at the last moment he must have heard the 'master's voice' for he said, no." Chafee, who always insisted that the State Department "strongly approved" of his efforts to develop friendly relations with Lomakin as well as every other member of the subcommission, was delighted when the Russian, back home after the session ended, sent him an illustrated Soviet calendar inscribed with his warmest regards. "I am much pleased by this evidence of a satisfactory personal relationship," he wrote to the delegate from Canada. "I wonder if he will turn up in Geneva also."[21]

Although the *Chicago Tribune* predicted that Chafee would not be chosen to go to Geneva because it believed the State Department was unhappy with his performance at Lake Success, Secretary of State George C. Marshall wired President Conant on 19 February 1948, expressing "hope that arrangements can be made for Professor Zechariah Chafee to serve as one of the United States delegates. His unique experience including recent service on the Commission on Freedom of the Press and on the United Nations Subcommission on

Freedom of Information and of the Press cannot be duplicated. He would make an outstanding contribution to the success of the United States in this difficult and important field which is crucial both to democracy and international understanding. It is hoped that Harvard University will want to associate itself with this subject of world freedom of information which will assume increasing importance in the years to come."[22] Despite the inconveniences posed by the request—spring semester was already underway and the conference was to begin in a month—the university on 8 March granted Chafee permission to be absent for seven weeks starting 12 March.

On that date he sailed for London aboard the Queen Elizabeth. Delighted at the prospect of seeing Europe again—he had not expected to, he told several friends—he was all the more pleased when the government agreed to find room (but not expense money) for his wife to make the trip. His mood was less buoyant concerning the outlook for the conference itself. "Although I do not expect that a great deal can possibly be accomplished during present conditions," he speculated a few days before sailing, "perhaps we can lay the foundations of something to be built in better times."[23] His skepticism was due not just to the abrasive relations between Russia and the West—relations made still worse by the recent fall of Czechoslovakia—but also to adverse press reaction to the article drafted by the subcommission for the International Covenant on Human Rights. "Since adjournment," he wrote Goedhart on 1 March, "I have been trying to remove misunderstandings of our Covenant Article in high quarters. The head of the United Press [Hugh Baillie] thought that Paragraph 2 was automatically law and rendered everything within the limitations a crime. Editor and Publisher [the newspaper trade magazine] says that the article is as trickily drafted as the Soviet Constitution . . . we have all been accused of selling out to the Soviet. As our former President, Mr. Lowell, used to say, 'you can either do a thing or have the credit for it, but you can't have both.' "[24]

After enjoying two days in London and one in Paris, the Chafees went to Geneva where the conference opened on 23 March. Other members of the American delegation were: William B. Benton, chairman; Sevellon Brown, editor and publisher of the *Providence Journal* and *Evening Bulletin*; Erwin D. Canham, editor of the *Christian Science Monitor*; and Harry Martin, president of the American Newspaper Guild. An alternate, Oveta Culp Hobby, replaced Canham when he had to leave a few days before the conference ended on 21 April.

The nature of this meeting was substantially different from that of the Lake Success sessions. Now there were more than 200 delegates from fifty-four nations, with most of the work conducted in four committees to which each country could send a delegate. The conference delegates functioned as representatives of their government, obliged to consult with their country's other delegates as well as with their government's permanent officials and subject to directives cabled from the home capital. There was little opportunity for the give and take that Chafee had enjoyed at Lake Success, where he said progress was sometimes made during informal meetings of "a few men from diverse countries who had got to know each other intimately." At Geneva committee sessions, he related,

> instead of twelve men sitting close together around a single table, forty or more delegates . . . occupied at least half a dozen tables with the chairman and other committee officers behind a raised desk. So one had the sense of addressing a mass meeting rather than trying to persuade individuals. Indeed, the speaker knew that there was little use in convincing his listeners, since the real decisions were usually not made by them but by hundreds of people outside the room. The necessity of a long interval for translating each speech broke the continuity of discussion, although it had the advantage of giving an opponent plenty of time to collect his thoughts for a reply. There was no danger of blurting out the first idea that came to mind, as with simultaneous translation [as used at Lake Success].

The committee structure used at Geneva had been suggested by Chafee at the first session of the subcommission the previous year.[25] Aware that at earlier UN meetings on the press separate committees on newspapers, radio, and movies had proved troublesome because common problems cut across the three fields, he proposed a different system for Geneva. Besides a committee on principles and general problems and the obligatory committee on law, there were two committees set up on a functional basis: one, on the gathering and transmission of news out of a country, and the second, on the reception and distribution of news in a country. This structure made it possible, for example, for all the work on foreign correspondents to be done in one committee, whereas the earlier scheme would have either split the subject among three separate committees or given it all to the general committee whose members had many other things to do.

Naturally, Chafee was assigned to the law committee, whose chairman was Sir Ramaswami Mudaliar, prime minister of Mysore and first chairman of the UN's Economic and Social Council. Chafee thought Mudaliar was the outstanding person at the conference and one of the greatest men he had known. Charged with drafting, among other things, article 17 of the International Covenant on Human Rights, the committee used the subcommission's draft as its point of departure. Some of the phrasing was improved, but several substantive changes also were made despite Chafee's objections. One change that particularly troubled him was made during a Saturday afternoon session that he skipped to be with Betty on her birthday. They went to the region around Interlaken, and, as he later recounted, while he was enjoying the view from Murren, his committee colleagues back in Geneva were weakening (unintentionally, he thought) the rule-of-law principle that, at Chafee's insistence, the subcommission had carefully embodied in its draft of article 17.[26]

The problem was this: As applied to freedom of speech, the doctrine of the rule of law means that a government official seeking to restrain discussion must be required to rely on a specific legal provision, either in a statute or a court decision. It is not enough, in other words, for the official to show that his action falls within one of the traditional limitations on freedom of speech and press, such as those dealing with criminal incitement or obscenity. At Lake Success, the subcommission had incorporated the rule-of-law principle into article 17 by providing that "penalties, liabilities or restrictions limiting this right [of freedom of information] may therefore be imposed for causes which have been clearly defined by law." But then at Geneva, while Chafee was playing hooky, that language was changed to "the right . . . may . . . be subject to penalties, liabilities or restrictions clearly defined by law."[27] So whereas the subcommission had circumscribed the causes for penalties, the new draft simply required the punishments to be clearly defined. Had he been present, Chafee said, he "would have called attention to the serious effects of this change."[28]

This change in language was not the only thing that bothered him during his five weeks in Switzerland. He was annoyed much of the time by the fact that the American view on limiting speech—a view he had to defend as a government representative—differed sharply from his own. Because officials of both the State Department and the Justice Department believed it would be difficult to include each specific limitation that might be desirable, the United States argued at Geneva for a single blanket limitation to the effect that "freedom of expression may be limited only to protect the rights of others and the freedom, welfare, and security of all." This proposal was voted down in the law committee, where Chafee had the schizoid experience of arguing for it while personally opposing it, and specific limitations were approved instead. However, the seven limitations originally drafted by the subcommission were expanded to include an eighth, sponsored by India, that Chafee disliked. Reminiscent of a viewpoint pushed by William Ernest Hocking on the Hutchins Commission, the Indian amendment called for punishing "systematic diffusion of deliberately false or distorted reports which undermine friendly relations between peoples and States."[29]

The Indian amendment did not represent just "one more" limitation, Chafee explained, because there were no precedents in American common law or legislation for such a restraint on discussion of significant public issues. By contrast, the other seven limitations dealt with problems familiar to American law: vital state secrets, direct incitement of criminal acts, direct incitement of violence against government, obscenity, statements impairing the fairness of judicial proceedings, copyright, and defamation. Perhaps the greatest difficulty with the Indian proposal concerned the matter of proof. "Since the proposal says 'false' reports shall be punished," Chafee pointed out, "it is easy to assume that true reports will be left alone, but the trouble is that there is no litmus paper or yardstick to tell what is true and what is false. We never know that a statement is really false, but only that the tribunal decides it is false. Experience with suppressive statutes like the Espionage Act [of 1917] shows that juries and judges sometimes call political discussions false because they dislike what is said. Yet it is really a matter of differences of opinion."[30]

As for the limitations of the type originally approved by the subcommission, he said the need for them lay in the legal difference between the U.S. Constitution and the covenant. The Supreme Court interprets the First Amendment in relation to the original Constitution, deriving limitations on it from the affirmative powers of Congress. Thus the First Amendment contains limitations even though it mentions none. But such a system of judicially imposed limits to a seemingly absolute freedom will not work for an international treaty like the covenant, which stands by itself. If it granted complete freedom of speech and press, there would be no underlying document like the U.S. Constitution to restrict that immunity.

Further, the framers of article 17 could take nothing for granted; they could not assume a background of familiar law because the covenant was intended to bind many countries, each with its own body of law. Accordingly, every signatory needed to be told exactly what was and was not being promised. "If we drafted a promise which left no opening for a government to punish a person who betrayed its secret plans of forts and airplanes," Chafee argued, "there was very little prospect that our government or the British government would sign it, to say nothing of others. So it was thought essential to permit governments to retain a reasonable power of control with regard to matters where serious danger from abuses of free speech has long been recognized and where some regulation of newspapers is customary in free societies like England and the United States."[31]

At the same time, Chafee emphasized, the article's limitations did not themselves impose restrictions on the press or news media; instead, they were permissive—merely providing that "penalties . . . *may* . . . be imposed" for the utterances specified. No government was required to punish, for example, the disclosure of state secrets or violent revolutionary talk or contempt of court. All that article 17 said was that a government could punish such behavior without violating the covenant. And if a blanket limitation were substituted for specific limitations—as urged by the U.S. government at Geneva—the result would be to make largely meaningless the first paragraph of article 17 containing this statement of an affirmative right: "Every person shall have the right to freedom of thought and expression without interference by governmental action." The trouble was that an open-ended phrase like the "welfare and security of all" in the blanket proposal could be used to justify practically any restriction that struck an official's or a legislature's fancy.

This question, of whether there should be a blanket limitation or specific limitations, Chafee described as "the most complex and baffling of all the legal problems raised by Article 17."[32] The blanket limitation was thoroughly aired at Geneva and repeatedly rejected by "irresistible majorities," with the result that Chafee became "very indignant at the unwillingness of Washington to accept repeated defeats on this point." Although he "joined in this because my government ordered me do so," he otherwise felt he had followed the example of Admiral Nelson at Copenhagen, when he placed his telescope to his blind eye so as not to see the official signal. "I was not built to represent any government," he complained. "I am too much of a lone wolf."[33]

The government's intransigence on this point was carried into the plenary session on article 17, where the American delegation joined the Soviet bloc in a minority of seven nations opposing the law committee's draft. "The occasion on which we added our vote to the six Soviet votes in opposing the rest of the free nations was a moment I do not like to remember," Chafee related to Arthur N. Holcombe of Harvard's government department. "The chief Indian delegate was ready to give up the clause about false and distorted reports in return for our supporting the [draft] in principle. Benton afterward said that we had made a mistake in not abstaining on this vote."[34] On the day before the conference ended, Benton, no doubt aware of Chafee's annoyance, sent him a cheery note:

> I am deeply mindful of the fact that, after devoting so much time and energy to the Sub-Commission, you were willing to make further sacrifices in order to take on this added responsibility.
>
> No one on the delegation has contributed more to our common effort than you have. Without your wisdom and learning, the delegation would have had a very much poorer grasp of the issues; without your conviction and your wit, it would have been very much duller.
>
> I hope and trust that you feel it has been worthwhile.[35]

His wit, at least, remained intact on the last day of the conference, when he drafted a confidential report of his reactions to the proceedings. Remarking on the "impressive tediousness" of the long speeches in the general committee and plenary sessions ("The same positions were expressed at length over and over by the same people"), he said he had worked out a remedy that he called the algebraic theory:

Let "A" represent the American position, "B" the French position, "C" the Russian position, et cetera. When a delegate from the United States makes a speech, he will just say "A" at the start. This will be understood as meaning that we have no censorship, that we admit that we have some bad editors and publishers, but we have many more good examples of both, that we have no real monopolies, that truth will prevail over falsehood in the end, et cetera. When the Frenchman says "B," this will be equivalent to saying that all freedom should be accompanied by responsibility, that the French have been attached to the liberty of the press since 1789, that they had some bad collaborationist newspapers before 1940, and they had determined that nothing like that shall ever occur again. When a Soviet delegate says "C," this means that the press is perfect in Russia, that it is devoted to the interest of the people, that every word is true, and that Western newspapers are entirely controlled by wicked capitalists who long for another war in order to multiply their millions. By this simple method, a great deal of time would be saved.[36]

Elsewhere, Chafee referred to this broken-phonograph repetition of each side's view as "the scold war."[37]

But the rest of his report was deadly serious, and the penultimate paragraph opened with a suggestion on a matter that "is probably none of my business": in Chafee's opinion everybody in Washington with power to make decisions on the subject matter of a forthcoming conference in Geneva of the Economic and Social Council should be present for the entire meeting. His explanation reverberated with the cry of the lone wolf: "As a novice in diplomacy, I was staggered by the frequency with which detailed instructions came from over three thousand miles away on matters where the wisdom of a particular course of action necessarily depended on immediate and intangible factors in the conference itself. How can atmosphere be sent through a cable? It would seem more natural that, except for novel or major questions, the men who are steeped in that atmosphere should be able to deal with the constantly shifting situations before them."

Unsurprisingly, in light of his service on both the Hutchins Commission and the subcommission, his report also contained tart comments about American media, especially newspapers. From conversations with representatives of nations sharing America's general concept of liberty, he said, he had discovered two apprehensions concerning the United States. The first was a fear of cultural imperialism—of being swamped by American movies, magazines, and press services: "If we allow ourselves to impair the vitality of the corresponding industries in the countries which share the common heritage, the world will be intellectually poorer. The ideal of diversity is worth considering in this connection."

The second was alarm over the growing rift between the United States and the Soviet Union: "They feel that in our remoter position we are somewhat blithely contemplating an armed conflict which would destroy them before reaching us . . . The reluctance of our newspapers to criticize each other, which was mentioned in *A Free and Responsible Press*, should be abandoned so far as reckless talk about war is concerned. Unless strong moral forces are operating against such reckless talk, friendly worried nations like the Australians, who want something really done to lessen the evil of provocation to war, may look more favorably on the use of the criminal law than they do now. The Australian repeated abstention on the Indian amendment was significant: they are with us but they need assurance that our reputable press is actually attacking the evils described in that amendment."

And, looking ahead, he suggested that "the American press needs more guidance about the issues in a conference like this and especially about the viewpoints of other countries within the common heritage." Had it been more enlightened in this respect, it might not have spread "the absurd idea" that every government at the conference except the United States was "trying to throttle the press" just as *Editor & Publisher*, in its editorial after the last meeting of the subcommission, had "assumed that men who conducted underground newspapers in Holland and Norway at the risk of their lives joined with the editor of the *Montreal Star* and [myself] in a nefarious conspiracy to subject the press all over the world to Soviet theories."

Although he was no great admirer of either the American press or the American Bar Association, it is doubtful that he could have anticipated the alliance these two forces of the status quo soon formed in opposition to the Human Rights Covenant and to a United States–sponsored treaty to facilitate the international flow of information, called the News Convention. Meanwhile, upon returning home, he often made the point that the conference had accomplished more than he originally thought possible, despite the added chill produced by the Czech coup. And he rated his service on the subcommission as "one of the most important pieces of work I have done."[38] But as for the possibility of continuing to sit on the subcommission, he was ambivalent.

Not long after the Geneva conference ended, he told Dean Griswold that they ought to discuss his future at the UN, adding: "Rather looks to me that I ought to slip out pretty soon rather than find myself serving two masters."[39] His mood may have been influenced by the fact that he was just out of the hospital—minor surgery almost kept him from giving the Radcliffe College commencement address, "Free Speech in the United Nations," on 9 June 1948—for he later indicated a willingness to serve again when the subcommission was reconstituted in the spring of 1949.[40] "I am prepared to continue meeting and talking every year as long as I live with Lomakin and the Bulgarians, etc.," he told Harry Martin, "because I believe that it will lead to something worthwhile after I am dead, but I don't expect to live to see an all inclusive body dealing effectively with the problems of freedom of the press. While we are waiting for that a great deal of good can be accomplished by informal bodies like the [newly established] International [Press] Institute through exchange of ideas, mutual acquaintance and raising of standards in the western countries."[41]

But he actually doubted that he would be reappointed because of his difficulty in taking orders at Geneva. When word came from the State Department that he was not being reappointed, the official explanation was that "now that the Subcommission . . . will be going into highly technical operating problems, it is desirable to have as the American member someone who has had wide experience in the field of international news operations."[42] So Chafee was replaced by a working journalist: Carroll Binder, an editorial writer for the *Minneapolis Tribune* and before that a foreign correspondent for the *Chicago Daily News*. Chafee believed that the choice was excellent and that the reason given for it made sense. But a former colleague on the subcommission, George Ferguson of the *Montreal Star*, thought that the underlying reason was quite a different one: the "smear" Chafee suffered as a result of his service on "the Chicago Commission" (the Hutchins Commission). "This is, in itself, a commentary on the press of this continent," he said in a letter expressing disappointment over Chafee's having been dropped in favor of Binder, "and I will not elaborate on a thesis which is even more familiar to you than to me."[43]

Though his UN service was officially over, his efforts on behalf of the world body actually intensified over the next few years as he defended the Human Rights Covenant and the News Convention from attacks by the press and bar. Much of this controversy became focused on the Bricker amendment (discussed in Chapter 11) calling for limits on presidential power to make treaties and executive agreements, around which coalesced isolationists and states' rightists of both major political parties. Of the subcommission's work, the amendment's author, Republican Senator John W. Bricker of Ohio, commented that "it is impossible to imagine a more legal basis for the most repressive measures of atheistic tyranny."[44] Chafee's defense of the covenant and the News Convention against what he called "the Hostile Critics" was carried on chiefly in the pages of law journals.[45] Eventually, he abandoned the covenant—he had always assumed it would not achieve wide acceptance anyway until "the better times ahead"—in order to defend the U.S. Constitution against the Bricker amendment.

And he followed the same course in respect to the News Convention. Although he had not worked directly on the news treaty at Geneva, he had prepared the way for its consideration by pushing hard to include it on the conference agenda drafted at Lake Success. An important part of his later work for the News Convention came during the early 1950s when he served for two years as chairman of the Press Freedom Committee of the ABA's Section on International and Comparative Law. In this role he achieved the section's approval of the treaty.

The News Convention may have been doomed simply because the press's leadership, which, in the afterglow of V-J Day had urged UN action on freedom of information, had grown increasingly suspicious of the world body as it became evident that the American way could not be imposed on all other nations. This attitude was reinforced in May 1949, when the General Assembly adopted the News Convention—officially known as the International Convention for the Transmission of News—in a form differing from that approved by the Geneva Conference a year earlier A prime indicator of press disaffection was the flip-flop done by Sevellon Brown, a friend of Chafee's from Providence who had worked on the original draft at Geneva. Without Brown's backing, Chafee believed, the News Convention would be "seriously handicapped."

Thus in February 1952, as he was preparing to go to Chicago where the News Convention was to be submitted to the ABA House of Delegates, Chafee wrote Brown seeking to regain his support. Sorry, Brown replied, but he felt he must oppose United States ratification of the treaty because he remained convinced that there was "danger" in its language. And he said President Truman's recent security order, "doubtless well intentioned," had reinforced his fear of how far peacetime censorship could be carried under such general language as "national defense."[46] (The "recent order" was Truman's Executive Order 9835 of 2 March 1947, creating the Federal Employee Loyalty Program and reviving the attorney general's list of subversive organizations. Chafee and other Harvard law professors, including Dean Griswold, had denounced the program for ignoring legal procedures and using as evidence the untested validity of the attorney general's list.)

To Lyman M. Tondel, Jr., chairman of the ABA's Section on International and Comparative Law, he earlier expressed doubts that Brown was honest about the reasons for his changed views: "I am inclined to suspect that somebody got to [him] between the time he wrote me with enthusiastic approval of the action of our Committee [apparently a reference to the section's approval of the Press Freedom Committee's recommendation of the treaty] and the moment, a fortnight ago, when he suddenly sent word to me that he did not like the final draft. His objections are so close to the points raised in the [New York Daily] News and the [Chicago] Tribune about the text of the Convention that everything indicates a common source of opposition. I am reliably informed that the United Press including Hugh Baillie and his assistant, Mr. Frye, are very active against the News Convention. In any event, I feel sure that certain portions of the press will do a good deal to influence members of the House of delegates against the News Convention."[47]

Prior to the Chicago meeting of the House of Delegates, Chafee did what he could to line up newspaper backing for the treaty. For example, in a letter to Irving Dilliard, an editorial writer for the *St. Louis Post-Dispatch* who had spent a year at Harvard as a Nieman Fellow, he noted that he was "up with the sun trying to develop support." And he asked Dilliard to endorse the News Convention in an editorial as well as in a letter to Tondel.[48] It proved to be another lost cause.

Even before Chafee boarded the train for Chicago, the ABA Board of Governors (executive committee) had recommended to the House of Delegates that the News Convention be rejected and the proposal that became the Bricker amendment be recommended to Congress for consideration. To Chafee's great surprise, there was no opportunity for the Section on International and Comparative Law to be heard. But what shocked him even more—he called it "particularly reprehensible"—was the fact that the vote on the incipient Bricker amendment was taken with no consideration given to a pending study, being done for the section under the direction of Harold E. Stassen, of the constitutional status of treaties and their relation to the Bill of Rights. Even Chafee's longtime cynicism toward the ABA had not prepared him for such developments. "I have heard of many dirty political tricks, but never have I come personally in contact with one which was dirtier than this," he told Erwin D. Canham in describing what happened at the meeting. "It is particularly tragic that lawyers should have done this because they are dedicated to the principle of hearing both sides before a decision is reached."[49]

As for the News Convention, Chafee had decided by the time he got to Chicago that there was no point in trying to save it. Letters from Canham and Brown left little doubt that journalists' views of this treaty "made by newspapermen for newspapermen" (as Chafee called it) had been "poisoned"; and Canham also had indicated that prospects were remote of getting it opened for signatures by the UN General Assembly.[50] It became plain, as he pondered such developments while riding the train to the heartland, that members of the international law section had a "terrible uphill fight" to save either the News Convention or the U.S. Constitution, and so "the only wise thing was to concentrate all our strength on saving the Constitution." Upon reaching the meeting site, he immediately met with the section's executive committee and advised "throwing the News Convention as a baby to the wolves." His willingness to abandon "something I had spent an enormous amount of effort upon was generously appreciated by my associates," he told Canham, "although the Chicago Tribune characteristically said that they 'repudiated' me."[51]

His efforts at the Chicago meeting to "save the Constitution" included distributing a statement he had prepared against the treaty-limiting proposal, and he along with others in the international law section also sought to postpone any vote on the proposal until the Stassen report was completed. "The hardshells refused to compromise," however, and so "the leading organization of lawyers in the United States decided in a few minutes to undo one of the main achievements of the Philadelphia Convention of 1787" by endorsing the idea that the treaty-making power should be curbed.[52] But Chafee's fight to preserve the spirit of the Philadelphia Convention had only begun, and during the next few years he became a leading critic of the various versions of the amendment introduced by Senator Bricker.

After Chicago, Chafee also became something of a "hostile critic" of the press. His service to both the Hutchins Commission and the United Nations had sensitized him to the growing need for media responsibility, and his own experiences with the press concerning documents and recommendations of these bodies had been disconcerting. It was not surprising, therefore, that he saw in a speech given by Philip L. Graham, *Washington Post* publisher and Harvard law alumnus, an excuse for flaying journalists. Seizing upon Graham's assertion that the bar had been timid in the face of abuses by legislative investigators, Chafee turned it back on him with the remark that "the press of this country has sometimes also run away. The glaring example of this was the recent attitude of newspapers toward the International Convention for the Transmission of News. When this was completed by the UN Assembly two or three years ago, the newspapers hailed the result in glowing terms. Yet last winter when I tried to get some help from the press in pushing through the American Bar Association's resolution supporting this treaty, I got practically no help. Even your notable organ, I am told, was unwilling to speak in its favor."[53]

Some five months later, Chafee delivered a similar but double-barreled attack on journalists at a meeting in Boston, with the second barrel containing ammunition fashioned from his Hutchins Commission experiences. He complained that the commission's general report had been largely ignored by newspapers except for "the final chapter of recommendations, which were unexciting because we rejected all sensational remedies as worthless," and explained that "the real value of the book lies in the two opening chapters which wrestle with the problem of what the American public needs from the press in our free society." Noting that its main conclusion was that the press should be both responsible and free he explained that the commission meant moral, not legal, responsibility. Then as an important example of press irresponsibility he again referred to its general lack of support for the News Convention as well as the Human Rights Covenant's article on freedom of information.[54]

Such journalistic behavior may have disappointed him most of all because of his belief, often expressed during deliberations of the Hutchins Commission, that the way to improve the media was through professional integrity, not government controls. But if he was frequently irritated by both the lack of press integrity and the threat posed by government regulation, still he often revealed considerable patience. For instance, in discussing the future of the United Nations, in which he believed strongly as he had in the old League of Nations, he concluded: "There is no simple solution. We ought to be patient and remember that cathedrals are rarely built by a single generation. We have to know much and hope much . . . To preserve the integrity and dignity of the individual human being through ever-increasing complexities is a baffling task. Yet it is our task. As DuPont de Nemours wrote from France to Jefferson: 'We are only snails with the peaks of the Andes to climb. By God, we must climb!' "[55]

CHAPTER 11

"Pulling Asses out of Pits" and Other Cold War Exertions

In April 1950 Chafee attained the summit of Harvard professordom when he was appointed a university professor, a rank allowing faculty of exceptionally wide learning to cross the boundaries of knowledge and teach in departments other than their own. His appointment and that of Percy W. Bridgman, a physicist perhaps best known for his 1927 book, *The Logic of Modern Physics*, brought the total number of university professors to six; the others were: Edwin J. Cohn, a biochemist; Werner Jaeger, a classicist and author of *Paideia*; I. A. Richards, a humanist and coauthor with C. K. Ogden of *The Meaning of Meaning*; and Sumner N. Schlichter, an economist. The appointment had special meaning for Chafee because his mentor Roscoe Pound had been the first recipient of a university professorship. From San Francisco, where he was then teaching at the Hastings College of Law, Pound wrote upon learning of the appointment: "No one could be better qualified. Please remember to help Greek, which suffers intolerably in the universities of today."[1]

Besides the prestige it carried with it, the university professorship made more bearable for Chafee the elimination of Equity from the law school curriculum. Indeed, Chafee suspected that the appointment had been arranged by Dean Griswold partly for this reason. "I think it can perhaps fairly be said," the dean told Chafee at the time, "that it would not have been made had I not nursed it along, although I do not mean by that that it was necessary to push or fight it through against opposition, or anything like that. At any rate, I do take personal pleasure in the event, which I know you will not mind. As far as I am concerned, and I know I speak for the rest of us, this is in no sense a detachment of you from the Law School, except to the extent that you wish to make it so. I could not think of you except as a part of the Law School, and I hope I shall not have to try."[2]

As a university professor, Chafee taught two undergraduate courses. One, Comparative Literature 181 (Legal Protection of Literature, Art, and Music), dealt with copyright and gave him an opportunity to combine his legal expertise with his love of English literature and interest in the arts. He had published an authoritative article on copyright (he had also written about, and taught, the related subject of unfair competition) that was distinguished as much by its understanding of artistic creation and concern for ideals as by its discussion of legal technicalities and clashes between commercial interests. In considering ways to improve the outdated Copyright Act of 1909, he described "a philosophical system" comprising these six ideals that the law should seek to attain: "complete coverage for all intellectual and artistic creations reduced to permanence; a monopoly against all forms of reproduction; international protection; absence of excessive protection for the monopoly; refusal to stifle independent creation; and legal rules convenient to handle."[3] As an author himself, he readily identified with authors' concerns about protecting their works, and his article drew freely upon the ideas about copyright of such luminous wordsmiths as Dr. Johnson and Macaulay.

Those were the emphases and interests that Chafee brought to the teaching of the comparative literature course, which was aimed at bridging the gulf between the law and humanities for nonlaw students. He had hoped to attract undergraduates "who would look at these problems from the viewpoint of the author or artist or composer or publisher, and not just as lawyers and judges see the problems."[4] Unfortunately, as he went on to explain to a music professor in a memo seeking to recruit some students from that department, the course attracted mainly government majors suffering from legal preoccupations. The course was also the source of what was the worst experience of his teaching career. According to his secretary at the time, he was horribly upset by the discovery that two students plagiarized a paper that they coauthored—on plagiarism.

He had much more fun with the second undergraduate course— Social Science 120 (Fundamental Human Rights), which gave him his first opportunity to teach a course in constitutional law. Calling his approach to the course "teaching history backward," he explained the method this way: "We have to go outside the operative bodies (the [constitutional] conventions and Congress) and look elsewhere in order to find out what the framers had in mind when they drafted these clauses and voted for them overwhelmingly. We have to ask what experiences and what previous writings were much in their thoughts. And that will not end matters. We shall want to know what the authors of those previous writings had in *their* minds. That will send us to still earlier experiences and discussions, and then we shall need to understand those too from what went before, and so on."[5] He had first tried this method, which he said disclosed "very little that is original with me," while teaching a course at the University of Colorado Law School during the summer of 1950, and then modified it for the nonlaw students in the general education course at Harvard.

In various forms, including several lecture series given at other law schools, the subject of fundamental human rights occupied a great deal of his time and energy during his last years on the faculty. It was a timely topic because the widespread fear of subversives was threatening to subvert the Constitution; but his journey backward in time also served as a temporary escape from the superpatriotic headaches of the present.

Upon being named a university professor, he alluded to his appointment by quoting this line from Milton's *Lycidas:* "Tomorrow to fresh woods and pastures new." The pastures, however, turned out to be pockmarked with pits into which a variety of "asses" had tumbled or were about to fall, and so the exalted teaching post proved in some respects to be just a rerun of his earlier rescue efforts. One of those who had suffered a great fall was Alger Hiss, a friend and former student. His devotion to Hiss alone would have ensured that he would be drawn into the controversy over Communism, a controversy that became cataclysmic after Hiss's conviction for perjury in early 1950. "Without the Alger Hiss case," one historian of the period has written, "the . . . controversy that followed might have been a much tamer affair, and the Communist issue somewhat more tractable."[6]

Underlying Chafee's reaction to the Hiss case as well as to the Communist controversy in general was his basic conception of Communism stretching back to 1920. "Objectionable as the purposes of the Communist Party are to all who have faith in our system of representative government and the possibility of progress through public opinion and the ballot," he wrote in *Freedom of Speech*, "those purposes are not within the Deportation Act of 1918, for they are altogether compatible with the absence of force and violence . . . There is a middle method of political change between the ballot and the bomb, namely economic pressure, and that, however unwise or injurious in nature, is the method of the Communist Party. It advocates the overthrow of our government, but not by force and violence."[7]

Those last two sentences, together with other reflections on Communism from his first book, he repeated two decades later in *Free Speech in the United States*, although one change in wording reflected a slight alteration in his thinking: The statement that "economic pressure . . . is the method of the Communist Party" was changed to "economic pressure . . . may very well be the method . . ." Elsewhere in the book, he declared that the Communist Party was not a conspiracy and argued that it should not be banned from the ballot.[8] In 1947 he recalled the position he had taken in *Free Speech in the United States* but added: "When it comes to the question of [Communists] holding office, I find it more difficult to form an opinion. A man whose primary loyalty is to Moscow cannot properly take office under the United States Government. On the other hand, [those whose main motive is resentment against the inequalities and suffering among us] may very well be useful public servants."[9]

He saw no clear and present danger in the party's American presence because of its comparatively small size: 70,000 members was the figure he cited, using a number taken from a 1947 wire-service report. Perhaps because of his mathematical bent, he liked to express that total as a percentage of the population so as to conclude that "the odds are over 1,999 to 1 in favor of free institutions." And, after noting that he had paid "considerable attention to the activities of Communists in this country" for more than thirty-five years, he offered his "considered opinion that they are far less dangerous today than they were in 1919–1920, soon after the Russian Revolution."[10] Such assertions made him vulnerable to the criticism that sheer numbers bore little relationship to the actual threat posed by Communism, and that such oversimplifications betrayed a serious lack of understanding of the theory, strategy, and tactics of Communism as expounded by Marx, Lenin, and Stalin.[11]

Understandably, a man whose basic notion of Communism had changed so little in a quarter-century found it hard, if not impossible, to imagine even the possibility that a bright, charming product of the law school like Alger Hiss could betray his country by becoming a Soviet agent. Thus when Whittaker Chambers, an ex-Communist then working as an editor at *Time*, pointed a pudgy finger at the urbane Hiss in front of the U.S. House Committee on Un-American Activities, Chafee was incensed.

Chambers first testified before the committee on 3 August 1948. By 15 December Hiss had been indicted on perjury charges by a federal grand jury in New York City; after a trial that ended in a hung jury on 8 July 1949, he was retried and convicted on 21 January 1950. Sentenced to five years in prison, he was released in 1954 after having served forty-four months; in 1957 he published a book proclaiming his innocence.[12] More than three decades later, Hiss was still seeking to clear his name, and in 1975 he did achieve a personal victory when he was readmitted to the Massachusetts bar. Meanwhile, books and articles have piled up "proving" either his innocence or his guilt. The research done by one historian served to change his own mind if not those of Hiss partisans. Allen Weinstein, whose *Perjury* first appeared in 1978, started his investigation believing Hiss innocent and ended up judging him guilty. "Those politically and temperamentally disposed to support Hiss," Weinstein writes, "generally relied on a welter of conspiracy theories, which shared an underlying theme: that Whittaker Chambers had perjured himself."[13] Chafee, too, took that position.

On 13 December 1948, two days before Hiss's indictment was handed down, a letter from Chafee questioning Chambers's veracity was printed in the *Washington Post*. Appearing under the heading "Pumpkin Melody" because it centered on Chambers's recent revelations about microfilms of documents allegedly stolen by Hiss and hidden by Chambers in a pumpkin on his Maryland farm, the letter rhetorically inquired if Chambers was not now "completely discredited" and concluded: "His own testimony shows that he double-crossed his former Communist associates. If he did not tell the committee about these documents during his close contact with it last summer, then he double-crossed the committee. It is hard to see that anything he says against Hiss should be believed. Before this, I was unable to understand why the statements of a former Communist are given 100 percent credit by many people who think that all Communists are the scum of the earth."[14] Chafee also tried to discredit Chambers by raising the possibility that the documents were either unimportant or that the microfilm copies had been made only recently, whereas Chambers alleged that he received them from Hiss in the latter 1930s.[15]

Elsewhere in the letter he sought to discredit the committee itself. He referred to it, as he habitually did, as "the Un-American Committee" (the official name is House Committee on Un-American Activities, but the common acronym—sometimes used pejoratively—is HUAC, not HCUA), and in an unusual public show of spleen he called its members "a stupid bunch of investigators" and "a bunch of babbling Congressmen." At the outset, the letter questioned the committee's motives in holding the hearing at all ("Is it possible that the real purpose . . . is, not to save the country, but to save the committee?"); and its penultimate paragraph questioned the motives of committee member Richard M. Nixon in flying back from a vacation cruise to take part in the investigation only after Chambers produced the pumpkin papers ("Was not the probability of a hearing [on these documents] known to the committee before Representative Nixon left for Panama, so that his return on a Government plane which took him off his ship is simply deliberate melodrama?").

There was some foundation for both of these charges. Prior to the Chambers-Hiss investigation, the committee had been having its troubles; one of them later resulted in the indictment of chairman J. Parnell Thomas for allegedly taking kickbacks from his employees. Chafee's letter referred to Thomas's difficulty (he was subsequently convicted and sent to prison) and correctly noted that President Truman was "hostile to the committee." Somewhat more tenuous were its pronouncements that HUAC—which had been established as a permanent committee only three years earlier—was "on its last legs before this affair broke" and that it was "very likely that the House at its next session would abolish the committee or at least drastically curtail its appropriations." (Thirty years later, Allen Weinstein wrote: "HUAC's tarnished reputation made it vulnerable by mid-1948, and Truman aides drafted a bill to abolish the Committee if the November election restored Democratic control of Congress.")[16] In any event, the Hiss case indubitably re-energized the committee.

As for Chafee's charge against Nixon (the *Post* on 16 December

1948 printed his lengthy reply to Chafee's nine numbered points; Nixon commented that "I believe I have established in my life in and out of Congress a reputation for honesty"), it proved to be partially correct. Here is Weinstein's assessment of this aspect of the case: "Nixon, who has never admitted this fact, was told in advance . . . about Chambers' having turned over stolen typed documents to Hiss' attorneys. Not waiting to see what a HUAC subpoena for additional documents might uncover, the cautious Nixon fled Washington on a cruise-ship vacation. Once HUAC staff members had obtained the microfilm and determined its importance, Nixon hurried back to steal the headlines and to claim credit for the coup: 'opportunistic' behavior surely, but hardly conspiratorial."[17]

Chafee's letter was originally aimed at the *New York Herald Tribune*—specifically at its distinguished columnist Walter Lippmann, who at times asked Chafee for background information on legal issues. He sent two copies to Lippmann, asking that the second be given to Bert Andrews, a reporter whose work Chafee admired and who had recently won a Pulitzer Prize for a series exposing abuses in the State Department's loyalty program and also criticizing HUAC's 1947 investigation of the motion picture industry.[18] Upon learning that Lippmann was out of the country, he wrote him again to explain that he had sent a revised version of the original letter to Philip L. Graham, the *Post's* publisher, who, he noted, was a Harvard law graduate. And on the day the *Post* ran his letter he wrote Andrews— who, without Chafee's knowledge, had advised Nixon to have a subpoena issued compelling Chambers to produce what turned out to be the pumpkin papers and who wired Nixon on the cruise ship urging his return[19]—explaining about the letters to Lippmann and Graham and saying he hoped the reporter would not think he was trying to bypass the *Herald Tribune*.

Referring to excerpts from some of the documents as published in the Sunday papers, he said, "When I was a teacher of evidence I used to give a good deal of thought to the inferences which could be properly drawn from a given document or piece of testimony. These Chambers revelations have set my mind running in the same way once more." He then offered his reflections on the documents he had read in the press and concluded: "We are asked to believe that Hiss was like an experienced burglar who leaves untouched a pearl necklace and a diamond tiara and walks off with a glass paperweight. On the other hand, a disloyal charwoman would turn over to Chambers everything in a figurative waste paper basket."[20]

Andrews was unimpressed: "I think that your reasoning is a good example of how one can draw inferences from given evidence, but I am sorry to say that I think there is much more to the case than careless dumping of documents or 'a disloyal charwoman.' " Stressing that there was "indisputable evidence" that microfilm copies of stolen State Department documents ended up in the hands of a confessed Communist agent, he said he believed that this fact "far transcends both Hiss and Chambers and whatever roles they had in the mystery." And he urged Chafee to write the committee for bound transcripts of the August-September hearings as well as the later ones and also for a copy of its forthcoming report, adding that he would like to read whatever analysis Chafee cared to make after reading all the testimony. Chafee's reply again raised doubts about when the documents were actually removed from the State Department and microfilmed and about the true manufacturing date of the film. But far more telling was his comment that "my own personal contacts with Hiss make it incomprehensible to me that he should be guilty."[21]

Chafee's belief in Hiss wavered slightly when, two months after his letter ran in the *Post*, he conceded that "subsequent disclosures make it probable that some of my conjectures are mistaken." But he immediately added: "Still I think that I am right for the most part. I know Hiss well and I am absolutely sure that he is innocent, but there is some bad evidence against him. It looks like Chambers had been laying for him for years." And some months after Hiss's perjury conviction at the second trial, he explained the verdict this way: "As always when Alger Hiss is mentioned, I am glad of an opportunity to say that I believe him innocent and that the jury simply made one of those terrible mistakes which have occurred from time to time in the past, as every lawyer and historian knows."[22] Chafee also helped organize and contributed to Hiss's legal defense fund, and when Hiss got out of prison in 1954 a "generous" check from Chafee awaited him.

If Chafee's largely visceral defense of Hiss left him teetering on the edge of the pit from which he sought to pull his former student, he might be said to have toppled in briefly while seeking to defeat anti-Communist legislation pushed by Hiss's principal HUAC persecutor, Nixon. In 1948 Nixon, together with fellow committee member Karl E. Mundt, sponsored the Mundt-Nixon bill, which became law as the McCarran Act two years later over President Truman's veto.

First word of the bill reached Chafee not long after he got back from Geneva when a Massachusetts congressman and Harvard law graduate asked for his comments on the measure. By the time he could respond, the bill had cleared the House, so he asked for a copy of it in order to prepare comments to send to his classmate Robert A. Taft and other senators. But without waiting for the copy to arrive, he questioned the need for such legislation: "I have enough confidence in the FBI to believe that they can take care of any really dangerous communists under the conspiracy statutes to say nothing of the Smith Act. The fact that the Smith Act has hardly ever been invoked supports my belief that the alleged national danger exists only in the minds of the Un-American Committee which has a vested interest in prolonging its own existence, and in the minds of citizens who have become a bit hysterical."[23]

Six days later, after studying the bill and while getting ready to go to the hospital for minor surgery, he sent a four-page single-spaced letter to Alexander Wiley, whose Senate Judiciary Committee was holding hearings on the bill. After preliminary remarks including his belief that the minuscule number of Communists in the country posed no real danger and that Communism was currently less of a threat than in 1910–20, he criticized the bill for requiring subversive organizations to register with the federal government and for imposing "many serious penalties upon the expression of opinions and upon membership in organizations which are stigmatized because of their opinions." Pointing out that much of the bill created guilt by association, he explained why his letter had said nothing about its constitutionality: "The main question before your committee is the wisdom of this Bill and not its validity . . . Are these novel penalties, is this novel machinery, required to save the country?"[24]

Thus Chafee had enlisted in the anti-Nixon forces even before the young California congressman had exploited the Hiss affair to his political advantage. But his opposition to the Mundt-Nixon legislation intensified after HUAC's pilloring of Hiss. So intense did it become that he was willing to go to any extreme in an effort to defeat the bill. This included serving as a sponsor of a controversial group known as the National Committee to Defeat the Mundt Bill.

Some indication of his feeling at the time, mid-May 1949, may be gleaned from a wire he sent a University of Wisconsin law professor who sought his advice about joining the committee: "Joining . . . Hope you will. Strong coordinating committee needed. This vicious bill has powerful support of American Bar Association. When bad fire raging don't bother about opinions of men carrying buckets of water. Imperative purpose counts more than some dubious associates. Otherwise I would resign from American Bar Association."[25]

A year earlier he had used a similar allusion to fire fighting in a letter to President Truman asking that he pardon the defendants in *Barsky v. United States*, an early postwar case involving contempt convictions for refusal to provide HUAC with requested information.[26] Barsky, a medical doctor, was president of the Joint Anti-Fascist Refugee Committee, an alleged Communist front organization whose stated purpose was to help Spanish Loyalists and German Communists who were refugees from fascist persecution. He and the other defendants argued that the resolution creating HUAC was unconstitutional because it allowed the committee to inquire into political opinion and expression and because its vagueness violated the Sixth Amendment. Chafee told Truman it was "undesirable" to send the defendants to jail for having performed "a public service" in bringing HUAC's activities before a court, and he asserted that "the defendants deserve leniency because of what their organization has done in liberating many persons from Fascist prisons and confinement. I do not know whether they have been helped by Communists in some of their work, but that seems to me rather irrelevant. When one is trying to put out a big fire, he does not inquire very closely into the political views of the man who is carrying a bucket of water beside him."[27]

This was not the first time, of course, that Chafee had urged the pardoning of persons known or thought to be Communists. He had contributed to his radical reputation through similar efforts on behalf of the *Abrams* defendants during the first red scare, and in the early 1940s he wrote to Attorney General Francis Biddle about freeing Earl R. Browder, the Communist Party's general secretary and presidential candidate, who was serving four years in prison for having lied on a passport application. President Roosevelt did pardon Browder, although Chafee said he had no idea if Biddle had shown Roosevelt his letter.

Chafee's interest in the matter caused his name to be linked to a group called Citizens to Free Earl Browder, which also appealed to the attorney general; Chafee said he declined to sign its petition because it said Browder should not have been convicted. His own letter, he explained, was written because he thought the four-year sentence was too severe.[28] Despite his recollection to the contrary, Chafee apparently signed the petition of Citizens to Free Earl Browder although he did decline to speak at a mass meeting sponsored by the committee to mark Browder's fifty-first birthday on 20 May 1942. After the committee (along with the Joint Anti-Fascist Refugee Committee) ended up on the attorney general's list of subversive organizations, Chafee noted that he had been accused of being a member of Citizens to Free Earl Browder and thus "I am said to be a bad security risk, next door to a Communist."[29]

Although Chafee had long been accustomed to criticisms from ultraconservatives and reactionaries, after he became identified with the national committee fighting the Mundt-Nixon legislation he found himself being chastised by friends and acquaintances of liberal repute. One was Arthur M. Schlesinger, Jr., then on the Harvard history faculty, who wondered if Chafee knew that the organization was "a Communist controlled outfit"; he listed nine sponsors "all of whom have been repeatedly identified with party line activities." Advising that "your weight and influence would be much better applied in assisting such non-Communist organizations as the American Civil Liberties Union, and the Americans for Democratic Action," Schlesinger strongly suggested that Chafee "check my account of this committee" with Roger N. Baldwin of the ACLU or Joseph L. Rauh, Jr., of the ADA.[30] Similar letters soon arrived from Baldwin and Rauh.

But it was Schlesinger, perhaps because of the patronizing tone of his remarks, who bore the brunt of Chafee's indignant response to such criticism. After noting that he did not know many members of the committee but knew and admired some of them, he said, "I do not find in your letter any statement that any of these men is a criminal, even under the ridiculous terms of the Smith Act. You just don't like the ideas of some of them and very likely I shouldn't like them either. But what of it . . . These people were the first in the field to write me and I felt it my duty to throw in my lot with a group on the spot which would do its best to kill these measures. I would even ally myself with an anti-vivisectionist to fight these bills." To Rauh—a former student who had written that he had "a deep admiration for your great fight for civil liberties" and hated "to see persons who do not share your devotion to civil liberties exploit your reputation and your integrity"—he sent a copy of his letter to Schlesinger, and added: "I am ready to join twenty groups to fight these bills if it will do any good."[31]

The same day he wrote Rauh and Schlesinger, he sent President Truman a copy of a forty-two-page statement opposing two versions of the original Mundt-Nixon bill. He urged Truman in an accompanying letter to veto any such legislation if Congress passed it and to "take advantage of your opportunity to give us the same kind of ringing proclamation of freedom that Jefferson gave in his First Inaugural." The president alone, he said, was in a position to do what Charles Evans Hughes did in 1920 when, as a former governor of New York and former Supreme Court justice, "he broke up the red hysteria of that period by his denunciation of the expulsion of the five Socialists from the New York Assembly."[32] Chafee had prepared his lengthy statement opposing the bills—the original went to James O. Eastland, chairman of the Senate Judiciary Committee, with copies to the committee members, other congressional leaders, the vice president as well as the president, and leading newspapers—after he had been asked by the National Committee to Defeat the Mundt Bill to testify. He declined, saying he could not go to Washington because it was the busiest time of year at the school and because of the impending marriage of his daughter Nancy, but offered to prepare a statement if he could be provided with copies of all the pending bills together with an indication of which of them deserved particular attention.

One copy of his statement went to Senator Taft, along with a note explaining that it was not "an extraordinary appeal" but mainly an argument that present laws were adequate to deal with any Communist threat.[33] Thus, in important respects, he was merely reiterating a view he had stated for years—that federal conspiracy laws, some of them going back to the Civil War, were adequate to deal with plans for the violent overthrow of the government.[34] It is not surprising that Taft, who a little later became a defender of Senator Joseph R. McCarthy after he emerged as a leading Communist hunter, seems not to have responded.[35] Chafee's statement did draw favorable comments—perhaps none more laudatory than those of the same Roger Baldwin who criticized him for joining the group fighting the Mundt bill. Calling Chafee's attack "overwhelming," Baldwin said: "As usual with you it is a gem of literature as well. It is a service nobody can render with your authority and effectiveness. We hear the bill is pretty well stuck in the Senate Committee, and it would take another Communist coup in the Czechoslovakia manner to bring it out."[36]

By the spring of 1950 the legislation still had not been enacted, although a version known as the Mundt-Ferguson bill had cleared the Senate Judiciary Committee. Chafee revised his earlier statement, adding a meaty section on provisions for the registration of Communist-front groups, and sent it to HUAC where the measure was being considered.[37] Once more, he sent a copy to the president, along with a letter expressing his hope that Truman would veto the legislation if it got that far and adding, "I should like to take advantage of this opportunity to express my gratitude for your vigorous support of the Secretary of State [Dean Acheson; both he and the State Department in general were early targets of McCarthy]. He was one of my very first students, and one of whom I have always been proud."[38] Again, Chafee was asked by the National Committee to Defeat the Mundt Bill to testify in Washington—this time at the HUAC hearing on the measure—and again he declined, explaining that his March-April schedule was too crowded. But he filed his expanded statement with HUAC.

His opposition efforts did not stop after the bill became law as Congress voted on 23 September 1950 to override President Truman's veto. In October he joined with Archibald MacLeish and Schlesinger, his critic of the previous year, in launching "The 1950 Civil Liberties Appeal"; its goal was to seek repeal of the McCarran Act by electing to the Senate three candidates who had voted against the bill: Representatives Helen Gahagan Douglas of California and John A. Carroll of Colorado and Senator Herbert H. Lehman of New York. Only Lehman was elected; Douglas's victorious opponent was Richard M. Nixon.

Chafee's alliance with Schlesinger did not signal the end of his relationship with the national organization that had fought the bill. When the new National Committee to Repeal the McCarran Act was being planned after the veto was overridden, he agreed to serve as one of the sponsors. But in February 1951, as a meeting in New York was being arranged to formalize the committee and outline its future program, he abruptly quit. "Of course, I am in strong sympathy with the purposes of this Committee," he explained, "but in this as in other organizations, I have made it a personal policy not to identify myself with any permanent group in the area of my research and writing. For instance, I have thought it wise not to join the Advisory Council of the American Civil Liberties Union, greatly as I value its work. I feel I can be most effective by preserving an independent position as a scholar and writer. For similar reasons, I have never taken a retainer or any sort of compensation in a civil liberties litigation."[39]

Not long after the November 1950 elections Chafee had made clear his intention to focus on other issues. As he explained to Thomas I. Emerson, a Yale law professor, civil libertarian, and budding First Amendment theorist, "I said all that lay in me, before the [McCarran] Act was passed. For the present, consequently, I feel the way a lawyer does after losing a big case. I better turn to other big cases. This Act is not the only important struggle for freedom which is now going on, and I am able to engage in just a few struggles . . . I am thinking of problems like the ABA test oath . . . and the UN Draft Covenant on Human Rights." And, with his sixty-fifth birthday just three weeks away, he added: "You are one of those who can do a lot in the thick of the fight. Thirty years ago I was one of a whole bunch of men so engaged, but now I know that I cannot repeat my experience at 35."[40]

Both the ABA oath and the Human Rights Covenant were issues of national scope that consumed much of his energy during the ensuing months and years. But even before writing to Emerson he had also been engaged in struggles right in Harvard's own historic yard. And he was troubled to see that, in contrast to the conditions under President Lowell he described in the preface to *Free Speech in the United States*, it was possible at times to "breathe the air of Harvard and not be free." Not that there was necessarily any outright emasculation of the liberal policy on academic freedom articulated by Lowell at the time of World War I. Indeed, the dean of Harvard College during the McCarthy era later said of his defense of a Communist's right to speak at the university: "It's easy to take a stand on principle at Harvard. You don't have to worry here, really, about the reactions of politicians and newspapers to what you say or do. Harvard is rich enough and strong enough to do what it feels is right, and weak little colleges are always thanking it for taking the stands it does. That makes it easier for them. The important thing is that Harvard will always back its people on controversial issues."[41]

Harvard took a major stand on principle during a 1949 controversy churned up by Frank B. Ober, a law classmate of Chafee's who was also the uncle of his son Zech's wife. Ober had achieved prominence by leading a Maryland commission set up by the state legislature in 1938 to create a package of anti-Communist laws.[42] The principal consequence of the Commission's recommendations was what became known as the Ober Act, a sedition law that Chafee called "unbelievably bad." Perhaps emboldened by his triumphs in Maryland, Ober informed Harvard President James B. Conant in the spring of 1949 that he would not contribute to the Law School Fund because of the extracurricular activities of two professors, John Ciardi and Harlow Shapley, in "giving aid and comfort to Communism."[43]

Conant asked Grenville Clark, a member of the Harvard Corporation, to deal with the matter; in turn, Clark asked for Chafee's ideas and for his reaction to a draft letter to Ober. In the letter Clark reminded Ober of Harvard's traditions—including Lowell's defense of Chafee. Noting that he did not know if the university gained money or lost it as a result of its policy on academic freedom (his "shrewd suspicion" was that it gained more than it lost in the long run), he stressed that the real point was that "Harvard, in order to *be* Harvard, has to hew to the line." After reading the draft, Chafee told Clark that his manner of dealing with Ober was splendid: "You have really hit the nail on the head. He has let himself be carried away by his Maryland Commission and is not really himself. At bottom he is a very high-minded, conscientious man."[44] Conant also discussed the matter with Chafee, who then wrote Ober's law partner asking that he try to persuade Ober to change his mind. He would not even try and instead responded with a stirring defense of Ober, who himself was unpersuaded by Clark's eloquent entreaty.

Coincidentally, on 20 June 1949, the day the initial Ober-Conant correspondence became public, Chafee delivered at Harvard his Phi Beta Kappa oration, "Freedom and Fear." His remarks, based on the statement opposing the Mundt-Nixon bill that he had filed with the Senate Judiciary Committee a few weeks earlier, drew many favorable comments; for example, Paul A. Freund, a law colleague and former student, told him: "Your oration, coming as it did with the release of the Ober correspondence, made June 20 *dies mirabilis*.

The hearing of your oration was a moving experience, and as I leave Cambridge for the summer I could do no less than tell you so."[45]

But President Conant thought less well of the speech—he was mainly troubled by its downplaying of the Communist threat because of the comparatively few party members—and he and Chafee argued about it during a stroll around the yard after the oration. Later that day, he sent Chafee a copy of Harold J. Laski's foreword to the *Communist Manifesto* of 1848 along with a letter: "I do not know whether you would accept Mr. Laski as an authority on the Communist Party, but at least he is not with the Un-American Committee." (Ironically, Laski had felt obliged to give up a Harvard teaching post thirty years earlier during the Lowell administration because of criticisms of his exercise of free speech during the infamous Boston police strike.) "I base my case partly on evidence of this type from those who have been fairly closely associated with Communism, from my experience during the war" as chairman of the National Defense Research Commission "when I knew something of the espionage work of party members, from reading the record of the Canadian spy case (with which I assume you are familiar), and from the clear statement of party doctrine in which it is frankly declared that the ethics of war are the prevailing ones vis-à-vis the bourgeois on one hand and the party on the other."[46] The president's letter had about as much impact on Chafee as Clark's letter had on Ober, for Chafee's last book, published in 1956, contains a version of the Phi Beta Kappa oration including references to the insubstantiality of the Communist menace owing to its small size.

Chafee had other differences with both the central administration and that of the law school over the Communist controversy and what the response should be to various aspects of it. He was upset by the fact that Conant had joined in a statement by university presidents opposing employment of Communist teachers. "I regret [it] very much," he told Clark, because the statement "will be interpreted with a very much wider scope than he intended. Thus it was meant to apply only to schools and yet Ober already construes it to apply to universities including Harvard."[47] Clark agreed and noted that he had not been consulted or informed about the matter until after the president had become a signatory. And when HUAC asked Harvard for lists of books used in courses, Chafee was, as he explained to Clark, "rather disturbed that [Dean] Griswold thought that we ought to comply with a summons in case it cannot be staved off by negotiations. My own feeling is that we should not yield an inch. It is the first step which counts . . . The printed reports of committees in the California legislature show exactly where this opening request is intended to lead. It is my view that no use could be made of these lists for investigatory purposes except in a way forbidden by the First Amendment. Therefore compulsion to get the lists for an unconstitutional purpose is in itself unconstitutional."[48]

At the same time that Harvard and other universities were under pressure to fire and not hire Communists and to provide government investigators with book lists, their faculties were often compelled to sign exculpatory oaths—oaths disclaiming past or present membership in subversive groups. This was not a fresh issue at Harvard because the Massachusetts legislature—despite the protests of Chafee and others—had enacted a teacher-oath law back in 1935. Commenting that "no class of people is more injured by repression than teachers," Chafee declared that if the "abomination of exculpatory oaths" was to be revived for teachers, then it should be imposed on other occupations: for example, congressmen might be required to swear that they had taken no bribes or kickbacks, lawyers that they had never indulged in ambulance chasing, businessmen that they had never violated the anti-trust laws.[49]

And when the American Bar Association—about six months after the McCarthy era dawned with the senator's 9 February 1950 speech at Wheeling, West Virginia, about Communists in the State Department—proposed an exculpatory oath for lawyers, Chafee led the opposition. Particularly outraged because the ABA adopted the oath without debate, he told Abe Fortas, who had served with him on the Bill of Rights Committee, that he "made up my mind that if nobody else stood up on his hind legs and yelled, I was going to do so."[50] His "yelling" consisted of making speeches as well as circulating widely a statement that he prepared. Calling the proposed oath "a plan to purge the American bar," he said it was "especially bad because of the vague behavior which a lawyer must disclaim, to avoid thorough investigation of all his 'activities and conduct.' [More important than] lawyers who are Communists . . . is the loyal lawyer, who is no Communist but has participated . . . in unpopular enterprises, especially those irresponsibly labeled as 'Communist fronts.' "[51]

Not long after he had stood up on his "hind legs," twenty-six leaders of the bar (including Charles C. Burlingham, Grenville Clark, John W. Davis, Whitney North Seymour, Harrison Tweed, and Chafee) signed a statement condemning the oath as a violation of "the American tradition that suspicion of disloyalty shall not be cast upon an entire class or profession upon the chance of catching a few random delinquents."[52] This proved to be a winning fight, although Chafee's campaign against the forces of reaction within the ABA was far from over.

The depth of his disdain for that organization is expressed in a letter to his friend Ernest Angell, written not long after the ABA's House of Delegates recommended the oath in September 1950. "On the day that the Senate over-rode Truman's veto of the McCarran Bill," he said, "I was taking my first drive in our new open convertible all alone, thinking about the enclosed Ear Association resolutions. I turned on the radio and heard a young woman singing the inscription on the Statute of Liberty, 'Give me your tired, your poor, your teeming millions struggling to be free.' My first impulse was to send in my resignation to the Bar Association, which is rapidly becoming legal advisors to the most reactionary elements in both political parties." He continued:

> What used to be the Committee on the Bill of Rights, with its magnificent work against Frank Hague and the compulsory flag salute, has now become a committee to nibble away the Bill of Rights. The Committee on Peace and Order through the United Nations is really a committee to combat the United Nations . . . This crowd deserves the lines of Carl Sandburg,
> > "Why does a horse snicker
> > Hauling a lawyer away?"
> So I started with a determination never to give another cent to support the activities of this bunch of thick-headed reactionaries. Then I thought that they would probably be very happy to get rid of me, and I did not see why I should afford them this satisfaction . . . I also thought that the Association, through its sections, is engaged in a good many legitimate and desirable activities which interest me . . . In spite of its sins, the ABA is the only organization through which nation-wide improvement in the law can be achieved.[53]

During the early 1950s his battle to save the UN Human Rights Covenant from reactionaries in and out of the ABA might have matched—if a heart attack had not slowed him down somewhat—the intensity of his struggle against the Mundt-Nixon bill. And it is important to note that much of the impetus against the covenant and for the Bricker amendment to limit the treaty-making power arose from the belief that President Roosevelt had sold out to the Russians at Yalta, where Alger Hiss was a key figure in the 1945 negotiations that quickly led to Soviet domination of Eastern Europe and to the descent of what Churchill called an iron curtain.

In its original form, the Bricker amendment had two principal aims: (1) to void all treaties, where the specific approval of the forty-eight states was absent, bearing on matters reserved to the states under the Constitution; and (2) to allow Congress to regulate and to approve or disapprove all executive agreements with other nations. Although the measure had both Democratic and Republican internationalists among its sixty sponsors in the Senate, its stoutest supporters were ultraconservative isolationists or states' rightists in both parties—including Democrats McCarran and Eastland and Republicans Mundt, McCarthy, and, prior to his death in 1953, Taft. "Almost all subscribed to the 'conspiracy' or 'sell-out' theory of Yalta," William Harbaugh writes in his biography of John W. Davis, who convinced President Eisenhower that the amendment was both harmful and unnecessary, "and they were determined to forestall a repetition of that 'tragedy' . . . They were equally determined, in Bricker's words, to prevent the imposition of 'socialism by treaty.' The Southerners, in particular, wanted to destroy all possibility of adherence to the United Nations Covenant on Human Rights—essentially the creation of Eleanor Roosevelt—because of the Covenant's implications to the maltreatment of Negroes in the United States."[54]

After the ABA's House of Delegates in February 1952 endorsed what became the Bricker amendment, Chafee called it a "dangerous proposal" and described the association's action as "the worst event which has happened in the law since I began to study it over forty years ago." He saw it as "a swing back toward isolationism which has not yet become a definite proposal to get out of the United Nations" and as a sign that the ABA had been "captured by this isolationist group." He was convinced that "the only way to prevent this [undoing of an important achievement of the Philadelphia Convention of 1787] is for a large number of lawyers and law teachers to speak out over and over again. The press of the country has already been poisoned by these people. [Arthur] Krock [a *New York Times* columnist] has come out with Bricker. A Louisiana editor received the Pulitzer Prize for a series of editorials telling how treaties could nullify the Bill of Rights. So we must stage a real fight to save the Constitution."[55] Chafee's main contribution was in the form of various articles, although he did go to Washington to testify against the proposal.[56]

The Bricker amendment never became law; one reason appears to have been John W. Davis's role in convincing President Eisenhower that it was a bad idea and that the president should not even seek a compromise solution as he originally wished to do.[57] But Chafee, by speaking out over and over again, no doubt had some influence; he was told by the chairman of the ABA's Section on International and Comparative Law: "Our Section is proud, and the American people are lucky, to have someone of your ability to show up the danger, not to say stupidity, of this proposal to amend the treaty-making power of the constitution."[58]

When he was not teaching or battling Mundt-Nixon or defending the Constitution from Senator Bricker, he concerned himself with still other controversies involving Communists—real or imagined. Having been critical of HUAC's methods and of its 1947 Hollywood investigation (he thought it would "render the treatment of significant social and economic problems on the screen even rarer and more timid than it is now"), he agreed in early 1950 to sign an amici brief asking the U.S. Supreme Court to review the contempt convictions of two screenwriters who refused to answer the committee's questions.[59] The court refused. Having been appalled by Senator McCarthy from the beginning ("he is the price we pay for having complete liberty of discussion"), he stood up for Owen J. Lattimore when McCarthy called the former State Department employee "the top Soviet agent in the United States" and the architect of the policy that "betrayed" the Chinese Nationalists to the Chinese Communists. Testifying before McCarthy's committee, Lattimore, then a Johns Hopkins University professor, said he had received 170 letters in his defense from "distinguished scholars and experts" including Chafee, who characterized the senator's methods as "a barbarous invasion."[60]

Two years later, Chafee's name turned up on a list compiled by

McCarthy of seven persons "dangerous to America." The senator's accusation against Chafee came the day before the Fourth of July 1952, during hearings before the Senate Rules Subcommittee. The committee had before it both a demand from McCarthy for a full investigation of the conduct of Senator William B. Benton of Connecticut and a resolution by Benton calling for McCarthy's ouster from Congress. McCarthy testified before the rules committee that Benton, while serving as assistant secretary of state from 1945 to 1947, had "sheltered" the seven (Chafee's "shelter" was his UN subcommission assignment), and he noted that Chafee had signed the petition in behalf of Earl Browder and had been "repeatedly" cited by HUAC. McCarthy asserted that all seven were "fellow travelers, Communists and complete dupes." And "putting it mildly," he continued, "they were very, very bad loyalty and security risks." In Chafee's defense Benton said, "There is no communist taint against [him] anywhere," and he characterized him as one who frequently engaged in "lost causes" but who ranked as "a world champion against the Communists on the subject of press freedom."[61]

A few months later, Chafee engaged in yet another lost cause— the effort to prevent the executions of Julius and Ethel Rosenberg, convicted of having passed atomic secrets to the Russians. Chafee said he arrived at his basic position on the Rosenberg case during talks with E. Merrick Dodd, possibly his closest friend on the law faculty, prior to the death of Dodd and his wife in an auto accident in November 1951. Writing to federal Judge Jerome Frank, the former Yale professor who was on the U.S. Court of Appeals for the Second Circuit when it upheld the Rosenbergs' conviction, Chafee explained that he and Dodd had agreed on this key point: the statutory provision for death for spying during wartime should as a matter of justice be enforced only when the secrets were given to an enemy in the war, whereas the defendants had been convicted of passing secrets to an ally. He was also concerned about the possibility that the Rosenbergs were less guilty than trial Judge Irving R. Kaufman had thought, and he wondered if Frank felt "that I should be trying to block a definitely deserved punishment if I should write Mr. Truman [requesting commutation of the death sentence] . . . In other words, would I be trying to save people from execution who richly deserve to be executed. I have not spoken to anybody about my thought of writing you and shall keep this letter and your reply entirely to myself."[62]

From Frank, the legal realist whose 1930 *Law and the Modern Mind* Chafee had intensely disliked, came the reply that he thought the defendants had received a fair trial—more fair, indeed, than many in which convictions had been affirmed. However, he added that if the appeals court had had the power to modify the sentence, he would have voted to do so because he found unconvincing the testimony that the conspiracy they allegedly took part in did not end in 1945 but continued into the cold war period. "To be sure, the statute offered the judge the curious alternative of sentences of thirty years in jail or death; one can understand his reluctance to choose the former. But you have in mind, I assume, urging the President to commute to imprisonment for life. (I express no opinion as to the legal validity of such action.) I see no reason why you should not so urge him."[63]

In his letter to Truman Chafee gave several reasons against executing the Rosenbergs. The first was the one he had shared with Dodd and had described to Frank. Furthermore, he questioned the severity of the sentence in light of the fact that several spies in England, including Klaus Fuchs, had received lighter sentences than the Rosenbergs although they had betrayed more valuable atomic secrets; he doubted the desirability of putting a woman to death for a federal crime; and he raised the possibility that they were less guilty than the trial judge thought at the time he imposed the death penalty.

Concerning the last point, he noted that the chief witnesses against the Rosenbergs were accomplices whose testimony showed that they took a much more active part in the transactions than the Rosenbergs: "[David] Greenglass, the most important of them, was a brother-in-law of Rosenberg. Judge Frank says . . . that if his testimony were disregarded, the conviction could not stand. It bothers me when a man accuses his brother-in-law, because of the frequency of grudges and quarrels in that relationship. At any rate, there is some possibility of an error about their guilt or at least a mistakenly excessive estimate of their guilt."[64] Since their electrocution the Rosenbergs' trial has become another "case that will not die" along with the Sacco-Vanzetti and Hiss cases. In 1983, the thirtieth anniversary of their deaths, at least two books, one a revision of a 1965 study, were published proclaiming their innocence, while another sought to demonstrate their guilt.[65]

In his opposition to governmental abuses during the second red scare Chafee reflected the classical liberalism he had always stood for. As he told his friend Harlow Shapley in declining to help sponsor a 1947 Conference on Cultural Freedom and Civil Liberties, "Naturally I am much in sympathy with the purpose of this conference . . . At the same time, I am doubtful about lining up with some of the backers of the conference [which included the Progressive Citizens of America] . . . [Albert] Beveridge met Tom Marshall, Wilson's Vice-President, on the street in Washington and said, 'I understand you used to be a Douglas Democrat.' Marshall replied, 'Yes, and by God I'm a Douglas Democrat now.' So I am inclined to say, 'By God, I'm a Cleveland Democrat now.' The idea that the government should support the people is off my beat. I still think it ought to be the other way."[66]

Consistent with this view was his belief that teachers and others called to testify before legislative investigative bodies had a duty to cooperate. Early in 1953 he joined his law colleague Arthur E. Sutherland in a statement to this effect, published in the *Harvard Crimson*, that received wide publicity ("Silent Witnesses / Held Unjustified" said a *New York Times* headline summing up the statement) and excited a minor controversy of its own.[67] Among those objecting to the statement, largely written by Sutherland, was Alexander Meiklejohn.

Not long after the Chafee-Sutherland statement was printed, the Chafees departed for Europe where they spent several months traveling in Italy. It proved to be his last trip abroad, and it afforded him some—but not total—respite from the exertions of McCarthyism. The sojourn ended with a stint teaching Fundamental Human Rights at the Salzburg Seminar in American Studies, started by a group of Harvard students in 1947 to provide a center where Europeans could discuss American society and culture. The faculty included four Harvard law professors besides Chafee: Kingman Brewster, Jr., later president of Yale University; Paul A. Freund; Henry M. Hart, Jr.; and Arthur T. von Mehren. The students included government lawyers, private practitioners, judges, professors, and administrators.

Despite the charming Old World setting and the air of *gemütlichkeit*, Schloss Leopoldskron, the castle at the city's edge where the seminar was held, was not invulnerable to the "barbarous invasion" sweeping through the New World. "It is extraordinary the interest, distaste and fears of freedom engendered over here by McCarthy," Brewster wrote to Dean Griswold. And he noted that at an evening session on congressional investigations, "Zach gave them the flavor of informed outrage."[68] He also gave them a delightful Fourth of July address entitled "The United States and Europe—1776 and 1953." But perhaps most important was the fact that through his overall demeanor, he made it clear that decency was not dead in America. That is evident from a German student's critique of the seminar's legal sessions: "I was deeply impressed by Mr. Chafee's personality. His very human ideas and attitude taught me more about democracy than I learned ever before. I chose his seminar because of his reputation, and I am very glad to have heard him, for in my opinion he is the best American representative [whose acquaintance] I have ever made. Moreover, his method was very vivid. By his numerous practical examples he [made] clear the striking point of the problems."[69]

Back in Cambridge he suffered his first heart attack on 28 July 1953. After a three-month convalescence, he resumed his law school duties on 1 November. He proudly noted that his activity was largely undiminished except for having to give up hiking in mountains. The following April his doctor pronounced him to be in "very satisfactory condition"—he had taken off a few pounds and his pulse and blood pressure were both "very satisfactory"—but he was advised to put one nitroglycerine tablet under his tongue whenever he experienced any tightening of the chest.[70]

Besides getting out two books of his own, *Three Human Rights in the Constitution* (based on lectures given at the University of Kansas in 1952)[71] and *The Blessings of Liberty* [a compendium of articles and speeches], he worked for several years on a book manuscript that Merrick Dodd had left uncompleted at his death. Despite the numerous other demands on his time and despite his waning energy, he dedicated himself to completing the volume by Dodd, the son of a Providence wool merchant whom he first met at Hope Street High School. Having prepared the manuscript for Harvard University Press before going to Europe, he spent part of his convalescence reading the proof. He also did the index for the book, published in 1954 as *Early History of American Corporations*.[72]

Whatever relief the Dodd book afforded him from the seemingly endless Communist controversy did not last long. By the summer of 1954 he found himself defending the Chafee-Sutherland statement of a year and a half earlier from the previously mentioned criticisms of Meiklejohn.[73] In a letter to Meiklejohn he emphasized that "my anxiety has been to do what little I can to prevent my university, and possibly others, from adopting the rigid position that a professor who goes outside his legal rights at a legislative hearing [by refusing to answer questions] should be automatically discharged." He explained that he favored an intermediate position on the part of governing boards between "this abhorrent extreme and the opposite extreme of ignoring the whole matter," adding that university officials were entitled to know a professor's reasons for not testifying even when he had legitimately exercised his Fifth Amendment right to remain silent. "I am very happy indeed that Harvard has taken pretty much the course that I have urged, although I do not agree with all the reasons advanced by [its] Fellows. Personally, I think that a present member of the Communist Party should not necessarily be discharged."[74]

The following October, in a Founders Day address at the University of Oregon entitled "If the Salt Have Lost His Savour—," he urged university administrators to show courage by making no more concessions to the witch hunters. After describing the various attacks being made on the educational system and after recalling his own "trial" in 1921, he delivered this peroration: "The time has come for the universities of the United States to stop retreating and carry the war into Africa. We ought to educate more than our students. 'We must educate our masters'—the legislators and the citizens who in the end make educational institutions possible. We need to persuade them to minimize the dangers of heterodoxy . . . We need to convince them of . . . the importance of intellectual freedom . . . We need to make our fellow citizens realize that freedom is not safety, but opportunity."[75]

In December 1954 Senator McCarthy was censured by the Senate, although he continued to serve until he died on 2 May 1957—three months after Chafee's own death. When McCarthy's censure failed to exorcise the spirit of McCarthyism, Chafee continued his efforts to educate legislators and citizens about fundamental human rights. One way he spread the word to the general public was through a pamphlet about freedom of speech and press, published in early 1955 as part of the Freedom Agenda program carried on by the League of Women Voters under grants from the Fund for the Republic.[76] Indeed, the pamphlet proved to have a far wider distribution than any of his other works—more than 50,000 copies ("I don't suppose that anything I ever wrote before has reached 4,000 copies except casebooks, which were mostly written by the judges and not by me").

The pamphlet also brought new attacks, many of them from members of the American Legion who seized on it as an excuse to revive charges about Chafee's association with groups listed by HUAC and the attorney general. The Un-Americanism Committee of the Westchester County (New York) American Legion went even further and assailed all six of the Freedom Agenda pamphlets as Communist tinged, although Chafee's pamphlet was particularly criticized for making "a profane attempt to suggest a similarity between the trial of Jesus Christ and the trial of Communists today."[77] And the American Legion was not the only group offended by Chafee's reference to the trial of Jesus. From some Jews came the objection that such allusions were apt to reinforce anti-Semitism, while the American Jewish Committee additionally complained that "your fine references [in the pamphlet] to David, Nathan, Elijah and Hillel make no reference to Jewish identification. The only specific use of the word is in a sentence involving derogation."[78]

But perhaps the unkindest cut of all came from the reactionary radio commentator Fulton Lewis, Jr., who, as part of a program condemning Chafee for his un-Americanism, called his pamphlet badly written. "That was the only statement which raised my blood pressure," Chafee told Dean Griswold.

Although the calumnies of Lewis perturbed him no more than those of the *Chicago Tribune* (he joked that having Lewis devote an entire program to him "was equivalent to an honorary degree"), he was not wholly immune to the great fear induced by the Communist controversy. "The only time I ever saw fear in his eye was during the McCarthy period," his sister Elisabeth said.[79] He was not troubled by McCarthy the man. Nor was he concerned for himself, having spent much of his professional life at the vortex of controversy. What worried him was the possibility that the anti-Communist plague might fatally infect American institutions.

So he persevered until the end, preaching the gospel of freedom of speech and other basic human rights. His last effort to educate legislators came on 14 November 1955, when he appeared before the U.S. Senate Subcommittee on Constitutional Rights, chaired by a McCarthy antagonist—Thomas C. Hennings, Jr., of Missouri.[80] Chafee, who based his remarks on his Freedom Agenda pamphlet, joined Meiklejohn, Morris L. Ernst, and Thomas I. Cook in a theoretical discussion of the extent to which Congress, in order to protect national security, could limit the freedoms of speech, press, and assembly. He was delighted by press coverage of the session, especially that of the *Washington Post,* and he thought the main benefit of the committee's work might prove to be its effect in educating citizens at large.[81] The only negative aspect of his Washington trip was a mix-up over expenses that delayed his reimbursement. Informed that he would not be paid until he submitted an itemized statement, he replied that he had earlier been misinformed. Because he had been told that no itemization would be necessary, he had eaten a "more bounteous" dinner at the Mayflower Hotel than he would have otherwise. "However, it is all rolled in on the statement I now enclose. I have sworn to this and, if necessary, I am ready to make an affidavit that I am not and never was a member of the Communist Party, although I did once hover on the outskirts of the National Association of Manufacturers."[82]

At the end of spring semester 1956 Chafee retired—four decades after Austin Scott went to Providence to offer him an assistant professorship. There were the customary parties, honors, and tributes. *Time* magazine, in a salute to Chafee and other luminous professors retiring at the time, noted that he "was so handy with the apt anecdote that he became known as 'the Scheherazade of the law school.' "[83] He had plenty of good humor left as he concluded his association with Harvard's high citadel. Expressing the hope that he could retain his office through the following winter, he told Dean Griswold: "It will take at least that long to get it straightened out. As the young man said to the girl's father, 'my intentions are honorable, but vague.' " To one well-wisher, he observed, "Somehow my last months have been fuller than usual. They say that a tree has an unusual number of blossoms before it dies. However, I am not ready to quit work yet."[84] And, as it turned out, he did not.

For he was almost immediately recalled to active service as Harvard's first Lowell television lecturer. Under the lectureship series—honoring the Lowell family for carrying "the major burden of adult education in Boston for more than a century"—one or more outstanding professors were to be chosen each year "to record for television a single course of instruction selected both for its intellectual content and for the excellence of its manner of presentation."[85] Unsurprisingly, his lectures were based on his undergraduate course in fundamental human rights; his salary while preparing and delivering them was based on the then new annual rate of $18,000 for university professors. The assignment was demanding: "The job of writing out sixteen lectures and then cutting them down again and again until they fitted into twenty-seven and a half minutes has taken sixteen times twenty-seven and a half hours or maybe more."[86] And, no doubt, the preparation was made still more difficult because the lectures were designed, in his words, "for thoughtful men and women who are not legally trained and may lack detailed historical knowledge. The chief purpose [was] to make such men and women understand why the framers wanted to protect these rights and, if possible, to make listeners want to protect them too."[87]

Much as he enjoyed the new challenge and important though he thought it was, he looked forward to the last lecture and to five months of traveling in Europe with Betty. After the lectures and prior to sailing, he planned to "work on nothing except improving my Italian for the purpose of ordering meals."[88] The itinerary included, besides Italy, two countries they had not visited before: Greece and Spain. Their departure date was 13 February—two weeks after the last lecture on 31 January. By 19 January he was confined to his home for several days under doctor's orders and in a fretful mood. "My chief concern just now is to be able to deliver my last two TV talks and get up the gangplank on the 13th," he wrote to a Brown classmate in explaining that he would be unable to take part in fiftieth-anniversary events of the class of 1907.[39]

He made it through the last lecture, described by his friend Louis M. Lyons, a Boston journalist well known for his news program on station WGBH where the Lowell series was produced, as "an experience to remember. For there was a ring to his words when he talked of the freedoms men have won and how they have won them."[90] His closing words were:

> This ends my talks. I have given them in the hope of helping men and women to remember how the human rights in our Constitution grew strong before they gained a place there. These things weren't found under a gooseberry bush. They were shaped and achieved through centuries of struggle, through the willingness of men to languish in prison and die there, through long thinking and endless tedious work. Others have labored and we have entered into their

labors. Generations gave these human rights to us, and it is for us in turn to "secure the Blessings of Liberty to ourselves and our Posterity," strengthened and enriched while in our hands.[91]

Two days later, on 2 February, he suffered a mild heart attack. Taken to Phillips House of Massachusetts General Hospital, he was placed in an oxygen tent. On 4 February he suffered a severe heart attack that would have left him an invalid. After having a reasonably good night on 5–6 February, he developed hiccoughs and his condition deteriorated. Death came on 8 February at the age of seventy-one. On the night before deterioration set in, he had asked for some passages from Herodotus to be read to him. It is possible, as some family members supposed, that his life would have been prolonged had he not chosen to deliver the Lowell lectures. But his sister Mary made the point that even if he could have foreseen the possibility of fatal consequences, "My guess would be that he'd have wanted to do those TV lectures, so as to reach another audience with the ideas of rights so vital to individual liberty."[92]

It was unfortunate that he could not have had one final chuckle from the *Chicago Tribune*, whose obituary was headlined: "PROF. CHAFEE, / DEFENDER OF / LEFTISTS, DIES." The *Tribune's* criticisms were themselves buried under the outpouring of praise from former students, colleagues, friends, editorialists, and others. Those tributes for the most part he would have found excessive if not downright embarrassing. But at least one—that of the Century Club of New York of which he was a longtime member—he almost certainly would have awarded a *B*-plus or *A*-minus:

> In 1952 Senator McCarthy, then at the height of his power, named Zack as one of the seven persons most dangerous to the United States. Zack couldn't have cared less, but it made the Senator highly ridiculous in the civilized regions of the country and certainly contributed to his ultimate downfall.
>
> Zack not only defended the freedom of the mind, but he cared about the mind—about its capacity, its inventiveness, its aspirations, its fantasies. Which is simply to say that he was a civilized man in a time when not many men were civilized.[93]

Upon his death, the FBI office in Boston sent to Washington copies of several obituaries with a memo saying the Chafee file could now be "completed." Among more recent entries in the file, started in the early 1920s, were: reports about the "Communist activities" and the "security matter" of Zechariah Chafee, Jr.; copies of several articles by him, including "Spies into Heroes" and "Freedom and Fear" (originally the Harvard Phi Beta Kappa Oration); a summary of the Fulton Lewis broadcast denouncing him; memos on his involvement with the Committee to Free Earl Browder; extensive correspondence about his statement for the Bill of Rights Committee on the detention of arrested persons, a statement whose "inaccuracies and innuendoes" had so rankled FBI Director J. Edgar Hoover; and clippings concerning his United Nations service. Alongside a newspaper account of Chafee's remarks at Lake Success advocating complete freedom for Americans to study and discuss Communism was a longhand notation: "What an 'expert' for U.N. to select!" It was signed "H"—for Hoover.[94]

The Chafee Legacy

Zechariah Chafee, Jr., used to say that he cared more about Bills and Notes than about free speech. History, however, has ignored his priorities, for he continues to be remembered primarily for his First Amendment scholarship. Just how influential was—and is—his work on freedom of speech?

Certainly some of Chafee's most influential work concerns the clear and present danger test and his controversial interpretation of it. His interpretation was more liberal than Holmes's original rendition, yet one that had a liberalizing effect on Holmes and Brandeis's post-*Schenck* dissents in the *Abrams, Gitlow,* and *Whitney* cases. Indeed, Brandeis made extensive use of *Freedom of Speech* in preparing his eloquent concurring opinion in the 1927 case of *Whitney v. California;* that opinion—amounting to a dissent—contains the last and most speech-protective of the two justices' various restatements of the danger test.[1] Eventually, a U.S. Supreme Court majority started using the test to protect expression, although it did so in late-1930s and 1940s cases not about subversive speech, but about such things as ordinances against distribution of leaflets and contempt of court by newspapers.[2] There were, however, few World War II radical speech cases for the court to review because the Department of Justice—in yet another indication of Chafee's influence—followed a more enlightened policy than it had in 1917–18 and initiated few prosecutions.

It is interesting that Chafee championed the danger test while insisting that he actually preferred the more protective objective standard test. His ambivalence helps explain the one effort he made, expressed in a letter to Learned Hand, to meld the two. He argued that courts should apply Hand's distinction between political agitation and incitement in a manner that would never punish agitation and would punish incitement only if it satisfied the danger test.[3] Such a formulation, which would have eliminated the possibility under Hand's test of harmless incitements being punished, in a way anticipated a Supreme Court decision a half-century later. In an important 1969 ruling the high court struck down an old state criminal syndicalism statute and declared: "The constitutional guarantees of free speech and free press do not permit a State to forbid or proscribe advocacy of the use of force or of law violation except where such advocacy is directed to inciting or producing imminent lawless action and is likely to incite or produce such action."[4] That opinion, combining key features of both the objective standard and danger tests, has been called "the most speech-protective standard yet evolved by the Supreme Court."[5]

Chafee's enthusiasm for the danger test was paralleled by his commitment to the concept of balancing interests. A leading contemporary version of this device, known as ad hoc balancing, was widely used by the Supreme Court in press cases after Warren Burger became chief justice in 1969. Like the danger test, it has often been criticized for being insufficiently protective of expression.[6] Chafee, despite his strong advocacy of balancing, recognized that the process carries with it the risk of automatically tipping the scales in favor of a public interest—the national security, perhaps, or the administration of justice—that may far outweigh any individual interest in speech. His solution was to put a thumb on the speech side of the scales in the form of a heavy social interest in truth—a corrective that is seldom used by the justices even when they protect expression from government interference and one that sounds quaint in an age characterized by relativism, subjectivism, and irrationalism.

Only an unreconstructed man of the enlightenment could go on insisting, as Chafee did even after conceding that man's reason is imperfect and that truth does not always triumph over falsehood, that "reason is still the best guide we have." Although his conception of balancing in the First Amendment field seems intellectually démodé because of its linkage to the search for truth, the balance-of-interests concept that he originally borrowed from Rudolf von Jhering via Roscoe Pound is almost perfectly suited to the pragmatic spirit of modern America. Similarly, it reflects, in a larger philosophical sense, the transitional period between individualism and collectivism.[7]

One scholar, describing how the formulation of the relation of the individual to the modern corporate state has been stalled during most of this century, calls World War I "an intellectual tragedy" because it aborted an emerging "model of political analysis and philosophical definition which saw the necessity and the significance of describing individual rights in the context of modern institutional social structure."[8] Itself a product of the social milieu that included World War I, Chafee's First Amendment application of balancing—which de-emphasizes individual rights and emphasizes instead the social as well as the individual interest in expression—symbolizes the uncompleted "formulation of the relation of the individual to the modern state."

Although Chafee was a classical liberal who described himself as "an old-fashioned American," his thinking also reflected important elements of collectivism. And both these strains in his thinking continue to exert an influence.

On the one hand, he accepted the traditional negative interpretation of the First Amendment by which press freedom is defined as freedom from government interference. This view is reflected in the following statement by Chafee, quoted in Chief Justice Burger's 1973 opinion voiding a state statute requiring newspapers to give space for reply to political candidates they attacked:

> Liberty of the press is in peril as soon as the government tries to compel what is to go into a newspaper. A journal does not merely print observed facts the way a cow is photographed through a plate-glass window. As soon as the facts are set in their context, you have interpretation and you have selection, and editorial selection opens the way to editorial suppression. Then how can the state force abstention from discrimination in the news without dictating selection?[9]

At the same time, as classical liberals also believe, Chafee thought that the government ought to protect individuals from interference by nongovernmental sources. Here again, his ideas have had an impact on the Supreme Court. As Chief Justice Burger wrote in a 1976 case about house-to-house canvassing by political candidates, Chafee had "articulated something of the householder's right to be let alone."[10] Indeed, a passage from *Free Speech in the United States* quoted by Burger had been relied on by a court majority twenty-five years earlier in an opinion stressing the importance of residential privacy as a limitation on First Amendment interests. In the 1951 case of *Breard v. Alexandria,* involving a perennial problem in the court of how far government can go in regulating door-to-door hawking of wares or ideas, Justice Stanley F. Reed quoted these words of Chafee as the court upheld an anti-solicitation ordinance:

> Of all the methods of spreading unpopular ideas, [residential canvassing] seems the least entitled to extensive protection. The possibilities of persuasion are slight compared with the certainties of annoyance. Great as is the value of exposing citizens to novel views, home is one place where a man ought to be able to shut himself up in his own ideas if he desires . . . So peddlers of ideas and salesmen of salvation in odd brands seem to call for regulation as much as the regular run of commercial canvassers . . . Freedom of the home is as important as freedom of speech. [1]

On the other hand, Chafee believed that freedom of expression defined solely in negative terms can be a meaningless freedom if people with something to say are denied access to public forums. Or as Laurence H. Tribe puts it: "If no one will rent an unpopular speaker a hall or print the speaker's views, it may be of little use that government has not gone out of its way to muzzle the speech." Tribe, professor of law at Harvard and author of a leading treatise on constitutional law, also notes that "in 1941 Professor Chafee identified what was to become among the most significant first amendment issues of the modern period: the need for affirmative governmental action to facilitate expression."[12]

Actually, Chafee had recognized much earlier the need for an affirmative, or positive, construction of free speech in addition to the traditional negative one. But this strand of his thought has had much less influence on the Supreme Court. It is true that the justices shared his view that the government could legitimately force the Associated Press to make its service available to all comers, but the court's decision rested on a restraint-of-trade justification rather than on the public-service theory espoused by Chafee. While he thought that there are some things the government can do to facilitate expression, he held the even stronger belief that the best way for the public to be adequately informed is for the press to accept a moral responsibility to carry a wide spectrum of news and opinion.

The obverse side of Chafee's belief that there are categories of content the media are morally obligated to disseminate was his conviction that there are categories undeserving of First Amendment protection. This idea, perhaps his most controversial one, was originally adopted by the Supreme Court but then largely repudiated in piecemeal fashion. Noting that criminal law is aimed chiefly at injuries usually committed by acts, he pointed out that it also punishes certain classes of words—"like obscenity, profanity, and gross libels upon individuals"—because they "inflict a present injury upon listeners, readers, or those defamed, or [make] highly probable an immediate breach of the peace." And, he proceeded to argue, "profanity and indecent talk and pictures, which do not form an essential part of any exposition of ideas, have a very slight social value as a step toward truth, which is clearly outweighed by the social interests in order, morality, the training of the young, and the peace of mind of those who hear and see."[13]

This view of Chafee's, as expressed in *Free Speech in the United States*, was relied on by Justice Frank Murphy, a Catholic known for his defense of civil liberties, in stating the so-called fighting words doctrine in the 1942 case of *Chaplinsky v. New Hampshire*.[14] Murphy's opinion for the court, upholding the conviction of a Jehovah's Witness for calling a policeman "a God damned racketeer" and "a damned Fascist," has been sharply criticized by constitutional scholars as well as substantially eroded by a series of later high court rulings.[15]

Obviously, Chafee's impact on Supreme Court decisions on First Amendment issues amounts to a mixed legacy. Much the same conclusion applies to his contributions to the broader field of free speech scholarship. If he ignored some disagreeable pre–World War I judicial decisions and gave the original danger test a more liberal inflection than it deserved, he did so out of a desire to ensure that the First Amendment law-in-the-making afforded expression protection from more than just prior restraints. If he failed to solve the free speech problem of where to draw the boundary line, he brought the issue into national focus for the first time. If *Freedom of Speech* was a nonbook, it was a seminal one that set the agenda for the continuing dialogue on the meaning of "Congress shall make no law abridging the freedom of speech or of the press." If the dialogue seems endless and if his own contributions are being increasingly dissected, he would not be displeased by these developments.[16] After all, he maintained that the First Amendment should be continually reinterpreted in light of changing social conditions and that the civil liberties struggle he engaged in should be carried on by younger men with interests different from his own.

In much the same spirit Chafee insisted that he was pleased that other teachers were interested in "new ways of making good lawyers" even though he was not. He referred to himself as "an old-fashioned law professor" because, during his forty years on the dais, he kept on asking "judgment for whom?" and stressing concepts over empirical data.

No appraisal of Chafee's work should fail to emphasize that he was first and foremost a teacher. For at least three decades he was known to Harvard law students as a teacher of Equity, and news accounts of law school class reunions still include references to him as "one of the Harvard greats." Because he was a great teacher at the nation's most prestigious law school, his widest influence was upon the thousands of students who sat in his classes as well as those at other institutions who studied his casebooks and articles. If his classroom method was conservative, the basic lesson of Equity—that justice must be done in the individual case—is a timeless one for a democratic society. And although he ceased working on his Equity casebook even before he retired, and although Equity as a separate course was interred years ago at most law schools, the pedagogical philosophy of Harvard's last chancellor endures in *Cases and Materials on Remedies* by Edward D. Re, chief judge of the U.S. Court of International Trade and professor of law at St. John's University.[17] For that volume is a direct descendant of Chafee and Simpson's *Cases on Equity*.

Teaching and writing about equity was his greatest love, of course, and some experts have argued that his scholarship in this area surpasses his work on freedom of speech. As a reviewer of Chafee's *Some Problems of Equity* expressed it, "His great contributions to the practical administration of justice would appear to be a service exceeding even that which he has rendered to the cause of free speech."[18] And his most notable contribution to the practical administration of justice was his drafting of the federal Interpleader Act of 1936. The best proof of its salutary effect on the vexations attending multiple claims against stakeholders is the fact that, in the words of Erwin N. Griswold, "these cases are now almost always settled, without too great difficulty, and without involving any appreciable litigation."[19] Yet despite the success of his statute, he remained frustrated by his failure to produce a book on the subject. He should not have been. Any such book would have been largely derived from his series of law journal articles, which themselves have been called "monumental."[20]

That a fundamentally old-fashioned professor could modernize this technical area of commercial law is another tribute to Chafee's multidimensional personality. Karl Llewellyn, his friendly adversary at Columbia, alluded to this quality in his unpublished "Review of Zechariah Chafee, Jr.," inspired by a request to review Chafee's *Reissued Notes on Bills and Notes*. After concluding that basic differences in outlook precluded his reviewing the pamphlet, he critiqued its author instead. "In the reprint, as in original publication, there is a craftsmanship, a nobly patient thoroughness, a drive forward," Llewellyn wrote. "As Chafee's edition . . . of Brannan's [*Negotiable Instruments Law*] showed,

> you have here a thorough [the word replaced "cautious," which was crossed out] and skillful craftsman, yet at the same time one of daring. He dares, for instance, to argue (since "title" must always be present, somewhere) that the thief or finder of bearer paper must have title. And this is typical. In a fashion which I can only remotely indicate this Zechariah Chafee represents our law at work: bound beyond all reason by the conceived conceptual traditions . . . Chafee nonetheless sees our law as our law should be seen: as a general system rightly to be directed, within its framework, toward full and human ends.[21]

A teacher of law could have no finer epitaph.

A Note on the
Chafee Papers

The principal manuscript sources for this biography are three collections of Chafee Papers. By far the largest comprising 22,000 items and covering 50 linear feet, is in the Manuscript Division of the Harvard Law School Library. These materials, beautifully arranged and with a detailed inventory to facilitate accessibility, deal almost entirely with Chafee's professional life, including academic service, research, and teaching. Also in the law school library are four boxes of materials pertaining to his service on the Bill of Rights Committee of the American Bar Association.

The second main collection of Chafee Papers, roughly half the size of the law school collection, is in the Harvard University Archives in Pusey Library. These materials, arranged with a great deal less exactness than the main collection because they follow Chafee's original filing system, are primarily personal in nature. However, they illustrate the extreme difficulty of drawing a clear line between personal and professional activities. I found many significant items bearing on Chafee's public life, for example, that are not in the law school. At the same time, there are inevitable duplications between the two collections. But predominating is the rich assortment of family correspondence, diaries, scrapbooks, and letters from friends. By carefully going through the personal materials in the archives, I gained an understanding of Chafee that would have been impossible to acquire in any other way.

The smallest collection of Chafee Papers, but by no means an insignificant one, is in the Archives of Brown University, Chafee's alma mater. Included are correspondence and other materials concerning his undergraduate education and activities, his service as an alumni trustee and fellow, and his (and the Chafee family's) overall interest in the university. Brown honored him with an honorary doctor of laws degree in 1937 and with its Susan Colver Rosenberger Special Honor Medal (for beneficial or meritorious achievement) in 1947. For anyone interested in press freedom, a particularly valuable part of this collection concerns his work for the Commission on Freedom of the Press.

Notes

I have used the following abbreviations when referring to works by Chafee and to collections of Chafee papers.

BL *The Blessings of Liberty* (New York: Lippincott, 1956)

BUA Chafee Papers, Brown University Archives

CST "A Contemporary State Trial—The United States versus Jacob Abrams et al.," *Harvard Law Review*, 33 (1920), 747–774

FS *Freedom of Speech* (New York: Harcourt, Brace and Howe, 1920)

FSUS *Free Speech in the United States* (Cambridge, Mass.: Harvard University Press, 1941)

FSWT "Freedom of Speech in War Time," *Harvard Law Review*, 32 (1919), 932–973

GMC *Government and Mass Communications*, 2 vols. (Chicago: University of Chicago Press, 1947)

HLL Chafee Papers, Harvard Law School Library

HUA Chafee Papers, Harvard University Archives

IM *The Inquiring Mind* (New York: Harcourt, Brace, 1928)

In citing the materials in HLL, I have used two numerals; the first refers to a box number, the second to a folder or file number. For example, the citation HLL 43-10 refers to the Chafee Papers, Harvard Law School Library, box 43, folder (or file) 10. Similar citations are used to refer to other collections in the law school; one exception is a citation to the Thomas Reed Powell collection, where the box bears a capital-letter designation rather than a numerical one.

Prologue

1. Letter from Chesley Worthington, *Providence Journal*, 2 June 1968.

Throughout, in direct quotations, I have corrected misspellings and minor inaccuracies without using the obtrusive (and sometimes confusing) *sic*.

2. See Jerold S. Auerbach, "The Patrician as Libertarian: Zechariah Chafee, Jr., and Freedom of Speech," *New England Quarterly*, 42 (1969), 511–531; Gerald Gunther, "Learned Hand and the Origins of Modern First Amendment Doctrine: Some Fragments of History," *Stanford Law Review*, 27 (1975), 719–773; Peter H. Irons, " 'Fighting Fair': Zechariah Chafee, Jr., the Department of Justice, and the 'Trial at the Harvard Club,' " *Harvard Law Review*, 94 (1981), 1205–36; Jonathan Prude, "Portrait of a Civil Libertarian: The Faith and Fear of Zechariah Chafee, Jr.," *Journal of American History*, 60 (1973), 633–656; David M. Rabban, "The First Amendment in Its Forgotten Years," *Yale Law Journal*, 90 (1981), 514–595, and "The Emergence of Modern First Amendment Doctrine," *University of Chicago Law Review*, 50 (1983), 1205–1355; and Fred D. Ragan, "Justice Oliver Wendell Holmes, Jr., Zechariah Chafee, Jr., and the Clear and Present Danger Test for Free Speech: The First Year, 1919," *Journal of American History*, 58 (1971), 24–45. Although I have profited from these articles and have undoubtedly been influenced by their authors' interpretations in ways I am unaware of, I have tried to reach my own conclusions concerning Chafee's First Amendment views and to offer original insights into the man and the influences on his legal writings in general.

3. Benjamin Kaplan, "Zechariah Chafee, Jr.: Private-Law Writings," *Harvard Law Review*, 70 (1957), 1347–48. Some of Chafee's writings, including several items on nonspeech subjects, have been collected in Edward D. Re, ed., *Freedom's Prophet* (New York, 1981). This book also contains articles about Chafee, an excellent bibliography of his writings, and interviews with colleagues and former students.

4. This quotation combines comments in two letters from ZC to Sayre MacNeil, 4 May 1922 and 9 October 1923, HLL 14-17. Chafee's compassion for defendants in free speech cases was mixed with disdain, as illustrated by a later reference to them as "very queer people." ZC to Daniel Doherty, 21 April 1941, HLL 31-3. His ambivalence in this respect is neatly captured in his correspondence over two decades with Robert Goldstein, convicted under the federal Espionage Act of 1917 and originally sentenced to ten years in prison for producing a film entitled "The Spirit of '76." See FS, 10, 60–61. He thought the conviction a travesty, and his sympathy for the filmmaker was rewarded with a slew of requests for help as Goldstein got into other legal scrapes, some of them abroad, and at times was confined in mental institutions. Chafee often did what he could to provide advice and names of lawyers who might assist Goldstein, although in a 1930 letter to his uncle Jesse H. Metcalf, a U.S. senator, he referred to him as "a crazy chap who . . . has been writing me interminable letters for several years." But in 1941, having suffered a nervous breakdown himself in the meantime, he wrote a warm letter to Goldstein, then a patient in a New York mental

hospital, saying he would as requested write his doctor "what I remember about your case, and I shall do so today." ZC to Jesse H. Metcalf, 17 January 1930; ZC to Robert Goldstein, 17 June 1941, HUA.

5. ZC to John Beardsley, 17 March 1931, HLL 30-10. The case was that of Stromberg v. California, 283 U.S. 359 (1931), in which the U.S. Supreme Court, with Chief Justice Charles Evans Hughes writing the majority opinion, ruled that the statute deprived Stromberg of her liberty as guaranteed in section 1 of the Fourteenth Amendment. The decision was consistent with the court's substantive due process ruling in the Gitlow case six years earlier; see note 23 to this chapter. Chafee discusses the case in *FSUS*, 362–366.

6. Chafee, manuscript of address prepared for *Boston Herald* New England Book Fair, 22 October 1941, HUA. The text of an otherwise identical talk, given later in Chicago, omits the racial anecdote.

7. Herndon v. Lowry, 301 U.S. 242 (1937). Among those criticizing Chafee's discussion of the case, which appears at 388–398 of the book, was Mark DeWolfe Howe in a review in *Harvard Law Review*, 55 (1942), 695–699. A book about the litigation is Charles H. Martin, *The Angelo Herndon Case and Southern Justice* (Baton Rouge, La., 1976).

8. ZC to Mark DeWolfe Howe, 27 January 1942, HLL 74-4.

9. ZC to Matthew W. Bullock, Jr., 13 May 1942, HLL 74-3.

10. The address was published posthumously as "Safeguarding Fundamental Human Rights: The Tasks of States and Nation," *George Washington Law Review*, 27 (1958), 519–539. The *Review*'s editors explained that Chafee had made some revisions in his original speech text but died before he could revise the manuscript for publication; they made minor corrections to supply citations but did not change the substance of his remarks. The article is reprinted in Re, *Freedom's Prophet*, 115–135; the quotations in the text are from the *Review* article, 534–536. It is interesting to note that a memo summarizing the article was prepared by a U.S. Justice Department official and placed in the Chafee file maintained by the FBI for more than three decades. But in contrast to most items in the file, this one was uncritical and cast no doubt on his loyalty. His Justice Department file is discussed in more detail in Chapters 2 and 11.

11. "Chafee Scores Failure to Plan Desegregation," *Harvard Law School Record*, 31 January 1957. The lower federal courts went on to do even more "dirty work" to achieve integrated schools, making wide use of equitable remedies such as the injunction and class action suits. Although Chafee as an expert on equity often touted these tools because their flexibility can be useful in adjusting the law to changing social needs, it seems unlikely that he would have approved of their free-wheeling use by federal courts in running local affairs. "The cities of the United States must be governed by themselves and not by the United States courts," he had declared years earlier in *FSUS*, 430. However, given the absence of presidential leadership and the intransigence of state and local officials, he was willing to coun-

tenance some role for the federal government in integration. Nonetheless, as he stressed in his Morgan State address, a balance must be struck to ensure that every instance of local action or inaction is not seen as an emergency calling for federal intervention. For further discussion of these issues in relation to Chafee's role as a teacher of Equity, see Chapter 7.

12. Arthur M. Schlesinger, *The American as Reformer* (Cambridge, Mass., 1950), 10–11.

13. *FSUS*, 194. See also *FS*, 189, 226.

14. Harold Laski to Oliver Wendell Holmes, Jr., 2 January 1921, in Mark DeWolfe Howe, ed., *Holmes-Laski Letters*, vol. 1 (New York, 1963), 244–245. Chafee's books of general interest are: *Freedom of Speech* (1920), *The Inquiring Mind* (1928), *Free Speech in the United States* (1941), *Government and Mass Communications* (1947), *How Human Rights Got into the Constitution* (1952), *Three Human Rights in the Constitution* (1956), and *The Blessings of Liberty* (1956). Alfred A. Knopf, who longed to add Chafee's name to his publishing firm's list of distinguished authors, said after Chafee's death, "I think it rather a pity that Zech didn't take his books more seriously. He should not have worked so much with scissors and paste pot." Knopf to Mark DeWolfe Howe, 1 May 1957, HLL 6-17.

15. Chafee, "Harold Laski and the Harvard Law Review," *Harvard Law Review*, 63 (1950), 1398.

16. Chafee, "The Law," in Harold E. Stearns, ed., *Civilization in the United States* (New York, 1922), 63 and passim.

17. Chafee, "The Law," in Harold E. Stearns, ed., *America Now* (New York, 1938), 298–299.

18. "Autobiographical Sketch of Z. Chafee, Jr.," written for the Stephen Wise Award Committee, ca. April 1952, HLL 15-26. The $1,000 award, given by the American Jewish Congress in honor of the founder of New York City's Free Synagogue, recognized his "consistent exposition and defense of the principles of free speech and civil rights in the United States."

19. Chafee, "The Disorderly Conduct of Words," *Columbia Law Review*, 41 (1941), 383.

20. Ibid., 391–394. The article is reprinted in Re, *Freedom's Prophet*, 35–56.

21. The Chafee committee's findings received fairly wide circulation in an ACLU-sponsored pamphlet by Winthrop D. Lane, *The Denial of Civil Liberties in the Coal Fields* (New York, 1924). See Chafee, "Company Towns in the Soft-Coal Fields," in *IM*, 172–182.

22. ZC to Clifford K. Shipton, 1 November 1944, HLL 21-10.

23. Gitlow v. New York, 268 U.S. 652 (1925). Chafee devotes chapter 9 of *FSUS* to the case. See also Chafee, "Walter Heilprin Pollak," *Nation*, 151 (12 October 1940), 318–319, and his profile of Pollak in *Dictionary of American Biography*, vol. 22, supp. 2 (New York, 1958), 534–535.

24. The third report, dealing with the controversial murder convictions

of West Coast labor leaders Thomas J. Mooney and Warren K. Billings, was not officially published and was alleged to have been suppressed. Chafee insisted that the report, mainly the work of Pollak, was not suppressed but simply a casualty of the last-minute rush to wind up various aspects of the commission's work. ZC to Morris R. Cohen, 28 October 1936; ZC to Robert L. Schuyler, 2 April 1956, HUA. The report, with the appendices of the official version omitted, was later published privately (apparently with help from the ACLU) as *The Suppressed Mooney-Billings Report* (New York, 1932). A scholarly examination of the whole affair is Richard H. Frost, *The Mooney Case* (Stanford, Calif., 1968), and a popular account is Curt Gentry, *Frame-up* (New York, 1967).

25. *BL*, 292. See also his "Remedies for the Third Degree," *Atlantic Monthly*, 148 (November 1931), 621–630.

26. Chafee, "Congressional Reapportionment," *Harvard Law Review*, 42 (1929), 1015. His other articles on the subject are: "Reapportioning the House of Representatives under the 1940 Census," *Proceedings of the Massachusetts Historical Society*, 66 (1942), 365–408, and "Reapportionment of the House of Representatives under the 1950 Census," *Cornell Law Quarterly*, 36 (1951), 643–665.

27. ZC to Carl Stern, 31 October 1941, HUA.

28. See Donald Johnson, *The Challenge to American Freedoms* (Lexington, Ky., 1963); Paul L. Murphy, *World War I and the Origin of Civil Liberties in the United States* (New York, 1979), *The Meaning of Freedom of Speech* (Westport, Conn., 1972), and "Communities in Conflict," in Alan Reitman, ed., *The Pulse of Freedom* (New York, 1975), 23–64. See also Peggy Lamson, *Roger Baldwin* (Boston, 1976); Walter Nelles, *A Liberal in Wartime* (New York, 1940), a biography of Albert DeSilver, civil liberties lawyer and ACLU patron; and W. A. Swanberg, *Norman Thomas* (New York, 1976).

1. The Early Years with Freedom of Speech

1. Chafee, "Propaganda and the Next War," *Locomotive Engineers Journal*, 60 (February 1926), 150.

2. The correspondence with Commonwealth Fund officials is in HLL 81-11 and -12. The excerpts include slight alterations: a few style changes have been made, some paragraphing has been omitted, and some ellipses have not been indicated.

3. Gitlow v. New York, 268 U.S. 652 (1925). The decision represented an early major step toward "incorporating" various guarantees of the Bill of Rights into the due process clause of section 1 of the Fourteenth Amendment. In a series of cases starting in the late nineteenth century, the court ruled that the clause protected property and business from sweeping state statutes (usually dealing with socioeconomic reforms); but it had steadfastly refused to extend this substantive due process interpretation to liberties

other than the liberty of contract. Accordingly, prior to the *Gitlow* decision, Chafee doubted that the justices would decide to expand First Amendment protection in that case.

On a related point, he believed that state governments lacked the power to legislate against sedition as soon as Congress entered the field by passing the 1917 Espionage Act. His views apparently influenced Justice Louis Brandeis, who presented a similar preemption argument in dissenting in Gilbert v. Minnesota, 254 U.S. 325 (1920). At the time Brandeis was working on his opinion, Chafee sent to Dean Acheson, the justice's clerk and a former student, his thinking on preemption in the form of proofs of relevant sections of *FS*. Acheson found the argument without merit but failed to convince Brandeis of this. ZC to Dean Acheson, 20 November 1920, Brandeis Papers, HLL 5-12; Lewis J. Paper, *Brandeis* (New York, 1983), 283–285. More than three decades later, a Supreme Court majority adopted a preemption viewpoint in the case of Pennsylvania v. Nelson 350 U.S. 497 (1956), by holding that a conviction for sedition against the United States under a state act was barred by the federal Smith Act and other laws.

4. See Alexis J. Anderson, "The Formative Period of First Amendment Theory, 1870–1915," *American Journal of Legal History*, 24 (1980), 56–75; Margaret A. Blanchard, "Filling in the Void: Speech and Press in State Courts Prior to *Gitlow*," in Bill F. Chamberlin and Charlene J. Brown, eds., *The First Amendment Reconsidered* (New York, 1982), 14–59; and David M. Rabban, "The First Amendment in Its Forgotten Years," *Yale Law Journal*, 90 (1981), 514–595. Rabban includes a section "Zechariah Chafee, Jr., and the Selective Use of the Prewar Tradition," 586–591.

5. FSWT, 944–945. In the opening line Chafee is quoting Justice Samuel F. Miller in Davidson v. New Orleans, 96 U.S. 97 (1877).

6. Statement of Z. Chafee, Jr., about his work on freedom of speech, HLL 29-22.

7. Rabban, "First Amendment," 589–591, criticizes Chafee for ignoring in FSWT this tradition of hostility as expressed in such cases as Fox v. Washington, 236 U.S. 273 (1915), and Turner v. Williams, 194 U.S. 279 (1904). *FS*, published a year after the article, does discuss those cases and other judicial opinions and statutes condemning words for their bad tendency. See *FS*, esp. 188, 275–283.

8. The ruling in Brandreth v. Lance, 8 Paige 24–29 (1839), decided in the New York Court of Chancery, was that an injunction against publication would infringe freedom of the press.

9. Thomas M. Cooley, *Constitutional Limitations*, 7th ed. (Boston, 1903). Ernst Freund, *Police Power, Public Policy and Constitutional Rights* (Chicago, 1904). Roscoe Pound, "Interests of Personality," pts. 1 and 2, *Harvard Law Review*, 28 (1915), 343–365, 445–456; "Equitable Relief against Defamation and Injuries to Personality," *Harvard Law Review*, 29 (1916), 640–682. Henry Schofield, "Freedom of the Press in the United States," *American Sociological Society: Papers & Proceedings*, 9 (1914), 67–116, reprinted

in Schofield, *Essays on Constitutional Law and Equity* (Boston, 1921), 510–571; Theodore Schroeder, *"Obscene" Literature and Constitutional Law* (New York, 1911); *Free Speech for Radicals* (New York. 1916). For a critique of these works, see Rabban, "First Amendment," 559–579.

10. ZC to Walter Nelles, 31 March 1925, HLL 83-3.

11. See Paul A. Freund, "The Great Disorder of Speech," *The American Scholar*, 44 (1975), 550.

12. For a brief history of early controls on the press in England and America, see Leonard W. Levy, Introduction to his *Freedom of the Press from Zenger to Jefferson* (Indianapolis, 1966), an anthology of original documents.

13. Chafee, "Freedom of Speech," *New Republic*, 17 [16 November 1918), 67.

14. Ibid.; FSWT, 946; *FS*, 32.

15. ZC to Edward S. Corwin, 16 November 1920 and 3 January 1921, HLL 14-7.

16. Leonard W. Levy, *Legacy of Suppression* (Cambridge, Mass., 1960), 2–3.

17. Levy, *Legacy*, viii and passim; Chafee, "Freedom of Speech," 67.

18. New York Times v. Sullivan, 376 U.S. 254, 276 (1964). See also Harry Kalven, Jr., "The New York Times Case: A Note on 'The Central Meaning of the First Amendment,'" *1964 Supreme Court Review* (Chicago, 1964), 191–221. The scholarly debate continues over the accuracy of Chafee's interpretation vis-à-vis Levy's; see David A. Anderson, "The Origins of the Press Clause," *UCLA Law Review*, 30 (1983), 455–541, a detailed criticism of Levy, and Levy's *Emergence of a Free Press* (New York, 1985), which admits he overstated some views in *Legacy* but leaves his basic thesis intact.

19. FSWT, 938–939.

20. Near v. Minnesota, 283 U.S. 697, 716 (1931).

21. ZC to Garfield H. Horn, 8 April 1942, HLL 56-8.

22. The Espionage Act is still in force during wartime; 18 U.S.C. § 2388(a) (1976). The sedition amendment of 16 May 1918 was repealed in 1921.

23. Hand's key sentence states: "If one stops short of urging upon others that it is their duty or their interest to resist the law, it seems to me that one should not be held to have attempted to cause its violation." Masses Publishing Co. v. Patten, 244 F. 535, 540 (S.D.N.Y., 1917).

24. Schenck v. United States, 249 U.S. 47 (1919).

25. For criticisms of Hand's test, see Lillian R. BeVier, "The First Amendment and Political Speech: An Inquiry into the Substance and Limits of Principle," *Stanford Law Review*, 30 (1978), 336–337; Martin H. Redish, *Freedom of Expression* (Charlottesville, Va., 1984), 197–200; and Laurence H. Tribe, *American Constitutional Law* (Mineola, N.Y., 1978), 615–616.

26. Paul A. Freund, *The Supreme Court of the United States* (Cleveland, 1961), 44. For a criticism of Freund's argument, see Redish, *Freedom of Expression*, 210–211.

27. ZC to Learned Hand, 6 January 1920, Hand Papers, HLL 15-26.

28. Brandenburg v. Ohio, 395 U.S. 444 (1969).

29. Gitlow v. New York, 268 U.S. at 673.

30. The correspondence has been published as an appendix to Gerald Gunther, "Learned Hand and the Origins of Modern First Amendment Doctrine: Some Fragments of History," *Stanford Law Review*, 27 (1975), 719–773. Gunther, William Nelson Cromwell Professor of Law at Stanford, is writing a biography of Hand. Although I have read the correspondence in the papers of Chafee, Hand, and Holmes in HLL, in the following notes I cite only the appendix to the Gunther article. It gives full citations to the manuscript collections.

31. Frohwerk v. United States, 249 U.S. 204 (1919); Debs v. United States, 249 U.S. 211 (1919). In FSWT Chafee did not discuss *Frohwerk* but merely cited it as a case in which the First Amendment was not involved. This surprised Alfred Bettman, who as a Justice Department lawyer had been in charge of many leading Espionage Act prosecutions. He wrote Chafee that he considered Frohwerk, the editor of a German-language newspaper, "one of the clearest examples of the political prisoner," explained that he urged that he be pardoned, and expressed puzzlement that Chafee had cited the case as an example of a justified conviction. Although he praised Chafee's article, he also disagreed with Chafee's view that indirect causation was not part of the criminal common law. He failed to change Chafee's mind. On this important matter, see David M. Rabban, "The Emergence of Modern First Amendment Doctrine," *University of Chicago Law Review*, 50 (1983), 1290–94. See also n. 43 to this chapter. The Chafee-Bettman correspondence is in HLL 14-3.

As for Chafee's reaction to the *Debs* decision, he wrote in FSWT, 967–968, that "it is hard to see how he could have been held guilty" if the Supreme Court had applied the danger test to his utterances. But see n. 48 to this chapter. For a valuable critique of the *Debs* decision, see Harry Kalven, Jr., "Professor Ernst Freund and *Debs v. United States*," *University of Chicago Law Review*, 40 (1973), 235–247. The article includes a reprint of a critical piece by Professor Freund in the *New Republic* of 3 May 1919.

32. Abrams v. United States, 250 U.S. 616 (1919).

33. Gunther, "Learned Hand," 742–743.

34. ZC to Hand, 2 December 1919, ibid., 762.

35. Hand to ZC, 3 December 1919, ibid., 763.

36. Hand to ZC, 3 December 1920, ibid., 768.

37. *FS*, 34.

38. FSWT, 957–960.

39. Ibid., 960.

40. "Freedom of Speech," 68; FSWT, 962; ZC to Hand, 25 October 1920, in Gunther, "Learned Hand," 766–767.

41. FSWT, 943–944, 967, 953. Some scholars have pointed out that the danger test as first stated by Holmes in *Schenck* did not amount to a rejection

of bad tendency but rather was tantamount to that test. See, e.g., Rabban "Emergence," 1295: "Attention to the probable effects of speech, however direct the relationship between speech and crime, is essentially a variant of the 'bad tendency' test."

42. Commonwealth v. Peaslee, 177 Mass. 267. Holmes also used the "proximity" and "degree" terminology in a still earlier Massachusetts case, Commonwealth v. Kennedy, 170 Mass. 18 (1897). The development of the test in Holmes's thought is lucidly traced in Rabban, "Emergence," 1265-83.

43. Chafee's assertion rested on an erroneous understanding of the common law, a misunderstanding that also led him to the inaccurate conclusion that both Hand's direct incitement test and Holmes's danger test were reflections of traditional common law doctrine.

44. FSWT, 968.

45. Ibid., 968–969.

46. Eustace Seligman to ZC, 12 October 1919, HLL 14-26; Harold Laski to ZC, 23 July 1919, HLL 14-15; Fred D. Ragan, "Justice Oliver Wendell Holmes, Jr., Zechariah Chafee, Jr., and the Clear and Present Danger Test for Free Speech: The First Year, 1919," *Journal of American History*, 58 (1971), 43.

47. ZC to Charles F. Amidon, 30 September 1919, HLL 4-1.

48. Chafee, *FSUS*, 86. He was commenting on the Supreme Court's decisions in the *Schenck*, *Frohwerk*, and *Debs* cases, which he said "came as a great shock to forward-looking men and women" particularly because the majority opinions were written by "the Justice who for their eyes had long taken on heroic dimensions." Referring to this passage, Morton White has written of "the godlike wisdom which some of Holmes' lawyer followers have assigned to him. It seems rather striking that a scholar as courageous and forthright as Professor Chafee should have been willing to sacrifice Debs in the interest of saving Holmes' reputation as a wise and just man." White, *Social Thought in America* (Boston, 1957), 177.

49. ZC to Holmes, 9 June 1922, HLL 14-12.

50. Holmes to ZC, 12 June 1922, ibid. Holmes's references need amplification: the *Patterson* case is Patterson v. Colorado, 205 U.S. 454 (1907). Parker is Isaac Parker, chief justice of the Massachusetts Supreme Judicial Court from 1814 to 1830, who accepted Blackstone's definition of press freedom. "My Common Law" refers to his celebrated book of that name, published in 1881 and originally the Lowell Lectures The Massachusetts case is Commonwealth v. Peaslee (cited in n. 42 to this chapter). The *Swift* case is Swift & Co. v. United States, 196 U.S. 375 (1905) in which Holmes, writing for a unanimous court, rejected the firm's claim that its livestock was bought and sold locally and thus was not in interstate commerce. Bishop refers to Joel Prentiss Bishop's influential textbook on criminal law.

51. *FS*, 15, 88. The annotated copy of FSWT is in HLL 44-12.

52. *FS*, 156.

53. Hand to ZC, 2 January 1921, in Gunther, "Learned Hand," 769–770.

54. ZC to Hand, 28 March 1921, ibid., 773.

55. *FS*, 89, 93, 15.

56. Chafee, *BL*, 70.

57. Gunther, "Learned Hand," 747–748. But see the criticisms of Gunther and other advocates of the objective standard test in Redish, *Freedom of Expression*, 198–199. See also Rabban, "Emergence," 1282–83 n. 471, who suggests that "Hand may not have been as libertarian as his decision in *Masses* and much of his related correspondence might indicate."

58. ZC to Felix Frankfurter, 29 August (completed 10 September) 1949, Frankfurter Papers, HLL 183-17.

59. FSWT, 951–952, 960. For a critique of Chafee's rejection of bad tendency, see Rabban, "Emergence," 1287–89.

60. FSWT, 958.

61. See Rabban, "Emergence"; pt. 6, 1283–1303, is called "Zechariah Chafee, Jr.: The Scholar as Advocate." Although he may protest too much that Chafee operated from dubious if not base motives ("After freeing himself from the burdens of history and precedent, Chafee, with even more ingenuity and disingenuousness, developed his clever and erroneous interpretation of 'clear and present danger' "), Rabban is not unsympathetic: Chafee, Brandeis, and other civil libertarians "tried to make the most of a bleak situation, in part by ignoring prior hostile decisions and in part by 'read[ing] . . . the dissenting *Abrams* eloquence . . . back into *Schenck* as though it had been there all the time.' " Rabban is quoting Harry Kalven, Jr.

2. Trials and Tribulations of a Justice Department Critic

1. Two books devoted to governmental spying and related abuses of civil liberties are: Frank J. Donner, *The Age of Surveillance* (New York, 1980), and Athan Theoharris, *Spying on Americans* (Philadelphia, 1978). Donner is a civil liberties lawyer and has served as director of the ACLU's Project on Political Surveillance.

2. *FS*, 268–269. Years later, an article by Chafee called "Spies into Heroes," *Nation*, 174 (28 June 1952), 618–619, ended up in the files of the FBI. See Chapter 11 n. 94 and corresponding text.

3. FSWT, 964, 972.

4. John Lord O'Brian to ZC, 14 August 1920, HLL 14-22; Alfred Bettman to ZC, 20 September 1919, HLL 14-3. Bettman, together with his superior in the Justice Department, O'Brian, prepared the government's briefs in the *Schenck*, *Frohwerk*, and *Debs* cases.

5. Austen G. Fox to ZC, 9 February 1920, HLL 14-10. The previously mentioned Brookline library banning also was linked to Fox's complaints about Chafee.

6. Fox to ZC, 13 June 1920, ibid.

7. CST, 774.

8. *FS*, 126.

9. CST, 755, 757 (paragraphing omitted). The article prompted this praise from Albert DeSilver, an independently wealthy lawyer who was the principal benefactor of the wartime National Civil Liberties Bureau and the postwar American Civil Liberties Union: "I read it with great satisfaction and admiration. I am particularly delighted that you have shown up that great jurist Henry D. Clayton in such an analytical and unanswerable style. I read the full record in the Abrams case shortly after the trial and I never felt a deeper sense of indignation." DeSilver to ZC, 10 May 1920, HUA.

10. ZC to Frederick Lewis Allen, 10 December 1931, HUA.

11. Peter H. Irons, " 'Fighting Fair': Zechariah Chafee, Jr., the Department of Justice, and the 'Trial at the Harvard Club,' " *Harvard Law Review*, 94 (1981), 1205–36.

12. J. Edgar Hoover to George E. Kelleher, 21 April 1920, Bureau of Investigation record group 65, reel 326-B, file OG 388026. National Archives, Washington, D.C.; memorandum to J. Edgar Hoover, 15 June 1920, ibid., reel 311, file OG 397228. All that Military Intelligence reported was that Chafee "sponsored" the meeting "Make Peace with Russia Too," with Frankfurter presiding, at Faneuil Hall in Boston in 1919.

13. Robert P. Stephenson to the Editors of *Harvard Law Review*, ca. April 1920, HLL 29-19.

14. The links between and among Fox, Stephenson, the U.S. attorneys in New York, and Justice Department officials in Washington are traced in detail in Irons, "Fighting Fair."

15. ZC to Upton Sinclair, 5 October 1922, HUA.

16. CST, 761; *FS*, 145–156.

17. The definitive study of nativism is John Higham, *Strangers in the Land* (New York, 1965). An excellent general account of the hysteria following World War I is Robert K. Murray, *Red Scare* (New York, 1964). See also William Preston, Jr., *Aliens and Dissenters* (Cambridge, Mass., 1963), for more detailed historical background than Murray provides.

18. Stanley Coben, *A. Mitchell Palmer: Politician* (New York, 1963), 197, 203–206.

19. Ibid., 207; Donner, *Age of Surveillance*, 32–35; Theodore Draper, *The Roots of American Communism* (New York, 1957), chap. 11.

20. *FS*, 231.

21. Coben, *A. Mitchell Palmer*, 217–218.

22. Ibid., 219–220.

23. Ibid., 222–230.

24. Ibid., 231–232. Post later published a book called *The Deportations Delirium of Nineteen-Twenty* (Chicago, 1923), which has been called "an apology for the Labor Department's complicity in these raids." Donald Johnson, *The Challenge to American Freedoms* (Lexington, Ky., 1963), 140.

25. National Popular Government League, *Illegal Practices of the Department of Justice* (Washington, 1920), 40–41 Editor's Note.

26. Coben, *A. Mitchell Palmer*, 232–234.

27. Memorandum to Lawrence G. Brooks, ca. 21 March 1920, Brooks Papers, HLL 6-13.

28. Irons, "Fighting Fair," 1220.

29. Judson King to Lawrence Brooks, 22 March 1920, Brooks Papers, HLL 6-13.

30. Colyer v. Skeffington, 265 F. 17 (D. Mass. 1920).

31. Interview with Lawrence G. Brooks, 20 May 1973; James E. Mooney, *John Graham Brooks* (Worcester, Mass., 1968; privately published).

32. *FSUS*, xiv–xv.

33. Interview with Lawrence G. Brooks, 20 May 1973.

34. Harlan B. Phillips, ed., *Felix Frankfurter Reminisces* (New York, 1960), 170.

35. Irons, "Fighting Fair," 1221.

36. *FS*, 243, 249.

37. ZC to Judson King, 17 January 1921, HLL 29-1.

38. Skeffington v. Katzeff, 277 F. 129 (1st Cir. 1922). Chafee and Frankfurter had not wished to take part in the appeal, Chafee explained to Katzeff, "unless a strong and definite invitation to that effect comes from the Circuit Court of Appeals." ZC to Morris Katzeff, 1 March 1921, HLL 29-4.

39. ZC to James C. Collins, 26 January 1922, HLL 14-6. Chafee did not think it desirable to carry the appellate court's decision to the U.S. Supreme Court. In a letter to Judson King of the National Popular Government League, who had told him Post believed such an appeal should be taken, Chafee said he feared the Supreme Court would say it was for Congress, not the courts, to decide if membership in the Communist Party was a deportable offense, and he wondered if it was worthwhile "to spend money on an appeal which might better be directed to enlightening public sentiment for more sensible legislation." ZC to Judson King, 26 January 1922, HLL 29-3.

40. Report of Special Agent John E. Farley to J. Edgar Hoover, 18 May 1920, Bureau of Investigation record group 65, reel 325-B, file OG 387089, National Archives.

41. Carl Gerusny, "Uphill Battle: Lucius F. C. Garvin's Crusade for Political Reform," *Rhode Island History*, 39 (1980), 72. A Democrat, Garvin served as governor of Rhode Island from 1902 to 1904. Chafee saw him at Radical Club meetings during the period 1907–1910.

42. Irons, "Fighting Fair," 1222. Ironically, Frankfurter later intervened with President Roosevelt during the early days of the New Deal to help save J. Edgar Hoover's job as FBI director. Frankfurter acted on a rumor passed along from Harlan F. Stone, former attorney general and then an associate justice of the U.S. Supreme Court. Alpheus Thomas Mason, *Harlan Fiske Stone: Pillar of the Law* (New York, 1964), 152; Max Freedman, ed., *Roosevelt and Frankfurter* (Boston, 1967), 129.

43. Johnson, *Challenge to American Freedoms*, 158; Coben, *A. Mitchell Palmer*, 138.

44. NPGL, *Illegal Practices of the Department of Justice*, 3.

45. *Attorney General A. Mitchell Palmer on Charges Made against Department of Justice by Louis F. Post and Others: Hearings before the House Committee on Rules*, 66th Cong., 2d sess., 1920, 73–74.

46. *Boston Transcript*, 2 June 1920.

47. Telegram from Felix Frankfurter and ZC to A. Mitchell Palmer, 2 June 1920; telegram from Palmer to ZC, 4 June 1920; telegram from Frankfurter and ZC to Palmer, 4 June 1920, HLL 29-1. A few days later, Chafee received a note from John M. Maguire saying he had the following comment from the Justice Department concerning recent events: "It is understood that the Attorney General never heard of Pound until the other day. Palmer thinks Felix a real anarchist while Chafee is only a led-astray parlor one." Maguire to ZC, 8 June 1920, HLL 14-18.

48. Swinburne Hale, Memorandum for the Signers of the Report on the Department of Justice, ca. early June 1920, HLL 29-1.

49. John M. Ryan to Robert P. Stewart, 22 January 1921, Department of Justice record group 60, file 197009-I, National Archives.

50. *Charges of Illegal Practices of the Department of Justice: Hearings before the Senate Judiciary Committee*, 66th Cong., 3d sess., 1921, 165–207 passim.

51. A. Lawrence Lowell to Austen G. Fox, 11 February 1921, Lowell Papers, HUA.

52. Austen G. Fox to Francis P. Garvan, 12 February 1921, Bureau of Investigation record group 65, reel 70, file BS 209115, National Archives; J. Edgar Hoover to Austen G. Fox, 28 February 1921, ibid.

53. Memorandum of John M. Ryan, 1 March 1921, in Statement for the Information of the President and Fellows of Harvard College and the Board of Overseers of Harvard College with Respect to Certain Teachers in the Harvard Law School, HLL Red Set. Hereafter, this is cited as the Fox Statement.

54. Fox Statement. The document was signed by twenty law school and university alumni whose names are listed in Henry Aaron Yeomans, *Abbott Lawrence Lowell* (Cambridge, Mass., 1948), 318.

55. Chafee to Upton Sinclair, 5 October 1922, HUA. Lowell's statement on academic freedom is printed in Yeomans, *Abbott Lawrence Lowell*, 308–312.

56. Names of the full committee are in ibid., 319. In his diary Chafee recalled that he was working in the library stacks on the afternoon of Monday, 9 May, when Judge Swayze and another member of the committee came to notify him of the charges and to give him a copy of the Fox Statement. He immediately got out his correspondence with Fox, then lit his pipe and read the statement while the two committee members met with Dean Pound. He said much of it consisted of "an incorrect account" of the "private conversations" he had had with John M. Ryan, and "this use of my talks with him made me very angry." When Pound came to see him,

the dean was "hot as could be, & proposed to ignore the whole business & resign himself . . . I replied I was a good deal of a fighter when I got started, and wanted to see this thing through to the finish." That night he told his wife that they had "a real fight on their hands." In good spirits at first, she later became "greatly depressed and desperate over the possibility of a fifth pregnancy . . . I cannot say I was facing the crisis well, but managed to get better hold of myself as the hours went by." His greatest worry lay in trying to find the reference for his statement about defendant Lipman's "wife"; not until the following Friday did he find the reference in the *New York Times*. By Saturday, the fourteenth, his wife knew for sure she was not pregnant, and he had "cleared the deck for the action" to come on Sunday, the twenty-second. Chafee Diaries, HUA.

57. ZC to Upton Sinclair, 5 October 1922, HUA.

58. Statement of Z. Chafee, Jr., about his work on freedom of speech, HLL 29-22.

59. ZC to Edward H. Warren, 5 December 1940, HUA.

60. ZC to Richard W. Hale, 9 November 1939, ibid. After reading Chafee's files on the trial, Hale, too, criticized his long-windedness: "I think you did yourself a serious wrong from over-conscientiousness when you produced so much paper work admitting, correcting, improving, but always neglecting to give the impression which is given by a steam hammer when it hits an eggshell." Hale to ZC, 2 November 1939, ibid.

61. A Lawrence Lowell to Thomas W. Perkins, 13 May 1921, Lowell Papers, ibid.

62. Felix Frankfurter to ZC, 12 May 1921; Frankfurter to Julian W. Mack, 12 May 1921, HLL 29-22.

63. Phillips, ed., *Felix Frankfurter Reminisces*, 176; Francis Sayre, *Glad Adventure* (New York, 1957), 79.

64. Chafee to Upton Sinclair, 5 October 1922, HUA.

65. Irons, "Fighting Fair," 1231.

66. Chafee, "List of Papers Bearing on Abrams Controversy," HLL 29-19.

67. Chafee to Upton Sinclair, 5 October 1922, HUA. Chafee's account of the trial, written with Lowell's consent, was prepared after Sinclair sent him clippings from the *Appeal to Reason*, a radical paper published in Kansas, of material about the Fox affair that Sinclair had written and that he intended to include in his book about higher education. He asked Chafee to correct any errors, and Chafee later expressed satisfaction with Sinclair's corrected version in *The Goose-step*—although he thought its references to Lowell made unfair inferences possible. Another account of the trial, much of which is also based on Chafee's letter to Sinclair, is in "A Fight for Freedom, 1921," *The History Reference Bulletin*, 8 (1934), 37–40. Unless otherwise indicated, the following account of the trial is based on the letter to Sinclair.

68. ZC to Richard W. Hale, 23 May 1939, HUA.

69. *Boston Sunday Herald*, 17 July 1921.

70. A. Lawrence Lowell to ZC, 27 June 1921; ZC to Lowell, 7 July 1921; ZC to Lowell, 30 September 1921; Lowell to ZC, 1 October 1921, HLL 14-16; "A Contemporary State Trial—The United States versus Jacob Abrams et al.," *Harvard Law Review*, 35 (1921), 9–14.

71. ZC to Richard W. Hale, 23 May 1939, HUA. In his diary Chafee noted that "Warren thinks from his recent luncheon with the signers . . . that Stephenson took no active part in helping Fox. If so he probably came on as a witness to my conversations with Ryan, but I think he must have had some share in the matter and certainly turned his correspondence over to those who prepared the pamphlet." In another diary entry, about the trial itself, he wrote: "Stephenson at times took an active and hostile part in questioning me. It is significant that my correspondence with him was the beginning of trouble." Chafee Diaries, HUA. The first printed acknowledgment of Warren's assistance to Chafee did not appear until after Warren's death a quarter-century later. See Chafee, "Edward Henry Warren," *Harvard Law Review*, 58 (1945), 1109–21.

72. ZC to Roscoe Pound, 28 April 1922, HLL 2-22.

73. Not long after *FS* was published, H. L. Mencken wrote: "This Chafee begins to emerge as the owner and operator of one of the sharpest and freest intelligences now in function in These States. At a time when the whole American people wallowed in a muck of fears and imbecilities he kept his head. In a day when it was the worst of felonies for an American to show the slightest sign of independence of judgment or common self-respect, he maintained the detachment of a true scholar." *Baltimore Evening Sun*, 7 February 1921.

74. ZC to Richard W. Hale, 9 November 1939, HUA. Elsewhere he wrote: "Although most of the 'Statement' was aimed at me, I was only a sentry to be picked off before the real assault was launched against Dean Pound and Professor Frankfurter." Chafee, "Edward Henry Warren," 1117.

75. The dedication reads: "To Abbott Lawrence Lowell whose wisdom and courage in the face of uneasy fears and stormy criticism made it unmistakably plain that so long as he was president no one could breathe the air of Harvard and not be free."

76. Erwin N. Griswold, "Zechariah Chafee, Jr.," *Harvard Law Review*, 70 (1957), 1338. Just before the trial, Chafee wrote: "Oddly enough, the ultimate result has been to make me much more inclined to remain in law teaching, and not return to practice, of which I have thought much lately." Chafee Diaries, HUA.

3. A Rhode Island Man

1. ZC to Arthur W. Machen, Jr., 4 January 1955, HUA.
2. ZC to James B. Littlefield, 13 June 1944, ibid.

3. Zechariah Chafee, Sr., to Gentlemen, n.d., ibid.

4. ZC to Henry S. Canby, 30 April 1928, HLL 3-5; Calvert Magruder to Chafee, 10 May 1920, HLL 2-14.

5. ZC to Winslow S. Coates, 25 September 1951, HUA.

6. See William H. Chafee, *The Chafee Genealogy 1635–1909* (New York, 1909).

7. Zechariah Chafee, Jr., *Weathering the Panic of '73* (Providence, 1942; privately published). The same material is in *Proceedings of the Massachusetts Historical Society*, 66 (1942), 270–293. The following account of his grandfather's role as trustee of the Sprague estate is drawn primarily from this pamphlet.

8. The Sprague litigation dragged on until 1927, when the Rhode Island courts ordered the burning of all estate records, perhaps to protect the prominent descendants, including Aldriches and Rockefellers, of some of the principals. Thus it is impossible to know the degree (if any) of Grandfather Chafee's criminal liability or the extent to which he benefited financially in addition to the salary he received as trustee. Chafee's role as trustee is discussed in some detail in Jerome L. Sternstein, "Nelson W. Aldrich: The Making of the 'General Manager of the United States,' 1841–1886" (Ph.D. diss., Brown University, 1968).

9. Zechariah Chafee, Jr., "Biographic Sketch of Zechariah Chafee, Sr.," n.d., Chafee Papers, HUA.

10. Interview with Chafee's sister, Elisabeth Chafee Gamble, 5 July 1973.

11. Interview (mail) with Chafee's brother, John S. Chafee, February 1982.

12. Interview (mail) with Chafee's sister, Mary Chafee Andrews, April 1982; interviews with Elisabeth Chafee Gamble and John S. Chafee. Unless otherwise indicated the following details about Chafee's childhood are taken from these interviews.

13. "Autobiographical Sketch of Z. Chafee, Jr.," written for the Stephen Wise Award Committee, ca. April 1952, HLL 15-26.

14. Ibid.

15. For an account of Dana's troubles at Columbia, see Carol S. Gruber, *Mars and Minerva* (Baton Rouge, La., 1975), 198–206.

16. *FSUS*, xiii; the idea is stated without reference to Dana. He is given credit for it in a biographical sketch of Dana that Chafee wrote for the class book of the Harvard class of 1903, the manuscript of which is in HUA.

17. "Autobiographical Sketch of Z. Chafee, Jr."

18. Unless otherwise indicated, the account of the California trip is derived from Chafee diaries, HUA.

19. Chafee, "Confessions of a Book Worm," *Brunonian*, 38 (1903), 1.

20. The information about his high school years is drawn largely from his diaries.

21. *1903 Blue and White* (yearbook), Hope Street High School, no page number.

22. Manuscript of commencement speech, HUA.

23. Most of the information about Andrews is from David Wigdor, *Roscoe Pound* (Westport, Conn., 1974), 105.

24. English 3 paper, April 1904, BUA.

25. English 1 paper, Fall 1903, ibid.

26. ZC to David A. Jonah, 21 April 1952, ibid.

27. Interview with Claude R. Branch, 8 June 1973.

28. ZC to William S. Bivens, 16 November 1955, HUA.

29. Zechariah Chafee, Sr., to Laura, 16 January 1909, ibid. (some paragraphing omitted). According to Chafee's son, Zechariah Chafee III, the addressee was probably Laura Whittemore, a longtime family friend.

30. "Autobiographical Sketch of Z. Chafee, Jr."

31. For background on Rhode Island's unsavory political life, see Marvin Gettleman, *The Dorr Rebellion* (New York, 1973); Richard A. Gabriel, *The Political Machine of Rhode Island* (Kingsport, R.I., 1970); and Lincoln Steffens, *The Struggle for Self-Government* (New York, 1968), 120-160, and *The Autobiography of Lincoln Steffens* (New York, 1958), 464-469.

32. The articles also formed the basis of two Dorr Pamphlets entitled "The Constitutional Convention that Never Met" (Providence, 1938, 1939; privately published).

33. ZC to Sinclair Lewis, 12 February 1942, HUA.

4. Interest Jurisprudence and the First Amendment

1. Chafee, manuscript of review of Thomas Nixon Carver, *Essays in Social Justice* (Cambridge, Mass., 1915) and *The Religion Worth Having* (Boston, 1912), HUA. A classic study of the shift from individualism to collectivism in England is A. V. Dicey, *Law and Public Opinion in England During the Nineteenth Century* (London, 1963), first printed in 1905. In a major study of the Western legal tradition, a Harvard law professor writes: "It is said that in all countries of the West, the law is moving away from the individualistic assumptions that accompanied the change from a 'medieval' to a 'modern' political, economic, and social order, and toward one or another kind of collectivism." Harold J. Berman, *Law and Revolution* (Cambridge, Mass., 1983), 34.

2. On the relationship of the social milieu to ideas, see Emile Durkheim, *The Rules of Sociological Method*, trans. S. A. Solovay and J. H. Mueller, ed. G. E. G. Catlin (Glencoe, Ill., 1950), 112-121, and Robert A. Nisbet, *The Sociology of Emile Durkheim* (New York, 1974), 13-24.

3. The following references to newspaper materials are based on an examination of issues of the *Providence Journal* for the period 1885-1890.

4. Lawrence M. Friedman, *A History of American Law* (New York, 1973), 563-564; Jerold S. Auerbach, *Unequal Justice* (New York, 1976), 211.

5. See Cincinnati, New Orleans, and Texas Pacific Railway Co. v. Inter-

state Commerce Commission, 162 U.S. 184 (1896); ICC v. Cincinnati, N. O., and TPR, 167 U.S. 479 (1897); ICC v. Alabama Midland Railway Co., 168 U.S. 144 (1897).

6. See, e.g., Robert G. McCloskey, *American Conservatism in the Age of Enterprise* (New York, 1964); Richard Hofstadter, *Social Darwinism in American Thought*, rev. ed. (New York, 1959); Felix Frankfurter, "The Zeitgeist and the Judiciary," in Philip B. Kurland, ed., *Felix Frankfurter on the Supreme Court* (Cambridge, Mass., 1970), 1–7.

7. *FSUS*, 508.

8. See, among other works, John Dewey, *Liberalism and Social Action* (New York, 1963), the second chapter of which is called "The Crisis in Liberalism"; Morton White, *Social Thought in America: The Revolt Against Formalism* (Boston, 1957); R. Jackson Wilson, *In Quest of Community* (New York, 1970); Charles Forcey, *The Crossroads of Liberalism* (New York, 1967); James Gilbert, *Designing the Industrial State* (Chicago, 1972); Ray Ginger, *Age of Excess* (New York, 1965); Harry K. Girvetz, *The Evolution of Liberalism* (New York, 1963); Eric F. Goldman, *Rendezvous with Destiny* (New York, 1955); Arthur S. Link, *Woodrow Wilson and the Progressive Era, 1910-1917* (New York, 1954); Henry F. May, *The End of American Innocence* (New York, 1959); Jean B. Quandt, *From the Small Town to the Great Community* (New Brunswick, N.J., 1970); Robert H. Wiebe, *The Search for Order* (New York, 1967).

9. Herbert Agar, *The Price of Union* (Boston, 1950), 554.

10. Forcey, *Crossroads of Liberalism*, xxiii–xxiv.

11. Ibid., esp. 181–182. See also Ronald Steel, *Walter Lippmann and the American Century* (Boston, 1980), chaps. 6–7.

12. White, *Social Thought in America*, 13.

13. Julius Weinberg, *Edward Alsworth Ross and the Sociology of Progressivism* (Madison, Wis., 1972), 57. See also Wilson, *In Quest of Community*, chap. 4, for another discussion of Ross.

14. Julius Weinberg et al., Introduction to *Social Control*, by Edward Alsworth Ross (Cleveland, 1969), viii.

15. Ross's legal ideas were set forth in *Social Control*, chap. 11.

16. David Wigdor, *Roscoe Pound* (Westport, Conn., 1974), ix.

17. Oliver Wendell Holmes, Jr., *The Common Law*, ed. Mark DeWolfe Howe (Boston, 1963), 5.

18. Oliver Wendell Holmes, Jr., "The Path of the Law," in Louis Blom-Cooper, ed., *The Literature of the Law* (New York, 1965), 202.

19. Wigdor, *Roscoe Pound*, 62.

20. E. A. Ross, *Seventy Years of It* (New York, 1936), 89.

21. Quoted in Wigdor, *Roscoe Pound*, 112.

22. Roscoe Pound, "Mechanical Jurisprudence," *Columbia Law Review*, 8 (1908), 609–610.

23. Max Fisch, "Justice Holmes, the Prediction Theory of Law, and Prag-

matism," *Journal of Philosophy*, 39 (1942), 89. For a valuable discussion of the Metaphysical Club and the relationship between Green's and Holmes's ideas, see Philip P. Wiener's *Evolution and the Founders of Pragmatism* (Philadelphia, 1972), esp. chaps. 2, 7, 8.

24. Wigdor, *Roscoe Pound*, 186.

25. Charles Morris, *The Pragmatic Movement in American Philosophy* (New York, 1970), 178.

26. Rudolf von Jhering, *Law as a Means to an End*, trans. Isaac Husick (Boston, 1913), 188. An excellent summary of Jhering's philosophy is in Julius Stone, *The Province and Function of Law* (Sydney, Australia, 1946), chap. 11.

27. Roscoe Pound, "The Scope and Purpose of Sociological Jurisprudence," pt. 2, *Harvard Law Review*, 25 (1911), 143.

28. Roscoe Pound, "Interests of Personality," pt. 2, *Harvard Law Review*, 28 (1915), 453–456.

29. ZC to Earl C. Borgeson, 15 May 1956, HUA.

30. Quoted in E. Merrick Dodd, "Portrait of Zechariah Chafee, Jr.," *Harvard Law School Bulletin*, 3 (April 1952), 9.

31. Chafee, "Freedom of Speech," *New Republic*, 17 (16 November 1918), 67; BL, 65.

32. See John Clive, *Macaulay* (New York, 1973), 480; Vincent E. Starzinger, *Middlingness: "Juste Milieu" Political Theory in France and England, 1815–48* (Charlottesville, Va., 1965); William A. Madden, "Macaulay's Style," in George Levine and Madden, eds., *The Art of Victorian Prose* (New York, 1968), 127–153. Interestingly, Starzinger, a political scientist at Dartmouth University, is the son of a law school classmate of Chafee's.

33. Wade C. Stephens, "Greece: The Birthplace of Western Civilization," in Stephens, ed., *The Spirit of the Classical World* (New York, 1967), 16. See also Gilbert Highet, *Man's Unconquerable Mind* (New York, 1954), 19–20: "A wise man of our own time was once asked what was the single greatest contribution of Greece to the world's welfare. He replied 'The greatest invention of the Greeks was [the words meaning on the one hand and on the other hand].' Without these two balances, we cannot think."

34. Pound helped arrange for the address to be published. See Chafee, "The People v. the Law," *The Green Bag*, 26 (1914), 153.

35. Chafee, review of *A Treatise on the Rescission of Contracts and Cancellation of Written Instruments* by Henry Campbell Black (Kansas City, 1916), *Harvard Law Review*, 30 (1917), 300–301

36. Chafee, "Do Judges Make or Discover Law?" *Proceedings of the American Philosophical Society*, 91 (1947), 420.

37. FSUS, 360. He referred to his place among the middle group in a letter to Edward H. Warren, 17 October 1941, HUA.

38. FSWT, 935, 937.

39. Ibid., 957–958.

40. Chafee, review of *Free Speech and Its Relation to Self-Government* by Alexander Meiklejohn (New York, 1948), *Harvard Law Review*, 62 (1949), 901.

41. ZC to Edward H. Warren, 17 October 1941, HUA.

42. ZC to Felix Frankfurter, 29 August (completed 10 September) 1949, Frankfurter Papers, HLL 183-17. Referring to the Supreme Court's use of the due process clause of the Fourteenth Amendment to extend the First Amendment guarantees to the states, Meiklejohn writes that the court "has thrust aside the 'privileges and immunities' clause of the Fourteenth Amendment and has chosen, in the state field, to protect both the freedom of speech of the First Amendment and that of the Fifth under the due process clause which is taken directly from the latter. That decision clearly reveals the point of view which the court had already adopted in dealing with federal legislation. The First Amendment had been swallowed up by the Fifth. The freedom of public discussion is, therefore, no longer safe from abridgment. It is safe only from *undue* abridgment. By judicial fiat, the Constitution of the United States has been radically amended." According to Meiklejohn, the words of the Fourteenth Amendment that actually reproduce in the state field the intention of the First Amendment are these: "No State shall make or enforce any law which shall abridge the privileges or immunities of citizens of the United States." Meiklejohn, *Political Freedom* (New York, 1960), 53–54. This book includes, with a minor change, the text of the volume that Chafee reviewed.

The "perplexities" of the privileges and immunities clause alluded to by Chafee have been crisply summarized by the authors of a leading constitutional casebook: "The framers of the 14th Amendment had great difficulty in articulating any specific content for [this] clause. The Justices of the Supreme Court have not been able to be much more concrete so far." Gerald Gunther and Noel T. Dowling, *Constitutional Law*, 8th ed. (New York, 1970), 795.

43. ZC to Alexander Meiklejohn, 23 November 1948, HLL 2-16.

44. Chafee, review of *Free Speech and Its Relation to Self-Government*, 901.

45. For a discussion of the distinction between public and private speech, see David M. Rabban, "The First Amendment in Its Forgotten Years," *Yale Law Journal*, 90 (1981), 564–568.

46. See, e.g., Martin H. Redish, *Freedom of Expression* (Charlottesville, Va., 1984), 205–206 and passim, and Laurence H. Tribe, *American Constitutional Law* (Mineola, N.Y., 1978), 578.

47. Chafee, review of *Free Speech and Its Relation to Self-Government*, 899–900.

48. Alexander Meiklejohn, "The First Amendment Is an Absolute," *1961 Supreme Court Review* (Chicago, 1961), 257. For criticisms of his expanded view, see, e.g., Lillian R. BeVier, "The First Amendment and Political Speech: An Inquiry Into the Substance and Limits of Principle," *Stanford Law Re-*

view, 30 (1978), esp. 316–317; Redish, *Freedom of Expression*, 14–15; and Tribe, *American Constitutional Law*, 577–578.

49. Chafee, review of *Free Speech and Its Relation to Self-Government*, 900. Although they were far apart on the issues of clear and present danger and balancing, Chafee and Meiklejohn held similar views of the need for citizens to know. Chafee emphasized that "the real value of freedom of speech is not to the minority that wants to talk, but to the majority that does not want to listen," and Meiklejohn stressed that "what is essential is not that everyone shall speak, but that everything worth saying shall be said"; "We listen, not because they desire to speak, but because we need to hear."

50. Ibid., 900.

51. *GMC*, I, 58; Mark DeWolfe Howe, review of *FSUS*, *Harvard Law Review*, 55 (1942), 695–699. I refer to another of Howe's criticisms in n. 7 to the Prologue.

52. *GMC*, I, 59.

53. Dennis v. United States, 341 U.S. 494 (1951). The statute's official designation is the Alien Registration Act, 18 U.S.C. § 2385 (1970). For a scholarly study of prosecutions under the Smith Act, see Michal R. Belknap, *Cold War Political Justice* (Westport, Conn., 1977).

54. *FSUS*, chap. 12.

55. 341 U.S. at 509–511; *GMC*, I, 54.

56. In endeavoring to restate the clear and present danger test in *Dennis*, Judge Hand wrote: "In each case courts must ask whether the gravity of the 'evil,' discounted by its improbability, justifies such invasion of free speech as is necessary to avoid the danger." 183 F.2d 201, 212 (2d Cir. 1950). On the similarity of this formulation, variously called the gravity of the evil or sliding scale test as well as clear and probable danger, to the bad tendency test, see, e.g., Walter Gellhorn, *American Rights* (New York, 1960), 77–78, and Martin Shapiro, *Freedom of Speech* (Englewood Cliffs, N.J., 1966), 65. Shapiro's assertion that clear and probable danger "is simply the remote bad tendency test dressed up in modern style" is rejected by Marvin Schick, *Learned Hand's Court* (Baltimore, 1970), 180–181. For a plausible explanation of why the same judge who produced the protective objective standard test in 1917 did an about-face in 1950 and produced the repressive gravity of the evil test, see Gerald Gunther, "Learned Hand and the Origins of Modern First Amendment Doctrine: Some Fragments of History," *Stanford Law Review*, 27 (1975), 752. See also Schick, *Learned Hand's Court*, 179–187.

57. There are many excellent discussions of the period from the late 1950s to the early 1960s, when the court often used a balancing test to uphold convictions of persons for contempt of Congress or a state legislature. See, e.g., Thomas I. Emerson, *The System of Freedom of Expression* (New York, 1970), chap. 8. See also the articles by Laurent B. Frantz and Wallace Mendelson amounting to a debate over the use of a balancing of interests test

in First Amendment cases: Frantz, "The First Amendment in the Balance," *Yale Law Journal*, 71 (1962), 1424–50, and "Is the First Amendment Law?— A Reply to Professor Mendelson," *California Law Review*, 51 (1963), 729–754; Mendelson, "On the Meaning of the First Amendment: Absolutes in the Balance," *California Law Review*, 50 (1962), 821–828; and "The First Amendment and the Judicial Process: A Reply to Mr. Frantz," *Vanderbilt Law Review*, 17 (1964), 479–485.

58. See, e.g., *BL*, 85. Chafee's activities during the cold war are the subject of Chapter 11.

5. A Public Service Theory of the Press

1. *FS*, 377. He mentioned these works as providing a politicophilosophical perspective: Plato's *Apology*, Milton's *Areopagitica*, Mill's *On Liberty*, James Fitzjames Stephens's critique of Mill entitled *Liberty, Equality and Fraternity*, Walter Bagehot's "The Metaphysical Basis of Toleration," J. B. Bury's *A History of Freedom of Thought*, Graham Wallas's *The Great Society*, and Harold Laski's *Authority in the Modern State*.

2. Chafee, comments on application of Fredrick S. Siebert for Guggenheim Foundation grant, 21 November 1932, HUA. Siebert was then contemplating the research that became *Freedom of the Press in England, 1476–1776* (Urbana, Ill., 1952). Siebert could not recall ever having seen Chafee's comments. Siebert to author, 18 July 1977. In any event, Siebert later wrote two influential essays on the philosophical aspects of press freedom; see his chapters on authoritarian and libertarian press theories in Siebert et al., *Four Theories of the Press* (Urbana, Ill., 1956).

3. Kenneth R. Minogue, *The Liberal Mind* (New York, 1963), 14. See also John Dewey, *Liberalism and Social Action* (New York, 1963), 29: "In a longer treatment, the crisis [in liberalism] could be depicted in terms of the career of John Stuart Mill, during a period when the full force of the crisis was not yet clearly manifest."

4. See Siebert, "The Libertarian Theory of the Press," in Siebert et al., *Four Theories*, 39–71.

5. See Theodore Peterson, "The Social Responsibility Theory of the Press," in ibid., 73–103.

6. Chafee, "Liberty and Law," in Horace M. Kallen, ed., *Freedom in the Modern World* (New York, 1928), 113.

7. Chafee himself never owned stock in the publishing company. His mother, Mary Dexter Sharpe Chafee, was one of the few stockholders in 1902; his uncle Henry D. Sharpe was a director from 1905 until his death in 1954, and served as vice president from 1906 to 1931 and 1942 to 1952; and his brother Henry S. Chafee became a director in 1942, and later served as vice president, president, and chairman of the board; but the Chafee-Sharpe family apparently never held a majority of the stock. Zechariah Chafee III to author, 17 May 1978; William G. Chafee to Zechariah Chafee

III, 9 May 1978, copy in possession of author. William Chafee was then secretary-treasurer of the *Providence Journal* and *Evening Bulletin*.

8. *Time*, 10 May 1943, 48.

9. Chafee discusses the *AP* case in *GMC*, II, 542–563. For a journalistic treatment of the case, see Mary Pat Murphy, "The United States vs. the AP," *1974 Montana Journalism Review*, 40–46.

10. At the time, 81 percent of the morning newspapers and 59 percent of the evening newspapers belonged to AP; in terms of aggregate circulation, the AP papers accounted for 96 percent of the total for morning papers and 77 percent for evening ones. See United States v. Associated Press, 52 F. Supp. 362, 366 (2d Cir. 1943).

11. For a discussion of the political controversy surrounding the case, see Murphy, "The United States vs. the AP," 42, 46.

12. Chafee, statement on *AP* case, *Chicago Sunday Tribune*, 18 April 1943.

13. Fredrick S. Siebert, statement on *AP* case, ibid. For an account of Siebert's role in the case, see his "My Experiences with the First Amendment," *Journalism Quarterly*, 56 (1979), 448–449.

14. 52 F. Supp. at 372–374. Hand undoubtedly was familiar with Chafee's published statement, but there is no known correspondence between them discussing the case.

15. Carl Stern to ZC, 13 October 1943, HUA.

16. 52 F. Supp. at 372.

17. Associated Press v. United States, 326 U.S. 1 (1945).

18. Gerald Dunne, *Hugo Black and the Judicial Revolution* (New York, 1977), 220.

19. See Margaret A. Blanchard, *The Hutchins Commission, The Press and the Responsibility Concept*, Journalism Monographs, no. 49 (Lexington, Ky., 1977). The study, consisting primarily of the background leading up to the creation of the commission and of press reactions to its report, makes no use of commission deliberations and documents. See also Jerilyn S. McIntyre, "The Hutchins Commission's Search for a Moral Framework," *Journalism History*, 6 (1979), 54–57, 63, which does draw upon documents in discussing the commission's emphasis on press accountability and its recommendation for a citizens' commission to make the press accountable.

20. Associated Press v. National Labor Relations Board, 301 U.S. 103, 132 (1937). A year earlier, in the case of Grosjean v. American Press Co., 297 U.S. 233 (1936), the Supreme Court ruled that newspapers may not be taxed in a discriminatory way without infringing the First Amendment. Justice George Sutherland's opinion for the court drew upon historical materials originally prepared by Fredrick Siebert for Eberhard Deutsch, a New Orleans lawyer, who incorporated them into the brief he wrote for the appellee. Deutsch had been referred to Siebert by lawyers for the *Chicago Tribune*, which earlier had been assisted by Siebert when its publisher, Colonel Robert McCormick, agreed to provide funds to appeal the Minnesota gag case

to the Supreme Court (Near v. Minnesota, 283 U.S. 697 [1931], referred to in Chapter 1). Siebert, "My Experiences with the First Amendment," 446–448. In preparing his brief in *Grosjean*, Deutsch also received help from Chafee concerning First Amendment law. Eberhard P. Deutsch to ZC, 13 February 1936; ZC to Deutsch, 17 February 1936, HUA.

21. Among the leading critics and their works were: Will Irwin, "The American Newspaper," fifteen articles published in *Collier's* between 21 January and 29 July 1911; Upton Sinclair, *The Brass Check* (Pasadena, Calif., 1920); Walter Lippmann, *Liberty and the Press* (New York, 1920); Ferdinand Lundberg, *America's 60 Families* (New York, 1935); and Harold L. Ickes, *America's House of Lords* (New York, 1939).

22. Blanchard, *Hutchins Commission*, 9.

23. An excellent summary of Hutchins's career as an educator is in Edward A. Purcell, *The Crisis of Democratic Theory* (Lexington, Ky., 1973), chap. 8.

24. See Robert Stevens, *Law School* (Chapel Hill, N.C., 1983), chap. 9.

25. Quoted in Purcell, *Crisis*, 145.

26. Quoted in ibid., 147.

27. Robert Maynard Hutchins, *The Higher Learning in America* (New Haven, 1936), 27.

28. Purcell, *Crisis*, 143. Hutchins spent his last years as the controversial head of the Fund for the Republic and its successor, the Center for the Study of Democratic Institutions, a role in which he allegedly suppressed a commissioned study prepared by Leonard W. Levy, whose *Legacy of Suppression* is discussed in Chapter 1. See "A Conversation with Leonard Levy," *Journalism History*, 7 (1980), 97, and Levy, *Emergence of a Free Press* (New York, 1985), vii–ix.

29. Blanchard, *Hutchins Commission*, 12–13.

30. Those not mentioned are Chafee; William Ernest Hocking, whose differences with Chafee are discussed in the following text; and Robert Redfield, an anthropologist and dean of social science at Chicago.

31. The MacLeish comment is from his *A Time to Speak* (Boston, 1941), 111. Two articles by Dickinson criticizing realism are "Legal Rules: Their Function in the Process of Decision," *University of Pennsylvania Law Review*, 79 (1931), 833–868, and "Legal Rules: Their Application and Elaboration," ibid., 1052–96.

32. See Harold D. Lasswell, "The Structure and Function of Communication in Society," in Lyman Bryson, ed., *The Communication of Ideas* (New York, 1948), 37. Merriam's *Political Power* (New York, 1934) is a major study of the role of small groups in politics.

33. Purcell, *Crisis*, 152, 156. Niebuhr's books include *Moral Man and Immoral Society* (New York, 1932) and *Beyond Tragedy: Essays on the Christian Interpretation of History* (New York, 1937).

34. William E. Hocking to ZC, 25 August 1947, HLL 13-11.

35. ZC to Yuckikaku Co., Ltd., 17 November 1954, HUA.

36. Chafee, "Do Judges Make or Discover Law?" *Proceedings of the American Philosophical Society*, 91 (1947), 420.

37. Chafee, "Comments on Professor [George H.] Sabine's Paper," presented at meeting of the American Political Science Association, December 1929, in New Orleans, HLL Red Set.

38. ZC to Farwell Knapp, 2 July 1938, HLL 19-12; Chafee, "Some New Ideas About Law," *Indiana Law Journal*, 11 (1936), 522.

39. Benjamin Kaplan, "Zechariah Chafee, Jr.: Private-Law Writings," *Harvard Law Review*, 70 (1957), 1347.

40. *GMC*, I, xiii.

41. ZC to Robert D. Leigh, 4 January 1947, BUA. The letter gives the actual identities of all discussants in *GMC*.

42. Unless otherwise indicated, the following discussion of the commission's work is based on a small collection of commission materials in the Chafee Papers at BUA.

43. See In re Summers, 325 U.S. 561 (1945), in which the Supreme Court ruled against the conscientious objector, Clyde W. Summers, who later became a professor of law at Yale. The case is discussed more fully in Chapter 9.

44. Commission on Freedom of the Press, *A Free and Responsible Press* (Chicago, 1947), 17–19.

45. Ibid., 20–21. Theodore Peterson is the leading interpreter of the commission's report, which provided a framework for the social responsibility theory of the press; see Peterson's chapter in Siebert et al., *Four Theories*, 73–103. In an unpublished paper written in 1979, Peterson observed that "overall the direct contributions of the Commission to improved media performance are scanty . . . As an integral part of press theory, 'social responsibility' remains little more than . . . a pious hope." In 1977 Lasswell commented: "I think that the report of the Commission served the purpose that most of the members subscribed to. They were without any illusions about impact. The idea was to have a challenging document that would serve as a continuing challenge and reminder to serious-minded persons connected with the media. Judging from the footnotes that I see from time to time the document continues to elicit comment. I was chiefly interested in stimulating the development of continuing self-appraisal on the part of the communications industries. To this day the objective has been obtained only in very limited ways. It is however fascinating to see how often an initiative is renewed in the direction of comprehensive coverage." Harold D. Lasswell to author, 25 July 1977 (paragraphing omitted).

46. The point was forcefully made by an editor of *Fortune* magazine, who called the report "open at two ends" and "a mess." Herbert Solow to ZC, 25 August 1948, HLL 13-13.

47. Ernst later wrote an introduction for an updated version of his book rewritten by another author. See Bryce W. Rucker, *The First Freedom* (Carbondale, Ill., 1968), xv–xvii.

48. See William Ernest Hocking, *Freedom of the Press: A Framework of Principle* (Chicago, 1947), esp. 186–188, and *GMC*, I, 139–144.

49. See Commission on Freedom of the Press, *A Free and Responsible Press*, 86–87.

50. *GMC*, II, 638.

51. Hocking, *Freedom of the Press*, esp. 59–63, 218–220. See also Peterson, "Social Responsibility Theory," in Siebert et al., *Four Theories*, 96–99.

52. ZC to Felix F. Stumpf, 4 January 1948, HUA.

53. The Chafee-Hocking disagreements apparently did not disrupt the commission's work sessions. "Professor Chafee did not allow his long-standing differences with Professor Hocking to interfere with the discussions . . . Since the members of the group were experienced participants in discussion they did not transgress on the time available to their colleagues and President Hutchins of course was a concise and adroit chairman who kept the flow of conversation on track." Harold D. Lasswell to author, 25 July 1977.

54. A quarter-century after the report came out, an agency similar to the type recommended by the commission was established. Called the National News Council, it was created in 1973 with financial support from the Twentieth Century Fund—which at least one commissioner had mentioned as a possible sponsor for such a group. Always lacking the support of some major media, the council died in 1984—thus ending a decade of controversy over whether there should be such a body.

55. Frank Hughes, "A More Responsible Book from 'Press Freedom' Group" (review), *Chicago Sunday Tribune*, 26 October 1947, pt. 4; article by Eugene Griffin, *Chicago Sunday Tribune*, 11 January 1948; news item quoting Chafee statement to *Tribune* denying Griffin's comment that Chafee did not agree with the general report, *Chicago Tribune*, 15 January 1948; ZC to Walter A. Edwards, 10 March 1947, HUA.

56. *GMC*, II, 674–675. While he was writing the book, he told Robert Leigh he considered the anti-trust laws to be "the most important and difficult topic" in it, adding that "it ought to have a great deal of study from the Commission . . . My method of attack is rather different from what I have done elsewhere, and indeed from any law book which I have ever seen. It ranges pretty far into the human problems involved and makes extensive use of the discussions at our conferences." ZC to Leigh, 4 January 1947, BUA.

57. *GMC*, I, 29.

58. *GMC*, II, chap. 24.

59. Ibid., 689.

60. Ibid., 717. In his lengthy discussion of the anti-trust laws, he expresses grave doubts about what these measures can do to improve media service to the public. And referring to the public service theory, he says: "My conclusion . . . is that for the most part it represents a moral and professional

obligation of the press, not a legal obligation. The law can take us only a little way toward the ideal of fairness to all. When a large-scale organization like the Associated Press or Paramount [film studio], undertakes to furnish service of an impersonal sort to a great many applicants—good, bad, and indifferent—and does so for many years, the law can prevent it from arbitrarily rejecting a few applicants. Yet because the Associated Press has to behave like a railroad, this does not mean that the *Chicago Tribune* must behave like a railroad. Here we are not concerned with selling or leasing at all." *GMC*, II, 643.

61. *GMC*, I, xii. Although Chafee considered *GMC* to be his best book, one portion of it caused him considerable embarrassment. This was material in part 3 ("The Government as a Party to Communications") based on a memorandum by a foreign adviser to the commission, John Grierson, a well known documentary filmmaker who was general manager of Canada's Information Board during World War II. Chafee received complaints from Canadian journalists and officials that the Grierson material overstated their government's information role after the war was over. In the late 1940s Grierson's leftist views and activities got him into trouble in both Canada and the United States. Although Chafee considered Grierson to be a "Griersonist" rather than a Communist, he vowed that he would omit the Grierson passages if *GMC* went into a second edition. That never happened; indeed, Chafee considered the sales to be disappointingly small. An appreciation of Grierson by television critic Michael Arlen appeared in the *New Yorker*, 10 March 1980, 73–88. Arlen comments: "It is clear from his writings that all along he remained an unreconstructed liberal, possessed of a hardheaded Jeffersonian sense of the need for intelligent, informed discourse in a democratic society."

62. ZC to William L. Prosser, 6 August 1945, HLL 8-3. The Negotiable Instruments Law of the latter 1900s was the first major effort to produce uniform state laws and was one of the most successful of such laws, winning almost universal acceptance before being replaced by the Uniform Commercial Code in the 1950s and 1960s. See Lawrence M. Friedman, *A History of American Law* (New York, 1973), 355. The Chafee article to which his letter refers is "Rights in Overdue Paper," *Harvard Law Review*, 31 (1918), 1104–49.

6. The View from the High Citadel

1. Roscoe Pound to ZC, 15 March 1916, HLL 2-22.

2. Interview with Austin W. Scott, 16 January 1976, in Edward D. Re, ed., *Freedom's Prophet* (New York, 1981), 226.

3. Betty Chafee to Austin W. Scott, 18 October 1957, Scott Papers, HLL 9-11; interview with Scott in Re, ed., *Freedom's Prophet*, 226.

4. Interview with Zechariah Chafee III, 30 April–1 May 1982.

5. Betty Chafee to ZC, 21 July 1938, HUA.

6. Interview with Francis H. Chafee, 5 July 1973.

7. Mary D. Chafee to ZC, 10 September 1911, HUA. A few weeks later, after visiting Betty in Troy, Chafee told his parents that they had decided they "just could not live any longer without each other. And so we are not going to, ever." ZC to Mr. and Mrs. Zechariah Chafee, Sr., 26 September 1911, ibid.

8. Various letters from ZC to his mother in ibid.

9. The speech was published in *The Green Bag*, 26 (1914), 150–153.

10. Roscoe Pound, "The Scope and Purpose of Sociological Jurisprudence," *Harvard Law Review*, 24 (1911), 591–619, and 25 (1912), 140–168, 489–516.

11. ZC to Roscoe Pound, 10 March 1948, HUA; ZC to Bertha A. Searle, n.d. (ca. 1 March 1916), HLL 3-6.

12. ZC to Zechariah Chafee, Sr., 13 October 1916, HUA; interview with Elisabeth Chafee Gamble, 5 July 1973.

13. For a recent biography of Frankfurter, see Michael E. Parrish, *Felix Frankfurter and His Times: The Reform Years* (New York, 1982), the first of two volumes. Other recent studies of Frankfurter are H. N. Hirsch, *The Enigma of Felix Frankfurter* (New York, 1981), a psychological analysis drawing upon the theories of Erik H. Erikson and Karen Horney, and Bruce Allen Murphy, *The Brandeis / Frankfurter Connection* (New York, 1982).

14. For a history of the school by a faculty member, see Arthur E. Sutherland, *The Law at Harvard* (Cambridge, Mass., 1967). Other background on legal education at Harvard may be found in Joel Seligman, *The High Citadel* (Boston, 1978); Scott Turow, *One L* (New York, 1978); William Twining, *Karl Llewellyn and the Realist Movement* (London, 1973), esp. 10–25; Robert Stevens, *Law School* (Chapel Hill, N.C., 1983), esp. chaps. 3–4; and Jerold S. Auerbach, "Enmity and Amity: Law Teachers and Practitioners, 1900–22," in Donald Fleming and Bernard Bailyn, eds., *Perspectives in American History*, 5 (1971), 551–601.

15. Twining, *Karl Llewellyn*, 14.

16. Sutherland, *The Law at Harvard*, 232.

17. Turow, *One L*, 264.

18. Chafee Diaries, 12 September 1916, HUA.

19. ZC to Earl C. Borgeson, 15 May 1956, ibid.

20. The fourth edition came out in 1926. The fifth edition, published in 1932, was edited by F. K. Beutel and called *Negotiable Instruments Law Annotated*, ed. Joseph Doddridge Brannan and Zechariah Chafee, Jr.

21. ZC to George A. Spiegelberg, 23 January 1928, HLL 69-24.

22. Quoted in Sutherland, *The Law at Harvard*, 215.

23. Chafee, notes on "Bills and Notes Casebook," 17 December 1918, HLL 70-2. He published *Cases on Negotiable Instruments* in 1919 as a supplement to James Barr Ames's *Cases on Bills and Notes*, first printed in 1881.

24. ZC to Francis Sayre, n.d. (ca. 1956), HLL 3-12. Sayre's autobiography is *Glad Adventure* (New York, 1957).

25. Quoted in Twining, *Karl Llewellyn*, 15.

26. Oliver Wendell Holmes, Jr., to Sir Frederick Pollock, 10 April 1881, in Mark DeWolfe Howe, ed., *Holmes-Pollock Letters* (Cambridge, Mass., 1941), I, 17.

27. Karl Llewellyn, *Jurisprudence* (Chicago, 1960), 496. See also Twining, *Karl Llewellyn*, 23.

28. See Roscoe Pound, "The Call for a Realist Jurisprudence," *Harvard Law Review*, 44 (1931), 697–711, responding to Karl Llewellyn, "A Realistic Jurisprudence—The Next Step," *Columbia Law Review*, 30 (1930), 431–465. In turn, Llewellyn (with major research assistance from Jerome Frank, then on the Yale faculty) published "Some Realism about Realism—Responding to Dean Pound," *Harvard Law Review*, 44 (1931), 1222–64. In 1930 Frank had published his book *Law and the Modern Mind*, a leading realist tract that used Joseph Beale, an influential Harvard law professor, as an important example of the conventional wisdom the realists found wanting. "I dislike Jerome Frank's book so much," Chafee remarked, "that my opinion of it is valueless, but very few want it." ZC to Ernest Angell, 21 January 1939, HUA.

29. See, e.g., Twining, *Karl Llewellyn*, 24.

30. Roscoe Pound, *An Introduction to the Philosophy of Law* (New Haven, 1955), 47. The book, first published in 1922, was originally the Storrs Lectures given at the Yale Law School during the 1921–22 academic year.

31. Quoted in Wilfrid E. Rumble, Jr., *American Legal Realism* (Ithaca, N.Y., 1968), 31–32. Rumble's first chapter includes an excellent discussion of how realism is related to, yet different from, sociological jurisprudence.

32. Twining, *Karl Llewellyn*, 23.

33. Sutherland, *The Law at Harvard*, 243; David Wigdor, *Roscoe Pound* (Westport, Conn., 1974), 249; Harlan B. Phillips, ed., *Felix Frankfurter Reminisces* (New York, 1960), 169–170; interviews with John M. Maguire, 11 June 1973, and Austin W. Scott, 29 May 1973.

34. Interviews with John M. Maguire and Austin W. Scott.

35. ZC to Felix Frankfurter, 15 November 1926, HUA.

36. ZC to Karl Llewellyn, 26 May 1930, ibid.

37. Although there was some anti-Semitic sentiment among the faculty, the law school was affected little if at all by Harvard's Jewish quota system. At the time President A. Lawrence's Lowell's quota became a public controversy in 1922, Chafee wrote his father: "I suppose you have seen in the newspapers about the Jewish row here. It hasn't affected the Law School as yet (we have no worries there anyway), but I have learned a good deal about the college row. The general impression here is that the matter was badly bungled. One man of good judgment thinks that an impartial committee to pass on the desirability of all applicants for entrance, Jew or Gentile, with absolute fairness, would remove all real difficulties, and that racial

discrimination should be tried only as a last resort." ZC to Zechariah Chafee, Sr., 11 June 1922, ibid. See also Parrish, *Felix Frankfurter*, 155–157.

38. Interview with Austin W. Scott, 29 May 1973.

39. Parrish, *Felix Frankfurter*, 151.

40. Phillips, ed., *Felix Frankfurter Reminisces*, 169.

41. Felix Frankfurter to ZC, 23 December 1926, HLL 4-11; ZC to Frankfurter, 15 November 1926, HUA (paragraphing omitted).

42. Interview with Austin W. Scott, 29 May 1973. But see Sutherland, *The Law at Harvard*, 288–289: "Some of the older professors tended to take sides, became to some degree Pound men or Frankfurter men. The juniors, busy learning the details of their courses and the mysteries of instruction, were more apt to stand aside." By the late 1920s, when relations between the dean and Frankfurter steadily deteriorated, Chafee had been on the faculty for a decade and was in his early forties.

43. Chafee, Memorandum of Conversation, HLL 60-1.

44. Felix Frankfurter to ZC, 27 February 1928, HLL 4-18; Felix Frankfurter to ZC, ca. February 1928, HLL 60-1. For other discussions of the Margold affair, see Parrish, *Felix Frankfurter*, 157–158, and H. N. Hirsch, *The Enigma of Felix Frankfurter*, 96.

45. For discussions of the controversy over whether Landis or Henry L. Shattuck, a prominent Boston lawyer and politician, should be appointed, see Donald A. Ritchie, *James M. Landis: Dean of the Regulators* (Cambridge, Mass., 1980), 35, and Joseph P. Lash, ed., *From the Diaries of Felix Frankfurter* (New York, 1975), 124–131. Frankfurter's diary entries describe in detail the efforts of Chafee and John Maguire in Landis's behalf. At one point, Chafee supposedly threatened to resign if Landis was not hired.

46. Wigdor, *Roscoe Pound*, 249–250.

47. See Felix Frankfurter, "Case of Sacco and Vanzetti," *Atlantic Monthly*, 139 (March 1927), 409–432, and *The Case of Sacco and Vanzetti* (Boston, 1927). Discussions of Frankfurter's role in the case are in Hirsch, *The Enigma of Felix Frankfurter*, 37–40; Murphy, *The Brandeis / Frankfurter Connection*, 78–79; Lewis J. Paper, *Brandeis* (New York, 1983), 256–257; Parrish, *Felix Frankfurter*, chap. 10; and Sutherland, *The Law at Harvard*, 259–262. For Frankfurter's reconstruction of events surrounding the case, see Phillips, ed., *Felix Frankfurter Reminisces*, chap. 20.

48. ZC to Felix Frankfurter, 6 August 1927, Frankfurter Papers, HLL 183-18.

49. Wigmore's letter appeared in the *Boston Evening Transcript* of 25 April 1927. Frankfurter replied on 26 April, Wigmore responded on 10 May, and Frankfurter ended the exchange with a letter in the *Transcript* on 11 May.

50. John M. Maguire to ZC, 19 May 1927, HLL 2-15.

51. John H. Wigmore to ZC, 8 July 1927, HLL 3-22.

52. ZC to Felix Frankfurter, 2 September 1927, Frankfurter Papers, HLL 183-18 (paragraphing omitted).

53. ZC to Leonard Bacon, 9 September 1946, HUA.

54. Quoted in Phillips, ed., *Felix Frankfurter Reminisces*, 202.

55. ZC to Leonard Bacon, 9 September 1946, HUA. Although Bacon was a widely published poet, he never published a narrative poem about the case—or at least none is listed in the Verse Index of the bibliography in Louis Joughin and Edmund M. Morgan, *The Legacy of Sacco & Vanzetti* (Princeton, N.J., 1978).

56. Chafee, review of Arthur Garfield Hays's *Let Freedom Ring* (New York, 1928), *Portland Evening News* (Maine), 18 September 1928, copy in HLL 86-8.

57. ZC to Harold Laski, 18 November 1927, HUA

58. ZC to Francis Sayre, ca. 1956, HLL 3-12. Sayre largely heeded Chafee's advice and, except for noting that Frankfurter was "greatly exercised" and wrote the article and the book, said nothing about the case's impact on the faculty. Sayre, *Glad Adventure*, 77.

59. ZC to St. John Perret, 27 July 1935, HLL 55-10.

60. ZC to Sidney Simpson, 19 February 1936, HLL 55-11.

61. ZC to Edmund M. Morgan, 29 June 1936, HLL 55-12.

62. ZC to James B. Conant, 22 June 1935, HLL 59-12; ZC to Conant, 20 March 1936, HUA.

63. Frankfurter's opposition to Landis is discussed in Ritchie, *James M. Landis*, 82.

64. Seligman, *The High Citadel*, 68.

65. ZC to Sayre MacNeil, 21 October 1936, HUA.

66. ZC to members of the class of 1913, 11 April 1938, ibid.

67. ZC to Frank E. Tyler, 23 January 1939, ibid.

68. Report of the Law School Dean to the President, 3 December 1937, HLL 54-9.

69. Chafee, "An Echo to the Report," ca. 1937, HLL 55-16 (paragraphing omitted). See Ritchie, *James M. Landis*, 88, for a summary of the committee's recommendations and of some compromises worked out by the dean.

70. ZC to members of the class of 1913, 11 April 1938, HUA.

71. Ritchie, *James M. Landis*, 80–81.

72. Ibid., 139.

73. Interview with John M. Maguire, 11 June 1973.

74. Interview with Austin W. Scott, 29 May 1973.

75. Seligman, *The High Citadel*, 71–72.

76. ZC to Sidney P. Simpson, 4 January 1949, HLL 67-18.

7. The Last of the Harvard Chancellors

1. ZC to David F. Cavers, 25 February 1954, HUA.

2. Ernest J. Wrage to ZC, 11 January 1953, HLL 76-20.

3. *IM*, 3, 16–17, 22, 32.

4. Chafee, review of Charles A. and Mary R. Beard, *The Rise of American*

Civilization (New York, 1927), *Harvard Law Review*, 41 (1927), 265–269.

5. The list appeared as a Note in *Harvard Law Review*, 58 (1945), 589–604. Rodell's review is in *Yale Law Journal*, 54 (1945), 897–901. A few months after the review appeared, Chafee referred to it as one reason among many why Louis H. Pollak, son of his friend and Wickersham colleague Walter Pollak, should attend Harvard Law School rather than Yale. ZC to Louis Pollak, 18 January 1946, HUA. Pollak, later dean of the University of Pennsylvania Law School and a federal judge, went to Yale, but he "greatly missed not studying under Chafee." Interview with Louis H. Pollak in Edward D. Re, ed., *Freedom's Prophet* (New York, 1981), 292.

6. The following text is based on a twenty-page, double-spaced memo from ZC to Edmund M. Morgan, 13 November 1941, HUA.

7. Interview with Paul A. Freund, 14 April 1976, in Re, ed., *Freedom's Prophet*, 281.

8. Interviews with David F. Cavers, 13 October 1978, and Bethuel Matthew Webster, 19 January 1978, in ibid., 328, 307. Webster formerly served as president of the Bar of the City of New York and as a member of the Permanent Court of Arbitration under the Hague Conventions.

9. Interview (mail) with Richard S. Schwartz, 25 June 1981.

10. Alexander E. Racolin to author, 16 April 1981.

11. Francis T. P. Plimpton, former ambassador to the United Nations, used the word "savageness" to describe Warren's teaching methods. Interview with Plimpton, 11 December 1977, in Re, ed., *Freedom's Prophet*, 301. Plimpton was something of a law school legend himself because of his witty poetry, notably *In Personam: A Lyrical Libel*, published in 1924. Chafee loved the poem's Capitulum IX, recounting the Trial at the Harvard Club and ending with this account of the corrections he made in his *Abrams* article: "Now Zach gave way before the strength / Of those irate grand-mommas,/In fact apologized at length—/For several misplaced commas." Quoted in Arthur E. Sutherland, *The Law at Harvard* (Cambridge, Mass., 1967), 259.

12. Interview with Richard S. Schwartz, who related another of Bull Warren's methods of humiliating students in class. Handing a student a nickel, he would say: "Call your mother and tell her you're never going to be a lawyer." Chafee, in a tribute published after Warren's death in 1945, called his former professor and colleague "a great first-year teacher," "ruthless in his denunciation of a sloppy answer" but "unusually appreciative of good work." He also recounted, as noted in Chapter 2, Warren's help at the time of Chafee's "trial." Chafee, "Edward Henry Warren," *Harvard Law Review*, 58 (1945), 1109–21. The faculty included another Professor Warren, whose polar personality earned him the nickname "Gentleman Joe." Like the better known Warren, he taught Property and once served as acting dean. Chafee said no man "was of finer grain."

13. Interview with Plimpton in Re, ed., *Freedom's Prophet*, 298.

14. Interview with Webster in ibid., 308; Erwin N. Griswold, Foreword, in ibid., xiv; W. Barton Leach, "Chafee," *Harvard Law School Bulletin*, 19 (March 1968), 12. Chafee was both companionable and somewhat aloof; his last secretary at the law school called him "a very private person": "He was warm but kept his distance from most people, and he never seemed to get too involved with associates. He was closer to Merrick Dodd [a colleague as well as a law classmate] than anyone else during the years I worked for him." Interview with Margaret Smith McManus, 30 March 1973.

15. Interview with Austin W. Scott, 29 May 1973; interview with J. Edward Lumbard, Jr., 13 January 1978, in Re, ed., *Freedom's Prophet*, 312. Lumbard formerly served as chief judge of the U.S. Court of Appeals for the Second Circuit. The observations of Scott and Lumbard were confirmed by Chafee's former secretary: "He was readily available to students. Appointments weren't necessary, and students dropped in quite often. He never complained that students took up too much of his time. He was strictly a scholar and a teacher; little of his time was taken up by administrative matters." Interview with Margaret Smith McManus, 30 March 1973.

16. Shortly before World War II, he sugested to the dean that women be admitted to help offset financial losses caused by the draft but also as a matter of justice. ZC to James M. Landis, 14 March 1941, HLL 2-7.

17. His contributions include pieces about Ezra Hervey Heywood, a free-love advocate and sex educationist; Judge Nathaniel Holmes; James Irving Manatt, chairman of Brown University's Greek Department; and Henry Schofield, professor of law at Northwestern and early scholar of free speech.

18. Interview with Elisabeth Chafee Gamble, 5 July 1973. He exchanged some especially tart letters with Carl B. Rix of the ABA and U.S. Senator John W. Bricker concerning the United Nations Covenant on Human Rights and the Bricker amendment, topics discussed in Chapters 10 and 11.

19. ZC to Roger Scaife, 29 March 1944; ZC to Edward H. Warren, 17 October 1941, HUA.

20. Benjamin Kaplan, "Zechariah Chafee, Jr.: Private-Law Writings," *Harvard Law Review*, 70 (1957), 1350.

21. ZC to Ruth Schechtman, 10 May 1954, HLL 49-2; ZC to Avram J. Goldberg, 7 June 1954, HLL 49-1; ZC to Christopher R. Knauth, 19 May 1954, ibid.; ZC to Joseph A. Califano, Jr., 9 June 1955, HUA.

22. ZC to Monroe L. Inker, 3 June 1954, HUA.

23. Jerome Spunt to ZC, 24 April 1953, HLL 48-20; Muriel Happel to ZC, 11 March 1952, HLL 50-9.

24. ZC to Herbert G. Telsey, 24 May 1940, HUA.

25. Zechariah Chafee, Jr., and Sidney P. Simpson, eds., *Cases on Equity*, 2 vols. (Cambridge, Mass., 1934).

26. ZC to Ernest Angell, 17 February 1954, HUA.

27. Interview with David Cavers in Re, ed., *Freedom's Prophet*, 326.

28. Chafee and Simpson, *Cases on Equity*, I, vii. This interest in producing

a casebook of value to practitioners represented a change from Chafee's earlier view, expressed in Chapter 6, that casebooks serve strictly a pedagogical purpose.

29. Ibid., I, viii.

30. Reviews by Edwin W. Patterson, *Harvard Law Review*, 48 (1935), 1261–64; Percy Bordwell, *Iowa Law Review*, 20 (1935), 860–864; and Donald F. Wise, *Notre Dame Lawyer*, 10 (1935), 469.

31. ZC to Blackstone Canal National Bank, 26 January 1935, HLL 66-1; Loren R. Darr to ZC, 16 November 1945, HLL 67-6. Darr was with the Foundation Press, which took over publication of the casebook with the second edition in 1946. That edition, produced with a third collaborator, John P. Maloney of St. John's University, had forty-one adoptions.

32. Interview with Margaret Smith McManus, 30 March 1973. Chafee "never threw anything out," she said, and was somewhat absent-minded—mainly because, in her view, he was so absorbed in his work that he seemed to be "more or less in a trance." But he never missed a class or was late for one. She described him as being "a marvelous boss" and "a wonderful person—thoughtful, considerate. He never found fault with me even when I made mistakes." He did not become angry even after she accidentally threw out a manuscript that he had spent considerable time in preparing (luckily, she recovered it a day or so later from the trash collection center in Langdell Hall). "He wouldn't think of having me work on Sunday even if I expressed a willingness to do so when we were very busy," she related. "He said his father never let people work on Sundays, and he was not about to do so. He sometimes worked on Sunday himself, but he slowed down a bit with the years and after suffering heart trouble. He was also good about letting me go home early if we weren't busy."

33. ZC to Francis S. Philbrick, 23 March 1934, HUA.

34. Chafee Diaries, ibid. In September 1932 he resumed keeping a diary after a ten-year hiatus. "The events of the interval stand out in my mind as follows," he wrote, and one of the first notations under 1922 referred to his return to practice on a part-time basis.

35. ZC to James C. Collins, 12 May 1922, HLL 3-16; Roscoe Pound to ZC, 18 July 1922, HLL 49-2.

36. Chafee Diaries, HUA.

37. Zechariah Chafee, Sr., to ZC, 23 April 1918, HLL 5-10.

38. Zechariah Chafee, Sr., to ZC, 2 May 1919, HLL 5-12. In 1920, when repeal of the 1919 Massachusetts Anarchy Act was being considered, Chafee explained to Albert DeSilver of the ACLU that the statute "in its present form, was to a considerable extent the result of [a] conference between Mr. Young, now Speaker of the House, and myself." Chafee to Albert DeSilver, 8 November 1920, HUA. The statute was not repealed, and in 1941, writing in *FSUS*, 164, he noted that it had "lain practically idle for twenty-two years since its passage."

39. Zechariah Chafee, Sr., to ZC, 28 February 1920, HLL 5-13. Chafee's

father worried not just about his liberal views on expression but also about some of his ideas on labor-management relations. For example, after Chafee had been teaching for three years, his father told him that his decision to become a professor had "cleared the air" because his "communistic and similar views" could not be tolerated if he were to be directly associated with the foundry. Those views, expressed particularly in his role as BIF director, consisted of urging his father to give senior employees a share in directing the business by inviting them to factory conferences, to adopt some system of profit sharing and in general to foster cooperation with labor. All the while, however, he kept reassuring his father that "I am for you and against Gompers and his gang [the American Federation of Labor]." Zechariah Chafee, Sr. to ZC, 11 September 1919; ZC to Zechariah Chafee, Sr., 18 August 1919, and other correspodence with his father, HUA.

40. E. Merrick Dodd, "Portrait of Zechariah Chafee, Jr.," *Harvard Law School Bulletin*, 3 (April 1952), 8.

41. ZC to Felix Frankfurter, 25 April 1944, HLL 4-15. Chafee borrowed the nautical metaphor from Justice Holmes, who liked to say he got "more from philosophy on the quarter than dead astern."

42. For a recent discussion of the system of writs and forms of action, see Charles Rembar, *The Law of the Land* (New York, 1980), chap. 7. See also F. W. Maitland, *The Forms of Action at Common Law* (Cambridge, England, 1971), a slender volume published posthumously and derived from a series of lectures given around the turn of the century, and the criticisms of the work in C. H. S. Fifoot, *Frederic William Maitland: A Life* (Cambridge, Mass., 1971), 97–98. The forms of action were interred piecemeal, starting in 1832–33, although, as Maitland observed, "The forms of action . . . still rule us from their graves." A recent influential study of early English law is S. F. C. Milsom, *Historical Foundations of the Common Law* (London, 1969).

43. Chafee, Foreword to Edward D. Re, ed., *Selected Essays on Equity* (New York, 1955) reprinted in Re, ed., *Freedom's Prophet*, 387.

44. Ibid.

45. Roscoe Pound, "The Decadence of Equity," *Columbia Law Review*, 5 (1905), 20–35.

46. ZC to Donald McClure, 31 October 1941, HLL 56-9.

47. ZC to Edgar N. Durfee, 10 November 1949, HUA.

48. Rembar, *The Law of the Land*, 279.

49. Chafee, "Does Equity Follow the Law of Torts?" *University of Pennsylvania Law Review*, 75 (1926), 1–35, reprinted in Chafee, *Some Problems of Equity* (Ann Arbor, Mich., 1950), 103–148.

50. Chafee, "Does Equity Follow the Law of Torts?" 1, 35.

51. Chafee, *Some Problems of Equity*, 2. Chafee's two lectures on the clean hands doctrine appeared as a two-part article in the *Michigan Law Review*, 47 (1949), 877–906 and 1065–1096. The five lectures in the series became chapters 1–3 and 6–9 of the book, which includes reprints of two

related articles—the aforementioned "Does Equity Follow the Law of Torts?" and "Bills of Peace with Multiple Parties," which originally ran in *Harvard Law Review*, 45 (1932), 1297–1332.

52. ZC to Henry L. McClintock, 2 January 1952, HUA. McClintock, professor of law at Mercer University in Macon, Georgia, and the author of works on equity, reviewed *Some Problems of Equity* in *Vanderbilt Law Review*, 5 (1951), 131–133.

53. ZC to George B. Fraser, Jr., 30 November 1951, HUA. Chafee said he was pleased because Fraser, professor of law at the University of Oklahoma, in a review in *Oklahoma Law Review*, 4 (1951), 519–522, had given attention to the two chapters (6 and 7) on class suits.

54. Chafee, *Some Problems of Equity*, 295.

55. See, e.g., Richard Reeves, *American Journey* (New York, 1982), 101.

56. The cases are commonly referred to as Brown I and Brown II. The official citations are Brown v. Board of Education, 347 U.S. 483 (1954), and Brown v. Board of Education, 349 U.S. 294 (1955). For a detailed historical study of the cases, see Richard Kluger, *Simple Justice* (New York, 1976). See also G. Edward White, *Earl Warren: A Public Life* (New York, 1982), chap. 6, and Bernard Schwartz, *Super Chief* (New York, 1983), chap. 3.

57. The story of the role in school desegregation of the judges of the fifth circuit is told in Jack Bass, *Unlikely Heroes* (New York, 1981).

58. Ibid., 21. For a favorable view of such latter-day uses of equity, see Owen M. Fiss, *The Civil Rights Injunction* (Bloomington, Ind., 1978); for a critical view, see Gary L. McDowell, *Equity and the Constitution* (Chicago, 1982).

59. The appellation comes from his friend and colleague John M. Maguire, in a tribute written upon Chafee's retirement in 1956: "Quite likely it is fitting to dub him the Last of the Harvard Chancellors. For in this School at least fate has dealt a shattering blow to the pedagogic integrity of Equity." John M. Maguire, "Zechariah Chafee, Jr.," *Harvard Law School Bulletin*, 7 (June 1956), 2.

60. Chafee believed that the dismemberment of Equity began while he was on leave during 1936–37 recovering from a nervous breakdown. In March 1941, four years after Landis became dean and began implementing the major curricular changes, Chafee sent him a memo complaining generally about their adverse effect on Equity instruction and specifically about how Equity III had been sliced in half and half of it thrown away: "My main point is that this was my favorite course among all I have ever taught, even though it may have been nothing more than the incarnation of my personality. It was mutilated while I was out sick, and now that I am happily back with reasonable vigor, I should like to restore the amputated limbs." ZC to James M. Landis, 3 March 1941, HLL 2-7. Landis had criticized Chafee's approach to Equity several years before he became dean. Objecting to Chafee's overemphasis on the various doctrines of mutuality, Landis told him: "Talking mutuality continuously tends to make [students] treat equity as

a mathematical science, instead of dealing with its problems in a realistic way." James M. Landis to ZC, 12 July 1929, HLL 2-6. Chafee's mathematical bent may help explain why a course reflecting his personality was so criticized. His personality was not one-dimensional, however, and other evidence shows that his teaching of Equity was comprehensive, fair and humanistic.

61. Chafee, *Reissued Notes on Bills and Notes* (Cambridge, Mass., 1943). Publication of the pamphlet prompted Karl Llewellyn, his friendly adversary at Columbia, to write what he called "a review of Zechariah Chafee, Jr.," which is quoted in the Epilogue. From 1937 to 1942 much of Llewellyn's energies went into drafting the Uniform Commercial Code (UCC), which, as one wag remarked, put Bills and Notes teachers out of business. As was explained in Chapter 5, Chafee's work on the Hutchins Commission kept him from becoming actively involved in the drafting process. Thus when the editor of *Law and Contemporary Problems* asked him to contribute to a symposium on the UCC, he declined on the grounds "that it would be rather unfair to make adverse criticisms in print about possible shortcomings after refusing the chance to remove those shortcomings in the first place." ZC to Robert Kramer, 8 March 1950, HUA. For a critique of the code, which was rather quickly adopted by every state but Louisiana, see Lawrence M. Friedman, *A History of American Law* (New York, 1973), 581–582.

62. ZC to Frederick G. Beutel, 22 May 1943, HLL 65-4.

63. Interview with David F. Cavers, in Re, ed., *Freedom's Prophet*, 325.

64. ZC to Sidney P. Simpson, 4 January 1949, HLL 67-18.

65. ZC to James B. Conant, 22 June 1949, HLL 34-19.

66. A copy of the Cavers memo is in HLL 1-19. Dean Griswold later appointed Cavers associate dean for research and development.

67. ZC to Erwin N. Griswold, 8 January 1951, HLL 1-19.

8. Pushing a Stone Up Capitol Hill

1. Martin Mayer, *The Lawyers* (New York, 1967), 51, 49.

2. The example is based on a letter from ZC to Jesse H. Metcalf, his uncle and a U.S. senator, 22 January 1932, HLL 22-6.

3. New York Life Insurance Co. v. Dunlevy, 241 U.S. 519 (1916).

4. The first federal statute on interpleader was 39 Stat. 929 (1917); the later version including casualty and surety companies was 44 Stat. 416 (1926), 28 U.S.C.A. § 41 (26) (1926). A statute also was enacted in 1925, 43 Stat. 976 (1925), 28 U.S.C.A. § 41 (26) (1926), but a mix-up in its passage had to be promptly straightened out in the 1926 act.

5. ZC to Harold Tanner, 25 January 1940, HUA. The article Chafee referred to is "Modernizing Interpleader," *Yale Law Journal*, 30 (1921), 814–844. To Justice James C. McReynolds, who wrote the Supreme Court's opinion in the *Dunlevy* case, Chafee commented that "I strongly approve

of the principles on which you decided it. Since that case shows that interpleader by a life insurance company in the state courts cannot be effective under the Constitution, the subsequent [1917] Act of Congress seems very desirable." ZC to McReynolds, 6 May 1924, HLL 22-2.

6. Chafee, "Interstate Interpleader," *Yale Law Journal*, 33 (1924), 685–727.

7. Chafee, "Modernizing Interpleader," 814.

8. Ibid., 821–822. The classic statement of these four limitations is in John Norton Pomeroy's *Equity Jurisprudence*, which Chafee quoted from.

9. Chafee, "Modernizing Interpleader," 824, 830.

10. Ibid., 824, 828. Strictly speaking, Chafee favored the outright abolishment of the identity and privity requirements, for which the test of mutual exclusiveness would be substituted. The third and fourth requirements "should remain only as considerations affecting the exercise of equitable jurisdiction and no longer bar the jurisdiction." Ibid., 844.

11. Chafee, "Interstate Interpleader," 724–725.

12. ZC to Joseph S. Conwell, 6 May 1924, HLL 22-2.

13. Joseph S. Conwell to ZC, 8 May 1924, ibid.

14. ZC to Conwell, 26 May 1924, ibid.

15. ZC to J. H. McChord, 19 January 1932, HLL 22-6.

16. ZC to Jesse H. Metcalf, 22 January 1932, ibid.

17. J. H. McChord to ZC, 25 January 1932; ZC to McChord, 28 January 1932, ibid.

18. Marine Midland Trust Co. v. Irving Trust Co., 56 F. 2d 385 (S.D.N.Y. 1932), aff'd *sub nom*. Marine Midland Trust Co. v. Eybro, 58 F. 2d 165 (2d Cir. 1932).

19. ZC to Julian Mack, 8 February 1932, HLL 22-6. Later, Chafee wrote Mack again, this time noting that he disagreed with the reason the judge gave for one point of his "very gratifying opinion" in the *Marine Midland* case. ZC to Mack, 1 April 1932, ibid.

20. J. H. McChord to ZC, 12 February 1932, ibid.

21. McChord to ZC, 24 March 1932; ZC to McChord, 28 March 1932, ibid. The article Chafee referred to was published in two parts as "Interpleader in the United States Courts," *Yale Law Journal*, 41 (1932), 1134–71, and 42 (1932), 41–65.

22. For a discussion of the problems in Kentucky, see Paul L. Murphy, *The Meaning of Freedom of Speech* (Westport, Conn., 1972), 239–244.

23. ZC to McChord, 28 March 1932, HLL 22-6.

24. Chafee, "Interpleader in the United States Courts," *Yale Law Journal*, 41 (1932), 1137.

25. ZC to Roscoe Pound, 1 November 1932, HLL 22-7.

26. ZC to Roscoe Pound, 6 November 1931, HLL 22-1.

27. ZC to J. H. McChord, 16 November 1932, HLL 22-7.

28. ZC to Jesse H. Metcalf, 1 May 1933, HLL 22-8.

29. State v. Butterworth, 104 N.J.L. 587 (1928).

30. For a biography of Vanderbilt, see Arthur T. Vanderbilt II, *Changing Law* (New Brunswick, N.J., 1976), written by his grandson.

31. Arthur T. Vanderbilt to ZC, 3 February 1934, HLL 22-1C.

32. Hobart S. Weaver to J. H. McChord, 2 February 1934; McChord to ZC, 5 February 1934, ibid. Weaver's letter to McChord quoted one insurance company lawyer, "who has had considerable to do with this law," as follows: "I was very much taken with the careful, thorough and capable presentation by Professor Chafee of the proposed bill and the pros and cons as he presents them, and I do not think I have ever seen a more thorough presentation of any matter of like character than has been developed by him in his explanatory notes."

33. ZC to Arthur T. Vanderbilt, 6 February 1934, ibid.

34. ZC to Vanderbilt, 20 March 1934, ibid.

35. ZC to W. Calvin Chesnut, 2 March 1938, HLL 24-1. Thanking the judge for sending a copy of his opinion in John Hancock Mutual Life Insurance Co. v. Kegan, 22 F. Supp. 326 (D. Md. 1938), Chafee said he was "much pleased with your liberal interpretation of the statute and grateful for your numerous references to my articles."

36. ZC to Arthur T. Vanderbilt, 6 February 1934, HLL 22-10; Chafee, Memorandum on his draft bill for ABA Insurance Law Section. May 1934, HLL 22-13; various other materials pertaining to interpleader in HLL. Chafee, "The Federal Interpleader Act of 1936: I," *Yale Law Journal*, 45 (1936), 963–990, includes much of the memo he originally wrote for the ABA. See also Chafee, *Cases on Equitable Remedies* (Cambridge, Mass., 1938), chap. 1.

37. Chafee, Memorandum for ABA Insurance Law Section.

38. Vanderbilt to ZC, 21 May 1934, HLL 22-12.

39. ZC to McChord, 2 February 1935, HLL 23-1.

40. ZC to McChord, 14 February 1935, ibid.

41. ZC to McChord, 3 February 1936, HLL 23-8. The Interpleader Act is 49 Stat. 1096 (1936), 28 U.S.C. § 41 (26) (1936), An Act to Amend Section 24 of the Judicial Code by Conferring on District Courts Additional Jurisdiction of Bills of Interpleader and of Bills in the Nature of Interpleader.

42. Interview with John M. Maguire, 11 June 1973; interview with Austin W. Scott, 28 May 1973.

43. Interview with Claude R. Branch, 8 June 1973; interview with Francis H. Chafee, 5 July 1973; interview with John M. Maguire, 11 June 1973; interview (mail) with Mary Chafee Andrews, April 1982.

44. Interview with Elisabeth Chafee Gamble, 5 July 1973.

45. Interview with Zechariah Chafee III, 30 April–1 May 1982.

46. Anne Chafee Brien, "Zechariah Chafee, Jr.," (unpublished manuscript, 1958; copy in possession of author); interview with Zechariah Chafee III, 30 April–1 May 1982.

47. Various items in family correspondence, HUA.

48. Interview with Zechariah Chafee III, 30 April–1 May 1982; Donald

A. Ritchie, *James M. Landis* (Cambridge, Mass., 1980), 34; quitclaim deed, dated 18 June 1928, on file in Register of Deeds Office, East Cambridge, Mass.

49. ZC to Theodore Emery, 1 November 1937, HUA.

50. Ernest Angell, "Zechariah Chafee, Jr.: Individual Freedoms," *Harvard Law Review*, 70 (1957), 1344.

51. Zechariah Chafee, Sr., to ZC, 14 July 1939, HUA.

52. ZC to Paul C. Wolfe, 17 February 1955, HUA.

53. Chafee, "Robert Searle Chafee," reprint from the Sexennial Report of the Harvard College Class of 1936, HUA.

54. ZC to Sayre MacNeil, 25 September 1941, HUA; ZC to Mrs. Herbert L. Dorrance, 26 September 1941, ibid. The Chafees, together with his father and his Aunt Ellen Sharpe, bought land at Northampton, Massachusetts, to establish a bird sanctuary in memory of Robert, an avid birdwatcher. This later became the Arcadia Wildlife Sanctuary of the Massachusetts Audubon Society.

55. ZC to Mrs. Alex Burgess, 24 September 1941, HUA.

9. Safeguarding the Bill of Rights

1. Grenville Clark, "Conservatism and Civil Liberty," *American Bar Association Journal*, 24 (1938), 644.

2. The Bill of Rights Committee was created 24 July 1938 by a resolution of the ABA's House of Delegates. Hogan's inaugural address recommending formation of the committee was published as "Lawyers and the Rights of Citizens," *American Bar Association Journal*, 24 (1938), 615–619; Vanderbilt's speech as outgoing president is "United We Stand," ibid., 597–601, 639. For a discussion of the committee's creation as a means for helping the ABA to regain public support after its opposition to President Roosevelt's New Deal legislation, see Paul L. Murphy, *The Constitution in Crisis Times 1918–1969* (New York, 1972), 175. See also Irving Dilliard, "Grenville Clark: Public Citizen," *American Scholar*, 33 (1964), 101, and Grenville Clark to Philip L. Graham, 26 November 1951, HLL 11-10.

3. ZC to Grenville Clark, 28 September 1938, ABA Bill of Rights Committee Papers 1938–1942 (ABA Papers), HLL 1-8.

4. Hogan, "Lawyers and the Rights of Citizens," 617.

5. *FSUS*, 410.

6. Hague v. Committee for Industrial Organization, 307 U.S. 496 (1939). The case bears the original name of the CIO, which in 1938 became the Congress of Industrial Organizations.

7. The Supreme Court case is Davis v. Massachusetts, 167 U.S. 43 (1897), upholding a decision by Oliver Wendell Holmes, Jr., while a member of the Supreme Judicial Court of Massachusetts. See 162 Mass. 510 (1895). Chafee discusses the *Hague* case in *FSUS*, 409–431. See also Glenn Abernathy, *The*

Right of Assembly and Association (Columbia, S.C., 1961), 53–54, 115–128.

8. CIO v. Hague, 25 F. Supp. 127 (D.C.N.J. 1938). Judge Clark did reject the plaintiff's contention that Mayor Hague had pressured owners of private halls to deny labor groups access to them. A Harvard Law School alumnus, Judge Clark was a native of Newark whom President Coolidge named to the federal bench in 1925. He had achieved national prominence in 1930 by ruling that the Eighteenth Amendment was unconstitutional.

9. William Clark to ZC, 28 October 1938, HLL 3-7.

10. This brief, slightly changed, was later filed with the Supreme Court. Excerpts appear in *FSUS*, 414–428; the full brief is reprinted in Philip B. Kurland and Gerhard Casper, eds., *Landmark Briefs and Arguments of the Supreme Court of the United States: Constitutional Law* (Arlington, Va., 1975), vol. 36, 867–914. The committee's decision to intervene came after careful deliberation from August to November of 1938; Grenville Clark later described the committee's approach as follows: "If there is one thing [it] can't do, it is to hurry. We are a cautious crowd, including the chairman, and disposed to decide anything important only after considerable deliberation—so that 'hurrying' is simply out of the question. I could not make the Committee hurry if I wanted to; but also I don't want to." Clark to Frederick H. Stinchfield, 21 August 1939, ABA Papers, HLL 1-10.

11. ZC to Grenville Clark, 13 December 1938, ABA Papers, HLL 3-2.

12. ZC to Grenville Clark, 7 December 1938, ibid.

13. ZC to Grenville Clark, 14 December 1938, ibid.

14. Hague v. CIO, 101 F. 2d 774 (3d Cir. 1938).

15. *FSUS*, 423. Grenville Clark thought the appellate court's broad holding "might be said to be dictum [and thus not binding] because the court also upheld the point that it had been unconstitutionally administered." Clark, Memorandum to Committee Members, 9 February 1939, ABA Papers, HLL 2-9.

16. *FSUS*, 416–428 passim; Grenville Clark, Memorandum to Committee Members, 24 February 1939, ABA Papers, HLL 2-9.

17. Hague v. CIO, 307 U.S. 496, 518 (1939).

18. *FSUS*, 430.

19. Report of the Special Committee on the Bill of Rights, 26 April 1939, ABA Papers, HLL 1-2.

20. For a comprehensive treatment of Gobitis and other flag salute cases, see David R. Manwaring, *Render unto Caesar* (Chicago, 1962). A brief popular account is Irving Dilliard, "The Flag Salute Cases," in John A. Garraty, ed., *Quarrels That Have Shaped the Constitution* (New York, 1966), 222–242. Chafee once said he thought Dilliard, who had a long career as an editorial writer and editor with the *St. Louis Post-Dispatch*, knew more about the Supreme Court than any journalist in the country.

21. Manwaring, *Render unto Caesar*, 56.

22. ZC to Robert S. Chafee, 15 January 1939, HUA.

23. The memorandum is summarized in the Report of the Special Committee on the Bill of Rights, 26 April 1939.

24. Johnson v. Deerfield (together with Gabrielli v. Knickerbocker), 306 U.S. 621 (1939). The earlier dismissals had come in Leoles v. Landers, 302 U.S. 656 (1937), and Hering v. New Jersey State Board of Education, 303 U.S. 624 (1938).

25. Gobitis v. Minersville School District, 24 F. Supp. 271, 274 (E.D.Pa. 1938).

26. Minersville School District v. Gobitis, 108 F. 2d 683, 692 (3d Cir. 1939).

27. ZC to Albert B. Maris, 15 January 1940, HLL 24-8.

28. Grenville Clark to Irving Dilliard, 23 September 1959, copy in possession of author.

29. Grenville Clark, Memorandum to Members of Committee, 21 March 1940, ABA Papers, HLL 3-3. See also Alpheus Thomas Mason, *Harlan Fiske Stone: Pillar of the Law* (New York, 1956), 531, 853 n. 57.

30. United States v. Carolene Products Co., 304 U.S. 144, 152–153 (1938). See also Mason, *Harlan Fiske Stone*, 512–516.

31. Grenville Clark to ZC, 18 January 1939; ZC to George K. Gardner, 19 January 1939, ABA Papers, HLL 3-3.

32. A copy of Gardner's memo, dated 3 February 1939, is in ABA Papers, HLL 3-4. The House of Delegates vote to intervene was 53 to 51. Manwaring, *Render unto Caesar*, 126.

33. ZC to Burton W. Musser, 3 December 1943, ABA Papers, HLL 2-5.

34. ZC to Grenville Clark, 28 March 1940, ABA Papers, HLL 3-3.

35. Brief for ABA Bill of Rights Committee as Amicus Curiae at 19–20, Minersville School District v. Gobitis, 310 U.S. 586 (1940); ZC to Grenville Clark, 28 March 1940, ABA Papers, HLL 3-3. Chafee noted his responsibility for pages 19–20 of the brief in a letter to Henry Washburn, dean of the Episcopal Theological School in Cambridge, 1 May 1940, ibid. The brief is reprinted in Kurland and Casper, eds., *Landmark Briefs*, vol. 37, 453–502.

36. For a careful critique of the religious freedom section of the brief, see Manwaring, *Render unto Caesar*, 130–131.

37. ZC to Charles E. Hughes, Jr., 16 April 1940, HLL 56-9. Chafee and Hughes were longtime friends. After graduating from Brown University in 1909 (two years after Chafee), Hughes attended Harvard Law School and was president of the Law Review Board at the time Chafee declined membership. During the 1930s, both served on the Brown Corporation.

38. Manwaring, *Render unto Caesar*, 134–135, remarks that the court's previous per curiam dispositions of such cases "probably represented [Hughes's] views more than those of any other justice," and that "Hughes 'ran' the Court to a degree probably unparalleled since [Chief Justice John] Marshall; in the general run of cases, his associates seem to have been content so to be 'run.' "

39. Minersville School District v. Gobitis, 310 U.S. 586 (1940). Although the literature includes many discussions of Frankfurter's opinion, there is no mention of it in Harlan B. Phillips, ed., *Felix Frankfurter Reminisces* (New York, 1960).

40. Joseph P. Lash, *From the Diaries of Felix Frankfurter* (New York, 1975), 68.

41. ZC to Grenville Clark, 5 June 1940, ABA Papers, HLL 3-3.

42. ZC to Felix Frankfurter, 5 June 1940; Frankfurter to ZC, 11 June 1940, ibid.

43. Felix Frankfurter to Harlan F. Stone, 27 May 1940, published as an appendix to Alpheus Thomas Mason, *Security Through Freedom* (Ithaca, N.Y., 1955), 217–220. See also Mason, *Harlan Fiske Stone*, 526–528.

44. Mason, *Harlan Fiske Stone*, 512.

45. Ibid., 525.

46. Quoted in ibid., 527.

47. Ibid., 528.

48. Manwaring, *Render unto Caesar*, 147.

49. Chafee, "Mr. Justice Parker" (unsigned editorial), *New Republic*, 62 (2 April 1930), 177–178. Professor Peter Finch of Duke University, who has done research on Parker's career, informed me that Frankfurter prevailed upon Chafee to take a harder line on the judge's qualifications than he had originally been inclined to do. Chafee acknowledged authorship of the piece in a letter to Frank W. Buxton, 28 March 1930, HUA. In a later letter to Buxton, a *Boston Herald* editor with whom he often corresponded, he commented: "We are very enthusiastic about [Owen J.] Roberts out here [at the law school]. Despite the slams on the Senate on your editorial page, that body has done the country a good service in exchanging Roberts for Parker." ZC to Buxton, 15 May 1930, ibid.

50. Chafee, "Mr. Justice Parker," 178. A copy of Chafee's memo summarizing the judge's opinions is in the Thomas Reed Powell Papers, HLL F-9.

51. Jones v. Opelika, 316 U.S. 584 (1942).

52. Jones v. Opelika, 319 U.S. 103 (1943). An explanation of the court's changed views is contained in the majority opinion of Justice William O. Douglas in a related case decided the same day, Murdock v. Pennsylvania, 319 U.S. 105 (1943).

53. Barnette v. West Virginia State Board of Education, 47 F. Supp. 251 (S.D.W.Va. 1942).

54. Ibid. at 253.

55. Ibid. at 254.

56. ZC to Douglas Arant, 5 March 1943, ABA Papers, HLL 4-2. Arant, of Alabama, was then chairman of the committee.

57. Grenville Clark to ZC, 2 February 1943, ibid. (paragraphing omitted).

58. Brief for ABA Bill of Rights Committee as Amicus Curiae at 3–4, 7, West Virginia State Board of Education v. Barnette, 319 U.S. 624 (1943),

reprinted in Kurland and Casper, eds., *Landmark Briefs*, vol. 40, 205–239. One member of the committee, George L. Buist of South Carolina, would not sign the brief. In a letter to Buist, whose objection was cast mainly in terms of states' rights, Chafee said he too believed that "a large scope should be given to the local determination of local matters" but that it was "pretty clear that this is not a local matter but a national matter." ZC to Buist, 26 February 1943, ABA Papers, HLL 4-2 (paragraphing omitted).

59. Brief at 10.

60. Ibid. at 26.

61. John Raeburn Green to ZC, 14 June 1943, ABA Papers, HLL 4-2. The article by Green, "Liberty Under the Fourteenth Amendment," appeared in the *Washington University Law Quarterly*, 27 (1942), 497–562.

62. West Virginia State Board of Education v. Barnette, 319 U.S. 624, 639 (1943).

63. Osmer C. Fitts to ZC, 14 June 1943, HUA; George K. Gardner to ZC, 16 June 1943, ABA Papers, HLL 4-1; Gardner to ZC, 8 March 1943, ABA Papers, HLL 4-2.

64. ZC to Douglas Arant, 16 June 1943, HLL 9-14. For a discussion of the limited influence on the justices of the ABA and other briefs, see Manwaring, *Render unto Caesar*, 234–235.

65. ZC to Harlan F. Stone, 2 July 1943, HLL 25-17; Harlan F. Stone to Chafee, 14 July 1943, HUA. However, Stone had reservations of his own about Jackson's opinion, as explained in Mason, *Harlan Fiske Stone*, 600–601.

66. 319 U.S. at 646. H. N. Hirsch, *The Enigma of Felix Frankfurter* (New York, 1981), 171, states that Frankfurter's dissenting opinion "hardened [his] stand on the question of judicial review and thereby set the tenor of his entire philosophy of law"; and Lash, *From the Diaries of Felix Frankfurter*, 73, concludes that the opinion, in which Frankfurter asserted that the court has no larger role in protecting civil rights than property rights, "uncoupled him from the locomotive of history." Joseph L. Rauh, Jr., "Felix Frankfurter: Civil Libertarian," *Harvard Civil Rights-Civil Liberties Law Review*, 11 (1976), 507–520, disputes Lash's conclusion.

67. Charles C. Burlingham to ZC, 18 June 1943; Carl S. Stern to ZC, 19 August 1943, HUA.

68. Grenville Clark to ZC, 22 October 1941, HLL 74-1.

69. Grenville Clark to Philip L. Graham, 26 November 1951, HLL 11-10.

70. ZC to Harold Evans, 13 March 1945, HLL 10-22.

71. The *Summers* litigation is discussed in Mulford Q. Sibley and Philip E. Jacob, *Conscription of Conscience* (Ithaca, N.Y., 1952), 442–444. Chafee, calling the behavior of the Illinois bench and bar "a disgrace," thought it "obvious that the Character Committee and the Supreme Court of Illinois did not turn him down because they genuinely thought that his beliefs would make him a bad lawyer, but simply because they did not like his beliefs . . . I hope that the Illinois Bench and Bar will wear sack cloth for

their action in this case no matter what the Supreme Court decides. The letters of recommendation which this boy had set a high-water mark. When I think of the hard-boiled and slick fellows who get into the bar, I think that both [the Illinois] Supreme Court and the Illinois Bar Association ought to be ashamed of themselves for keeping out this able man of high ideals, just because he seems to them over conscientious." ZC to Charles P. Megan, 13 June 1944, HLL 10-19; ZC to Walter T. Fisher, 24 April 1945, HUA. Megan was a former president of the Illinois Bar Association; Fisher was a Chicago lawyer.

72. Julien Cornell, an ACLU lawyer for Summers and author of *The Conscientious Objector and the Law* (New York, 1943), wrote Chafee that it had "never been necessary within the memory of anyone in the office of the Clerk of the Supreme Court to issue a writ of certiorari compelling the certifying of a record until this case arose." Cornell to ZC, 8 March 1945, HLL 10-22.

73. ZC to Harold Evans, 10 April 1945, HLL 10-23. The brief is summarized in Sibley and Jacob, *Conscription of Conscience*, 443–444.

74. ZC to Clyde W. Summers, 7 March 1945, HLL 10-22.

75. In re Summers, 325 U.S. 561 (1945).

76. ZC to Harold Evans, 13 June 1945, HLL 10-24.

77. ZC to Grenville Clark, 28 May 1940, ABA Papers, HLL 2-1 (paragraphing omitted).

78. McNabb v. United States, 318 U.S. 332 (1943); Anderson v. United States, 318 U.S. 350 (1943). A copy of the memo, bearing the names of Chafee and four other committee members, is in HLL 10-1 along with the shorter statement of opposition, signed by all committee members.

79. 318 U.S. at 347.

80. Felix Frankfurter to ZC, 15 June 1944, HLL 10-3; J. Edgar Hoover to ZC, 21 November 1944, HLL 10-7; ZC to Jerome Michael, 21 December 1949, HLL 10-9. Chafee had sent Hoover a copy of the memo containing corrections of some statements to which Hoover and other Justice Department officials objected. Hoover replied, "I regret that the changes made do not correct all the inaccuracies and innuendoes included in the initial publication." Many items concerning this memo were placed in the Chafee file at FBI headquarters; see Chapter 11 n. 94 and corresponding text.

81. Mallory v. United States, 354 U.S. 449 (1957). For a discussion of congressional efforts to counter the *McNabb* and *Mallory* rules, see G. Theodore Mitau, *Decade of Decision* (New York, 1967), 178–183.

82. On racial and ethnic prejudice in the legal profession, see Jerold S. Auerbach, *Unequal Justice* (New York, 1976).

83. Report of Committee Meeting, 17–18 April 1942, ABA papers, HLL 2-3.

84. ZC to Douglas Arant, 13 June 1942, ibid. Elsewhere, Chafee commented: "The war power now used against second-generation Japanese may be stretched to include ninth-generation English [of whom Chafee was one],

and any of us who voices vigorous disapproval of heavy taxes or unwelcome priorities may be informed that national safety requires him to depart from his house and occupation in New England and settle on some Iowa farm. Thus what starts as regulation of freedom of movement may become regulation of freedom of speech as well . . . The [current] situation is not like the last war, it is like the Civil War . . . The forcible migration from California offers analogies to the administrative arrests of numerous citizens of Maryland . . . The vital question will not be how far judges and juries may go in sending citizens to prison but how far officials may go in confining citizens without judges and juries." Chafee, extract from unpublished article, ca. 1 March 1942, HLL 9-10.

85. Korematsu v. United States, 323 U.S. 214 (1944); Ex parte Endo, 323 U.S. 283 (1944). Early in 1983, a congressional commission issued a report concluding that the relocation program was "a grave injustice"—not motivated by military considerations but by "racial prejudice, war hysteria and failure of political leadership." *New York Times*, 25 February 1983. Late in 1983, a federal judge overturned the conviction of Fred Korematsu. *New York Times*, 11 November 1983. For a thorough discussion of legal aspects of the relocation program, see Peter Irons, *Justice at War* (New York, 1983). Irons was among counsel for Korematsu and other Japanese Americans.

86. Quoted in ZC to Charles P. Megan, 14 April 1943, ABA Papers, HLL 4-2.

87. ZC to Douglas Arant, 30 April 1943, ibid.

88. ZC to Burton W. Musser, 3 December 1943, ABA Papers, HLL 2-5.

89. Smith v. Allwright, 321 U.S. 649 (1944). This and other voting rights cases are discussed in Richard Kluger, *Simple Justice* (New York, 1975), 233–237.

10. Free Speech in the United Nations

1. ZC to Bitner Browne, 27 September 1939, HUA.

2. Hartzel v. United States, 322 U.S. 680 (1944). In reviewing the Justice Department's improved record during World War II, Chafee commented: "Not only have there been very few recent prosecutions, but also the [Espionage] Act has been much more strictly construed by the Supreme Court. In June 1944, while our troops were still struggling to gain Normandy, the majority of the Court gave greater protection to freedom of speech [in the *Hartzel* case] than their predecessors of 1919–20 thought safe long after the last gun was fired . . . All the Justices looked solely into the question [of] . . . intent . . . If Hartzel's case had come before the Court which sent Debs to prison, he would not have had a ghost of a show. The majority have at last made the Espionage Act mean what it says." *GMC*, I, 450–452 (paragraphing omitted).

3. For a biography of Coughlin, the first prepared with his cooperation,

see Sheldon Marcus, *Father Coughlin* (Boston, 1973). See also Alan Brinkley, *Voices of Protest* (New York, 1982) for a discussion of Coughlin, Huey Long, and other demagogues during the Great Depression.

4. *BL*, 79. For Biddle's account of the period, see *In Brief Authority* (New York, 1962), esp. chap. 15 (which also recounts his experiences with Father Coughlin). Under Attorney General Jackson shortly before the war, consideration was given to setting up an advisory committee on civil liberties. Jackson discussed the idea with Grenville Clark, who recommended several possible members with Chafee's name at the top of the list. Clark to Robert H. Jackson, 16 April 1940; Jackson to Clark, 20 April 1940, ABA Papers, HLL 2-1.

5. Chafee, manuscript of "The Bill of Rights Belongs to the People" (address to Chicago Civil Liberties Committee, 15 December 1941), HUA. The speech was printed in *Bulletin of American Association of University Professors*, 28 (1942), 92–101.

6. Wendell Berge, copy of "Freedom of Speech in Time of War" (speech on WWDC, Washington, 11 January 1942), HLL 32-4. Berge's speech, printed in *Bulletin of AAUP*, 28 (1942), 239–246, quoted Chafee's belief in fighting words with words, not force. See CST, 773; FS, 158; FSUS, 139.

7. Franklin S. Pollak to ZC, 26 January 1942, HLL 32-4.

8. ZC to Wendell Berge, 16 May 1944, HLL 10-1.

9. ZC to Barry C. Smith, 26 October 1943, HLL 81-11.

10. ZC to Monte Lemann, 13 November 1944, HLL 10-7.

11. See Donald J. Kemper, *Decade of Fear: Senator Hennings and Civil Liberties* (Columbia, Mo., 1965); Robert Griffith, *The Politics of Fear: Joseph R. McCarthy and the Senate* (Lexington, Ky., 1970), and David Caute, *The Great Fear: The Anti-Communist Purge under Truman and Eisenhower* (New York, 1978).

12. ZC to Scott Buchanan, 3 November 1945, HLL 35-7.

13. ZC to A. J. Carlson, 20 December 1935, HUA.

14. For his views of the League of Nations and other proposals for world organizations, see his "International Utopias," *American Scholar*, 2 (1942), 275–291.

15. ZC to William Benton, 5 June 1950; Benton to ZC, 14 June 1950, HUA. A page-one story by Chesly Manly, published 4 September 1948, had said: "As head of the [State] Department's U.N. affairs office, Hiss put over the appointment of Prof. Zechariah Chafee of the Harvard law school as this country's representative on [the subcommission]. Hiss, a Harvard law graduate, had studied under Chafee." Strictly speaking, members of the subcommission were nominated by their governments, then elected by the Human Rights Commission headed by Eleanor Roosevelt. Thus she was technically Chafee's "boss" while he sat on the subcommission, and he had the highest regard for her.

16. Most of the correspondence pertaining to Chafee's UN work is in

HLL, boxes 16–18; see also *BL*, chap. 11. In the following text, direct quotations without specific notations are from *BL*, 303–304; HLL 18-12; and *BL*, 304.

17. *New York Herald Tribune*, 23 January 1948; *Time*, 51 (2 February 1945), 53; Chafee, copy of Statement Before Subcommission, 22 January 1948, HLL 18-11.

18. Chafee, copy of Statement Before Subcommission, 27 January 1948, HLL 18-6 (some paragraphing omitted).

19. *Chicago Tribune*, 2 February 1948.

20. ZC to William M. Tugman, 15 November 1954, HUA.

21. Lomakin did not turn up at Geneva. He did return to the United States, serving as Soviet consul general in New York City until August 1948, when he was expelled from the country. He was ordered to leave after a Russian school teacher jumped to her death from a window in the Soviet consulate rather than return home as he had instructed her to do. However, Chafee had not heard the last of Lomakin, who in a well-publicized speech in Moscow on 15 March 1949 quoted Chafee as "admitting to me personally that the United States has the worst censorship" in the world. The story was on the front page of the *New York Times*, 16 March 1949. In a letter to the *Times*, 17 March 1949, Chafee said: "At Lake Success [Lomakin] repeatedly used the word 'censorship' to include control of newspaper owners over subject matter. I always insisted on limiting the word to control by government officials . . . Finally, even using the word 'censorship' in Lomakin's warped meaning, I never said the United States had the worst. I strongly believe governmental censorship [is] far worse than any evils of American private control. I do not remember ever making any comparison to him, but if I did I told him exactly that."

22. Telegram (typed copy) from George C. Marshall to James B. Conant, 19 February 1948, HUA.

23. ZC to Walter A. Edwards, 8 March 1948, ibid.

24. ZC to G. J. Van Heuven Goedhart, 1 March 1948, HLL 13-9.

25. Chafee said he made this suggestion after consulting with Byron Price, who had headed both the Associated Press and the wartime U.S. Office of Censorship. ZC to George A. Finch, 23 June 1949, HLL 19-6.

26. ZC to Carl B. Rix, 6 March 1950, HLL 18-17; ZC to Robert U. Brown, 3 March 1948, HLL 13-9. Chafee told Brown he considered this emphasis on rule making his "most useful service" to the subcommission.

27. The subcommission and conference drafts of article 17 appear in Appendix II of Chafee, "Legal Problems of Freedom of Information in the United Nations," *Law and Contemporary Problems*, 14 (1949), 545–583.

28. ZC to Carl B. Rix, 6 March 1950. In an earlier explanation of possible effects of this language change, Chafee said, "It is not enough to demarcate the punishment if the wrong itself be left vague. The Conference draft would permit a statute to impose a penalty of five years for the disclosure of 'any

matters which ought to remain secret in the interests of national security.' " See Chafee, "Legal Problems of Freedom of Information in the United Nations," 578.

29. Chafee, "Legal Problems of Freedom of Information in the United Nations," 583.

30. Ibid., 579.

31. Ibid., 568.

32. Ibid., 570.

33. ZC to George Ferguson, 1 March 1949, HLL 16-7; ZC to Charles E. Hughes, Jr., 18 May 1948; ZC to Arthur N. Holcombe, 24 November 1948, HUA.

34. ZC to Holcombe, 24 November 1948, HUA. Article 17 was later redesignated article 14, and the specific limitations were replaced by a blanket limitation as favored by the U.S. government.

35. William Benton to ZC, 20 April 1948, HL 21-15.

36. Chafee, "General Observations of the Conference," 21 April 1948, HLL 21-16.

37. *BL*, 316.

38. ZC to A. N. Marquis Co., 15 November 1950 HUA. In this letter about updating his entry in *Who's Who in America*, he said, "I very much want you to retain mention of my membership in the United Nations Subcommission."

39. ZC to Erwin N. Griswold, 4 June 1948, HUA.

40. In February 1948 Chafee had experienced some urinary disturbance, and later in Geneva a Swiss doctor had "unnecessarily alarmed" him. Soon after his return, he met with his physician, Dr. Richard B. King, and Dr. Fletcher H. Colby, described by King as the leading urologist in New England. A letter from King to ZC, 28 April 1948, notifying him of this consultative meeting, is in HUA. His Radcliffe address was abstracted in *Radcliffe Quarterly* (August 1948) and printed in full as "Channels and Chances for World-Wide Growth of Understanding" in *Dun's Review* (December 1948); it later formed the core of chapter 11 of *BL*.

41. ZC to Harry Martin, 9 February 1949, HLL 16-7. Martin, a member of the American delegation to Geneva, was then labor adviser to Averell Harriman with the Economic Cooperation Administration in Europe.

42. Lloyd Free to ZC, 18 March 1949, ibid.

43. George Ferguson to ZC, 20 May 1949, HLL 16-6.

44. Quoted in *BL*, 307.

45. See, in addition to the piece in *Law and Contemporary Problems* (cited in n. 27), these articles by Chafee: "Federal and State Powers Under the UN Covenant on Human Rights," *Wisconsin Law Review*, 1951, I, 389–473, and II, 623–656; "Amending the Constitution to Cripple Treaties," *Louisiana Law Review*, 12 (1952), 345–382; and "Stop Being Terrified of Treaties: Stop Being Scared of the Constitution," *American Bar Association*

Journal, 38 (1952), 731–734. See also his "Some Problems of the Draft International Covenant on Human Rights," *Proceedings of the American Philosophical Society*, 95 (1951), 471–489.

46. Sevellon Brown to ZC, 14 February 1952, HLL 8-1.

47. ZC to Lyman Tondel, Jr., 28 September 1951, HLL 8-7. Because both the *Chicago Tribune* and the *New York Daily News* were owned by the family of Colonel Robert R. McCormick, it is unsurprising that they expressed nearly identical views on this issue.

48. ZC to Irving Dilliard, 5 October 1951, ibid.

49. ZC to Erwin D. Canham, 3 March 1952, HLL 11-8.

50. Shortly before the Chicago meeting, Cranston Williams, general manager of the American Newspaper Publishers Association (ANPA), sent to its membership a memo containing the opinions of Carl B. Rix, one of the ABA's harshest critics of the treaty and of the Human Rights Covenant. This was not the first time the ANPA circulated ABA statements against the UN. For instance, in the fall of 1950, Williams sent members copies of a report by the ABA's Committee for Peace and Law through the United Nations—the focal point, despite its name, of bar attacks on the world body—alleging that the covenant, if ratified by the Senate, "would make possible the destruction of the rights of free speech, to have a free press, of peaceable assembly, of freedom of religion, and of petition as guaranteed in the First Amendment to the Constitution." Cranston Williams to ANPA members, 27 October 1950, copy in HLL 19-7.

51. ZC to Canham, 3 March 1952.

52. Ibid.

53. ZC to Philip L. Graham, 20 June 1952, HLL 11-10. Asked to comment on Chafee's letter to Graham, Erwin Canham—who did much of the redrafting of the News Convention in the General Assembly the year after the Geneva sessions—said: "I doubt if the Convention could have been saved no matter what the press had done." Canham to author, 15 September 1975.

54. Chafee, manuscript of "An Outsider Looks at the Press" (address to Associated Press Managing Editors Association, 14 November 1952), HUA. The speech was printed under that title in *Nieman Reports*, 7 (January 1953), 5–7.

55. *BL*, 321 (paragraphing omitted). This passage originally formed the conclusion of an Honors Day address entitled "Watchman, What of the Night?" and given at Brown University on 25 November 1947; it was published as *Brown University Papers XXI*. He used the same title for the opening chapter of *BL*.

11. "Pulling Asses out of Pits" and Other Cold War Exertions

1. Roscoe Pound to ZC, 31 May 1950, HLL 2-23.

2. Erwin N. Griswold to ZC, 12 April 1950, HLL 1-19 (paragraphing omitted).

3. Chafee, "Reflections on the Law of Copyright: I," *Columbia Law Review*, 45 (1945), 515. The two-part article was concluded in ibid., 719–738. See also Chafee, "Unfair Competition," *Harvard Law Review*, 53 (1940), 1289–1321. On the one hand, when the U.S. Copyright Act was finally updated effective 1 January 1978, it adopted several specific changes favored by Chafee including extending the duration of copyright from a maximum of fifty-six years to the length of the author's life plus fifty years. On the other hand, one part of the old statute that he strongly criticized was extended until 1 July 1986—the clause mandating that certain textual literary works be manufactured in the United States.

4. ZC to Randall Thompson, 25 February 1954, HLL 50-19.

5. Chafee, *How Human Rights Got into the Constitution* (Boston, 1952), 10. The book was originally the Gaspar G. Bacon Lectures, delivered in November 1951 at Boston University.

6. Earl Latham, *The Communist Controversy in Washington* (Cambridge, Mass., 1966), 10.

7. *FS*, 260. See also Benjamin E. Lippincott, *Democracy's Dilemma: The Totalitarian Party in a Free Society* (New York, 1965), 58–62, for a summary of Chafee's views on Communism. Lippincott calls Chafee "the most authoritative spokesman" of the traditional liberal position on how a democracy should deal with totalitarian ideas.

8. *FSUS*, 222, 474, 491. His exhaustive criticism of the Smith Act is in *FSUS*, chap. 12. He said he was unaware of this statute, the first peacetime federal sedition law since 1798, at the time of its enactment as a rider to the Alien Registration Act.

9. ZC to Osmond K. Fraenkel, 25 March 1947, HLL 31-4. Fraenkel, a lawyer for the ACLU, was among persons testifying against the Smith bill at the time hearings were held on it.

10. *BL*, 126–127.

11. One of Chafee's harshest critics was the well known anti-Stalinist Sidney Hook, professor of philosophy at New York University. See his joint review of *BL* and Felix Frankfurter's *Of Law and Men* (New York, 1956), in "Liberalism and the Law," *Commentary*, 23 (January 1957), 46–56, reprinted in Hook, *Political Power and Personal Freedom* (New York, 1959), 252–267. For a more temperate critique of Chafee's views on Communism by a leading spokesman of conservatism, see Russell Kirk's review of *BL*, *University of Pennsylvania Law Review*, 105 (1956), 290–293. For a balanced appraisal of Chafee's views, see Lippincott, *Democracy's Dilemma*, 147–150.

12. Alger Hiss, *In the Court of Public Opinion* (New York, 1957). In 1984 Hiss donated to the Harvard Law School Library forty-four cartons of materials—more than 30,000 items, about a third of them concerned with the

Hiss-Chambers case and obtained by Hiss under the Freedom of Information Act. For Chambers's version of events, see his *Witness* (New York, 1952). The main evidence against Hiss was State Department materials from early 1938, which provoked a controversy over whether they were typed on a Woodstock owned by the Hisses or whether they were forged by Chambers or possibly by the FBI. In 1984 it was reported that an American Communist Party official had obtained items under the Freedom of Information Act documenting that the FBI "has for many years had the ability to commit forgery by typewriter." See Gil Green, "Forgery by Typewriter," *Nation*, 239 (10 November 1984), 468–469, and the accompanying article by William A. Reuben. Also in 1984 President Reagan awarded Chambers a posthumous Presidential Medal of Freedom, the nation's highest civilian award.

13. Allen Weinstein, *Perjury: The Hiss-Chambers Case* (New York, 1979), xvi. Weinstein, who assesses the major conspiracy theories in an appendix, refers to the "partisan exhortation [that] has characterized almost every book written on the case, with the notable exception of Alistair Cooke's early study." Cooke's book, which Chafee admired and which contains a chronology of the case at 342, is *A Generation on Trial* (New York, 1950). A book defending Hiss is John Chabot Smith, *Alger Hiss: The True Story* (New York, 1976).

14. Chafee, Letter to *Washington Post*, 13 December 1948.

15. Controversy over the dates and authenticity of the films continued for years, fueled partly by the fact that in December 1948 an Eastman Kodak official erroneously gave 1945—which was promptly corrected to 1938—as the manufacturing date of some of the microfilm. See Weinstein, *Perjury*, 272–273.

16. Ibid., 4. HUAC was finally abolished in January 1975, after having undergone a name change to the House Internal Security Committee some years earlier. For a scholarly study of the committee, see Robert K. Carr, *The House Committee on Un-American Activities* (Ithaca, N.Y., 1952). A popular history is Walter Goodman, *The Committee* (New York, 1968). See also Frank J. Donner, *The Un-Americans* (New York, 1961) for an indictment of the committee by an ACLU lawyer.

17. Weinstein, *Perjury*, 581. At 190 he writes: "According to William 'Fishbait' Miller, doorkeeper of the House, Nixon confided shortly before leaving on the boat trip that he expected to be summoned back because of dramatic developments in the Hiss-Chambers probe."

18. The Hollywood inquiry is the subject of Victor Navasky's *Naming Names* (New York, 1980).

19. See Weinstein, *Perjury*, 189–193. At 27 Weinstein calls Andrews one of Nixon's three main advisors on the case. Andrews's account of his role in the affair is given in a posthumously published book: Bert Andrews and Peter Andrews, *A Tragedy of History: A Journalist's Confidential Role in the Hiss-Chambers Case* (Washington, 1962). John Chabot Smith, a colleague of Andrews at the *Herald Tribune*, writes that Andrews "enjoyed

the reputation of being a go-getter who would do anything for a good story," and that at one time Hiss had "respected [Andrews] as a good newspaperman, one who had often come to him for background information about Dumbarton Oaks and other matters." But their relationship went sour, according to Smith, after Andrews broke a story in March 1945 that "marked the beginning of a campaign by hard-line anti-Communists to denounce the whole Yalta agreement as a sellout to the Russians." See Smith, *Alger Hiss: The True Story*, 127–128, 190–192.

20. ZC to Bert Andrews, 13 December 1948, HUA.

21. Bert Andrews to ZC, 21 December 1948; ZC to Andrews, 4 January 1949, ibid.

22. ZC to George Ferguson, 1 March 1949, HLL 16-7; ZC to Katherine B. Hunt, 7 November 1950, HLL 34-2. Many other illustrious public figures—not all of them Harvard law graduates—lined up in support of Hiss; among them was John W. Davis, whose law degree was from Washington and Lee. For an account of Davis's relationship with Hiss and for a list of prominent persons who testified to his character and reputation, see William H. Harbaugh, *Lawyer's Lawyer* (New York, 1973), 451–452.

23. ZC to John W. Heselton, 20 May 1948, HUA.

24. ZC to Alexander Wiley, 26 May 1948, HLL 33-8.

25. ZC to William G. Rice, 18 May 1949, HLL 33-10. The bill underwent numerous name changes but at this time was being referred to simply as the Mundt bill.

26. Barsky v. United States, 167 F.2d 241 (D.C. Cir. 1948).

27. ZC to Harry S. Truman, 16 June 1948, HUA. The letter quoted from an article highly critical of HUAC's methods that he often cited during this period: Walter Gellhorn, "Report on a Report of the House Committee on Un-American Activities," *Harvard Law Review*, 60 (1947), 1193–1234.

28. Chafee, "The Encroachments on Freedom," *Atlantic*, 197 (May 1956), 42. Chafee also had written a letter in Browder's behalf to Biddle's predecessor, Robert H. Jackson; in a postscript, he said: "In order to avoid any possible misapprehension, I want to let you know that this idea is entirely my own and has been in my mind for a long time. Of course Browder's counsel, Carl Stern, is an old friend of mine, but this letter is sent because of my own reactions to the sentence and it is not due to any suggestion from him." ZC to Jackson, 22 April 1941, HLL 31-5.

29. Chafee, "The Encroachments on Freedom," 42. In that article and elsewhere Chafee said he declined to sign the petition. But in a letter to Carl S. Stern at the time of the Browder controversy, he said, "To judge from my fan mail, which might better be called brickbat mail, my signature to the Browder petition seems to have made some people very angry. Better be damned than mentioned not at all!" ZC to Stern, 23 March 1942, HLL 31-5. His refusal to speak at the New York rally is in ZC to Elizabeth Gurley Flynn, 8 May 1942, HLL 31-6. Still later, he also declined to assist Browder's wife in fighting a deportation order. ZC to A. B. Magil, 6 January 1944 and

21 January 1944, HLL 31-7. The Chafee-Browder connection accounted for several items being placed in the Chafee file at FBI headquarters in Washington.

30. Arthur M. Schlesinger, Jr., to ZC, 10 June 1949, HLL 33-12.

31. ZC to Arthur M. Schlesinger, Jr., 17 June 1949, ibid. (paragraphing omitted); ZC to Joseph L. Rauh, Jr., 17 June 1949, HLL 33-13. Committee members included Thurman Arnold, former U.S. assistant attorney general; Stringfellow Barr, former president of St. John's College in Annapolis; Alexander Meiklejohn; Louis Untermeyer and Mark Van Doren, literary critics; and Harlow Shapley, controversial head of the Harvard Observatory. Chafee said he was "proud to be associated with such men." ZC to Doris Cammett, 3 October 1955, HUA.

32. ZC to Harry S. Truman, 17 June 1949, HLL 33-13. Chafee discusses the case of the New York Socialists in FSUS, 269–282.

33. ZC to Robert A. Taft, 21 June 1949, HLL 33-13.

34. See FS, 166–167. Chafee's statement, the roots of which lay in his 1948 letter to Senator Wiley, was filed with the Senate Judiciary Committee on 4 June 1949. It served as the basis of a Harvard Phi Beta Kappa Oration he gave a fortnight later, and subsequently appeared in chap. 5 of BL. It was also excerpted in the Harvard Alumni Bulletin, 51 (9 July 1949), 781–785, and printed in full in Bulletin of the American Association of University Professors, 35 (1949), 397–433.

35. For Taft's views on McCarthy, see James T. Patterson, Mr. Republican (Boston, 1972), 594–595, and Thomas C. Reeves, The Life and Times of Joe McCarthy (New York, 1982), 269–270.

36. Roger N. Baldwin to ZC, 23 June 1949, HLL 33-13 (paragraphing omitted).

37. The portion of the statement on registration became an article, "The Registration of 'Communist-Front' Organizations in the Mundt-Nixon Bill," Harvard Law Review, 63 (1950), 1382–90, and later was incorporated into chap. 5 of BL. The full statement formed an ACLU pamphlet, The Free and the Brave (New York, 1950).

38. ZC to Harry S. Truman, 30 March 1950, HLL 33-17.

39. ZC to Olive Van Horn, 10 February 1951, HLL 34-4.

40. ZC to Thomas I. Emerson, 15 November 1950, HUA. Emerson later published two influential books on freedom of speech, Toward a General Theory of the First Amendment (New York, 1966) and The System of Freedom of Expression (New York, 1970).

41. Quoted in E. J. Kahn, Jr., Harvard: Through Change and Through Storm (New York, 1969), 101.

42. See William B. Prendergast, "Maryland: The Ober Anti-Communist Law," in Walter Gellhorn, ed., The States and Subversion (Ithaca, N.Y., 1952), 140–183.

43. Frank B. Ober to James B. Conant, 26 April 1949, copy in HLL 34-18.

Other letters pertaining to the controversy created by Ober are in the same location. Correspondence between Ober and Conant and between Ober and Grenville Clark, representing the Harvard Corporation, was printed in *Harvard Alumni Bulletin*, 51 (25 June 1949), 729–736, and in *Bulletin of the AAUP*, 35 (1949), 313–334.

44. ZC to Grenville Clark, 20 May 1949, HLL 34-19.

45. Paul A. Freund to ZC, 21 June 1949, HUA.

46. James B. Conant to ZC, 20 June 1949, HLL 34-19.

47. ZC to Grenville Clark, 14 June 1949, ibid.

48. ZC to Clark, 22 June 1949, ibid. The most notorious of the California legislative committees was the Tenney Committee, headed by Jack B. Tenney, a lawyer who had been a piano player and song writer ("Mexicali Rose"). See Edward L. Barrett, Jr., "California: Regulation and Investigation of Subversive Activities," in Gellhorn, ed., *The States and Subversion*, 1–53, and Barrett, *The Tenney Committee* (Ithaca, N.Y., 1951). Chafee, in a review of the Barrett book, *Northwestern University Law Review*, 47 (1952), 270–283, mentions his own listings by the committee as well as by HUAC.

49. *BL*, 241, 246.

50. ZC to Abe Fortas, 10 January 1951, HLL 85-6.

51. *BL*, 167. Chapter 6 of *BL*, "Purges Are for Russian Lawyers, Not American Lawyers," was originally a leaflet he distributed under the title "A Statement to My Fellow-Lawyers Who Have Sworn to Uphold the Constitution of the United States Urging Painstaking Scrutiny and Long Deliberation on the Resolution of the American Bar Association to Require Every Lawyer to Take Periodic Oaths."

52. The statement appears in *BL*, 177–178.

53. ZC to Ernest Angell, 20 October 1950, HLL 85-9.

54. Harbaugh, *Lawyer's Lawyer*, 434–435.

55. ZC to Willard B. Coles, 3 March 1952, HLL 11-8. When Krock later changed his mind, Chafee commended him for his willingness "to revise your views on the Bricker proposal in the light of discussion . . . I can't recall in our time another example of open-mindedness in the press such as you have shown." ZC to Arthur Krock, 2 February 1954, HLL 12-8. He did object to several points Krock made in his column of 28 January 1954, the same day a letter by Chafee opposing the amendment ran in the *Times*.

56. See Chafee, "Amending the Constitution to Cripple Treaties," *Louisiana Law Review*, 12 (1952), 345–382, and "Stop Being Terrified of Treaties: Stop Being Scared of the Constitution," *American Bar Association Journal*, 38 (1952), 731–734. Articles of related interest are cited in Chapter 10 n. 27 and n. 45. Chafee appeared before the Senate Judiciary Committee on 21 May 1952, after expressing an interest in testifying in a letter to Senator Leverett Saltonstall of Massachusetts. ZC to Saltonstall, 17 March 1952, HLL 11-8.

57. Harbaugh, *Lawyer's Lawyer*, 436. Harbaugh also describes, at 435,

Davis's role as joint chairman (with General Lucius D. Clay and Professor Edward S. Corwin of Princeton) of a committee formed by the Association of the Bar of the City of New York, the nation's lone bar group opposing the amendment, to study the senator's proposal. The committee concluded that the amendment would make the country's procedure for carrying out treaty obligations "the most cumbersome in the world," and its report "profoundly influenced" the president. But at that point Eisenhower clung to the hope of finding a compromise solution.

58. C. W. Tillett to ZC, 1 May 1952, HLL 11-9.

59. Chafee joined Osmond K. Fraenkel and Arthur Garfield Hays, both ACLU lawyers, in signing the brief in behalf of John Howard Lawson and Dalton Trumbo. A copy of the brief, dated 24 February 1950, is in HLL 34-13. Albert Maltz, another of the so-called Hollywood Ten convicted of contempt for refusing to answer the committee's questions, wrote Chafee several times asking for his intervention. In one letter he said: "If you should decide that the issues warrant your entering an amicus brief, we would regard it as about the best thing that had happened to our case in two years. This is crudely stated but . . . deeply felt. It . . . involves the fact that ten men entered the witness box before Mr. Thomas [HUAC Chairman J. Parnell Thomas] with hands still warm from 'Free Speech in the United States.' " Maltz to ZC, 4 June 1949, HLL 34-15.

60. *New York Times*, 3 May 1950. When Lattimore was indicted for perjury, Chafee contributed to his legal defense fund; he also had some correspondence with him (each greeted the other as "Mr.") and once invited him to his home for dinner. A recent scholarly account of Lattimore's case is in Thomas C. Reeves, *The Life and Times of Joe McCarthy* (New York, 1983), chap. 12. For Lattimore's account, see his *Ordeal by Slander* (Boston, 1950).

61. *New York Times* and *Washington Post*, 4 July 1952. See also Reeves, *The Life and Times of Joe McCarthy*, 404, and Archibald MacLeish's letter to the *New York Times*, 9 July 1952, declaring that "to call Zechariah Chafee 'dangerous to America' is either to insult the common sense of the country or to confess one's self ignorant of what America is."

62. ZC to Jerome Frank, 14 November 1952, HLL 35-21 (paragraphing omitted). For a discussion of Frank's role in the Rosenberg case, see Arthur Kinoy, *Rights on Trial: The Odyssey of a People's Lawyer* (Cambridge, Mass., 1983), chap. 4.

63. Jerome Frank to ZC, 18 November 1952, HLL 35-21.

64. ZC to Harry S. Truman, 26 November 1952, ibid.

65. Kinoy, *Rights on Trial*, chap. 4; Walter and Miriam Schneir, *Invitation to an Inquest*, rev. ed. (New York, 1983); and Ronald Radosh and Joyce Milton, *The Rosenberg File* (New York, 1983). Both the Schneir and the Radosh-Milton studies used materials obtained under the Freedom of Information Act in reaching opposite conclusions. Although some reviewers concluded that Radosh and Milton had demonstrated the Rosenbergs' guilt,

most Rosenberg partisans appeared unconvinced and some accused the authors of manipulating their data.

66. ZC to Harlow Shapley, 16 October 1947, HLL 35-23. Earlier, Chafee had advised Shapley about an impending appearance by the latter before HUAC.

67. *New York Times*, 11 January 1953. The statement, printed in the *Crimson* of 8 January 1953, served as a partial basis for chapter 7 of *BL*. At the time it appeared, Chafee was preparing to go abroad; before his departure he pledged $1,000 to Sutherland so that, if the need arose, "you and other members of the faculty [may] obtain the services of a lawyer to advise members of the Harvard faculty who are concerned in a possible congressional investigation." ZC to Sutherland, 14 January 1953, HLL 35-19.

68. Kingman Brewster, Jr., to Erwin N. Griswold, 28 June 1953, HUA.

69. Karl Jeck to Salzburg Seminar, 14 August 1953, copy in ibid.

70. Correspondence and records pertaining to Chafee's health are in ibid.

71. Chafee, *Three Human Rights in the Constitution* (Lawrence, Kan., 1956). This work, like the earlier *How Human Rights Got into the Constitution*, was spun off from his teaching of the general education course at Harvard. For that course he also compiled and published *Documents on Fundamental Human Rights*, several pamphlets distributed by Harvard University Press.

72. E. Merrick Dodd, *Early History of American Corporations* (Cambridge, Mass., 1954). He did many other things for the book, including preparing a table of New England corporations that he hoped "would excite the interest of readers."

73. Meiklejohn's criticisms appeared in the *Harvard Crimson*, 25 January 1954; see also his *Political Freedom* (New York, 1960), 148–155. Meiklejohn expressed chagrin over the influence of the statement on a "destructive" document issued 30 March 1953 by the Association of American Universities and entitled "The Rights and Responsibilities of Universities and Their Faculties."

74. ZC to Meiklejohn, 14 June 1954, HLL 2-16 (paragraphing omitted). Sidney Hook published two books bearing on the question of Communists in teaching: *Heresy, Yes—Conspiracy, No!* (New York, 1953) and *Common Sense and the Fifth Amendment* (New York, 1957). Much of the latter attacked a book by Dean Griswold, *The Fifth Amendment Today* (Cambridge, Mass., 1955), but included criticisms of Chafee.

75. Chafee, manuscript of "If the Salt Have Lost His Savour—" (address at University of Oregon, 18 October 1954), HLL Red Set. The speech was printed as "The Freedom to Think," *Atlantic*, 195 (January 1955), 27–33, and later as chapter 8 of *BL*.

76. Chafee's pamphlet was reprinted in Alfred H. Kelly, ed., *Foundations of Freedom* (New York, 1958), 52–87. The volume contains other Freedom Agenda pamphlets, some of them (but not Chafee's) extensively rewritten.

77. *New York Times*, 17 July 1955.

78. Edwin J. Lukas to ZC, 19 September 1955, HUA.

79. Interview with Elisabeth Chafee Gamble, 5 July 1973.

80. See Donald J. Kemper, *Decade of Fear: Senator Hennings and Civil Liberties* (Columbia, Mo., 1965), 115 and chap. 6 passim.

81. ZC to Philip Graham, 18 November 1955; ZC to Lon Hocker, 16 November 1955, HUA.

82. ZC to Benjamin Ginzburg, 30 December 1955, ibid.

83. *Time*, 68 (16 July 1956), 62.

84. ZC to Erwin N. Griswold, 11 January 1956, HLL 1-20; ZC to John G. Buchanan, 20 June 1956, HUA.

85. David W. Bailey to Nathan M. Pusey, 10 February 1956, copy in ibid.

86. ZC to Arthur Fisher, 30 January 1957, ibid.

87. ZC, prospectus for TV lectures "The Constitution and Human Rights," ibid.

88. ZC to Louis Schneiderman, 6 December 1956, ibid.

89. ZC to William P. Burnham, 19 January 1957, ibid.

90. Quoted in Anne Chafee Brien, addendum to unpublished 1952 "Autobiographical Sketch of Z. Chafee, Jr.," copy in possession of author.

91. Chafee, manuscripts of Lowell Television Lectures, HUA.

92. Interview (mail) with Mary Chafee Andrews, April 1982.

93. Century Club Memorial to Zechariah Chafee, Jr., from the club's 1958 yearbook, copy in HUA.

94. Copies of materials in the FBI's Chafee file were obtained by me under the Freedom of Information Act. A total of 187 pages was released, with 19 pages being withheld "in the interest of the national defense or foreign policy, for example, information involving intelligence sources or methods." The FBI in Washington confirmed that the sarcastic note about Chafee is in the handwriting of Director Hoover.

Epilogue

1. Whitney v. California, 274 U.S. 357, 372 (1927). Brandeis's opinion was originally written as a dissent in Ruthenberg v. Michigan, a similar case that the court dismissed after Ruthenberg died. The draft of his *Ruthenberg* dissent contains several dozen page citations to *FS*. Later, in a reference to his *Whitney* concurrence, he told Chafee: "You will see how much I have borrowed from you." Louis D. Brandeis to ZC, 5 May 1927, HLL 4-4. Materials pertaining to the justice's work on Ruthenberg and Whitney are in the Brandeis Papers, HLL 44-5 and 44-9.

2. The post-*Schenck* cases in which a Supreme Court majority used the danger test to protect expression include Schneider v. State, 308 U.S. 147 (1939)—street littering, and Bridges v. California, 314 U.S. 252 (1941)—contempt.

3. ZC to Learned Hand, 6 January 1920, in Gerald Gunther, "Learned

Hand and the Origins of Modern First Amendment Doctrine: Some Fragments of History," *Stanford Law Review*, 27 (1975), 764. I referred to this letter in Chapter 1 as part of the discussion of the correspondence between Hand, Holmes, and Chafee.

4. Brandenburg v. Ohio, 395 U.S. 444, 447 (1969). For a discussion of the high court's "long-delayed vindication" of the objective standard test in *Brandenburg* and several earlier cases, see Gunther, "Learned Hand," 750–755.

5. Gunther, "Learned Hand," 755. But see Martin H. Redish, *Freedom of Expression* (Charlottesville, Va., 1984), 186, for criticisms of *Brandenburg* and of Gunther's liberal reading of it: "It might be thought that the 'directed to inciting or producing imminent lawless action' language represented adoption of the *Masses* requirement of direct advocacy. But the Court's language should more likely be given a different interpretation. The Court's use of two words, 'inciting' and 'producing,' seems to indicate that by the phrasing of the test itself it intended to make possible convictions for indirect ('producing') as well as direct ('inciting') advocacy. Illegal action may certainly be 'produced' by indirect statements."

6. A more speech-protective form of balancing, known as definitional balancing, has been proposed by some scholars. A leading article advocating it is Melville B. Nimmer, "The Right to Speak from *Times* to *Time*: First Amendment Theory Applied to Libel and Misapplied to Privacy," *California Law Review*, 56 (1968), 935–967. Whereas ad hoc balancing considers the relevant specific interests in a particular case, the definitional form seeks to transcend the merits of a particular case by considering the general future value of a particular speech or speaker. Although Chafee's version of balancing has been considered in the ad hoc category, it actually appears closer to the definitional form because he emphasized the need to weigh the social interest in truth—an interest that would seem to transcend a particular case. For a thoughtful critique of balancing concepts, see Gerald Gunther, "In Search of Judicial Quality on a Changing Court: The Case of Justice Powell," *Stanford Law Review*, 24 (1972), 1001–35.

7. The most sophisticated work on the relationship between concepts of expression and philosophical systems may be found in Jay W. Jensen, "Liberalism, Democracy, and the Mass Media" (Ph.D. diss., University of Illinois, 1957).

8. Glenn Negley, "Philosophical Views on the Value of Privacy," *Law and Contemporary Problems*, 31 (1966), 324.

9. Miami Herald Pub. Co. v. Tornillo, 418 U.S. 241, 258 n. 24 (1974), quoting *GMC*, II, 633.

10. Hynes v. Mayor of Oradell, 425 U.S. 610, 619 (1976).

11. Breard v. Alexandria, 341 U.S. 622, 639 (1951), quoting *FSUS*, 406–407.

12. Laurence H. Tribe, *American Constitutional Law* (Mineola, N.Y., 1978), 693.

13. *FSUS*, 149–150. See also *FS*, 170–171. This distinction between categories of words that are constitutionally protected and those that are not has been called the two-level speech theory. See, e.g., Harry Kalven, Jr., "The Metaphysics of the Law of Obscenity," *1960 Supreme Court Review* (Chicago, 1960), 10–11.

14. Chaplinsky v. New Hampshire, 315 U.S. 568, 572 (1942). The Supreme Court used the same rationale in several later cases to place beyond First Amendment protection other classes of words: Beauharnais v. Illinois, 343 U.S. 250 (1952)—criminal libel of a group, and the companion cases Roth v. United States and Alberts v. California, 354 U.S. 476 (1957)—obscenity.

15. The critics include Kalven, "Metaphysics," 10–11, who calls the two-level theory "difficult to accept as doctrine" and "a strained effort to trap a problem." See also the criticisms by Murphy's biographer, J. Woodford Howard, Jr., *Mr. Justice Murphy* (Princeton, N.J., 1968), 256, and those by Franklyn S. Haiman, *Speech and Law in a Free Society* (Chicago, 1981), 19–25. Haiman, professor of speech communication at Northwestern University and board member of the ACLU, notes at 21: "To conclude, as many have done, including the U.S. Supreme Court, that there can be such a thing as speech which is devoid of ideational content is therefore not only to misunderstand the consciousness-mediated nature of symbolic transactions but to ignore the qualifying phrases in the original Chafee statement" (relied on in Chaplinsky). Chafee's qualifications consisted of the words "essential" and "slight" in his statement that "profanity and indecent talk and pictures, which do not form an essential part of any exposition of ideas, have a very slight social value as a step toward truth." The later Supreme Court decisions eroding two-level categorization include: New York Times v. Sullivan, 376 U.S. 254 (1964)—libel, and Cohen v. California, 403 U.S. 15 (1971)—profanity.

16. He would probably be both pleased and amused to see that one scholar, in reformulating the danger test to reflect a protectionist approach, has recently concluded that "the clear and present danger test is the worst method for determining the degree of constitutional protection of unlawful advocacy, except for all the other ways." See Redish, *Freedom of Expression*, 174, who is paraphrasing Churchill's famous comment about democracy. He also refers to Chafee's advocacy of the test.

17. Edward D. Re, *Cases and Materials on Remedies* (Mineola, N.Y., 1982). Chafee selected Re in the mid-1950s to assume responsibility for preparing future editions of the equity casebook. An account of Re's meeting with Chafee to discuss the details is in Edward D. Re, ed., *Freedom's Prophet* (New York, 1981), 349–352.

18. Henry L. McClintock, review of *Some Problems of Equity, Vanderbilt Law Review*, 5 (1951), 133. McClintock was disagreeing with this judgment by Chafee's friend Edgar N. Durfee in the Foreword to the book: "It is by

[*FS*] that he is most widely known, and it is by this that he has best served his country."

19. Erwin N. Griswold to author, 25 September 1975.

20. Erwin N. Griswold, "Zechariah Chafee, Jr.," *Harvard Law Review*, 70 (1957), 1338.

21. Karl Llewellyn, manuscript of "Review of Zechariah Chafee, Jr.," HUA.

Index